WATCHING

AMERICAN POLITICS

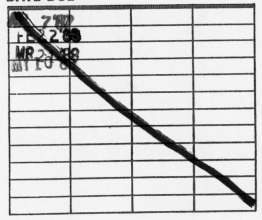

WATCHING
AMERICAN POLITICS

Articles and Commentaries
About Citizens, Politicians,
and the News Media

Edited by

Dan Nimmo
University of Tennessee

&

William L. Rivers
Stanford University

Longman
New York & London

WATCHING AMERICAN POLITICS
Articles and Commentaries About Citizens, Politicians,
  and the News Media

Longman Inc.; 19 West 44th Street; New York, NY 10036
Associated companies, branches, and representatives
throughout the world.

Developmental Editor: Irving E. Rockwood
Editorial and Design Supervisor: Joan Matthews
Interior Design: Dan Serrano
Cover Design: Graphikann
Manufacturing and Production Supervisor: Maria Chiarino
Composition: Book Composition Services, Inc.
Printing and Binding: The Book Press

Library of Congress Cataloging in Publication Data

Main entry under title:

Watching American politics.
    1.   Political participation—United States—Addresses,
essays, lectures.   2.   Political parties—United States
—Addresses, essays, lectures.   3.   Electioneering—
United States—Addresses, essays, lectures.   4.   Mass
media—Political aspects—United States—Addresses,
essays, lectures.   I.   Nimmo, Dan D.   II.   Rivers,
William L.
JK1764.W37   324'.0973   80-23788
ISBN 0-582-28197-0

Manufactured in the United States of America

9 8 7 6 5 4 3 2 1

Contents

Tables and Figures

TABLES

FIGURES

Preface

Confronted with what can only be called a glut of textbooks, readings books, and anthologies in the field of American politics and government from which to choose for instructional purposes, a teacher is tempted to yield to despair at the thought of trying to make an appropriate selection. But choice is unavoidable, for what the student can and does learn, the success of the course, and the contribution of the instructor are all on the line. Hence, we believe that when two editors offer yet another volume demanding both teachers' and students' inspection, justification is in order. What makes this book so different and where can it fit into current course needs?

We believe *Watching American Politics* differs from other volumes of readings and articles in a variety of ways. Taken together, they suggest the purposes our effort can serve for both instructor and student. At the outset one point must be clear; i.e., we take our book's title seriously. Our intent is to assist readers in becoming more effective observers of politics. The focus on politics is conscious and therefore we do not include selections or commentaries on governmental structures, formal institutions, and principles. These matters are adequately covered in all basic texts and, hence, need not be repeated in these pages. What basic texts too often fail at is providing students with the flavor of contemporary processes joining citizens to their political environment. Hence, we place considerable emphasis upon why and how people become politically involved, electoral politics, and aspects of national political campaigns. In addition we explore at length what politicians do, who the key power holders are, the new politics, and special interest, single-issue politics. Finally, we take account of the increased political role of the mass media and their influence upon each person's political life.

Our focus upon watching is also intentional. To improve the watching skills of students we have done two things. First, we have taken our selections from two major sources available to students. One consists of the kinds of popular reports about politics that flow from journalists. The role of the journalist is broadly conceived and, hence, we include articles by working reporters, political columnists, free-lance writers, pollsters, political consultants, and other nonacademic persons. Each chapter is devoted to a topic of contemporary political importance and contains one selection from a journalist. Paired with that selection is an article from a scholarly journal, a second key source of political information for students. This pairing permits illustration of the similarities and differences in the way nonscientists and scientists observe politics, thus providing students with the realization that they may round out their political watching by adding scholarly insights to more readily available news reports. This pairing and comparison provides a central theme that integrates all of the book's chapters, a theme explained in the prologue and reanalyzed in a concluding epilogue.

In addition to pairing selections from alternative types of information sources we have done something else to assist students in honing their skills of political observation. Along with the paired selections in each chapter there is an introductory note and a commentary written directly to the student. The introduction precedes the chapter's two articles. It describes the topical area of the chapter, relates the two selections to the topic, provides information about the authors of the chapter's articles, and suggests points readers should look for and questions worth raising about the material. The commentary to the student follows the chapter's selections. It reviews key points made in each selection, discusses and clarifies technical points, explains any methodological niceties, and compares the similarities and differences in approach and content of the chapter's articles. We feel the proper place for this type of discussion is after rather than before the articles, for two reasons. First, discussion and clarification is best undertaken when concrete examples from the articles can be cited, illustrations the student has already encountered and puzzled over. Second, placing the commentary after the selections invites the student to go back and reread portions employed for illustrative purposes. The commentary also has other purposes, namely, to update, critique, and personalize the chapter content. Again we raise questions for the student to ponder, both about the selections and about their implications for the student's political role. Rather than list these questions separately, they occur within the context of the commentary at appropriate points. Finally, a list of related articles and/or books appears, and students are invited to explore the chapter's topic in greater detail from both journalistic and academic perspectives.

The articles in this anthology touch upon important dimensions of politics as practiced today. They also suggest leading controversies that divide political observers. For example, why don't more Americans take part in politics? Some political watchers blame restrictive laws; others cite a lack of economic incentive or personal motivations. Other areas of disagreement include: Who rules America? What is the future of American political parties? Does political reform improve or weaken popular control of politics? What is the impact of television on politics?

We have organized the chapters in this book along three lines. Part 1 looks at what political observers know and don't know about citizens in the political process. The articles in Part 2 shift the focus to politicians of various stripes—power wielders, partisans, political consultants, reformists, etc. Part 3 focuses upon the role of the news and publicized events in politics—i.e., the effects of news on people's views about politics, the force of television, and the influence of publicized polls. As noted, these three parts are supplemented by a prologue and an epilogue exploring news and science as aids to political watching.

Many of the articles in this volume are of recent vintage, yet touch upon matters of continuing import. When students have read them, they will have both a sense of what political observers have seen and the vantage points they have taken. More importantly, readers will develop a grasp of how they can become seasoned political watchers themselves.

One final prefatory comment is in order. As editors of this volume each of us recognizes the importance of citations, footnotes, and other forms of documentation to the scholarly enterprise. Indeed such paraphernalia are an essential ingredient of publications in scholarly journals. For students endeavoring to fathom for the first time the intricate explanations of things provided by social scientists, however, they sometimes constitute overkill. Hence, in many cases we have displayed our editorial license and exorcised citations and footnotes where such documentation was not demanded for the reader's understanding.

In the preparation of this volume we have been greatly assisted by the encouragement and good humor of Irving Rockwood, executive editor of the College and Professional Books Division of Longman. Thurbon Tukey, assistant editor, kept us well informed about the continuing adventures surrounding publication. Finally, Joan Matthews was as helpful, gracious, and patient a production editor as we could ever have asked of any publisher.

Dan Nimmo
William L. Rivers

WATCHING
AMERICAN POLITICS

PROLOGUE

WATCHING POLITICAL WATCHERS

INTRODUCTION

Either you are now, or soon will be, a political observer. If you already follow politics closely, it may be due to a political interest developed earlier in school or perhaps passed along to you by family, friends, coworkers, or others. If until now you have been unconcerned with politics, the very fact that you are reading these words suggests you are enrolled in a college course which gives you the opportunity, even requires you, to pay attention to politics.

Our purpose in this book is to help you become an informed political observer and to sharpen your skills at watching politics. What do we mean by politics? We mean simply all those things people do—you and we—that tie them to what other people occupying positions in government do. Our emphasis is upon American government at the national level. We want you to look at how citizens such as yourself think about politics, get involved, and do or do not vote. And, we invite you to observe the politicians who exercise political power in the United States and how they try to organize and persuade you on their—and perhaps your—behalf. Finally, we hope that you will think about where you learn about politics, how well the news media serve your needs to know about yourselves and politicians, and how you might learn more.

We are particularly concerned about how each of us learns about politics. Chances are, if you are like most Americans, most of what you know about daily political goings-on comes from the news. Approximately two-thirds of us rely primarily upon television for political information, about one-third solely upon TV news. One-half of us rely upon newspapers, one in five doing so exclusively. Radio, news magazines, books, and conversations with other people are principal sources of detailed information about politics for relatively few of us.

But you are not like most Americans. You have an opportunity through your college course work to add another vital source of political information to your repertoire that most Americans miss. That source lies in articles and books about politics written by lifelong students of the subject—political scientists, sociologists,

1

psychologists, and others. We make no argument that what they have to say is "better" than what you find in the news, only that social scientists offer alternative, sometimes different, ways of watching politics. In fact, if you are to become a skilled political observer, we think you need to consult both the daily news and scholarly material. The articles in this volume provide you freedom to sample both. Each chapter offers the viewpoint on a topic of contemporary political importance of a journalist, public affairs reporter, or free-lance writer specializing in politics, and of a professional social scientist. As editors of this book we introduce you to the authors of each chapter, highlight some of the points you should look for in their articles, ask you to read their selections, then close each chapter with a commentary that compares what the authors have said, updates some of the information, raises a key issue or two, and suggests other things you might want to read by journalists and social scientists that can help you polish your talents of political observation.

But, first, to assist you in understanding the kinds of information available to you in watching politics, we invite you to think about the people who make a living out of being political observers. For you, watching politics may be an avocation, but for them it is their bread and butter. So let us take a look at these political watchers, who they are and what they do.

As noted, two sets of political observers supply us with information about public affairs—journalists and social scientists. Each author of each of the selections that follow has been both during his career. Bill Rivers, coeditor of this book and author of the first article, "The Social Scientist and the Journalist," is now a professor in the Department of Communication at Stanford University. He has taught also at Louisiana State University, the University of Miami, and the University of Texas. He has B.A. and M.A. degrees from Louisiana State University and a Ph.D. (in political science) from American University. Numerous book-length studies about politics and the press, reporting, and journalism roll from his typewriter, including *The Opinionmakers, The Adversaries, The Mass Media and Modern Society,* and *Writing: Craft and Art.*

But academic credentials alone do not qualify Bill Rivers to write about journalists and social scientists. Earlier in his career he was Washington correspondent for *The Reporter,* a politically oriented magazine, and worked on newspapers in Baton Rouge, Louisiana. His byline on political articles has appeared in *The Reporter, The Progressive, Nation, Harper's,* and other magazines.

Gerald Grant, author of "Journalism and Social Science: Continuities and Discontinuities," is now a professor in the department of sociology and cultural foundations of education at Syracuse University. He too holds academic degrees, a Ph.D. in education, and has written numerous books, including *On Competence* and *The Perpetual Dream: Reform and Experiment in the American College.* But like Rivers, Grant did not start out as a social scientist. He worked as a journalist for several years, winning a Nieman Fellowship (an award to permit deserving journalists to pursue advanced studies at Harvard) in 1968. Hence, he also is particularly equipped to compare the crafts of journalism and social science.

Both Rivers and Grant compare and contrast what it is that journalists do, and how, with what social scientists do, and how. Do these two sets of political watchers really differ from one another, or are they merely working for different kinds of organizations? Is the difference simply one of rumpled suits and academic gowns? Do they go about their work differently? Does what they present to you, the reader and viewer, provide alternative kinds of information about politics? Reflect upon these questions as you turn first to Bill Rivers, then Gerald Grant.

THE SOCIAL SCIENTIST AND THE JOURNALIST

William L. Rivers

Edited and reprinted from William L. Rivers, Finding Facts *(Englewood Cliffs, N.J.: Prentice-Hall, 1975): 11–17, 160–169.*

The Social Scientist's Approach

Sketching the approach of the social scientist follows naturally the approaches of historians and natural scientists, for fact-finding in the social sciences is riven by leanings in both directions. Some sociologists, anthropologists, psychologists, political scientists, and communication specialists are drawn to the research techniques of the historian, some to the methods of the scientist. Given the rapid growth of the leaning toward science, however, it seems obvious that those who think of themselves as social *scientists* are winning the day—or at least the most attention. They can be distinguished from the others by the title *behavioral scientists.*

The behavioral scientist seeking to construct methods like those used by natural scientists faces a critical problem: If the distinguishing feature of science is the ability to state general propositions—Galileo's laws of falling objects, for example—how is he to state the *laws* of human action? Kenneth Colby tells an apocryphal story of an object that reaches Earth from outer space and defies the efforts of physicists and astronomers to analyze its composition, structure, or function. At last, a social scientist asks, "What's your name?" and the object answers, "Ralph." The fable is designed to suggest that the nature of the behavioral scientist's work allows him research techniques denied to natural scientists. But, of course, the techniques create infinite problems.

The mission of all social scientists is to examine mankind, and not only have they found it impossible to establish a universal proposition, or law, for any human behavior, the prospect for establishing one is nowhere in sight.

From time to time, a behavioral scientist will claim to have established a universal, as when Clark Hull published in *The Scientific Monthly* an article titled "A Primary Social Science Law."[1] It states that human responses to stimuli, physical and verbal, diminish with increasing distance from the point of stimulation. For example, if an aunt lives with or near a mother and assists the mother in caring for a child, the child will regard the aunt as a mother, and less so—or not so at all—if the aunt lives at a distance. Like the other "laws" of human action that are occasionally set forth, this one has not been accepted by behavioral scientists.

It is not true, however, that behavioral scientists have no real mission, because human behavior is not always individual and particular, with every human reacting differently and unpredictably. Although universals that will enable us to predict all human action are neither established nor in prospect, it is obviously absurd to argue that there are no patterns of human behavior. Mail a dollar bill in an envelope with no return address to an American, and he is almost certain to spend it. Mail a dollar under the same conditions to an Australian aborigine; he may convert it to money that he can use, discard it, or burn it.

The behavioral scientist cannot begin his sentences "Whenever," "If ever," "Any," "No," and "All," but he can sometimes assert with confidence that in given circumstances most people will usually react in a predictable way. In some instances, the behavioral scientist can also explain why most of the others react differently.

It is not possible to explore in a short space all the methods through which the behavioral scientist makes judgments. Increasingly, some behavioral scientists are using content analysis, a research technique that enables them to study written works systematically and quantitatively. For example, psychologists Richard Donley and David Winter, both of Wesleyan University, analyzed the inaugural addresses of twelve United States presidents to try to measure the need for power versus the need for achievement of each president. The researchers considered words indicating strong action, aggression, persuasion, and argument as showing need for power. Words such as "good," "better," "excellent," and "high quality" were analyzed as showing a need for achievement. Theodore Roosevelt and John F. Kennedy were judged to have the strongest need for power. The inaugural addresses of each contained 8.3 power images per 1,000 words. Only three presidents were judged to have a greater need for achievement than for power: Herbert Hoover, Lyndon Johnson, and Richard Nixon.

Most behavioral investigation, however, has long been based on two methods, *survey research* (commonly referred to as polling, which is based on interviews, questionnaires, or both) and *experiments,* and on two techniques, *asking questions* and *observing actions.* Many researchers prefer laboratory experiments because of the many problems of "field work." (Some experiments are conducted in the field; most survey research is.) Leonard Sellers describes the field work problems he and his colleagues experienced in conducting a survey when he was a graduate student:

> We randomly pulled some 300 names from the mailing lists of the two local Sierra Club chapters. This was for a survey of "eco-activists"—defined as any members of a conservation group—to find where they got environmental information.
>
> First, we had to word the introduction very carefully to convince people that we weren't selling something. This worked for most people, but we still had to spend time with some assuring them that we were not selling magazines.
>
> Second, the demographics of our population—high education and income—caused some problems. There was a high percentage of unlisted telephone numbers and, with M.D.'s, answering services. Additionally, because of the high education, some respondents were very hip to what we were doing. We were asked astute questions about our sampling procedure, questionnaire construction, and intended method of data analysis. The range of "experts," from biologists to statisticians, was wide and more than a little unsettling. To have your questionnaire critiqued while in the process of administering it is unnerving.
>
> Because of the mixture of demographics and the survey area, which included Palo Alto and Berkeley, we also had a strange but rare problem. Graduate students administering the survey would sometimes find themselves dealing with "academic giants." At least one student completely blew a questionnaire because the respondent turned out to be the man who had written the main textbooks in his undergraduate major; the student was so rattled by personally talking to the man that the survey was worthless.

This is only one aspect of the range of problems in field work that runs from irritations to injuries. Perhaps the greatest obstacles researchers encounter are that survey findings cannot establish causality and that all field work is so little subject to control that it seldom yields findings in which they can place complete confidence. As one put it, "The real world is a messy place."

By contrast, a researcher *can* control human subjects in a laboratory experiment, but in controlling them he takes them out of the real-life situations:

As long as we test a [broadcast] program in the laboratory we always find that it has great effect on the attitudes and interests of the experimental subjects. But when we put the program on as a regular broadcast, we then note that the people who are most influenced in the laboratory tests are those who, in a realistic situation, do not listen to the program. The controlled experiment always greatly overrates effects, as compared with those that really occur, because of the self-selection of audiences.[2]

Another example of how experimental work can lead to misinterpreting facts is the Hawthorne effect, which took its name from a classic study of the effect of various working conditions on rate of output at the Hawthorne plant of Western Electric Company. The experimenters varied the number of rest periods and lengths of rest periods and working days over several weeks for six women, expecting that this would determine which kinds of conditions promoted work and which interfered with it. Regardless of conditions, however, the women worked harder and more efficiently with each succeeding experimental period. The most important reason was their feeling that, having been chosen for an experiment, they were special people and should perform exceptionally.

In experiments, the researcher tries to control and manipulate some factors, called "variables," so that he can focus on the effect of one factor (or a few). But this increases the probability that he will find an effect for the factor he has isolated; it does not share influence with other factors in the same way that it does in life.

There are other problems with laboratory experiments, and although researchers have devised ingenious methods of discounting them or allowing for them, a few always exist to a degree that mars the findings.

The problems that spring from studying people who are aware that they are being studied—in the field as well as in the laboratory—have led some behavioral scientists to devise techniques that allow unobtrusive investigation. The best summary of them is a readable book entitled *Unobtrusive Measures* [3] by Eugene J. Webb and three colleagues. To ask visitors to the Museum of Science and Industry in Chicago which exhibit they prefer, for example, would undoubtedly cause many to name one that might confer distinction on them (just as unbelievable numbers of respondents in surveys claim to read prestigious but not widely read magazines like *Harper's* and *The Atlantic*). A research committee that was formed to set up a psychological exhibit at the museum learned, however, that vinyl tiles around the exhibit containing live, hatching chicks had to be replaced every six weeks or so; tiles in other areas of the museum went for years without replacement. The conclusion is obvious.

Unobtrusive Measures carries hundreds of other examples of studies that avoid the most evident difficulty in human research: The act of measuring may change the measurement. Such methods are valuable but somewhat limited. The behavioral scientist must continue to refine his methods of studying the subjects who are all about him.

The Journalist's Approach

More often than any other serious researcher, the journalist pursues facts for their own sake, many of them amounting to information that may have neither value nor significance. This is an inevitable result of the work of journalists—at least those who face daily deadlines. A reporter can seldom know as he sets out to cover an event whether it will be banal or significant, nor can he always judge its value in the hot moment of occurrence. Indeed, the value of many of the events the journalist reports can be judged only by specialists. At least occasionally, the reporter relates events whose significance he will never know. Some are certain to be insignificant. The criteria of newsworthiness include that which will interest or titillate some large portion of the public for a passing moment, and thus much of the journalistic mission comes to little.

But if most journalism produces a mass of information, much of it *mere* information, the immensity of that mass coupled with the fact that journalists pursue significances as well as trivialities indicate that their reports can be mined profitably. It would be odd if this were not true, for the journalist has entrée to great events and to decision-makers ("a right to butt in," one has called it) seldom granted to any other researcher.

Because journalists are so often eyewitnesses to history, most of us are forced to depend on the mass media for current information. Newspapers and magazines, radio and television tell us most of what we know about public figures and public affairs. We are always subject to journalism and incapable of doing much about it because we can see too little for ourselves. Days are too short and the world is too big and complex for anyone to be sure of much about the web of government. What most of us think we know is not known at all in the sense of experience and observation.

We get only occasional first-hand glimpses of government by catching sight for a moment of a presidential candidate in the flesh, by shaking hands with a senator (or talking with one while he absently shakes hands with someone else), by doing business with the field offices of federal agencies, by dickering with the Internal Revenue Service—all the little bits and pieces of contact with officialdom that are described, too grandly, as "citizen participation in government."

We learn more at second hand—from friends, acquaintances, and lecturers on hurried tours, especially those who have just come from Washington or the state capital and are eager to impart what they consider, perhaps erroneously, to be the real story of what is going on there.

Yet this is sketchy stuff, and it adds only patches of color to the mosaic. Most of our knowledge of public affairs comes from the mass media. There simply are no practical alternatives to living in a synthetic world.

A distinguished political scientist, Harold Lasswell, has urged that his colleagues collaborate with journalists, rather than merely use their reports, because a journalist is often stationed at a vantage point that allows him to provide a first-hand account of the birth of a new elite or the demise of an old regime:

> Attuned to the immediate, he is impatient of delay. Accustomed to coping with tacticians of deceit, he is a sophisticated assessor of false witness. A journalist is also aware of who knows what, since his dramatizing imagination often perceives the relationship of every participant to the central action, recognizing potential informants who would otherwise be overlooked.[4]

Like the social scientist, the journalist most often pursues fact by interviewing and observing. Here, we should focus on an important aspect of journalism: how raw, unevaluated facts are reported for the sake of timeliness.

The assassination of President Kennedy in 1963 is an excellent case. Dozens of reporters were in the motorcade with the president when he was shot. Hundreds of others had descended on Dallas a few hours after the shooting. In the inevitable confusion, the accounts varied alarmingly.

Item. The rifle from which the bullets came was found by the window on the second floor of the Texas Schoolbook Depository Building. Or it was found in the fifth-floor staircase. Or it was hidden behind boxes and cases on the second floor. Ultimately, all reports agreed that it had been found on the sixth floor.

Item. The rifle was first reported to be a .30 caliber Enfield. Then it was a 7.65mm Mauser. But it was also an Army or Japanese rifle of .25 caliber. Finally, it became an Italian-made 6.5mm rifle with a telescopic sight.

Item. There were three shots. But some reports mentioned four bullets: one found on the floor of the president's car, one found in the president's stretcher, a third removed from Governor Connally's left thigh, and a fourth removed from the president's body. There was even one report of a fifth bullet, which was said to have been found in the grass near the side of the street where the president was hit. Finally, there was general agreement that there were only three bullets.

Item. The first reports of the president's wounds described a "bullet wound in the throat, just below the Adam's apple" and "a massive, gaping wound in the back and on the right side of the head." The position of the president's car at the time of the shooting, seventy-five to one hundred yards beyond the Texas Schoolbook Depository Building, explains the head wound. But how does one account for a bullet in the throat?

Item. The shots were reported to have been fired between 12:30 and 12:31 P.M., Dallas time. It was also reported that Lee Oswald, who was accused of the shooting, dashed into the house at Oak Cliff where he was renting a room "at about 12:45 P.M." Between the time of the assassination and the time of his arrival at the rooming house. Oswald reportedly (1) hid the rifle, (2) made his way from the sixth floor to the second floor of the building, (3) bought and sipped a Coke (lingering long enough to be seen by the building manager and a policeman), (4) walked four blocks to Lamar Street and boarded a bus, (5) descended from the bus and hailed a taxi, and (6) rode four miles to Oak Cliff. How did he accomplish all this in fourteen minutes?

The confusing array of misleading reports is easily explained. *Reporters* did not say on their own authority that a bullet had entered the president's throat; they quoted Drs. Malcolm Perry and Kemp Clark of the Parkland Memorial Hospital in Dallas, who turned out to have been wrong. The Dallas police first identified the rifle as a .30 caliber Enfield and a 7.65mm Mauser. A Secret Service agent said he thought the weapon was a .25 caliber Army or Japanese rifle. The housekeeper at the Oak Cliff rooming house said that Oswald had come dashing in at about 12:45. And so on.

The most that one can charge the journalists with is haste, which gave equal status to everything posing as fact. Some errors were inevitable. Texas Governor John Connally said that the president's car had just made the turn at Elm and Houston Streets when the firing began. Mrs. Connally said that the car was nearing the underpass— 220 yards beyond the turn. Both cannot be right. In fact, the consensus of other observers indicates that both were wrong; the car was about midway between these points.

Such discrepancies mar the work of the reporter who is on a deadline. He observes what he can and relies on authorities, or purported authorities, for the rest. The nature of journalism makes it obvious that although such methods cannot be supplanted, they can be refined to yield closer approximations of fact—for example, by choosing authorities more wisely.

Increasingly, another kind of journalism seeks to go beyond reporting random facts. More and more journalists are linking, combining, and interpreting facts to paint coherent pictures. Although they cannot have the long perspective that is available to most historical writers, the effect and value of their work is much like that of the historian. In a few cases, journalists employ the methods of survey research developed by behavioral scientists. Again, systematic research enables the journalist to pursue and report relevant information.

Kinds of Research Reports

Research is reported in hundreds of forms, from memos to multi-volume books. Even if it were possible to describe all of them, the result would be longer than it would be useful. One who knows where and how to find facts can learn to report them in any of the appropriate forms by analyzing a few of the most important.

Journalistic Forms

When a prominent industrialist refused a reporter's request for an interview, the reporter asked why.

"Because of that editorial," the industrialist replied, referring to one opposing the industrialist's favorite project. The reporter protested that he had had nothing to do with the editorial—that, indeed, he had never written *any* editorial—but the industrialist went on, "I don't mind if you fellows slant news stories, but you shouldn't do that to editorials."

Like the industrialist, most people are confused about journalistic jobs and forms of reporting. Only in extraordinary cases does any reporter ever write an editorial. More important, most reporters try to present news objectively, leaving it to editorial writers to state opinions, to editorialize—to "slant." True, reporters may be as fallible as other humans, but their training and their objectives are different. Perhaps the chief problem in understanding what reporters do and how they do it grows out of the fact that they report in several forms.

The most common is the *straight news report*—also known as the *objective report*—which is a timely account of an event. A newspaper report of a speech is usually straight news. Because it covers only what happened during a brief period, straight news provides a valuable focus. It is also valuable because it makes such limited demands on the reporter that he can come close to presenting an objective report of verifiable fact. Straight news is written by a formula which requires that the first few sentences (in some cases the first sentence alone) report at least the who-what-when-where of an event, with the details strung out in descending order of importance. Because this formula gives the reporter little leeway to express himself—and especially because the reporter is instructed neither to editorialize nor to use words that even hint at his opinion—the report usually lives up to its name: straight.

But if writing according to the formula prevents the reporter from editorializing, it also prevents him from helping readers understand events. Because straight news isolates a small slice of life at a particular time and reports none of the surrounding facts that might provide meaning, it is usually superficial. That is why many reporters argue that nothing like the full truth can emerge from such reports, that straight news is a straitjacket. They are aware, of course, that some events are not *worth* more time and attention than a straight news report provides, but their arguments for more complete reports on important events are the principal reason other forms have emerged.

The *depth report* takes a step beyond straight news. Instead of trying merely to mirror the highlights of an event, the reporter gathers additional information that is independent of the event but related to it. A reporter who covers a speech on medical practices in China may consult experts and reference sources, then present the speaker's words in a larger framework. In some cases, additional information is placed in the speech report; in others, it is reported separately. In either case, depth reporting calls for transmitting information, not the reporter's opinion. Verifiable fact is as pivotal in depth reporting as it is in straight news reporting.

Although the writer's opinion has no place in a depth report, the facts he gathers may rebut or refute the speaker—in which case the speaker or his supporters may charge that the report is slanted. Perhaps it is. The crucial point is *which* of the many available facts a reporter uses to build the larger framework.

Interpretive reports—also known as *news analyses*—are another step beyond straight news. They usually focus on an issue, problem, or controversy. Here, too, the substance is verifiable fact—not opinion. But instead of presenting facts in straight news or depth report fashion and hoping that they will speak for themselves, the interpretive reporter clarifies, explains, analyzes. The interpretive report usually focuses on *why:* Why did the president take that trip, appoint that man, make that statement? What is the real meaning of the event?

Whatever his intention, a reporter who is given the leeway to interpret events may inadvertently offer his opinion; he is always in danger of using words that steer his readers toward his desires and beliefs. Because clarification, explanation, and analysis require that the reporter weigh and filter facts, the interpreter enters the reporting process much more personally than other reporters. And because an interpretation is not written by formula, the reporter has latitude that makes it easier for him to disguise his opinions.

Investigative reporting, which some call "muckraking," is the practice of opening closed doors and closed mouths. As in interpretive reporting, the focus is on problems, issues, and controversies. In fact, interpretive and investigative reports are the same in cases in which the reporter must dig up hidden information in order to clarify, explain, and analyze. In most cases, though, an interpretive reporter has relatively little trouble because he is explaining public events and can find many sources who are happy to help him. (In fact, one of the chief dangers in all reporting is that some sources want to provide information that will serve their own interests.) In contrast, the investigative reporter must try to dig up facts that have been hidden for a purpose—often an illegal or unethical purpose.

Features differ from news reports primarily in their intent. Whereas a news report ordinarily presents information that is likely to concern readers, a feature is usually designed to catch their interest. The feature reporter casts a wide net in his search for facts, sometimes pulling in and using things a news reporter would consider frivolous. The feature writer's report provides a reading experience that depends more on style, grace, and humor than on the importance of the information. (This difference is reflected in the fact that those who produce features exclusively are called "feature writers," not "reporters.")

To understand all these journalistic forms, consider a hypothetical case. Imagine that university administrators, discovering that too little dormitory space is available for all the students who want to live on the campus, have leased one hundred trailer homes and have parked them on the edge of the dormitory area to house four hundred students.

Assigned by the editor of the campus paper to write a straight news report, a reporter would quote the speech or the press release in which the administration announced the establishment of "Trailer Dorm." If student leaders spoke for or against the conditions of trailer living, the writer would quote them as well. If students held a protest rally, the writer would report its highlights dispassionately.

Assigned to write a depth report, one might gather opinions by questioning students, compare home campus housing to that at a nearby university, or report the results of any or all of a dozen quests related to student housing. The limit is marked only by the imagination the reporter brings to his research.

Assigned to write an interpretive report, one might interview administrators to determine why they decided to lease trailers rather than make other arrangements and interview student leaders to determine why they support or oppose the trailer park. Again, the reporter can use many approaches to gathering information that will enable him to clarify, explain, and analyze.

Assigned to write an investigative report by an editor who suspects that the administration was lax in not planning for more dormitory space, or that an administrator's brother owns the trailers, a reporter must interview widely and adroitly and check financial records. The most difficult kind of journalism, investigative reporting requires a researcher who is imaginative, industrious, and aggressive. He must write a hard-fact report, not speculation.

Assigned to write a feature, the writer looks for the color and flavor of trailer life. Do trailer residents live differently from other students? How? Have they painted their homes in wild colors? Are they planting gardens? Who does the cooking—and with what results?

These are not rigid categories. Like all other writing, journalistic forms sometimes overlap. Traces of depth or interpretive reporting may appear in a straight news report. An interpretive report may have investigative elements. A feature may seem to be weighted as heavily with matters of concern as with matters of light interest. But occasional mixtures are not as important as the fact that definable forms exist. Nearly every large newspaper carries reports in these forms. Reading them will show how journalists use different kinds of information to shape the structure of each kind of report.

Academic Forms

William James once said that there is only one kind of scholarly report: the research paper. If the paper is short, it is an article; if long, it is a book. Established scholars can talk off-handedly with one another about the length of their writing; most of it is article or book length. But unless they are having trouble trimming an article to size for publication or deciding whether to devote another year to expanding a long article into a book manuscript, they regard discussions of the length of their work as little more than cocktail party talk.

Unfortunately, the proper length sometimes seems to be the principal concern of students. Most seem to resemble the amateur writer who called a publisher and asked, "How long is the average novel nowadays?"

"Oh, between 75 and 90 thousand words."

"Well, then, I've finished!" [5]

Perhaps he had actually finished, perhaps he should have written more—or perhaps he should never have written a word. In any case, length was not the proper criterion. There is no appropriate length for novels in general. Ernest Hemingway's *The Old Man And The Sea* is fewer than thirty thousand words. Tolstoy's *War and Peace* is more than three hundred thousand. Similarly, student research reports should cover the subject, whatever the length.

The trouble is, of course, that students are accustomed to having the lengths of their reports prescribed—or at least the minimum length. That is probably inevitable. Ideally the instructor in any course would have to do no more than say that he expected a research paper. Each student would soon become so caught up in the substance of the course that he would read widely, noting how, and at what length, different researchers treat different topics. Then the student would say, "The topic that intrigues me is this, and I can treat it that way if I do this and that." By the middle of the term, each student would be able to outline his topic; the instructor would do little more than nod approvingly to encourage each student to develop his excellent idea. One student's report would cover twenty pages, another ten, another fourteen—each an appropriate length because it suited the topic and the purpose of the assignment.

But an instructor is fortunate to find one or two such students in the average course. As a result, he must assign topics and lengths to everyone and encourage those who are caught up in their own ideas to develop them. An instructor may sigh and assign his students to prepare for more demanding work by writing finger exercises: papers that do not demand the time, the attention, or the sophisticated understanding of research and writing that go into a research paper.

The simplest kind of academic paper is the *precis*. Pronounced *praysee,* it is a specialized summary of a passage from a book or article. Written in the basic order of the passage, it also maintains the same proportions of part to part.

Next is the *summary,* which is usually a compact version of an article or book. It covers all the main points and reports them in the same relation to one another found in the work.

The *book report* is both summary and something more. Most instructors require some information on the author and much more on the book itself—identification of it as novel, biography, etc., its subject, the author's theme and interpretation, the organization, and the tone or style. Because few books carry enough on their author's background, other writings, and reputation (some that *do* carry enough background material tend to make the author more important than he is), the student must find the relevant reference sources described in the preceding chapter of this book.

Book reports should not be confused with the *book reviews* published in newspapers, magazines, and professional journals. Reviewers and critics seldom provide all the detailed information about author and book that can be found in a formal book report. Although they are likely to provide much of it, they usually have a larger purpose: comparing the book to similar works and assessing its value.

Nor should book reports and book reviews be confused with *Reports,* which were once formal documents like research papers (the capital "R" is to distinguish this use of the word from the other references to "report"). Some instructors still require formal Reports properly footnoted and spell out everything that must be included.

Formal Research Papers

A fun-loving professor once gave a class a list of topics for a research paper, all but one of which were reasonable. That one was:

Describe the history of dramatic poetry from its origins to the present, concentrating especially but not exclusively on its social, political, religious, and philosophical impact on Europe, Asia, America, and Africa.

To the professor's dismay, most of the students considered that to be seriously intended as a topic. Three chose to write on it. Perhaps nothing else could have demonstrated more clearly that the students did not understand the goals and limitations of research. Unless a teacher explains them in some detail, few students ever seem to understand, if one judges accurately by the many who sigh, "I have to write a paper tonight," as though a research paper represented only meaningless hard labor that actually could be completed properly in one night.

Considered as a negative example, the grotesque topic quoted above shows the goals and limitations of research papers. The most important point is that the topic is impossibly broad. If it can be undertaken successfully, only a specialist should try it, one who is prepared to spend years—probably decades—writing several volumes. A student could do little more with it than pull scraps of information from several books, quote several passages and paraphrase several more, then use a few of his own sentences to string the hodge-podge together.

That approach points up flaws common to many research papers that cover reasonable topics. Written by a student who does not understand what he is about, even a paper on a topic narrow enough to provide a suitable foundation for research and writing is likely to be made up of pieces of the findings and ideas of others. This process can be described as transferring bones from one graveyard to another. Instead, the student should *use* the writings of others, but produce a research paper that bears the clear mark of his own thoughts. That is the scholar's way.

Why should a student who cares not at all about becoming a scholar imitate one? The answer lies at the center of learning. To mingle the works of others in a form whose only claim to originality is that no one has ever placed them in quite the same order is to learn nothing of much value. But a student who analyzes the research and insights of others and responds to them creatively is engaged in the best kind of education. He may undertake research paper after research paper in course after course without reading anything or developing any ideas that will seem to him in later life to have practical value. That is much less important than the real value: learning to think. Gail Thain Parker, who became president of Bennington College when she was 30, said that "The best ideas I have about college administration came from courses in nineteenth century novels. They taught me to think."

References

1. Clark L. Hull, "A Primary Social Science Law," *The Scientific Monthly* 71 (October 1950): 225.
2. S. M. Lipset, "The Psychology of Voting: An Analysis of Political Behavior," in G. Lindsey, ed., *Handbook of Social Psychology,* Vol. 2 (Reading, Mass.: Addison-Wesley, 1954): 1124.
3. Eugene J. Webb, Donald T. Campbell, Richard D. Schwartz, and Lee Sechrest, *Unobtrusive Measures: Nonreactive Research in the Social Sciences* (Chicago: Rand McNally, 1966).
4. Harold D. Lasswell, *The Future of Political Science* (New York: Atherton, 1963): 190.
5. Jacques Barzun and Henry F. Graff, *The Modern Researcher* (New York: Harcourt, Brace and World, 1957).

JOURNALISM AND SOCIAL SCIENCE: CONTINUITIES AND DISCONTINUITIES

Gerald Grant

Edited and reprinted from Herbert J. Gans, Nathan Glazer, Joseph Gusfield, and Christopher Jencks, eds., On the Making of Americans: Essays in Honor of David Riesman (*Philadelphia: University of Pennsylvania Press, 1979*): 291–313.

Critics of the mass media seem obsessed of late with the performance of the journalist as an actor and thinker. There has been a rather extraordinary shift of attention away from questions of context, content, and control. An earlier generation of critics wrote about managers, advertisers, and owners who set the context of the news and determined what appeared in print. The reporter was something of a pawn in the process. Much of the academic criticism of recent years has focused on the shortcomings of the journalist as a thinker and knower. Journalism has been portrayed as the "underdeveloped profession," staffed by idealogues who are untrained, uncritical, or lacking the methods to ascertain truth. The comparison, whether implied or explicit, has often been with the work of the social scientists who authored these critiques.

The criticism of the journalist comes after a decade of enormous inflation in the ranks of social scientists and at a time when the social sciences have fallen into basic disputes about what they teach and who is qualified to teach it. Not surprisingly, social scientists have become more sensitive to the distance between themselves and journalists at a time when it is more difficult to draw precise boundaries. As academic *arrivistes,* social scientists may be eager to separate themselves from their journalistic origins, and, like any newly arrived class, are likely to distort their origins and natural affinities and to act as if there were no commonalities, when of course there are. I say this with some authority, since I am writing about an earlier version of myself, when, after earning a doctorate, I was much too sensitive about references to my status as a "former journalist."

One of the aims of this essay is to show that recent critiques are misleading precisely because the discontinuities between the work of the social scientist and that of the journalist are overdrawn, and the continuities are scarcely recognized. Many critics fail to distinguish between types of journalists, treating a part for the whole. Nor do they take adequate account of significant improvements in resources devoted to more intelligent analysis of many issues, or of rising levels of expertise and knowledge on the part of many journalists.

Types of Journalists

The category "journalist" is not unitary and homogeneous, but as wide as the census category of "managers" that includes candy-store proprietors and managers of highly technical industrial enterprises. If we restrict the term "journalist" to daily print journalism, as is intended here, it includes reporters on small dailies who earn $7,500 a year and journalists on elite papers where minimum wages for journeymen now exceed $25,000.

In terms of their roles and cognitive styles, however, there are three types of journalists. Type I is the pressroom or police reporter, who is dependent upon official sources: this is the classic reporter who accepts the official version of events, or agrees to operate within the definitions of reality that officials provide, even if he or she is skeptical about what the official sources have said. This view characterizes much reporting from the White House as well as from police headquarters. Such reporters seldom assume personal responsibility for what they write. If challenged as to the accuracy or truthfulness of what they have written, they will tend to point to the official who said it or failed to say it as the culpable party, not themselves. The reporter's world tends to be defined by the "sources" he is assigned to cover, and a collection of sources defines a "beat." The subject matter of the "news" tends to be patterned on official activity: a campaign to snag scofflaws, a narcotics raid, an investigation of youth gangs. Much effort is expended in predicting the pattern of official activity, such as appointments of important persons, and scooping the opposition.

The story does not arise from an independent assessment of events or a question in the writer's head; the argument among reporters is not about what the "story" is but, given what has been said, or handed to them, what is the lead. The reporter is thus a transmission belt; he or she writes reports about events as defined by others. The job is to convey this information clearly and quickly. It is an important function. Although some reporters spend a lifetime in such work, pure types are hard to find. Even the most hard-bitten police reporter will occasionally decide on his or her own that conditions in the local jail are intolerable and ought to be exposed, or that a police chief's new policy of "preventive detention" violates civil liberties. This may be written on the reporter's own authority, but usually an "official source," such as the local American Civil Liberties Union lawyer, will be found as a peg on which to hang such a story.

Veteran White House reporters convince themselves that they are not really passive receptors by telling about the telephone calls they made to lower-echelon officials, resulting in modifications of the story the press secretary wanted them to put out. But most of the time, they put it out; that is their function. They are to some degree propagandists for the party in power, or, more benignly, dissemination is a legitimate function of journalists who report on democratically elected officials. A few, of course, are more than conduits, these are usually journalists from papers large enough to double-staff the White House, thus leaving one person free to forage and to think.

Just such suspicions—and they occurred long before Watergate—gave rise to the Type II journalist, the inside dopester and investigative reporter who develops sources he or she can trust. The Type II journalist works by personal, confidential contacts. In the case of the investigative reporter, these are usually antiestablishment or undercover sources, but the inside dopester is characterized by having back-door access to important informants who relay privileged information to the anointed. Social standing, the right address, and invitations to the right clubs and cocktail parties are essential passports to success for the inside dopester. Charles Bartlett, a little-known reporter on the *Chattanooga Times* who had been an old school friend of John F. Kennedy's, was suddenly offered a syndicated column when Kennedy moved to the White House. Elite journalists in Washington formed various insiders' clubs where leading political figures could furnish inside dope. In the 1960s, Godfrey Sperling of the *Christian Science Monitor* initiated a breakfast club, at first limited to a handful of leading political reporters, where Robert Kennedy, Spiro Agnew, Nelson Rockefeller, and others shared some of their first formulations of campaign strategies on an off-the-record or not-for-attribution basis. Jack Germond of the Gannet newspapers initiated a rival supper club limited to fourteen capital correspondents.

Investigative reporters also work essentially by establishing confidential sources and following up inside tips, but they are more likely to be mavericks and underdogs than members of a social elite. Jack Anderson and Les Whitten have their counterparts on every newspaper. These are reporters who are known as crusaders or have a reputation for ferreting out evidence of corruption or wrongdoing. Aggrieved parties, those with an axe to grind, or simply persons with a keen sense of justice will leak information to them on a confidential basis.

Good reporters of this type work for their salary, however, since after days of checking and cross-checking, a tip may prove to be malicious or unfounded. Some investigative journalists were themselves members of a deviant community or had special links to one: for instance a reporter with relatives in the Mafia. More often, however, an investigative reporter works by slowly establishing confidence with a source, in the way that Woodward and Bernstein describe repeated trips to the homes of secretaries who worked for the Committee to Re-Elect the President. In one case, they returned fifteen times. The secretary finally talked to them on the night they helped her clear the dishes after waiting for her party guests to leave.

Investigative journalists, operating without powers of subpoena and without the buffer of lapsed time that helps to open attics and locked drawers for historians, resemble private detectives more than either scholars or journalists of the first type. Type I journalists are lap dogs, generally content with what they are fed, whereas journalists of the investigative type are hound dogs willing to bite the hand that feeds them. Yet while investigative reporters are more critical than pressroom types, their adversary styles and topics of investigation are predictable, and they are highly dependent on handouts, even if undercover. Although some investigative reporters rise to Holmesian heights of deductive reasoning, they are less often capable of systematic analysis of complex problems.

It is the capacity for such complex and creative intellectual activity that distinguishes Type III, the analytical journalist. Once quite rare, limited to an occasional columnist or editorial page writer, the analytical journalist now constitutes an emerging and significant type on the staffs of elite newspapers. And here we are talking not just about the *New York Times* and the *Washington Post,* but about more than a dozen serious papers in major cities (but by no means in all, for New Orleans, San Francisco, and Cincinnati, for example, have none). These journalists are better paid (on the best papers, with salaries as high as those of professors at major universities) and better educated (often with graduate training and occasionally a Ph.D.) than their cohorts a generation ago. Differences in educational levels between journalists on elite and nonelite media are particularly significant (with elite media defined here as those regarded as "the fairest and most reliable" news organizations by journalists themselves). About 80 percent of the elite journalists are college graduates (with proportionately more graduating from the most selective colleges), and 17 percent have graduate degrees. Among the nonelite, only half have college degrees and less than 5 percent have graduate degrees.

The general increase in educational attainment throughout the society has undoubtedly had some effect in creating a demand for more intelligent journalism at the same time that it has provided higher levels of training for those entering the field. Newspapers have been influenced in their forms of coverage by the unexpectedly large audiences drawn to new mediating journals in the social sciences—such as *Psychology Today*—and by the advances demonstrated by educational television. New salary levels and the increased willingness on the part of elite media to offer more space and other resources to more serious forms of journalism have created new opportunity structures for those with advanced training in the social sciences.

For example, Michael T. Kaufman, a *New York Times* correspondent in Nairobi, focused on a debate over a proposed change in marriage laws that would give wives a veto over a husband's polygamous plans and permit them to share control of family property. The attention to such an issue is itself a significant indicator of the shift to more analytical journalism, and the quality of the analysis was penetrating. Here is the third paragraph of Kaufman's report:

> African tribal society is by no means monolithic. There are more cultural, linguistic and even physiological differences among black Africans than there are among white Europeans. But one component of African cultures that is fairly universal is the extended family system, which through an intricate blend of rights and responsibilities assured the continuance of the family and security for its members. Sex roles were clearly defined. The system tended to be polygamous and was adapted to rural and agricultural settings where people lived in relative isolation.[1]

Kaufman's story went on to discuss the ways in which increasing social mobility, socialist regimes, and Western influences have eroded the cultural legacy of African traditions. His analysis was sociologically and anthropologically informed; he drew on scholarly sources and independently paid careful attention to changing images of marriage and the family as they were portrayed in the popular press and television in Nigeria. Other examples could be cited. The hard-drinking foreign correspondent who slammed out copy on the basis of a few English-speaking contacts has been largely replaced today by journalists who have some academic preparation for their assignments, usually speak a foreign language, and, like Michael Kaufman, would regard the spot news and travelogue coverage of an earlier day as unworthy of their talents.

Evelyn Waugh described the trench-coat types of an earlier era in his novel *Scoop,* which Phillip Knightley argues was no fictional parody of the foreign correspondent but rather close to a factual account of the antics of reporters covering the Italian invasion of Addis Ababa in 1935. Waugh's protagonist, Corker of the *Universal News,* speaks for the art of journalism in that day:

> You know, when I first started in journalism I used to think that foreign correspondents spoke every language under the sun and spent their lives studying international conditions. Brother, look at us. On Monday afternoon I was in East Sheen breaking the news to a widow of her husband's death leap with a champion girl cyclist. Next day the chief has me in and says, "Corker, you're off to Ishmaelia." "Out of town job?" I asked. "East Africa," he said, just like that, "pack your traps." "What's the story?" I asked. "Well," he said, "a lot of niggers are having a war. I don't see anything in it myself, but the other agencies are sending feature men, so we've got to do something."

Knightley concludes his study of 120 years of war correspondence with the observation that not until the Vietnam War did the war correspondent begin to emerge as a "partisan for truth," and that it was in Vietnam that "correspondents began seriously to question the ethics of their business." It was one of the few instances where an American correspondent (Harrison Salisbury reporting from Hanoi for the *Times*) made an objective effort to assess civilian damage in enemy territory, forcing publicists in the Pentagon to reverse themselves.[2] I do not think that Henry Kissinger was merely trying to court favor with the press when he said that "the more sophisticated of the journalists often have a reservoir of knowledge and continuity that is better than that of many of the top officials [in the State Department]. I could name individuals who, on arms control, on Vietnam negotiations, could spot subtleties that many of the officials could not see." Of course Kissinger was talking only about some journalists when he made this comment midway in his term of office. In his farewell talk to the Washington press corps he concluded, "I will think of you with affection tinged with exasperation." [3]

Differences between Journalists and Social Scientists

If it is true, as I have argued thus far, that distinctions between journalists and social scientists are overdrawn rather than spurious, what distinctions are valid? It seems to me that the most useful way to examine these distinctions is to look at them not as sharp breaks, but as spectra. There are differences of orientation along several dimensions, with Type I journalists usually at one end of the spectrum and Type III journalists often approaching the boundaries of social science at the other. Four such dimensions will be examined here. These are qualities of time, voice, knowledge, and reference group.

Time. The Type I journalist is typically breathless, in pursuit of the ephemeral event. The social scientist may plan his observations to coincide with the natural cycle of human action or, when dealing with events that are either physically or historically remote, devote time to more leisurely and prolonged analysis and searches of relevant literatures and comparative frameworks.

Many social scientists defend their months or years in the field against "mere journalists who drop in for a day or two" and scribble hasty impressions. They overlook journalists like Joseph Lelyveld of the *Times,* who repeatedly visited a Harlem classroom over the course of a year and perceptively wrote about the struggles the teacher encountered. Similarly, Donald Bartlett and James B. Steele of the *Philadelphia Inquirer* spent the autumn of 1972 coding for computer analysis more than ten thousand criminal records. They examined twenty thousand pages of courtroom testimony and hundreds of psychiatric and probation reports in order to analyze discriminatory patterns in the adjudication of 1034 cases in the Philadelphia courts. Some reporters on the *Los Angeles Times, Wall Street Journal,* and *Washington Post* are allowed months to work up major analyses. Such generous leads have not become the norm, even among elite newspapers, but these examples are no longer rare occurrences.

Voice. A sense of personal responsibility for what is written marks the work of the Type III journalist. In this he or she lies close to the social scientist, who is scrupulous about distinguishing his own analysis from that which is borrowed, and far from the Type I journalist, who is generally a mouthpiece for others. The Type II journalist, or investigative reporter, lies between the two in that he or she engages in independent analysis and speculation, but most often relies on an inside source. The *Philadelphia Inquirer's* Steele rejects the description "investigative reporter" on just such grounds: "The challenge is to gather, marshal, and organize vast amounts of data already in the public domain and see what it adds up to. Inside sources can't always do that for you. They're too involved." [4] Steele exemplifies the Type III journalist, who takes pride not in achieving a scoop, or grooming a confidential source, but in the quality of his analysis.

Knowledge. The kind of knowledge the writer possesses is a critical distinction. Compared with other journalists, the analytical or Type III journalist possesses greater breadth of general knowledge and often has depth in an area of specialization. Architectural writers today often have some training in architecture. Journalists with training in law, economics, and the social sciences are no longer rarities. Institutes and training programs for science writers are increasingly common. The *Times* has employed a medical doctor to write medical news.

Yet when compared to social scientists, Type III journalists differ on two critical dimensions of knowledge: theory and method. The pure social scientist holds theoretical knowledge most dear. He or she aims first at the development of theory, second at the development of method. In the workaday world, however, most academics do not expect to make major contributions to theory. Their claims lie in the less exalted domain of method; they take pride in having mastered methods for gathering and sifting evidence, for establishing standards of reliability and validity. Even among social scientists who do not aspire to the mantle of the great man of theory, one can discern differences in theoretical awareness, or in the degree to which their investigations are theoretically informed. Good social scientists are conscious of the variety of theoretical lenses through which one may examine the social world. Three different theorists sitting in the same classroom would "see" three different worlds.

The theoretically informed person is at once conscious of how his or her own theoretical presuppositions influence what is observed, and of what aspects of that social world would appear in a different light if refracted through another theoretical lens. Analytical journalists differ sharply from social scientists in that their choice of vocation signifies that they have no aspirations of contributing to theory as theory. They differ less sharply, although still considerably, on the question of theoretical awareness. Hilton Kramer on art, Wolf Von Eckhardt on architecture, Leonard Silk on economics, and David Broder on politics are theoretically informed. The newspaper audience limits a writer's appetite for theory and abstraction; such readers are often in search of information or escape. Yet, as the quotation from Michael Kaufman's article and the accompanying notes illustrate, what editors regard as the tolerable limits of a more theoretically informed style have been broadened appreciably.

Of course, most Type I and Type II journalists remain random empiricists, focused on particular events, operating without any general framework of ideas or consciousness of their own theoretical orientations. They operate on the assumption that the facts are sufficient for understanding. It may be that reporters ignore the truth that all facts are "theory-laden" out of a subconscious wish to avoid ideological conflict or to reinforce commonly accepted notions of the status quo, but I suspect it is less that than reinforcement of traditional notions of descriptive storytelling, where the emphasis is placed on colorful, readable accounts of events regarded as unique rather than as recurring as part of larger patterns. Young reporters with literary aspirations idealize their work as a defense of the concretely human against what the humanist feels as "the mostly violent and stupid formulations about the abstractly human." Social scientists, however, are inclined to view facts as mostly propaganda in the absence of any theoretical frameworks (that is, abstractions) for making sense of them.

The analytical journalist is to some degree theoretically informed, but is oriented more to the world and to action than to structures of knowledge. He or she is neither consciously testing theory nor primarily interested in the cumulative programs of the academic disciplines. But such journalists are beginning to be in some degree conscious—in the way just noted—of the different lenses through which one may view the occurrences of the social world. Similarly, their reading habits differ significantly from those of Type I and Type II journalists. They do not read the academic journals in the basic disciplines or, generally, works of pure theory. But they are likely to be critical consumers of midrange literature of the social and behavioral sciences and to read those journals edited for creative intellectuals and those concerned with critical analysis of public affairs: *Foreign Affairs, The Public Interest, Transaction and Society*, the *New York Review of Books*, and professionally oriented academic journals within their fields of interest. Such journalists have a general framework of ideas, though not a precise theoretical scheme. The analytical journalist is an eclectic—a fox, not a hedgehog—who has begun to develop a larger view. They have partially realized Robert E. Park's hope that journalists might be capable of viewing daily events in "their more general bearings." Park, one of the founders of American sociology, had himself been a newspaperman before turning to the University of Chicago, and he believed that the newspaper could be a "powerful agency" for education and reform. Park said he had been influenced by the notion "that thought and knowledge were to be regarded as incidents of and instruments of action, and I saw in the newspaper, responsible for its mission, an instrument by which this conception might be realized in action, and on a grand scale." [5]

Journalists who are theoretically informed are also attentive to data and are becoming more adept at generating data for analysis. The sophisticated social surveys by Philip Meyer of the Knight newspapers following the 1967 Detroit riots were a breakthrough. But modern survey techniques have now been adopted by a number of elite newspapers, and they are no longer restricted to election polls. For example, a recent story in the *New York Times*, drawing on technical assistance from a Princeton social scientist, analyzed a *Times* poll of 593 randomly selected residents of a Queens school district that had refused to supply the federal government with ethnic breakdowns of its staff members and students, thus jeopardizing programs to aid disadvantaged students. Prior to the poll, the Queens community school board had been portrayed as racist. The poll analysis, with accompanying charts, showed that 70 percent of the residents, 40 percent of whom were Jewish and 40 percent Catholic, backed the board. The analysis then turned to an examination of why this might be so and raised the possibility that it was not raw prejudice, since most of the residents were not opposed to integrated education, but evidence of increased middle-class resentment over social policy that excludes their children from federal programs their taxes support. In recent years, the quality and frequency of such analysis has increased appreciably. Certainly one index of analytical journalism ought to be a decrease of anecdotal evidence and some increase in quantifiable data. As a very rough indicator, I totaled the space given to charts and graphs and other quantified data in the *Times* for the month of September in 1935, 1955, 1965, and 1975. Excluding weather charts, stock tables, the sports pages, and other repetitive material, I found that nearly twice as much space is now given to quantified material as in previous decades:

Year	Column Inches of Charts and Graphs
1935	128
1955	150
1965	122
1975	283

The complexity of treatment of the data and the quality of analysis in recent years, while impossible to quantify, have been impressive. For example, in the midst of the New York City teacher negotiations and with a strike threatened, Edward Fiske of the

Times surveyed teacher benefits in ten large cities. His data—arrayed in matrix spread across four columns—compared teachers on thirteen complex variables, including class size, preparation periods allowed, sabbaticals, pensions, length of working day, and relative cost of living.[6] Election polls have moved far beyond the straw vote stage or mere predictions of who is ahead. The *Washington Post* has employed Louis Harris, and the *Times* has employed a variety of social scientists to assist its own staff, including Garry Orren of Harvard and Michael R. Kagay of Princeton. In the last presidential primary, the *Times's* new sophistication was illustrated by its poll of voters as they came out of the booth in order to analyze the results by ideology, religion, occupation, age, education, and race.

   The influence of analytical journalists on papers like the *Washington Post, Los Angeles Times,* and some other elite newspapers has increased in the last decade as these papers established news services serving hundreds of provincial papers. This reduces the reliance of the latter on the Associated Press and United Press International, which formerly dominated the field with what I have described here as Type I coverage. In an analysis of the press's handling of concern about the possibility of a swine flu "epidemic," David Rubin noted the contrast in reporting between a number of elite papers and the standard wire services. While science reporters on some elite papers provided coverage of "depth and sophistication," the routine wire service coverage was "exceedingly superficial," focusing on the "defenses of the public health establishment rather than on the underlying logic of the entire program." Rubin found that the science and medical background of the analytical reporters was the "single most important variable in the quality of coverage," whereas the wire service reporters "were not equipped to ask basic scientific questions about the vaccine, its administration, its composition, and the inoculation programs as a whole." Second, Rubin found a direct correlation between the quality of coverage and the number of sources cited in the coverage. The *New York Times* drew on twenty-two sources, the *Washington Post* seventeen, and the *Miami Herald* twelve, compared with the *Denver Post's* two and the *Caspar* (Wyoming) *Star Tribune's* one.[7]

Reference Group. The cooperation between reporters and social scientists on survey teams indicates a small but important shift in the character of the analytical journalists reference group—that loosely defined group of significant others whose expectations influence one's performance in a role. The significant others for the Type I reporter are sources on his beat whom he tries to please and editors who assign stories and (sometimes without even consulting him) rewrite his copy. The significant role models for the Type II reporter are the muckraker and prize-winning journalist stereotypes—the reporter whose exposé puts wrongdoers behind bars. The Type III or analytical journalists, by virtue of their educational background and their need to be critical consumers of a wide range of reports written by social scientists, are more inclined to compare their work to social science models. One salient model is provided by the social scientist who does not write primarily for his or her academic peers but for a more general intellectual audience of whom fellow social scientists are but one subset. Social scientists of this generalized type (although not only them) are strong influences on analytically oriented journalists.

   Other models are also having an impact as the exchanges between journalists and social scientists have increased and new relationships have been created. Analyses written by academics appear more frequently in newsprint (as contrasted with the earlier practice of restricting such contributions to signed opinion pieces opposite the editorial page). The Russell Sage Foundation has sponsored internships on newspapers for doctoral candidates, and academic sabbaticals for journalists are more plentiful. Newspapers have brought academics into the newsroom for short-term projects and have commissioned research. Academics have been more hospitable to contributions from analytical journalists on some journals and have occasionally invited journalists to participate in research projects. These new networks and affinities are creating new standards of comparison.

But reference groups have a normative as well as a comparative aspect; that is, they shape the values by which judgments are made as well as provide standards against which to measure oneself. One of the ways in which analytical journalism is growing closer to the norms of science is in its willingness to examine its own performance. The most striking evidence of a more reflexive attitude is found in the appointment of staff critics or ombudsmen who have the power to investigate complaints about the newspaper's performance and publish the results. The first such position was created by the *Louisville Courier-Journal and Times* in 1967. Within a decade, fifteen papers have followed suit. Corrections are now published more readily, and in a less aggrieved tone.

The National News Council, with its broad oversight powers, had a slow birth, greeted skeptically by some leaders in journalism, welcomed by others, and opposed by a few (including the *New York Times*). Since its establishment in 1973, it has won the endorsement of the American Society of Newspaper Editors. Now the Council's often witheringly critical reports of individual papers and journalists are regularly published in the *Columbia Journalism Review* in the manner of censures reported by the American Association of University Professors. The News Council has had some influence in elevating the discourse on ethical issues—a topic sorely in need of discussion when a major newspaper publishes a column defending its "journalistic enterprise" by arguing that "a newspaper should . . . stick to what it does best—which is to steal other people's books." [8]

The *Columbia Journalism Review* was itself a lone voice when established in 1961 "to assess the performance of journalism in all its forms, to call attention to its shortcomings and strengths, and to help define—or redefine—standards of honest, responsible service." But more than a dozen such reviews have come into existence since, most on a regional or local level.

All this is not to argue that journalism is a science or that analytical journalists are colleagues of social scientists in a formal sense. A reference group is not a peer group. The work of journalists is not refereed by colleagues in the way that manuscripts are passed upon by social scientists. And despite liberalizations in both the length of newspaper articles and the length of time given to prepare them, and improved educational levels of analytical journalists, the audience for which they write does not have the tolerance for ambiguity and complexity that social scientists may take for granted.

Journalists as Social Scientists

The qualities just discussed define a new class of journalists—as yet a tiny minority. These journalists are educationally prepared to engage in analysis. They are not mere functionaries, but thoughtful social observers who have developed their own intellectual agendas. Although they vary greatly in the degree to which they are theoretically informed, they are oriented to social science methods, and their search for evidence is increasingly scrupulous, if not yet deserving the description "scientific." The acknowledgment of this new class has been obscured by increased attention to the real shortcomings of the press in other respects and a failure to distinguish among the multiple realities that go by the name of "journalism." The analytical journalist is not yet fully institutionalized, and the role has created some dynamic tensions within journalism and in its relation to social science. Predictions are always risky, but several developments seem probable in the next decades.

The traditional rugged individualism of the reporter's trade will be in conflict with the need for teamwork and new forms of group journalism influenced by social science methods. Elite journalism is intensely competitive. After a year-long immersion in the newsroom, Chris Argyris concluded that life at the *New York Times* was characterized by high competition and low trust. He noted this typical comment by an editor about reporters: "They're competitive as the devil, they're competitive for a sandwich, they're jealous of each other. . . ." [9] Journalists who are out to best the competition and each other concentrate more on winning than on cooperating, yet analytic journalism adopting social science methods requires cooperation in teams. The new italic prefaces delineating the various contributions of reporters on team-written stories are one indication of the rise of analytic journalism. The italic replaces the larger boldface bylines, reflecting in typesize the reduction of ego required in cooperative modes. This tension between individualism and cooperative enterprise will not be easily overcome. Even when it does not mean working in teams, analytic journalism means that a reporter's name does not appear in the paper as often, and that his or her articles will more likely appear inside than "out front" on page one.

As more persons with advanced training in the social sciences are drawn into journalism—as I believe more should be and will be in a time of "excess capacity" in the nation's graduate schools—tensions between generalists and experts will increase. The generalist philosophy that any staffer should be ready on demand to cover any assignment or chase any fire engine remains potent. The new experts of analytical journalism have won privileges and exemptions informally, on a case-by-case basis. But pressures will increase to define their statuses and privileges in more formal ways. In the future, analytical journalists will seek more clearcut protection against irrelevant assignments and unauthorized changes in their copy—if not some journalistic analogue to formal rights of academic freedom.

These tensions will be played out in the executive suites in the next decade as new editors are selected. If they come from the ranks of generalists, analytical journalism may continue to be seen as important, but somewhat of a deadend. If analytical journalists rise to the top, its practice will be rewarded. The feelings will be not unlike those expressed by academics about the appointment of a dean or president—will he or she be one of us, nourishing the values we respect, or just another "manager"? The economics of modern journalism will play a critical role, with many profit-minded publishers seeking leadership that will increase circulation and advertising revenue. One of the strongest countervailing pressures to the advance of a more analytical journalism will come from such publishers, who will want gossipy features and splashy new sections devoted to hobbies or housewares rather than an increase in the allotment of serious journalism. Serious journalists of the type I have described are going to become more militant about trivialization of the news. But the powers of journalists and publishers are unequal. The outcomes are highly uncertain.

In addition to the foregoing, which are struggles within the journalistic profession, tensions between this emerging class of journalists and social scientists may also increase. In an earlier time, social scientists were wary of popularizations and oversimplifications of their work in the mass media. Journalists were viewed as the boobs who might hold them up to ridicule. Now the concern is that journalists will cream off their work without giving proper credit, a concern highlighted recently when a UCLA psychiatrist sued a journalist, Gail Sheehy, for plagiarizing his work. Resolution of these tensions will draw journalists into consideration of more thoughtful codes of ethics and more careful attribution and acknowledgment of sources. The *New York Times* will never appear with footnotes, but the day may not be far off when some stories will end up with a paragraph or two of agate type giving a more careful account of interviews and scholarly sources that cannot be easily acknowledged in the body of an article.

The kind of interaction that journalists and social scientists achieve will bear importantly on the development of the Type III journalist. This new form of journalism seems likely to develop in one of two ways: toward the analytical style sketched out here, heavily influenced by social science models, or toward free-standing social criticism. Although social criticism has a long and honorable tradition, it is also much more open to abuse. The social critic gives dominance to personal expression. What matters is filtering a question through his or her sensibility and expressing an opinion about it. It can easily degenerate into the application of a fairly predictable ideological stance. What is often missing in social criticism is a certain kneading of the dough, a submission to disciplined interaction with others. Analytical journalists who are oriented to social science models will give dominance to the quality of the data, tests for it, synthesis, reading into and around a topic, and exploration of the complexities. They will be distinguished by greater detachment and more careful acknowledgment of sources. In the writings of the social critic, voice dominates data, whereas the contrary is true for the analyst.

Journalists are not fixed in typologies, but develop in dynamic relationship to opportunities and interactions with significant others, most of which still occur after entry rather than in formal training prior to launching a career. Social scientists can influence that dynamic process toward the analytical model in several ways. They can be more circumspect in using the word "journalism" as a pejorative and acknowledge the real achievements of many analytically oriented journalists as persons who, if they are not colleagues, are fellow members of a fraternity of scrupulous observers and interpreters of the social world. Instead of putting up fences and drawing moats around an illusory world of pure social science, they can recognize the commonalities and the possibilities of cooperation. More sabbaticals for journalists are needed, and more social scientists should venture into newsrooms and television studios as members of survey teams or as advisers and subeditors. Serious journalists should be welcomed into professional academic associations as associate members. Graduate students with a bent for journalism should be encouraged to experiment in that direction without feeling they have made an unalterable choice or turned their backs on "science." Social scientists should provide more responsible criticism of media performance, giving recognition to exemplary performance, perhaps by establishing awards that would rival the Pulitzers, and providing specific and detailed analyses of the shortcomings of the press along with suggested practicable remedies. In short, there has been too much condemnation of the press, some of it self-serving, and too little appreciation of the actualities and imaginative possibilities of more productive interactions between journalists and social scientists. What is at stake is nothing less than securing a basis for more intelligent human action in a democratic society.

References

1. Michael T. Kaufman, "Tradition a Big Barrier in Kenya's Marriage-Reform Drive," *New York Times,* October 23, 1976.
2. Phillip Knightley, *The First Casualty* (New York: Harcourt Brace Jovanovich, 1975): Chs. 8, 16.
3. Transcript of an interview published in *Newsweek,* December 30, 1974: 32; and a report of his farewell talk at the National Press Club, *New York Times,* January 10, 1977.
4. Leonard Downie, Jr., *The New Muckrakers* (Washington, D.C.: New Republica Book Co., 1976): 99–100.
5. Robert E. Park, "Life History," *American Journal of Sociology* 79 (1973): 255.
6. Edward B. Fiske, "City Rated High in Teacher Pay," *New York Times,* September 8, 1975.
7. David M. Rubin, "Remember Swine Flu?," *Columbia Journalism Review* 16 (July/August 1977): 42–46.
8. Richard Cohen, "Haldeman Book Creates a Journalistic Stir," *Washington Post,* February 21, 1978.
9. Chris Argyris, *Behind the Front Page* (San Francisco: Jossey-Bass, 1974): 10.

TO THE STUDENT: A COMMENTARY

Bill Rivers is saying to us that social scientists and journalists may be interested in the same thing, say politics, but approach it in different ways. For example, take the outcome of the 1980 presidential election. A political scientist specializing in the study of voting behavior will probably look at the pattern of votes and the kinds of survey data Rivers alludes to in hopes of explaining what happened by developing a general theory of voting behavior that would cover a variety of electoral outcomes or, if such a theory already exists, fitting the 1980 results into that theory—either substantiating or modifying the theory as facts dictate. The political scientist may even have grander goals in mind, such as deriving a general theory of politics or even of human choice. In any case, a search for law-like behavior motivates many a social scientist. But, notes Rivers, "facts for their own sake" goad the journalist. This is not to say that reporters don't try to explain the facts in a more general way, for many do (Grant's Type III journalist is a case in point). But Rivers is arguing that on a day-to-day basis the facts you see and hear through TV news or read in the newspapers are frequently "raw, unevaluated" and lacking the "long perspective." Rivers, like Grant, recognizes that an increasing number of journalists are interpreting facts to provide coherent pictures, but the pressures of deadlines and the necessity for timeliness—so well illustrated in Rivers' example of reporting of the assassination of President John F. Kennedy—make coherence difficult in accounts of breaking events.

Thus, for Rivers the *approach* of most journalists to a topic will not be that of a social scientist. Grant basically would agree. By his own account neither the Type I (beat reporter) nor Type II (investigative reporter) journalist approaches a topic with the analytical style that Grant associates with social science. Moreover, Grant clearly distinguishes Type I (and for that matter Type II) journalists from social scientists on "qualities of time, voice, knowledge, and reference group." Note the parallels of Rivers and Grant on each of these. Both see most journalists as pressed by needs to report timely pieces (Rivers speaks of timeliness, Grant of reporting by Type I journalists as breathless). With respect to "voice" Grant says that beat reporters pass along to us the facts given them by informants (so do investigative reporters after more searching). Rivers captures this idea when he notes with respect to confusion regarding the Kennedy assassination that *"reporters* did not say on their own authority" anything. "They quoted." Again, on Grant's quality of "knowledge" we find him echoing a point parallel to Rivers, i.e., social scientists are interested in systematically derived facts contributing to theories and law-like propositions; journalists (especially of Type I) are theoretically naive and, unless of Type III, not specialized in the subject they report about. Finally, Rivers speaks little of Grant's "reference group" quality. But wait a minute. Does not his discussion of journalistic and academic forms make a point similar to Grant's? Both of our sets of political watchers couch their reports in styles they deem appropriate for winning the approval of others. Hence, journalists write for other journalists, editors, and their readers, and social scientists for their fellow academicians.

To assist you in summarizing the key points made in the Rivers and Grant articles comparing and contrasting the kinds of political watchers you will find represented in this book, consider a distinction offered more than four decades ago by a scholar attempting to distinguish between "news" and social science "knowledge." [1] In 1940 sociologist Robert Park, who incidentally had also been a journalist before becoming an academician, relied upon a distinction made by the American social psychologist-philosopher William James between "acquaintance with" and "knowledge about."

Through your daily experience you become acquainted with a variety of things—that it is raining or sunny, that a professor did not show up for class, that the U.S. Congress passed a tax cut. Granted you learn of these things; what do you really know about them? Knowledge implies some theoretical grasp of the whys and wherefores of the weather and climate making for rain or clear skies; of the occupation, social role, psychology, economics, and organizational position of being a college teacher (social psychology); or of the political and/or economic motives and consequences of congressional actions (political science).

News, thought Park, provides you and us acquaintance with a lot of things—probably more now than when he wrote in 1940, perhaps through the "miracle of television." But, does news increase knowledge about those things as well? Perhaps, perhaps not.

In providing us acquaintance with people and events, news is strongly affected by "now-ism." [2] Now-ism is the tendency for the news to take current events of a timely but ephemeral nature and read all manner of implications into them for our past, present, and future. Consider the melancholy plight of President Jimmy Carter's press coverage in 1979–1980 when Carter was challenged for the Democratic presidential nomination by Senator Edward Kennedy. When Kennedy first hinted he might seek the nomination, journalistic accounts in the spirit of now-ism quickly stressed Carter's plight. Unable to deal with Congress, trailing Kennedy badly in public opinion polls, dogged by diplomatic failures, Carter received the verdict of much of the now-news media: because of his lack of leadership in national affairs, Carter's likelihood of surviving the Kennedy challenge was so slim that withdrawal from the nomination race might even be appropriate. Yet, within two weeks of Kennedy's entrance into the nomination sweepstakes, events had taken a new turn. Carter discovered himself lauded in news accounts for his "temperate" handling of the seizure of U.S. embassy officials in Iran, a leadership coup "propelling" him upward in public opinion polls and in the assessment of congressional leaders. The new and now estimate was that, if Kennedy showed poorly in early head-to-head contests with the President, the Senator would withdraw from the race.

In short, now-ism can be likened to "an irresistible urge to extrapolate tiny momentary changes into Necessary Historical Tidal Forces."[3] This is not to say that social scientists are free from the affliction. As you will see in many of the chapters that follow, many a supposed scientific theory of politics falls victim to being premature, a hasty conclusion based on too little, or invalid, data. We invite you to be especially sensitive to this problem as you reflect upon the essays in this book; i.e., are you merely becoming acquainted with politics or genuinely acquiring knowledge about political life?

Another aspect of the kinds of political watching by social scientists and journalists deserves your attention. Both Rivers and Grant allude to it in passing, but explicit mention is required. Suppose people march in protest in front of the White House in an effort to halt the building of any more nuclear power plants. The social scientist may ask several questions about the demonstration: Who took part and why? What effect did the protest have on changes in public policy regarding nuclear power? How did the President respond and what does that response say about presidential leadership and character? How did congressional committees react and what does that tell us about patterns of congressional behavior? Whatever the question (let us assume it is who took part and why), the social scientist probably has an educated guess (called a hypothesis) about it. To see if that hypothesis is correct or not, the social scientist asks certain things about the people involved in the protest—their characteristics such as age, sex, educational background, and so forth; their motives, attitudes, and how they see things; their relations with other protestors and nonprotestors. These qualities the social scientist considers to be "variables," i.e., factors that differ in certain ways from person to person. The social scientist will probably examine these variables, measure them, and try to relate them one to another. Thus, the social scientist's approach is to isolate key variables that help explain the nature of the protest.

Variables are, of course, the facts or data of social science. As Rivers stresses, facts are also important to journalists. But the news reporter, especially the beat or investigative reporter, is less interested in isolating key factors that vary from person to person and relating those variables than in isolating major leaders and typical participants in an event. For the journalist a protest demonstration unfolds as an event to be narrated in dramatic form. The focus is not upon characteristics of persons so much as the persons themselves: protest leaders, such as actress Jane Fonda; major public figures, such as Governor Jerry Brown of California; representative protestors, including a college student, a concerned scientist, a housewife who does not want a nuclear facility built near her home; or whomever.

The differing emphases of social science and journalism—the former on variables and the latter on events involving key actors—appear in the principal elements that enter into the social scientist's and journalist's respective accounts of "what happened." As you will note in many of the selections written by social scientists in this book, the academic format of reporting, as Rivers suggests, is predictable. Typically the scholarly article states the "research problem" followed by the "theoretical framework" to which it relates, the "hypotheses" tested, the "methods of gathering data," "findings," and ends with a discussion of "interpretations" or "conclusions" about how the stated problem, theory, and evidence relate to one another. The sequence of presentation may vary slightly or the labels may change, but the overall presentation follows a ritual that aids social scientists in communicating to one another and makes it easier for one scientist to redo (or "replicate") another's work.

As Rivers indicates, much of news reporting also follows a formula, one in keeping with narrating the drama surrounding a newsworthy event. Emphasis is upon the who, what, when, where, and how of the event. As reporting grows more analytical and interpretative, the "why" of the event also intrudes into the news story. For the journalist the craft is, as Shakespeare's Hamlet intoned, one where "the play's the thing," i.e., the story comes before any guiding theories.

Now what does all this imply for you as one seeking to become a keen observer of political life? We think two things. First, most journalistic accounts of events in TV news and metropolitan dailies still emphasize beat, investigative, depth, and interpretive reports and features that highlight dramatic qualities of events. If you are aware of that, you can look for such story elements and better evaluate whether you are actually getting knowledge about political events or merely added acquaintance with them. If knowledge seems to be lacking, your experience in reading the social scientist's analyses of problems presented in this book may suggest (1) whether that is truly knowledge or simply a better than nodding acquaintance, and (2) if knowledge, where you might turn in the future to round out your understanding of politics.

Second, if Grant is correct that an increase in analytical reporting is facing you as a citizen concerned with political events, then the likelihood is that more and more journalists will incorporate social science theories, variables, methods, and data into their accounts. Some may even flirt with adapting the academic format to their reporting. If you wish to become an informed watcher of politics (and we invite you to do just that!), it behooves you to familiarize yourself with social scientists' reports and to compare them with what journalists are saying to you. By providing you with both a journalist's and social scientist's account in several crucial areas of American politics we offer you that opportunity and challenge.

Our plan is simple. This book consists of three parts. The first asks you to think about citizens such as yourself and their role in politics. The second invites you to observe the activities of politicians. The third urges you to become familiar with the ever more influential role of the news media in American politics, a role that makes journalists both political watchers and doers. As you read the chapters in each part harken back to what we have said here about how journalists and social scientists may shape what you see as you watch this nation's politics. In our epilogue you will be invited to rethink that question in even more general ways.

Perhaps by now you have given thought to reflecting in more detail about how social science and journalism compare with one another as sources of political information. If you want to do so, we think you will find the following materials helpful.

By social scientists:

Herbert J. Gans, *Deciding What's News*

Gaye Tuchman, *Making News*

Edward Epstein, *News From Nowhere*

"Approaches to Objectivity" by E. Barbara Phillips in Paul Hirsch, Peter Miller, and Gerald Kline, eds., *Strategies for Communication Research*

"What IS News," a symposium in the *Journal of Communication,* Volume 26 (Autumn 1976): 86–123

"News as a Form of Knowledge" by Robert E. Park in the *American Journal of Sociology,* Volume 45 (March 1940): 669–86

"What Is News" by J. Herbert Altschull in the *Mass Communication Review,* Volume 2 (December 1974): 17–23

By journalists/former journalists:

James Reston, *The Artillery of the Press*

Tom Wicker, *On Press*

Bernard Roshco, *Newsmaking*

"The New Journalism" by Robert D. Novak in Henry M. Clor, ed., *The Mass Media and Modern Democracy*

Walter Lippmann, *Public Opinion*

References

1. Robert E. Park, "News as a Form of Knowledge," *American Journal of Sociology* 45 (March 1940): 669–86.
2. Dan Nimmo and James E. Combs, *Subliminal Politics* (Englewood Cliffs, N.J.: Spectrum Books, 1980).
3. Everett Ladd, Jr., Charles Hadley, and Lauriston King, "A New Political Alignment," *The Public Interest* 23 (Spring 1971): 46–63.

PART 1 LOOKING AT CITIZENS

1 America and the Americans

INTRODUCTION

Politics does not occur in a vacuum. Political activity is what it is because people are what they are. Our social and personal attributes help shape politics and, in turn, are influenced by our political lives. How each of you gets involved and takes part in politics, votes, responds to politicians, and follows political events is partly a reflection of what you are socially, believe, value, and expect out of life.

Such an observation is scarcely startling. We all know it to be so. Yet think how often politics seems remote from our lives, not much more than a set of abstract public figures and governmental institutions wrapped in the labels of "President," "Congress," "bureaucracy," or "Supreme Court." Because it is so easy to slip into that feeling and to forget that *politics is what we are* rather than an abstract idea, it is worthwhile to begin your watching of politics by looking first at the people who make American politics possible—Americans! The two selections in this chapter permit that.

The character of a nation's people—that is, who they are, their age, sex, where they live, and what they think and feel—says a lot about their politics. Politicians recognize this and are sensitive to any changes in population attributes affecting their fortunes. In "A New Country: America, 1984" Ben Wattenberg identifies one population shift that may have considerable bearing on our electoral politics in the 1980s. The article is brief, but provocative. Read it with an eye toward relating how the population change he is talking about forebodes a change in our presidential and congressional politics. Wattenberg even provides a "blaze of questions" that will surely stimulate your thinking.

Who is Ben Wattenberg? He is a little bit of everything. For one, he is a committed Democrat who worked on behalf of Senator Henry Jackson's efforts to win presidential nominations in 1972 and 1976, and helped write the Democratic party platforms in those years. For another, he is a television producer—creator and narrator of the series "In Search of the Real America." He may have found it, for even earlier in another of his many roles he wrote a book entitled *The Real America*. And he is a novelist, coauthor of *Against All Enemies,* published in 1977. If that is not enough, he has also been a business consultant for well over a decade and was an assistant to President Lyndon Johnson from 1966–1968. Finally, although not technically a journalist by trade, he certainly plays the social role labeled by Gerald Grant in the selection you just completed in the prologue of this book, that of the analytical journalist. His articles appear in a variety of magazines, chiefly *Public Opinion,* from which this selection was taken.

Americans, however, are more than people residing in different places from time to time—the focus of Wattenberg's analysis. They also know what they want and how they feel about things. That is the subject of Milton Rokeach's article "Change and Stability in American Value Systems." Read it and reflect upon how Americans purportedly feel about equality and freedom and how those feelings have influenced our politics in the past decade. Do you think Americans value the same ideals today? And, most importantly, do you share the consensus Rokeach seems to have found regarding Americans' values?

Rokeach is a preeminent student of how people organize their personal systems of beliefs and values and how they respond to the ideas of others. His deserved high regard among social scientists was solidified in 1960 with the publication of *The Open and Closed Mind,* an examination of prejudice and dogmatic thinking. The work was nine years in preparation and is now a classic. Rokeach has also written other notable works, including *The Three Christs of Ypsilanti* that explores fixed and changing beliefs, a 1968 study of *Beliefs, Attitudes, and Values,* a major book-length work in 1973 entitled *The Nature of Human Values,* and most recently *Understanding Human Values.* He has taught courses in social psychology at major universities and currently directs the Unit on Human Values at Washington State University.

Clearly, then, both Ben Wattenberg and Milton Rokeach have considerable experience in looking at Americans, our characteristics, beliefs, and values. Consider what they say.

A NEW COUNTRY: AMERICA, 1984

BEN J. WATTENBERG

Edited and reprinted from Public Opinion 2 *(October/November 1979): 20, 41.*

It seems now that Senator Edward Kennedy has indeed decided to seek the presidency in 1980. Why did Senator Kennedy make his decision to run? Much has been written about it; many reasons have been advanced.

One reason, a sound one, has drawn no attention. Perhaps Senator Kennedy and his advisors paid no attention to it; if they didn't, they should have.

Nineteen eighty is more than just an election year. It is also a decennial census year. Our Constitution stipulates that the House of Representatives be reapportioned every ten years to reflect the population shifts recorded in the decennial census. By 1982, the House will be reapportioned. In 1984—the presidential year immediately following the 1980 one—the electoral college will be reapportioned to reflect those House changes. The number of electoral votes given to a state, remember, is simply the total of its Senate and House seats.

So what?

Well, population has been shifting in the United States. The population of the "Sun belt," we've been informed, has been growing. (What it actually means is the South-and-West belt, which includes some now-and-again cold and un-sunny places like Oregon and Washington.) The population of the "Frost belt" has been getting relatively smaller. Consider for a moment how the picture looks if one uses the standard Census Bureau regional breakdowns as the delineators: "Northeast" and "North Central" equating as "Frost belt," and "South" and "West" as "Sun belt." [See Table 1.]

When John Kennedy was elected President in 1960, the "Frost belt" had 286 electoral votes, the "Sun belt" only 245. The "Frosties" led by *forty-one*. When Lyndon Johnson was elected in 1964, the "Frostie" lead had already shrunk to only *twelve*. When Richard Nixon won in 1972 the South and West states had, for the first time in American history, more electoral votes than did the "Frost belt" states, but by only a slim *four*-vote lead. That is still where the situation stands today.

But what about 1984, the other year Ted Kennedy might have chosen for his run for the roses?

According to the Census Bureau projections, when voters go to the polls in 1984, the South-and-West belt will have twenty-six more electoral votes than the "Frost belt"—a twenty-two vote shift from 1980!

It creates a new political terrain.

The changes in the political map from the time of the election of John Kennedy to the putative candidacy of Ted Kennedy in 1980 have already been great. By 1984 they will be enormous.

Why?

The rate of political change is particularly quick right now. This is so, first, because the population shift has been large. But second, by quirk of the Constitution, the twenty-four year span from 1960 to 1984 will reflect apportionment changes spanning *four* censuses—those of 1950, 1960, 1970, and 1980. The rate of change is compressed.

The magnitudes are massive. The twenty-four year change amounts to a loss of thirty votes for the "Frost belters" and a gain of 37 for the "Sun belters."

A loss of thirty electoral college votes is as if Pennsylvania and Rhode Island disappeared suddenly from the "Frost belt" one morning. A gain of 37 electoral college votes is as if a new Florida and Tennessee were created overnight in the "Sun belt." The *swing* of sixty-seven electoral college votes, representing the real value of

TABLE 1 Electoral Vote Change Over Time

	"Frost belt"	"Sun belt"	"Frost" "Sun" Balance
1952	286	245	+41
1964	275	263	+12
1972	267	271	− 4
1984	256	282	−26
Gain or loss	−30	+37	
"Swing"		67	

the four reapportionments, would constitute roughly the combined populations of Florida, Colorado, Michigan, and Virginia. A big move in just twenty-four years.

It is not a random move, politically speaking, just as it is not random geographically. Public opinion data show conclusively that the states of the West and South are substantially more conservative than those of the "Frost belt."

This might not have hurt the candidacy of John Kennedy. He was regarded as somewhat to the right of the liberal wing of the Democratic party. The Stevensonians, recall, attacked him during his fight for nomination.

Ted Kennedy is another matter. He is regarded, and his voting record bears it out, as the standard-bearer of the lefter side of the Democratic party. His Americans for Democratic Action rating, for example, is substantially higher than that of George McGovern.

* * *

These data fuel a blaze of questions and speculations.

- Did Senator Kennedy consider this equation in his deliberations? Did he decide to run now, in part, because it might be "now or never"?
- Won't these trends—even in 1980—make it more difficult for a Kennedy candidacy to succeed—as a primary candidate, as a candidate in the general election, as a president?

Suppose, for example, Senator Kennedy is elected president. By 1982 the House of Representatives will be reapportioned. The more conservative states will be gaining seats; the more liberal states losing seats. From John Kennedy to Ted Kennedy, New York will have lost nine congressmen, Texas gained four. Even if the second President Kennedy *wants* to wage a fight for liberal programs, does he have a chance of success? Will political America turn permanently semi-conservative, semi-permanently conservative, or any permutations thereof?

- What about "Quad-Cali"? That was the psephological doctrine espoused by Richard M. Scammon and this author in the 1970 book, *The Real Majority*. That thesis said that the presidential candidate who carried Quad-Cali—the industrial *quad*rangle, east of the Mississippi River and north of both the Ohio River and the Mason-Dixon line, south of upper New England, *plus Cali*fornia—would have enough votes to carry the electoral college. Although these states are still potent, *that will not be true in 1984; it is only barely so in 1980, but only if one counts in Indiana.* But when did Indiana last go Democratic?
- California. Always critical—now super-critical. When John Kennedy ran, California had thirty-two electoral votes and so did Pennsylvania. In 1984, California will have forty-seven votes and Pennsylvania twenty-six! But California is *not* a politically "conservative" "Sun belt" state the way, say, Texas is. It swings in national elections. A growing Hispanic population further clouds the crystal ball. But so massive is the movement of voters that one can begin to play games that lead toward the possibility that the more liberal candidate can *carry* California *and* the traditionally liberal areas—and *still lose* a national election!

* * *

Many, many questions. Fuel for the political hot stove league for the next five years at least. That way, it should be noted, lies a pleasant madness for those equipped with pocket calculators and a penchant for speculation. And all keyed to the fact that tens of millions of Americans decided to move in recent decades, changing the demographic map and thereby, the political map as well.

TABLE 2 Electoral Votes

First Election Reflecting Electoral College Reapportionment		1952	1964	1972	(Projected change in House seats)	1984 (projected)
Northeast	Connecticut	8	8	8		8
	Maine	5	4	4		4
	Massachusetts	16	14	14		14
	New Hampshire	4	4	4		4
	New Jersey	16	17	17		17
	New York	45	43	41	−4	37
	Pennsylvania	32	29	27	−1	26
	Rhode Island	4	4	4		4
	Vermont	3	3	3		3
North Central	Illinois	27	26	26	−2	24
	Indiana	13	13	13		13
	Iowa	10	9	8		8
	Kansas	8	7	7		7
	Michigan	20	21	21	−1	20
	Minnesota	11	10	10		10
	Missouri	13	12	12		12
	Nebraska	6	5	5		5
	North Dakota	4	4	3		3
	Ohio	25	26	25	−2	23
	South Dakota	4	4	4	−1	3
	Wisconsin	12	12	11		11
South	Alabama	11	10	9		9
	Arkansas	8	6	6		6
	Delaware	3	3	3		3
	Florida	10	14	17	+2	19
	Georgia	12	12	12		12
	Kentucky	10	9	9		9
	Louisiana	10	10	10		10
	Maryland	9	10	10		10
	Mississippi	8	7	7		7
	North Carolina	14	13	13		13
	Oklahoma	8	8	8		8
	South Carolina	8	8	8		8
	Tennessee	11	11	10	+1	11
	Texas	24	25	26	+2	28
	Virginia	12	12	12		12
	West Virginia	8	7	6		6
	District of Columbia *		3	3		3
West	Arizona	4	5	6	+1	7
	California	32	40	45	+2	47
	Colorado	6	6	7		7
	Idaho	4	4	4		4
	Montana	4	4	4		4
	Nevada	3	3	3		3
	New Mexico	4	4	4		4
	Oregon	6	6	6	+1	7
	Utah	4	4	4	+1	5
	Washington	9	9	9	+1	10
	Wyoming	3	3	3		3
	Hawaii *		4	4		4
	Alaska *		3	3		3
		531	538	538		538

* Between the presidential elections of 1956 and 1964, the electoral college was increased from 531 to 538 by the addition of Alaska, Hawaii, and the District of Columbia.

Source: Figures compiled from U.S. Bureau of the Census information.

CHANGE AND STABILITY IN AMERICAN VALUE SYSTEMS

Milton Rokeach

Edited and reprinted from Public Opinion Quarterly *38 (Summer 1974): 222–238.*

The main purpose of this article is to report the value stabilities and changes that have been observed in American society over a three-year period, 1968-1971. A second purpose is to report on the underlying structure of American values over the same three-year period.

In the spring of 1968 and again in the spring of 1971, value measurements were obtained from a national area probability sample of Americans over 21. The test employed was the Rokeach Value Survey,[1] on both occasions administered by the National Opinion Research Center (NORC).

The Rokeach Value Survey consists of 18 terminal values—ideal end-states of existence—and 18 instrumental values—ideal modes of behavior. Respondents were instructed "to arrange them in order of their importance to YOU, as guiding principles in YOUR life."

The average adult requires about 15 to 20 minutes to complete the rankings. Form D of the Value Survey, which employs pressure-sensitive gummed labels, has been successfully employed with respondents ranging in age from 11 to 90. The 18 labels are presented alphabetically on the right-hand side of the page; the respondents' task is merely to rearrange them in order of importance into boxes 1 to 18 printed down the left-hand side of the page. The gummed label technique gives the Value Survey a highly motivating, game-like quality that is distinctly superior to the more usual paper-and-pencil tests.

In previous research, various subsets of the 18 terminal and 18 instrumental values have been found to distinguish significantly between men and women, rich and poor, educated and uneducated, and among persons varying in age, occupation, and life-style.[2] Various terminal and instrumental values are significantly correlated with logically related attitudes and, far more important, with logically related behavior. On the average, approximately one-third of the 36 values have been found to distinguish at statistically significant levels (a) among persons varying in attitude (for example, toward blacks, American presence in Vietnam, religion); and (b) among persons varying in behavior (for example, joining or not joining a civil rights organization, cheating or not cheating on an examination).

Consistent with a theory of cognitive and behavioral change proposed elsewhere, previous experimental research has demonstrated that long-range changes in values, attitudes, and behavior are possible as a result of objective feedback of information about one's own and others' values and attitudes.[3] Such feedback made many of the experimental subjects conscious of certain contradictions existing within their own value-attitude system, resulting in long-term cognitive and behavioral changes. There is also evidence that the basic psychological mechanism that initiates or generates such a process of change is the arousal of an affective state of self-dissatisfaction, the source of which is highly specific and identifiable.

Feedback of information led many of the experimental subjects to become aware that they held certain values and attitudes or had engaged in certain behavior that was contradictory to self-conceptions, thus arousing an affective state of self-dissatisfaction. To reduce such self-dissatisfaction, the subjects reorganized their values, attitudes, and behavior to make them all more mutually compatible and, even more important, to make them all more compatible with self-conceptions.

There is no reason to think that long-term changes in values, attitudes, or behavior that might occur naturally in one's everyday life would occur by processes any different from those that we have observed in more controlled experimental settings. During the particular period under consideration, 1968-1971, a number of specific issues were at the forefront of attention in the minds of many Americans: the continuing American involvement in Vietnam, institutional racism, an emerging awareness of institutional sexism, and the problem of pollution. To be sure, not all Americans were willing to recognize all these as genuine problems requiring solution. Many, no doubt, felt that these issues were overblown or exaggerated, that they did not really require any special attention, action, or solution. But the more these issues were in the news, the more salient they became for more people, and the greater the receptivity to consider solutions. It is within such an everyday context of issue salience that certain values, attitudes, and behavior—those most logically related to these issues—are especially vulnerable to change, either in American society as a whole or in those segments of American society that perceive themselves to be the most affected by these issues.

Moreover, it is reasonable to expect certain values to undergo change in an opposite direction: a social problem or issue that has been previously salient may become less salient, perhaps because it has been alleviated in whole or in part. For instance, if, as a result of legislation, social security or medical care benefits became routinely extended to all, we would expect this to be reflected in a lowered concern over certain values, such as economic security. Less concern over security-related values should, in turn, pave the way for the emergence of an increased concern with higher-order values.[4]

However, not all of a society's values are expected to undergo change. Values not related to the emergence or alleviation of major societal problems should remain relatively stable. Thus, we may expect that only those values directly related to the particular economic, political, and social issues confronting American society during the relatively brief time interval under consideration will have undergone measurable change.

Results

Value Change in American Society as a Whole

Table 3 shows the changes and stabilities in the 18 terminal and 18 instrumental values obtained for the national sample during the period from 1968 to 1971. This table, like all the others presented in this article, shows the median ranking for each value and, in parentheses, its composite ranking. For instance, Table 3 shows that *a world at peace* had a median ranking of 3.3 in 1968 and 2.9 in 1971. This terminal value had the highest median rankings for both years, indicated by a composite ranking of 1, which is shown in parentheses. Conversely, *an exciting life* had the lowest median rankings on both occasions, indicated by a composite ranking of 18.

Before proceeding to a consideration of the specific value changes that took place, it is perhaps worth noticing that the value hierarchies found for the whole American sample were remarkably stable between 1968 and 1971. The composite ranking of the terminal value *a world at peace* was first in 1968 and first again in 1971; *family security* was second and *freedom* third on both occasions; *an exciting life, pleasure, social recognition,* and *a world of beauty* were at the bottom of the national sample's terminal value hierarchy in both 1968 and 1971. For both years, the most important instrumental values were *honest, ambitious,* and *responsible;* the least important were *imaginative, logical, obedient,* and *intellectual.*

These findings may be summarized somewhat as follows: more than anything else, adult Americans perceived themselves as peace loving, freedom loving, family oriented, honest, hardworking, and responsible; they perceived themselves neither as hedonistic, aesthetically, or intellectually oriented; nor, at least consciously, as status oriented. To what extent would these self-reported value patterns coincide with those reported by objective observers? More important, to what extent would these value patterns turn out to be similar to and different from those that might be obtained from other major cultural or national groups? [5]

TABLE 3   Changes in Terminal and Instrumental Values for Entire Adult American Sample, 1968– 1971 [a]

Values	1968 (N = 1,409)	1971 (N = 1,430)	*p*
Terminal Values			
A comfortable life			
(A prosperous life)	9.0(9)	10.6(13)	.01
An exciting life			
(A stimulating, active life)	15.3(18)	15.2(18)	—
A sense of accomplishment			
(Lasting contribution)	9.0(10)	9.6(11)	.01
A world at peace			
(Free of war and conflict)	3.3(1)	2.9(1)	.05
A world of beauty			
(Beauty of nature and the arts)	13.6(15)	12.5(15)	.01
Equality			
(Brotherhood, equal opportunity for all)	8.5(7)	7.6(4)	.01
Family security			
(Taking care of loved ones)	3.8(2)	4.2(2)	.05
Freedom			
(Independence, free choice)	5.5(3)	5.3(3)	—
Happiness			
(Contentedness)	7.6(4)	7.7(6)	—
Inner harmony			
(Freedom from inner conflict)	10.5(13)	10.2(12)	—
Mature love			
(Sexual and spiritual intimacy)	12.5(14)	11.9(14)	.05
National security			
(Protection from attack)	9.5(12)	9.0(8)	—
Pleasure			
(An enjoyable, leisurely life)	14.6(17)	14.7(16)	—
Salvation			
(Saved, eternal life)	8.8(8)	9.2(9)	—
Self-respect			
(Self-esteem)	7.7(5)	7.7(5)	—
Social recognition			
(Respect, admiration)	14.4(16)	14.9(17)	.05
True friendship			
(Close companionship)	9.3(11)	9.4(10)	—

TABLE 3 (*continued*)

Values	1968 (N = 1,409)	1971 (N = 1,430)	p
Wisdom			
(A mature understanding of life)	8.0(6)	8.2(7)	—
Instrumental Values			
Ambitious			
(Hard-working, aspiring)	6.5(2)	6.9(3)	—
Broadminded			
(Open-minded)	7.5(5)	7.5(5)	—
Capable			
(Competent, effective)	9.5(9)	9.4(9)	—
Cheerful			
(Lighthearted, joyful)	9.9(12)	10.4(13)	—
Clean			
(Neat, tidy)	8.7(8)	9.5(10)	.05
Courageous			
(Standing up for your beliefs)	7.8(6)	8.1(6)	—
Forgiving			
(Willing to pardon others)	7.2(4)	7.2(4)	—
Helpful			
(Working for the welfare of others)	8.2(7)	8.7(7)	—
Honest			
(Sincere, truthful)	3.3(1)	3.3(1)	—
Imaginative			
(Daring, creative)	15.4(18)	15.2(18)	—
Independent			
(Self-reliant, self-sufficient)	10.5(13)	10.2(12)	—
Intellectual			
(Intelligent, reflective)	13.0(15)	12.7(15)	—
Logical			
(Consistent, rational)	14.2(17)	13.4(17)	.01
Loving			
(Affectionate, tender)	9.7(11)	8.7(8)	.01
Obedient			
(Dutiful, respectful)	13.3(16)	13.3(16)	—
Polite			
(Courteous, well-mannered)	10.8(14)	11.0(14)	—
Responsible			
(Dependable, reliable)	6.7(3)	6.5(2)	—
Self-controlled			
(Restrained, self-disciplined)	9.6(10)	9.6(11)	—

[a] Figures shown are median rankings and, in parentheses, composite rank orders.

Let us now consider the changes found between 1968 and 1971, as reported in Table 3. Twenty-five of the 36 values show no statistically significant changes for the national sample as a whole, while 11 of them do show significant changes. Significantly more important in the American value hierarchy in 1971 compared with 1968 were *a world at peace, a world of beauty, equality, mature love,* being *logical,* and *loving;* significantly less important were *a comfortable life, a sense of accomplishment, family security, social recognition,* and being *clean.*

A major question is whether these changes were manifested in all segments of American society or occurred only in certain segments. To answer this question the value rankings obtained in 1968 and 1971 were further analyzed for Americans varying in sex, race, race and sex, income, education, and age.

Value Changes in American Men and Women

Over the three-year period, seven values changed significantly for men, and six changed significantly for women (Table 4). Comparing these two sets of changes, it becomes apparent that the results are the same for only two values: American men and women both placed significantly more importance on *a world of beauty* and significantly less importance on *a comfortable life* in 1971 than they did in 1968.

The remaining changes are different for the two sexes. *A world at peace*, although ranked as the most important terminal value by American men in 1968, became even more important for them in 1971; *mature love* was also ranked higher by American men in 1971. Three other values—*a sense of accomplishment, social recognition,* and being

TABLE 4   Changes in Terminal and Instrumental Values for American Men and Women, 1968–1971 [a]

	American Men			American Women		
Values	1968 (N = 665)	1971 (N = 687)	p	1968 (N = 744)	1971 (N = 743)	p
Terminal Values						
A comfortable life	7.8(4)	9.2(9)	.01	10.0(13)	11.7(13)	.01
An exciting life	14.6(18)	14.6(17)	—	15.8(18)	15.6(18)	—
A sense of accomplishment	8.3(7)	9.3(10)	.01	9.4(10)	9.8(12)	—
A world at peace	3.8(1)	3.2(1)	.05	3.0(1)	2.6(1)	—
A world of beauty	13.6(15)	12.8(15)	.05	13.5(15)	12.4(14)	.01
Equality	8.9(9)	8.0(6)	—	8.3(8)	7.4(4)	.05
Family security	3.9(2)	4.0(2)	—	3.8(2)	4.4(2)	.01
Freedom	4.9(3)	5.1(3)	—	6.0(3)	5.5(3)	—
Happiness	7.9(5)	7.6(4)	—	7.3(5)	7.8(8)	—
Inner harmony	11.1(13)	11.0(13)	—	9.8(12)	9.5(11)	—
Mature love	12.6(14)	11.4(14)	.01	12.3(14)	12.4(15)	—
National security	9.2(10)	9.0(8)	—	9.8(11)	8.9(9)	—
Pleasure	14.1(17)	14.3(16)	—	15.0(16)	15.1(17)	—
Salvation	9.9(12)	10.9(12)	—	7.3(4)	7.6(6)	—
Self-respect	8.2(6)	7.9(5)	—	7.4(6)	7.4(5)	—
Social recognition	13.8(16)	14.6(18)	.01	15.0(17)	15.1(16)	—
True friendship	9.6(11)	9.4(11)	—	9.1(9)	9.5(10)	—
Wisdom	8.5(8)	8.9(7)	—	7.7(7)	7.7(7)	—
Instrumental Values						
Ambitious	5.6(2)	5.4(2)	—	7.3(4)	8.0(6)	—
Broadminded	7.2(4)	7.1(4)	—	7.6(5)	7.8(5)	—
Capable	8.9(8)	8.7(6)	—	10.1(12)	10.3(12)	—
Cheerful	10.4(12)	11.0(13)	—	9.4(10)	9.8(10)	—
Clean	9.4(9)	10.2(11)	—	8.1(8)	9.0(9)	—
Courageous	7.5(5)	8.0(5)	—	8.1(6)	8.2(8)	—
Forgiving	8.2(6)	8.8(7)	—	6.4(2)	5.9(2)	—
Helpful	8.4(7)	9.2(9)	.05	8.1(7)	8.0(7)	—
Honest	3.4(1)	3.3(1)	—	3.2(1)	3.2(1)	—
Imaginative	14.3(18)	14.5(18)	—	16.1(18)	15.8(18)	—
Independent	10.2(11)	9.9(10)	—	10.7(14)	10.4(13)	—
Intellectual	12.8(15)	12.5(15)	—	13.2(16)	12.9(15)	—
Logical	13.5(16)	12.8(16)	—	14.6(17)	13.9(17)	.05
Loving	10.9(14)	10.6(12)	—	8.6(9)	7.3(4)	.01
Obedient	13.5(17)	13.4(17)	—	13.1(15)	13.2(16)	—
Polite	10.8(13)	11.2(14)	—	10.7(13)	10.8(14)	—
Responsible	6.6(3)	6.2(3)	—	6.8(3)	6.7(3)	—
Self-controlled	9.6(10)	9.2(8)	—	9.6(11)	10.0(11)	—

[a] Figures shown are median rankings and, in parentheses, composite rank orders.

helpful—turned out to be significantly less important for them in 1971. For American women, *family security* became significantly less important in 1971, and *equality*, being *logical*, and *loving* became significantly more important.

Value Changes for White and Black Americans

Table 5 shows the comparable changes found for white and black Americans. Ten of the 36 values changed significantly among whites, and six changed significantly among blacks. The fact that more values changed significantly for white Americans is not particularly surprising; it was probably due to the fact that there were many more whites than blacks in the total sample—about 85 per cent compared with 15 per cent

TABLE 5   **Changes in Terminal and Instrumental Values for White and Black Americans, 1968–1971** [a]

Values	White Americans			Black Americans		
	1968 (N = 1,195)	1971 (N = 1,205)	p	1968 (N = 202)	1971 (N = 213)	p
Terminal Values						
A comfortable life	9.6(12)	11.2(13)	.01	6.6(5)	7.1(5)	—
An exciting life	15.3(18)	15.3(18)	—	15.3(18)	14.8(18)	—
A sense of accomplishment	8.8(8)	9.4(10)	.05	10.2(11)	11.3(12)	—
A world at peace	3.2(1)	2.8(1)	.05	3.5(1)	3.3(1)	—
A world of beauty	13.4(15)	12.4(15)	.01	14.1(16)	13.5(16)	—
Equality	9.5(11)	8.1(6)	.01	4.6(2)	5.0(4)	—
Family security	3.6(2)	4.1(2)	.05	5.1(4)	4.8(3)	—
Freedom	5.6(3)	5.5(3)	—	5.0(3)	4.7(2)	—
Happiness	7.5(4)	7.8(5)	—	7.6(7)	7.2(6)	—
Inner harmony	10.3(13)	9.9(12)	—	10.9(12)	12.1(13)	.05
Mature love	12.0(14)	11.8(16)	—	13.7(14)	12.4(14)	.05
National security	9.1(9)	8.7(8)	—	11.4(13)	10.2(11)	—
Pleasure	14.6(17)	14.9(16)	—	14.3(17)	13.7(17)	—
Salvation	8.5(7)	9.1(9)	—	9.4(9)	9.4(10)	—
Self-respect	7.7(5)	7.5(4)	—	7.5(6)	8.3(7)	—
Social recognition	14.5(16)	15.0(17)	.05	13.7(15)	13.5(15)	—
True friendship	9.2(10)	9.5(11)	—	9.8(10)	9.2(8)	—
Wisdom	7.9(6)	8.1(7)	—	8.5(8)	9.3(9)	—
Instrumental Values						
Ambitious	6.7(3)	6.8(3)	—	5.2(2)	7.9(6)	.01
Broadminded	7.3(5)	7.2(4)	—	8.0(8)	8.8(8)	—
Capable	9.4(10)	9.3(9)	—	10.4(13)	10.6(13)	—
Cheerful	9.8(12)	10.4(13)	—	10.2(12)	10.1(11)	—
Clean	9.2(8)	10.1(12)	.01	5.2(3)	6.3(2)	—
Courageous	7.8(6)	8.1(6)	—	7.8(7)	8.6(7)	—
Forgiving	7.0(4)	7.4(5)	—	7.6(5)	6.7(3)	—
Helpful	8.3(7)	9.0(8)	.05	7.8(6)	7.3(4)	—
Honest	3.1(1)	3.1(1)	—	3.8(1)	4.8(1)	.05
Imaginative	15.3(18)	15.4(18)	—	15.8(18)	14.6(17)	.01
Independent	10.6(13)	10.3(12)	—	10.2(10)	9.6(10)	—
Intellectual	13.1(15)	12.8(15)	—	12.6(16)	12.4(16)	—
Logical	13.9(17)	13.1(16)	.01	15.1(17)	15.0(18)	—
Loving	9.3(9)	8.5(7)	—	11.9(15)	9.2(9)	.01
Obedient	13.4(16)	13.6(17)	—	11.5(14)	11.8(15)	—
Polite	10.8(14)	11.2(14)	—	10.2(11)	10.2(12)	—
Responsible	6.5(2)	6.3(2)	—	7.6(4)	7.6(5)	—
Self-controlled	9.4(11)	9.4(10)	—	10.1(9)	10.9(14)	—

[a] Figures shown are median rankings and, in parentheses, composite rank orders.

in both years. More noteworthy is the fact that white and black Americans changed significantly on completely different values; not a single one of the changes were the same for the two races.

White Americans attached significantly more important in 1971 to *a world at peace, a world of beauty, equality,* and being *intellectual;* they attached significantly less importance to *a comfortable life, a sense of accomplishment, family security, social recognition,* being *clean,* and being *helpful.* Black Americans apparently had other preoccupations: *mature love,* being *loving* and *imaginative* became significantly more important; *inner harmony,* being *ambitious* and *honest* became significantly less important.

Value Changes in Americans Varying in Sex and Race

We also analyzed the value changes from 1968 to 1971 separately for white men and women and for black men and women. White men and women both significantly increased their regard for *a world of beauty* and *equality;* both significantly decreased their regard for *a comfortable life.* They manifested other changes, however, that they did not share with each other: white men regarded *mature love* as more important in 1971 were just as likely to occur among the poor or uneducated as among the affluent white women regarded being *logical* and *loving* as more important in 1971 and *family security* as less important.

Whereas white men and women had both increased their ranking of *equality* in 1971, black men and women both decreased their *equality* rankings, although not significantly so. Black men changed significantly with respect to only one value: *inner harmony* became less important. And black women changed significantly by increasing their rankings of *mature love* and *loving* and by decreasing their rankings of *ambitious.*

Education, Income, and Age as Determinants of Value Change

The extent to which the observed changes were a function of socioeconomic level or age may also be questioned. Further analysis revealed that neither education nor income were determinants of value change. The values that changed from 1968 to 1971 were just as likely to occur among the poor or uneducated as among the affluent and educated.

The findings did differ with respect to age, however. These data, which are not presented here to conserve space, show that younger adults within the national sample underwent more extensive value changes than older adults. Respondents in their twenties, thirties, forties, fifties, sixties, and those over seventy manifested, respectively, 10, 4, 2, 0, 2, and 0 significant value changes over the three-year period. Americans in their twenties attached significantly greater importance in 1971 to *a world at peace, a world of beauty, equality, inner harmony,* and being *logical;* they attached less importance to *a comfortable life, salvation,* and being *clean, obedient,* and *polite.* Those in their thirties showed considerably fewer significant changes: *a world at peace, a world of beauty,* and *national security* had increased and *family security* had decreased in importance. The significant value changes found for persons beyond the thirties are few in number and could easily have arisen by chance.

Additional analyses, again too complex to present here, revealed that these age-related changes were found primarily among white men and women and not among black men and women. Moreover, as previously stated, they were not related to differences in socioeconomic status.

Structure of Values, 1968 and 1971

The significant value changes found between 1968 and 1971 should not obscure the fact that most of the 36 values did not change, as even a cursory inspection of Tables 3 through 5 will reveal. As already stated, the over-all value patterns in 1968 and 1971 look very similar. Are the underlying structures also similar?

Table 6 shows the range of correlations obtained in 1968 and 1971 for the total national sample and, separately, for the four subsamples. The highest positive correlation found in all ten matrices was .41, between *a comfortable life* and *pleasure;* the highest negative correlation was –.38, between *an exciting life* and *salvation.* Since the average correlation between values was close to zero both in 1968 and in 1971 a conclusion reached earlier on the basis of the 1968 sample alone is now doubly reinforced: "The ranking of any one of the 36 values is for all practical purposes unrelated to the ranking of any other value, and it is therefore unlikely that the 36 values can be effectively reduced to some smaller number of factors." [6]

Nonetheless, factor analyses of these ten matrices provide us with some additional insights into the underlying structure of American values. Previously reported factor analyses of the 1968 data yielded six factors. These six factors have previously been identified as follows: immediate vs. delayed gratification, competence vs. religious morality, self-constriction vs. self-expansion, social vs. personal orientation, societal vs. family security, and respect vs. love. These factors described not only the total 1968 national sample but also the male and female, white and black subsamples considered separately.

The comparable factor analyses carried out with the 1971 data yielded results that are essentially the same as those found for 1968. Moreover, the findings are essentially the same in 1971 for the four subsamples of men and women, whites and blacks as they were for the total national sample. And all these findings for the total sample and for the four subsamples are, in turn, highly similar to those already reported for 1968. Thus, no useful purpose would be served by reporting them in detail here.

Discussion

Survey research has long been concerned with the assessment of attitude changes over time but not with the assessment of value changes, perhaps because simple methods for measuring values have previously not been available. This article represents, as far as is known to the present writer, a first quantitative attempt to measure value change and stability in American society.

Moreover, the data reported here may reasonably be regarded as social indicators of the quality of life in American society. For instance, decreases in the perceived importance of having *a comfortable life* and being *clean* could be interpreted as social indicators of an improved socioeconomic status; increases in the importance of *a sense of accomplishment* and being *capable* could be interpreted as indicators of increased strivings for achievement or self-actualization; increases in the importance of *equality* could be interpreted as an indicator of an increased egalitarianism; increases in the importance of *a world of beauty* could be interpreted as an indicator of an increased willingness to sacrifice material comforts in return for a less polluted environment.

It perhaps goes without saying that the statistically significant differences in values reported in this article are not large. It is not reasonable to expect large value changes over so short an interval as three years of a society's history. Nonetheless, the fact that

TABLE 6 Highest and Lowest Correlations Found within 36-Value Matrix for Total National Samples, American Whites and Blacks, and American Men and Women, 1968 and 1971

Group	N	Highest Correlation (between)		Lowest Correlation (between)	
Total NORC sample, 1968	1,409	.35	(A comfortable life—Pleasure)	−.32	(A comfortable life—Wisdom)
Whites, 1968	1,195	.38	(A comfortable life—Pleasure)	−.32	(An exciting life—Salvation)
Blacks, 1968	202	.31	(Obedient—Polite)	−.35	(A comfortable life—Wisdom)
Men, 1968	665	.30	(Cheerful—Clean)	−.38	(An exciting life—Salvation)
Women, 1968	744	.41	(A comfortable life—Pleasure)	−.32	(A comfortable life—Wisdom)
Total NORC sample, 1971	1,429	.32	(A comfortable life—Pleasure)	−.34	(An exciting life—Salvation)
Whites, 1971	1,204	.37	(A comfortable life—Pleasure)	−.34	(An exciting life—Salvation)
Blacks, 1971	213	.32	(Happiness—Cheerful)	−.35	(Broadminded—Obedient)
Men, 1971	687	.33	(A comfortable life—Pleasure)	−.36	(An exciting life—Salvation)
Women, 1971	743	.35	(A world at peace—National security)	−.34	(Clean—Logical)

we did find statistically significant changes in several values during this period suggests, at least, that: (a) the value measure employed is sufficiently sensitive to register short-term changes, (b) certain values had in fact undergone change in American society between 1968 and 1971, and (c) more clear-cut trends are likely to become discernible with measurements over longer time intervals.

The significant value changes between 1968 and 1971 reported for the total adult American sample are, for the most part, reflections of selective, rather than ubiquitous, changes that had taken place in various strata of American society. They are attributable mainly to differential changes occurring among Americans varying in race, sex, or age.

Consider first the changes that were found for the terminal value *equality*. *Equality* had increased significantly between 1968 and 1971 for white Americans but had decreased for black Americans. This suggests that the civil rights movement had a significant impact on white Americans during this period. In contrast, the decreases in *equality* among black Americans, although nonsignificant, reflect a change in the direction of separatism, perhaps as a result of the impact of the black power and black nationalist movements, and perhaps also because of a growing despair or impatience over a loss of momentum during the Nixon years.

The fact that the terminal value *equality* increased significantly for white Americans between 1968 and 1971 is consistent with the long-term increases between 1942 and 1970 in pro-integration attitudes that have been reported by Greeley and Sheatsley.[7] Placing their findings alongside those reported here it now becomes possible to assert that not only are racist attitudes in American society undergoing change, at least for the time intervals under consideration, but so, too, is the main value known to underlie such attitudes.

Moreover, white, but not black, Americans exhibited statistically significant increases in the importance they attached to *a world of beauty*. This finding suggests that concern about ecology between 1968 and 1971 was a preoccupation mainly of white Americans, and was not especially salient for black Americans. Pollution of the environment is not likely to become a salient issue or to affect values when there are more pressing needs and values concerning safety and security.

Consistent with these findings are the comparable changes for white, but not for black, Americans concerning having *a comfortable life* and being *clean*. Previous research has shown that rankings of these two values are the two best predictors of socioeconomic status: the higher one's socioeconomic status the lower the rankings of these two values (not so much because these are no longer important but because they are taken for granted). This suggests that socioeconomic level may have improved more for white than for black Americans. Partial evidence that this may have been the case comes from a 1972 Census Bureau report to the effect that the number of poor blacks had increased in the preceding year while the number of poor whites had decreased. In any event, we have found that the two main economic values had become significantly less important in 1971 for white, but not for black, Americans.

What are we to make of these and other findings showing that white and black Americans had changed for the most part in different ways, implicating different values? Did the values of black and white Americans converge or diverge from one another between 1968 and 1971? The findings are ambiguous on this point because the terminal values of black and white Americans became more similar from 1968 to 1971 (the rho correlations between the composite rankings of white and black Americans increased from .815 to .88), and the instrumental values became more dissimilar (the rho correlations decreased from .88 to .78). Thus, it is not possible to answer this question in any definite way until more extensive data become available.

Other significant value changes found in the total national sample can be traced mainly to changes occurring only among white women or white men. White women downgraded the importance of *family security* and upgraded the importance of being *logical*, a change that can reasonably be attributed to an increasing awareness between 1968 and 1971 of institutional sexism as a national problem and to the concomitant rise of the women's liberation movement—a movement that was probably more salient for American women than men, and perhaps more salient for white women than for black women.

On the other hand, white men exhibited a nearly significant increase in their ranking of *a world at peace* and significant decreases in *a sense of accomplishment* and *social recognition*. This suggests that white American men were more preoccupied with problems of war and peace and devoted less attention to their traditional pursuits of education, career, and social status. These value changes can possibly be attributed to the Vietnam war, the Cambodian invasion, the antiwar protests, the Kent and Jackson shootings, and, perhaps, to a fear of being drafted. It will be interesting to see if these particular changes persist now that the Vietnam war and the draft have ended.

Other significant value changes are more difficult to interpret: white men and black women both increased their rankings of *mature love;* white and black women both increased their ranking of *loving;* black Americans decreased their rankings of *honest* and increased their rankings of *imaginative;* black women decreased their rankings of *ambitious.* It is hard to say what these findings mean. Most were not statistically significant for the total sample. Various *post hoc* interpretations are possible but would not be intuitively appealing; they may or may not represent chance differences. Further research should enable us to sort out which of these significant value changes are replicable and thus to be taken seriously.

Finally, attention should be drawn to the fact that most of the significant changes found between 1968 and 1971 for the national sample are traceable to changes occurring among white Americans in their twenties and, to a lesser extent, in their thirties. The findings suggest that this subgroup of adult Americans may be undergoing more extensive value changes than any other segment: toward a lesser emphasis on tradition and religion; toward greater concerns with racial and sexual egalitarianism, ecology, peace, and peace of mind.

It is not clear from these latter data, however, whether the changes between 1968 and 1971 actually occurred among adults in their twenties or, alternatively, whether they were a result of the movement of persons between 18 and 21 in 1968 into the 21-30 age category in 1971, or both. Future research with respondents under 21 years of age should help us answer this question.

Turning to the factor analytic findings, two interrelated conclusions seem warranted. First, the fact that the intercorrelations among the 36 values were uniformly negligible for both years suggests that the way a respondent ranks any one value is a rather poor predictor of the way he will rank any other value. Even logically related values are negligibly related to one another. For instance, the average correlation between rankings of *salvation* and *forgiving* is only about .25; the average correlation between rankings of *freedom* and *equality* is only about .11. Second, the same half-dozen factors obtained for 1968 and 1971 seem to possess little "explanatory power" since taken together they account for well under half of the total variance, with no one factor accounting for more than 10 per cent. Thus, the findings suggest that the 36 values cannot safely be reduced to some smaller number of values.

Returning to the main findings, it should perhaps be reiterated that what has been reported thus far about value changes and stabilities in American society is based only on two points in time, obtained three years apart. But, even within such a short interval, we found that certain values underwent significant change. These changes seem to be a result of economic factors and the emergence of various issues concerning war and peace, racism, sexism, and ecology, all of which became salient and thus a source of dissatisfaction for various subgroups of adult Americans.

It would be helpful to see these data supplemented at regular intervals in the future. This would provide a more continuous monitoring of values in American society and, it is hoped, would guide social policy and help set national priorities.

In conclusion, it might be appropriate to mention some logical next steps in our ongoing research program on values as social indicators of the quality of life. First, there is no compelling reason why we should not also monitor the stabilities and changes of those who are well below the age at which they become eligible to vote. As previously stated, the Rokeach Value Survey has been successfully employed with persons ranging in age from 11 to 90.

Second, there is no reason why social indicator research should focus only, or mainly, on stabilities and changes within a single country. If values are indeed meaningful indicators of the quality of life, then attempts should be made to determine to what extent they might also turn out to be useful as international social indicators. It would, for instance, be interesting to compare the relative importance of certain political, religious, or self-actualization values across various national samples and, moreover, to plot their stabilities and changes over time. Ultimately, we might seek to develop global social indicators that would allow us to assess stabilities and changes in quality of life across cultural space as well as across historical time.

References

1. Milton Rokeach, *Value Survey* (Sunnyvale, Cal.: Halgren Tests, 1967).
2. Milton Rokeach, *The Nature of Human Values* (New York: The Free Press, 1973).
3. *Ibid.*
4. A. H. Maslow, *Motivation and Personality* (New York: Harper and Row, 1954).
5. Rokeach, *The Nature of Human Values.*
6. *Ibid.*: 44.
7. A. M. Greeley and P. B. Sheatsley, "Attitudes Toward Racial Integration," *Scientific American* 225 (1971): 13–19.

TO THE STUDENT: A COMMENTARY

Ben Wattenberg's article is so brief and clearly written that you probably had little difficulty with it. Remember that a President of the United States is not elected directly by the votes we cast on election day. Rather, your vote goes to select a slate of electors. As Wattenberg recalls, each state has a number of electors equal to the number of members for that state in the House of Representatives and the Senate. Each state has two members in the Senate, but House membership depends on the state's population. Since each state receives a number of members in the House proportionate to the state's population, the more people a state has the larger its House membership relative to other states. Thus, a state's influence in the House and in the Electoral College that chooses the President may depend upon the size of its population. That is why presidential candidates court the more populous states in campaigning. Since the candidate that gets the most of the popular votes cast in your state receives *all* of the state's electoral votes, numbers of people and where they live are very important.

Wattenberg's basic assumption and the point he derives from it are simple: population shifts between regions of the country affect the presidential aspirations of politicians; hence, whether or not Senator Edward Kennedy was correct in challenging President Jimmy Carter in 1980, he may have made the only choice possible.

Do you agree? Wattenberg's analysis appeared in November, 1979, one full year before the 1980 presidential election and during the month Kennedy announced his bid for the Democratic nomination. You now have the benefit of hindsight, you know what happened. In that light, and assuming for the moment that for Kennedy it was "now or never," what do you think of Wattenberg's analysis? If it holds up, the implications for presidential and congressional politics in this decade are enormous.

Think about the politics of your own state and region. Changes in what happens in presidential politics can filter down to statewide races for governor and other officials; the U.S. Senate and House races; and myriad local contests. Moreover, if incumbent presidents seeking reelection don't consider your state essential to victory, they may smile with less favor on your state when bestowing the bounty of the federal government. So if you are a "frostie" (both as to region of residence and because you are suffering from a lack of federally allocated heating oil), don't expect to be as warm in the 1980s as you were in the '70s. If you're a "sunny" (as are both the editors of this volume), expect to see a lot more presidential candidates wandering through your state in 1984 and 1988 than you did in the past.

As Wattenberg notes, changes in the demographic map raise "many, many questions" about potential changes in the political map as well. Are changes also occurring in the value maps of Americans that have potential political import? The article by Milton Rokeach addresses that question.

Rokeach's discussion really has five parts. You probably recognized the format of his report quickly for it parallels the academic-scientific style described in the prologue. The five parts reflect that format. In the first he describes how he undertook a survey of a nationwide sample of Americans in both 1968 and 1971. He asked people to rank, in order of importance to each person, eighteen "terminal" and eighteen "instrumental" values; that is, values that are ends in themselves and values that are means of achieving such ends. The evidence he accumulated helped him to describe how the values of Americans changed over a three-year period. It was a tumultuous era of American politics marked by civil rights demonstrations, urban unrest, programs to cure poverty, a war in Vietnam, and the assassinations of Robert Kennedy and Martin Luther King, Jr.

The second portion of Rokeach's article simply tells you what he found. You may be impressed with the remarkable stability in the way two different samples of Americans in two different years ranked both terminal and instrumental values. The goals valued most and least in 1968 were the same that Americans prized most and least in 1971. And there was virtually no change in the ranking of instrumental values in that period. In teaching courses in public opinion in the 1970s, one of the editors of this book had students take the Value Survey. Although such samples of students are scarcely representative either of college students generally or of the American population, it is noteworthy that year in and year out the rankings proved consistent with Rokeach's findings.

Saying that nationwide samples of Americans generally rank values in the manner revealed by Rokeach's research does not, of course, mean that everyone ranks things the same way. Think about your own views, and even conduct your own mini-study. Rank the two sets of values and have others do so. See if your findings agree with what Rokeach is telling you. We suspect that you will find that *in general* your results will agree with Rokeach but you will uncover a sufficient number of people with unique rankings to demonstrate the wisdom of singer Ray Charles' admonition, "different strokes for different folks."

Nor does stability in rankings across a three-year period mean that nothing changes. Rokeach reports significant changes in the rankings of a few values. Particularly noteworthy is the change in *equality*. Ranked seventh in 1968, it moved up to fourth in 1971. Rokeach offers no evidence of stability and/or change in value rankings of Americans in more recent years derived from nationwide surveys, but he has reported the results of twenty-three experiments indicating that under certain conditions people will alter their value systems to increase the priorities of values such as *equality*. If people are confronted with how they have ranked values, then made aware of how others have done so, they may change their value rankings *if* they feel a sense of dissatisfaction at the contrast between themselves and others.[1]

An aside is necessary. When we say that Rokeach found "significant" changes in the ranking of *equality*, the term refers to *statistical* significance. Social scientists use "tests of significance" to find out if the differences between people on a variable (recall our discussion of variables in the prologue) are actual differences as such or are the result of chance. In taking a sample of Americans, for example, from our nationwide population there is always the possibility that the differences between people uncovered by the sample are due to chance. Had other people been included in the sample and those made part of the sample thereby excluded, the differences might not emerge. Tests of significance are statistical measures to gauge the degree of such a chance. Look again at Table 3 in Rokeach's article. In the right-hand column note the designation p. Below are listed numbers such as .01, .05. Not every value has such a number accompanying it. The number should be read as saying that the difference in the ranking of a given value from 1968 to 1971 was "significant at the .01 (or .05) level." Simply put, this means that the differences in rankings of the value in the two years could be expected to have occurred *by chance alone* only one time in a hundred (in the case of .01) or five in a hundred (in the case of .05). If there is no number listed in the p column, the differences in rankings were so likely to have been the result of chance alone as to be "not significant." In many of the social science articles you will read you will find significance tests reported in this way. Remember: they help you evaluate how much confidence you can place in the findings you read!

A third aspect of Rokeach's report outlines the value changes among specific segments of society. His discussion is straightforward and you probably had no difficulty with it. It is no surprise, for example, that in the era of the feminist movement American women placed significantly less importance on *family security* in 1971 than in 1968 and that they elevated *equality* from eighth to fourth by 1971. It is surprising that, in the wake of the civil rights movement of the 1960s, both black men and women ranked *equality* lower in 1971 while white males and females ranked the value higher. The changes were not statistically significant, but warrant your thought. Was the civil rights movement successful enough so that blacks felt equality was being achieved, thus valued it less? Or, was it a matter of lack of success and a tendency to channel efforts into more fruitful paths? Were whites confronted with their 1968 rankings, embarrassed, and dissatisfied, hence changed? Such questions invite your pondering.

The fourth part of Rokeach's analysis is a little confusing. He reports an attempt to discover an "underlying structure" in American values and changes in that structure. By structure he means how closely the values are tied to one another. If closely tied, a change in the ranking of one should be accompanied by a change in ranking of other values. To explore this problem Rokeach used two techniques. First, he correlated the scores of each of the thirty-six values with one another (each of the eighteen terminal and eighteen instrumental values). Correlation is a statistical technique describing how closely two things are related to one another. "Correlation coefficients" tell you how close the relationship is. If two things are closely related in a positive way (say that the more you eat for lunch goes hand-in-hand with increasing drowsiness in the class lecture that immediately follows) the coefficient may approach +1.00. But if two things are negatively related (say you drink a lot of coffee before class to ward off drowsiness), the coefficient approaches –1.00. If two things are largely unrelated (you go to sleep in class no matter what you have for lunch, or whether you eat or not), the coefficient is 0. In sum, a correlation coefficient ranges from +1 through 0 to –1 depending upon how closely things are associated.

Table 6 presents Rokeach's correlations for his two national samples and various subsamples. Note that the highest correlation (between a *comfortable life* and *pleasure*, among women in 1968) is only –.41. Since most of his correlations were near zero, Rokeach concluded there may be little underlying structure in the values of Americans. But such a conclusion invites an additional check, another technique. Factor analysis is a complicated and sophisticated technique. Let it suffice to say that factor analysis is a procedure to reduce a large body of quantitative data about several variables to a smaller number of basic types, called factors, that are closely interrelated. In both 1968 and 1971 Rokeach found the same six basic types of values. But the types are not sufficiently clear-cut and easily distinguished as to indicate a sharply defined structure in the American value "hierarchy."

Rokeach concludes with a brief summary of his findings and a discussion of their implications. You will note that he is impressed with changes in the relative ranking of *equality* from 1968 to 1971. One reason probably lies in the results of other research he published in 1968.[2] Then he compared four ways people might relate the values of freedom and equality:

1. Highly value freedom and equality
2. Value neither freedom nor equality
3. Value equality but not freedom
4. Value freedom but not equality

He went on to analyze the content of various political writings: two socialists, Norman Thomas and Eric Fromm; Nazi dictator Adolf Hitler; Bolshevik dictator of the Soviet Union Nikolai Lenin; and conservative U.S. Senator Barry Goldwater. By comparing the number of favorable and unfavorable references to freedom and equality for each writer with references to other values in the Value Survey, Rokeach calculated the value rankings of each political leader. He found that socialist writers valued both freedom and equality, ranking them one and two respectively. Hitler devalued both: freedom ranked sixteenth and equality seventeenth in his writing. Lenin's works placed equality number one, freedom last. And Goldwater's writing ranked freedom first, equality second to last. Now consider that in the 1968 survey Americans ranked freedom third, equality seventh; in 1971 freedom again ranked third, equality fourth. Are Americans becoming more socialist, less conservative? Would a nationwide survey in the 1980s yield a similar picture? Are politicians aware of such shifts in value sentiment and do they trim their sails accordingly?

Such questions as those posed by both Wattenberg's and Rokeach's analyses of America and Americans suggest the importance of knowing who we are and what we think, feel, and expect. Our social and personal identities are frequently projected into the political arena, changing the face of electoral politics and, perhaps, contributing to greater demands for equality, freedom, security, peace, well-being, and other ideals. In turning next to who among you watches and participates in politics you'll do well to remind yourself from time to time of what Wattenberg, the jack-of-all-trades analytical journalist, and Rokeach, the professional social psychologist, have told you about yourself and your fellow Americans.

If you would like to know more about Americans and their views consult any of the following materials.

By social scientists:

Milton Rokeach, *Understanding Human Values*

Richard E. Dawson, *Public Opinion and Contemporary Disarray*

Rita James Simon, *Public Opinion in America: 1936–1970*

Robert Weissberg, *Public Opinion and Popular Government*

By journalists/pollsters:

Samuel Lubell, *The Hidden Crisis in American Politics*

Louis Harris, *The Anguish of Change*

William Watts and Lloyd Free, *State of the Nation*

References

1. Milton Rokeach, "Value Theory and Communication Research," in Dan Nimmo, ed., *Communication Yearbook 3* (New Brunswick, N.J.: Transaction Books, 1979), 7–28.
2. Milton Rokeach, "A Theory of Organization and Change Within Value-Attitude Systems," *Journal of Social Issues* 24 (January 1968): 13–33.

2 Citizens' Responses to Politics

INTRODUCTION

Where were you on the evening of September 23, 1976? If you were like 100 million other Americans you were doing something you might do any evening of any year—watching television. But on that night you were viewing something special. You were watching the first of a series of televised debates between two men. One was Gerald Ford, President of the United States who wanted to remain so, and Jimmy Carter, the nominee of the Democratic party who wanted Ford's job. Interest in the confrontation was so great that an estimated 90 percent of the nation's TV households were tuned to it as the antagonists opened their exchange at 9:30 EST that evening.

The debate ranged over a variety of topics. At its close each candidate had the opportunity to sum up his viewpoint about America and its current condition. In light of the years to come the words of candidate Jimmy Carter were interesting: "Our system of government is still the best system of government on earth. And the greatest resource of all are the two hundred and fifteen million Americans who have within us the strength, the character, the intelligence, the experience, the patriotism, the idealism, the compassion, the sense of brotherhood on which we can rely in the future to restore the greatness of our country. . . . we can once again have a government as good as our people."

Carter went on to win the presidential election and to try his hand at managing "the best system of government on earth" and its "greatest resource": Americans. But on July 15, 1979, three years to the day after accepting the nomination of his party to seek the presidency, Jimmy Carter spoke solemnly in a nationwide televised address:

> I want to talk to you right now about a fundamental threat to American democracy. . . . The threat is nearly invisible in ordinary ways. It is a crisis of confidence. It is a crisis that strikes at the very heart and soul and spirit of our national will. We can see this crisis in the growing doubt about the meaning of our own lives and in the loss of a unity of purpose for our Nation. . . . Our people are losing . . . faith, not only in government itself, but in the ability as citizens to serve as the ultimate rulers and shapers of our democracy.

53

Carter detected symptoms of the crisis everywhere—in nationwide polls showing Americans were more gloomy about the nation's future than ever before, in the failure of two-thirds of Americans to vote in elections, in falling productivity of our workers, and in a growing disrespect for government, churches, schools, the news media and other institutions. In short, things were bad and getting worse.

Carter's dreary assessment did not go unnoticed, or unchallenged. Were citizens' responses to politics really so negative, wondered some analysts? Were they really losing faith in themselves, asked others? And how could one be so optimistic about Americans as Carter had in 1976 only to be so pessimistic so quickly?

This chapter offers you two views regarding how Americans responded to politics in the 1970s, and perhaps still do today. In the first selection David Gergen speaks directly to the question raised by President Carter, that is, is there a crisis of confidence? Gergen is managing editor of a publication entitled *Public Opinion,* a magazine published bimonthly by the American Enterprise Institute for Public Policy Research. The American Enterprise Institute has a reputation for being a conservative "think tank." Established in 1943, it brings together scholars, policy makers, businessmen, journalists, and others to discuss and analyze social problems, recommend solutions, and publish their views.

In "A Crisis of Confidence?" David Gergen carefully describes the results of public opinion polls that tap how citizens feel about their government and themselves. As Gergen notes, President Carter has his own personal pollster and he relies on poll results for gauging the mood of Americans. Gergen contrasts the evidence used by Carter with the results of other opinion surveys, then asks if we indeed have a crisis or a "funk," a general feeling of concern and dismay. As you read Gergen's report pay close attention to the specific question he asks—is there truly a crisis of the spirit, is it overblown, what's bugging people, and is the mood unique?

Gergen's questions are cast in an entertaining way, and in the fashion of the journalist alluded to in our prologue they make otherwise dry statistics come alive through the use of dramatic ploys—emphasizing the "inside" information on which the President relies, stressing conflicts between those who do and don't see a crisis of confidence, and setting the controversy against the larger stage of recent history. One aspect of that larger stage is what citizens think of their own lives and capacities. President Carter alluded to that in 1979 when he spoke of "the growing doubt about the meaning of our own lives" and a loss of "faith . . . in the ability as citizens to serve as the ultimate rulers and shapers."

As Roberta Sigel's "The Psychology of Political Involvement" illustrates, the search for meaning and control in your life extends beyond the now-ism reflected in the shift of presidential concerns or the midsummer controversy over a crisis of confidence aired by Gergen's selection. Recall from our prologue that now-ism is the tendency for the news to focus upon current events, give them unique status, then forget them. If Roberta Sigel is correct, however, the factors that make you and me politically involved transcend the here and now, indeed linger on in our personal lives for very long periods.

Who, in fact, controls your life—you, others, outside forces, the fates? Are you so confident of the future that you plan ahead to live your life as you want, or do you so despair at failing that you just give up trying to plan? Is it planning, experience, or just luck that makes a difference in your life? How people answer these questions provide social psychologists with measures of what they call "locus-of-control." Roberta Sigel thinks that the locus-of-control of your life, indeed anybody's, has a great deal to do with what you know, feel, and do in politics.

Roberta Sigel is a professor of political science at Rutgers University. She was born in Berlin, Germany, but grew up in this country. She received her B.A. from Greensboro College, M.A. from Syracuse, and her Ph.D. from Clark University. She has taught at Indiana University, Smith College, the University of Detroit, Wayne State University, and the State University of New York. Over those years of teaching and research she has become a foremost scholar in studying how children learn about politics, how they view political leaders, how political leaders present themselves to citizens, and how personality influences political actions. She has published numerous articles and two of her book-length works include *Political Socialization: Its Role in the Political Process* and *Learning About Politics*. So she has a great deal to say about how people learn to control their political lives.

Sigel's "The Psychology of Political Involvement" appeared before President Carter concluded that Americans were losing their locus-of-control, before pollsters decried the crisis of confidence. As you read her selection consider how well her thoughts square with those voiced by political leaders—such as Carter—and pollsters about citizens' responses to politics. Was her analysis a forecast of the future or a snapshot of an enduring pattern?

A CRISIS OF CONFIDENCE?

DAVID GERGEN

Edited and reprinted from Public Opinion 2 (*August/September 1971*): 2–4, 54.

Trading in his cardigan sweater for sackcloth and ashes, Jimmy Carter came down from the mountaintop this summer to deliver the bleakest assessment of the American spirit of any President in modern times. By all accounts, it was his most effective speech. Yet within less than a week, just as Mr. Carter himself was caught up in a new swirl of controversy, the speech itself was enveloped in debate about the depth and nature of the national malaise.

Are Americans as despairing as Mr. Carter said? If so, what lies at the core of their anguish? And if not, was the President simply engaging in rhetorical overkill to catch the nation's attention—or to serve political purposes?

Evidence from a variety of public opinion polls, including those taken by the President's personal pollster, Patrick H. Caddell, is not conclusive, but it provides a good deal of guidance in looking for answers. For a starting point in defining today's national mood, most survey researchers turn to the mid-1960s, for it was then, they agree, that the country turned a psychological corner. As Seymour Martin Lipset and William Schneider wrote in an earlier issue of this magazine (July/August 1978), "The Vietnam involvement, the explosion of antiwar protest, and the rise of militant social movements concerned with the status of various minority groups . . . and women seemingly changed the perception which Americans had of their country. Various pollsters registered a steady decline in the public's confidence in the country's institutions and the people running them." Between 1966, when Louis Harris began the first inquiry, and 1971, the number of Americans expressing "a great deal of confidence" in the people running institutions as diverse as the executive branch of government, major companies, and the military dropped by more than 20 points; as confidence faltered, cynicism mounted rapidly so that within a few years time, those who felt isolated from the political process expanded from one to two-thirds of the population, and some four Americans out of five came to think they could not trust political leaders.

Since the early 1970s, confidence levels have remained in a valley, but on at least two occasions they began to climb upward again, only to tumble under a torrent of bad news. The first upward march occurred in 1972. But then between 1973 and 1974, under the pressures of Watergate, the oil embargo, and the onset of serious stagflation, the numbers fell backwards once more. According to Harris, George Gallup, and a variety of other surveys, the election of Jimmy Carter—along with the end of the recession—gave confidence levels a second upward bounce in 1976–77, but in 1978 and early 1979, optimism receded sharply again—with consequences that Mr. Carter could hardly ignore.

The President's Private Polls

Apparently, Mr. Carter's concern with the nation's spirit was stirred by a lengthy memorandum sent to him this April by Mr. Caddell. The *Washington Post* has reported that the paper, warning that large numbers of Americans were losing faith both in the future and in his own stewardship, "somewhat stunned" the President and was a major factor in sending him up to Camp David for ten days of introspection. The memorandum was based in large part upon the findings of Mr. Caddell's survey firm, Cambridge Reports, Inc., based in Massachusetts. While the memorandum remains private, it can be reliably reported that among its central findings were these:

—For the first time since Cambridge Reports began asking in 1972, the pollsters found in the first quarter of 1979 that on the average, Americans thought the nation would be worse off in the future than it is today. The Cambridge firm was employing a "self-anchoring scale," a test that was developed by Lloyd Free and Hadley Cantril in the late 1950s and has become a familiar tool for survey researchers. In that test, an individual is shown a ladder from 0 to 10 (ten highest) and asked to rate the nation on the ladder five years ago, today, and five years from today. In the early 1979 survey, respondents put the nation's past at 5.7 on the scale, the present at 4.7, and the future at 4.6—a downward curve that set off alarm bells in the Carter camp. Moreover, the number of pessimists (those who see the nation on a downward slope) had swollen to 48 percent, compared to 16 percent who were considered optimists.

—A less dramatic, but in Caddell's view probably more significant, erosion was found in the way that people viewed their personal futures on the ladder scale. In its measurements since 1972, Cambridge Reports had previously found that optimists far outnumbered the pessimists and there was little rise among the pessimists, even during the 1973–74 recession. Since the fourth quarter of 1978, however, the firm has registered a near doubling in the ranks of the pessimists so that there are almost as many pessimists (32 percent) as optimists (38 percent). Caddell is deeply concerned about the velocity of the recent change—it's unprecedented in his surveys, he says—and the fact that personal pessimism is now seeping into the elite structure of society.

—Still a third area of serious concern to both Caddell and the President has been a series of Caddell measurements of "personal efficacy"—that is, the ability of the individual to affect the political system and the responsiveness of that system to his needs. In Caddell's view, "efficacy levels" remained relatively constant during the mid-70s, even during the recession, but dropped precipitously between December 1976 and December 1978. He points to a series of results from his polls to bear out that contention:

Do you agree or disagree that most politicians today are so similar that it doesn't really make much difference who gets elected?

	Agree	Disagree
1976	39%	57%
1978	48	43

People like me don't have any say about what government does.

	Agree	Disagree
1976	40%	55%
1978	57	35

In his December 1978 survey, Caddell also asked a series of questions about major issues facing the country. He found that 46 percent of his respondents thought the government could do "a lot" to bring down inflation and 52 percent thought it could do "a lot" to reduce taxes significantly. Only 10 percent, however, thought it "very likely" the government would act effectively against inflation and only 11 percent anticipated large tax cuts. Even fewer were "absolutely certain" that effective action would be taken on the inflation and tax fronts in the next four to five years.

The Caddell memorandum to the President did not dwell on consumer confidence figures or the President's own approval ratings—both of which have also dropped in recent months—but all in all, it painted a very gloomy picture. At the very least, then, it would appear that in deciding the country is suffering from "malaise," Mr. Carter came by his judgments honestly.

Yet, questions persist. While authorities in the survey field and in politics respect Mr. Caddell's findings, they are openly skeptical about some of the conclusions. Let's consider the questions one by one.

It May Be a Funk, But Is It a Crisis?   The answer seems to rest in the eye of the beholder. Those who wish to see a "crisis of the spirit" can find many other surveys to buttress their claims. A year ago, Albert and Susan Cantril, under contract from the U.S. Labor Department, asked people to rate the nation's past, present, and future and found signs of pessimism that closely paralleled those of the Cambridge survey team. More recently, some 67 percent told researchers from Yankelovich, Skelly and White that "the country is in deep and serious trouble"; some 65 percent told the Roper Organization that "things in the country have pretty seriously gotten on the wrong track"; and 69 percent told the Gallup poll that, in general, they were "dissatisfied with the way things are going in the U.S. at this time." Just after the President's speech, the CBS News/*New York Times* survey team went into the field and found 77 percent agreeing with him that the nation is experiencing a "crisis of confidence." NBC and *Newsweek* polls reported almost identical results.

An Overblown Crisis?   Despite this long, grey line of numbers, however, there are many other findings that suggest the idea of a "crisis" is badly overblown. Social scientists have long pointed out, for example, that at the same time that Americans are expressing a sour note about the country, they usually feel much more buoyant about their private lives. This past February, in a Gallup survey that found 69 percent dissatisfied with national life, no less than 77 percent said they were generally satisfied with their own personal lives. In fact, the last time Gallup asked people of several nations about "life as a whole"—a survey taken in late 1977—the level of satisfaction in the United States (69 percent) was higher than anywhere in Europe; only 41 percent of West Germans expressed such satisfaction and even fewer, 26 percent, had much *joie de vivre* in France. Americans may have become more somber about their personal lives in recent months, but nowhere is there any evidence that people's personal satisfaction or confidence in themselves has collapsed.

Social scientists also carefully point out that while Americans are less confident than in the mid-60s of their leaders in political and other major institutions, they have retained their faith in the institutions themselves. Daniel Yankelovich has noted, for example, that after a decade when public confidence in business leaders plummeted from 70 percent to about 15 percent, some nine out of ten Americans were still so attached to the free enterprise system in the mid-70s that they were willing to make personal sacrifices in order to preserve it. Even in the rising hostility toward the oil companies this year, there has been little public demand for nationalization or more rigorous government regulation.

It is this unshaken belief in the institutional arrangement of society, both politically and economically, that in the view of some observers, like Seymour Martin Lipset, has made the United States more impervious to socialism and to vast internal upheavals than any European democracy.

There are two other distinctions worth making here, and they emerge most clearly in the way that Harris and Gallup ask people about their confidence in institutions. Harris poses his confidence question this way:

> As far as *people* in charge of (read list) are concerned, would you say you have *a great deal of confidence,* only some confidence or hardly any confidence at all in them? (Italics added)

Gallup asks his confidence question this way:

> I am going to read a list of *institutions* in American society. Would you tell me how much confidence you, yourself have in each one—*a great deal, quite a lot,* some, or very little? (Italics added)

By asking in terms of people running institutions and restricting his confidence measurement to only those who say they have "a great deal," Harris consistently comes up with much lower levels of public confidence than Gallup, who asks about the institutions themselves—always more trusted—and measures confidence in terms of those who answer "a great deal" or "quite a lot."

In the first three months of this year, both pollsters sent teams into the field. Harris found that confidence in "the military" stood at 29 percent, Gallup found it at 54 percent; Harris found confidence in the U.S. Supreme Court at 28 percent, Gallup at 45 percent; Harris found confidence in "organized religion" at 20 percent, Gallup asked about "the church or organized religion" and found 65 percent expressing confidence. They agreed on almost nothing, underscoring an old axiom that slight changes in question wording can produce enormous changes in outcomes and showing once again how dangerous it is for anyone, including a President, to read too much into single sets of survey numbers.

It can also be argued, as scholars such as Amitai Etzioni have done, that measuring how many people have "a great deal of confidence" in institutions is not the only relevant way to look at the issue. Etzioni points out that in the Lou Harris surveys between 1966 and 1975, the number expressing "a great deal" of confidence in American institutions (based on an average of all institutions) fell by twenty-two points, but the number expressing "no confidence" moved up a bare seven points, from 12 to 19 percent. In other words, the seismic shift in confidence that has occasioned so much debate in recent years was more than anything else a movement from the "great deal of confidence" to "some confidence" column, rather than to "no confidence."

What's Bugging People?   In his July 15th speech, Mr. Carter pinpointed five different causes of the "malaise": the assassinations of the early 1960s, Vietnam, Watergate, ten years of inflation, and the series of oil shocks that began in 1973. Conveniently, all of those root causes predated his own entry into office, a theme that is sure to be repeated on the campaign trail. In the wake of the President's speech, one of his White House advisers went so far as to tell a *Wall Street Journal* reporter that Mr. Carter was elected "to be the national psychologist, to put the country on the couch, and provide reassurance and therapy" after the traumas of Vietnam and Watergate.

Mr. Caddell entertains more complicated views—views that are of some significance because, from news reports, it appears he has an intellectual influence upon the First Family that has stretched far beyond his polling numbers. In essence, he holds that events like Vietnam and Watergate have had a cumulative effect, eroding the core of people's belief systems about society, so that the onset of more distressing events such as inflation can "trigger" a very rapid loss of faith and confidence. He thinks that Americans are confused in their values and uncertain of purpose. He is not sure how all the pieces fit together—"I'm baffled by the way that some of the numbers have changed so rapidly in the past two years," he says—but he is convinced that society's malaise runs far deeper than concerns such as inflation and Mr. Carter's leadership.

Other observers are quick to disagree. While conceding that events such as Vietnam and Watergate took a heavy toll (and some refuse to go that far), they argue that recent trends in confidence are tied not to earlier times but to the ups and downs of the economy. Since 1973, at least, nearly all of the general confidence levels measured by Yankelovich, Roper, and others have closely paralleled economic trends. Indeed, to a rough eye, there appears to be an interesting parallel between the consumer confidence index of the prestigious University of Michigan survey and the national ladder ratings of Mr. Caddell's own firm. In early 1975, when the Michigan consumer confidence index was in a trough (that was the end of the recession), the number of optimists about the nation's future stood at 12 percent in the Caddell studies. As the nation pulled out of the recession, consumer confidence climbed upward, reaching a peak in the spring of 1977—and the number of optimists in the Caddell survey then hovered around 40 percent. Over the next two years, from May 1977 to May 1979, consumer confidence plunged 20 points—and the number of optimists also dropped about 20 points, hitting 16 percent in the first quarter of 1979. The opposition case thus seems strong, but based on his own regression analyses, Caddell remains convinced that the link between inflation and the "crisis of confidence" is not as powerful as it looks.

The Carter Issue—Mr. Carter's critics are also determined not to let him off a political hook by conceding the point that the nation's "malaise" started before he came into office and is unrelated to his own leadership. Some have pointed out that it was only when the President suffered a "crisis" in his political polls that he found a "crisis" in the nation; others have insisted there is no "crisis of confidence," only a "crisis of leadership." One poll employed in such arguments was that taken by Lou Harris in December 1978, asking people how much confidence they had "in the President" and "in the country." Some 28 percent said they had "a great deal" of confidence in the President; 74 percent said they had "a great deal" of confidence in the country.

A more scholarly statement on the matter was offered this summer by Arthur H. Miller of the Center for Political Studies at the University of Michigan. Writing in *Economic Outlook USA,* he states that "1978 brought not an upsurge in political trust but the lowest level of confidence in government during the past twenty years. . . . What is the explanation for the continued low regard for government? . . . Clearly, the public's current lack of confidence in government does not reflect perceptions of the personal appeal or integrity of the incumbent. A better explanation of political distrust stems from the public's evaluation of how well the Carter administration has performed in handling national problems. The American people expect their government to solve the nation's social problems, and our politicians foster these expectations with their campaign promises." Jimmy Carter, in Miller's view, is only the most recent in a series of presidents who have promised to solve various social problems and have failed, causing more and more voters to question whether their ballots make any difference anymore.

Has Pessimism Become a Drag on the Nation?   One of the more arresting points that Mr. Carter made in his July address is that the public's lack of confidence is now the source of many national difficulties. "Why have we not been able to get together as a nation to resolve our energy problems?" he asked, and then he went on to answer by describing people's loss of faith.

To some, that argument was the most dubious of all, for it turned common sense on its head: confidence has dropped because of the inability of the nation's leaders to solve problems, not the other way around. That is one debate, at least, that can't be settled by polls.

Is Today's Mood Unique?   Still another question that cannot be easily addressed with survey data is whether there are historical parallels to the nation's mood. Robert Lane, a political scientist at Yale University, has investigated public opinion data from the 1930s to the 1960s and concluded that public confidence did plummet to low levels during the Great Depression, only to rise steadily for the next quarter of a century on a crest of growing affluence and well-being. Other than Lane's work, however, there are few comprehensive studies of the public mood in earlier years, especially before polling became popular during the 1930s. French writer and philosopher, Jean-Francois Revel, asserts that people have been decrying "crises of confidence" for centuries, but the definitive history of malaise has yet to be written. It sounds like a dissertation in search of an author.

In the meantime, as Americans grapple not only with the problems of energy, inflation, and a recession but with the new questions about their own self-confidence, what conclusions can be drawn about the national mood? The one certainty is that President Carter will continue to say there is a crisis of confidence; a majority of

Americans will continue to agree with him; but others, especially in the survey field, will disagree about the severity of that judgment.

Whether one chooses to characterize the nation's mood as a "crisis of confidence," a malaise, or just a funk, however, is not as important as understanding the dimensions and nature of the problem. Those dimensions seem clear: there are large numbers of Americans today, perhaps as many as half or more of the population, who have turned pessimistic about the future of the economy and of the nation. Public confidence in the leaders of our institutions is both volatile and fragile. But so far, Americans remain relatively optimistic about their own personal lives and express continuing faith in institutions themselves.

No doubt, it would be extremely unhealthy to allow today's pessimism and cynicism to fester for another five years; yet there also seems little doubt that if, instead, the country enjoyed five years of continuing prosperity—something that Americans haven't seen, after all, for more than a decade—the public opinion polls would suddenly blossom with good news and the "crisis of confidence" would be quietly forgotten.

THE PSYCHOLOGY OF POLITICAL INVOLVEMENT

Roberta S. Sigel

Edited and reprinted from Social Science Quarterly 56 (*September 1975*): 315–323.

The point of departure for this investigation is the fact that individuals vary in the extent to which they become politically involved. The explanation we wish to offer for such variation is a psychological one. We will test the proposition that individual differences in locus-of-control explain differences in political involvement. Locus-of-control is a construct developed by Rotter who observed that

> . . . people differ in the tendency to attribute satisfactions and failures to themselves rather than to external causes. . . . Some persons are confident that they control themselves and their destinies. . . . They are Internals. Other persons feel that their fates are in the hands of powerful others, that they are pawns. . . . They are Externals.[1]

Following Rotter's lead, it might be possible to explain involvement or lack of involvement with politics on the basis of a person's felt reward expectancies. Externals are politically uninvolved because they consider it futile to try to influence government by their own behavior. Internals, because they feel themselves in control, are politically involved.

This link between politics and locus-of-control was first explicated by Seeman who described locus-of-control as "an important corollary of powerlessness,"[2] and powerlessness in turn was seen by him as a dimension of political alienation. Whereas Rotter stated that Internals are better learners than Externals, Seeman added a qualification to this generalization by asserting that they are better learners only when the information to be gained seems control-relevant to them.

Although Seeman stressed the importance of control-relevance, he tended not to determine which areas were control-relevant for the individual. Instead he designated *a priori* certain ones as control-relevant. In this paper we address ourselves to the problem of operationalizing this feature since control-relevance is of crucial importance to any political analysis. Politics has such low salience for most Americans that it would be unrealistic to expect high levels of involvement with the political domain unless it were demonstrated to be control-relevant.

Seeman equates political involvement with information and interest. Our cognitive definition of political involvement adds two dimensions to his cognitive one, namely affect for the political system and political participation in it. We contend that under conditions of relevance, Internals will be politically more involved in all three dimensions than will Externals. From this is derived:

Hypothesis 1—Cognitive Dimension.   Internals will not differ from Externals in the cognitive dimension of involvement unless they see politics as a control-relevant domain. They will, therefore, score higher on knowledge and interest since Internals acquire more information which to them has "high potential utility for altering the individual's outcomes in a given domain." [3] Externals should not be affected by differences in relevance since they feel they cannot influence the political environment anyway. Hence, they will see no need for acquiring information which could equip them to exercise influence over government.

Hypothesis 2—Activism Dimension.   Under conditions of relevance Internals will differ from Externals in their propensity to become politically active. For example, Internals who want certain things from government—such as a policy change—will increase their activity level. This prediction fits in with Gore and Rotter's description of Internals as people who "expect reward in a large variety of situations to be the function . . . of their own behaviors. . . ." [4]

Hypothesis 3—Affect Dimension.   Under the same control-relevance conditions Internals also will exhibit higher positive affect toward government. Since Internals are inclined to see people as trustworthy, predictable, and motivated by good will toward their fellowmen, we expect them to generalize this inclination to the government and its officials. Officials will be seen as trustworthy, non-corrupt and responsive to their wishes and/or control attempts. Consequently, Internals will score lower on political cynicism and higher on political efficacy than Externals.

Design of the Study

346 public school seniors and sophomores, randomly selected from the class lists in two Western New York communities were chosen to test the above three hypotheses. During the spring of 1971 these students were interviewed at length about their political involvement and affiliative patterns. [5] In addition to the personal interview, several psychological and political scales were administered to them by means of a pencil and paper questionnaire filled out in the presence of the interviewer. All interviewers were experienced members of a state university's field staff.

Internality/Externality was ascertained through the 14-item version of the Rotter I-E Scale (none of them fillers) validated by Bachman in a study of tenth grade boys. This version of the scale emphasizes personal and social (not political) control, success in planning one's life, popularity, success in school, and chances for personal leadership.[6] On the basis of the distribution, the sample was divided into three groups,[7] but analysis reported here deals only with the two extreme groups: the External and the Internals.

Measures of Involvement

Involvement was measured in the following ways:

Cognitive Dimension.   We as Seeman used two indicators, interest in politics and information about current events,[8] adding a third indicator of 25 items which measured a respondent's *understanding* of important political principles, such as majority rule, due process of law, etc.

Activist Dimension.   Behavioral indicators were developed, but since school youths are not yet likely to have become politically involved, these indicators included questions about the future as well as current activities. Students were asked to reflect on the likelihood of becoming participatory when confronted with government actions which might affect them adversely. In addition, they were offered a list of eight types of political action and were asked to indicate how appropriate it was for them "as citizens" to engage in such action under the above contingencies. The eight actions varied in forcefulness from passivity ("do nothing; the government has more information") to militancy ("use violence if all else fails"); and in "social respectability" (from voting to violence).

Affective Dimension.   Two measures of affect for the government were used: a six-item Political Cynicism Scale previously used with public school youth[9] and the Easton-Dennis version of the Michigan Sense of Political Efficacy Scale. Relevance of government was determined on the basis of the answer to the question: "Do you think the government has much to do with the way the average man runs his life?"[10]

Results

Youth tends to feel moderately in control of self and environment (45 percent). Less than one-quarter (23 percent) feels very high in personal control, and one-third feels powerless. Grades in school, age, and sex do not affect this distribution.[11]

Hypothesis 1—Cognitive Dimension.   Internals who saw government as relevant scored significantly higher on the three cognitive indicators of *political interest, knowledge,* and *comprehension.* Among Externals relevance of government makes little or no difference in their scores which are generally low. These findings are in keeping with our hypothesis that Internals will, under conditions of control-relevance, exhibit more political interest and acquire more information than Externals.

Hypothesis 2—Activism Dimension.   Our prediction that Internals would be more sympathetic to active participation or intervention into politics when confronted with governmental action which they judged harmful was generally not confirmed. Internals who saw government as relevant did not differ greatly from other Internals in only three instances but, contrary to our predictions, did not differ with respect to the remaining five.[12] For Externals, as predicted, relevance of government did not affect approval or rejection of the eight activities (except, unexpectedly, in the case of forming a pressure group).

Why, however, on the five remaining items are Internals not behaviorally far more involved than Externals? The answer might well lie in the items chosen by us. The five items are highly consensual. Of these, three are generally rejected, especially resort to violence and complete passivity (demonstrating is the third). Two are highly sanctioned, i.e. voting and writing letters to officials. Agreement on these five items is so great in the total sample that they seem to constitute non-differentiating items, reflecting the prevailing political culture rather than individual feelings of control. Under such circumstances, personality variables are not likely to predict who will be politically active and who will not.

But why do personality variables predict in the case of three activities? What specifically makes the three so different that Internals—under conditions of control-relevance—are more apt to accept them than are the Externals or the remaining Internals? The activities share three features: (1) they require more effort and determination than pulling a lever; (2) they require individual initiative in that the individual must set the agenda; (3) they are directly related to specific goals or rewards one wishes to obtain, i.e. the goal is control-relevant.[13] Under the latter conditions Internals will engage in behavior which requires more than minimal effort. Motivation to control plus Internals' conviction that they have the power to control explains why Internals behave differently from Externals and from those Internals for whom government is not relevant. Control-relevance in short furnishes the crucial motivation.

While the findings with respect to the activism dimension thus do not entirely confirm the hypothesis, they do provide a basis for qualification. In addition, we are alerted to the possibility that political actions are not all of the same cloth. Locus-of-control possibly may be related to those actions requiring considerable individual initiative and which are engaged in to make government *respond directly* to citizen requests. To test this interpretation, future measures of involvement should be so designed to distinguish clearly low initiative and effort activities from more strenuous ones.

Hypothesis 3—Affect Dimension. The prediction that Internals who see government as relevant would show more affect for government than the remaining Internals was confirmed in both instances: They scored lower on political cynicism and higher on the political efficacy scale. Turning first to political cynicism, relevance makes no significant difference for Externals but it does for Internals. Our findings suggest that the Internal's high trust in people is generalized to politicians when politics becomes relevant—probably because without such trust, the Internal's control attempts would be useless.

Moreover, when *all* Internals are compared with *all* Externals (without controls for relevance), Internals also are less cynical than Externals. While neither group is highly cynical (6 percent and 18 percent respectively), Internals are significantly more positive in their trust in officials (lower in cynicism) than Externals (40 percent and 18 percent respectively).[14]

The second affect indicator reveals similar relationships. Control-relevance is not related to political efficacy among Externals, but it is among Internals. This finding demonstrates that Internals' political involvement is highly affected by the relevance government has for them and is compatible with the accepted image of the Internal as a person who sees himself as skillful and powerful enough to elicit appropriate responses in a variety of social situations.

Finally a comparison of *all* Internals with *all* Externals reveals Internals to feel politically significantly more efficacious (67 percent to 39 percent respectively). Low feelings of efficacy are quite exceptional for them (Internals, 10 percent; Externals, 38 percent). The fact that locus-of-control relates to political cynicism and sense of political efficacy even without imposition of controls seems indicative of the Internal's tendency to generalize to the political environment the feelings he has about self and the general environment. He trusts self and others; government and politicians constitute no exception for him.

The fact that Externals, lacking trust in people [15] and confidence in their own capacity to control the environment, evidence more political cynicism and lower sense of political efficacy, corroborates that feelings of low personal competence as measured by Rotter's scale of internality/externality do tend to depress an individual's inclination for political involvement. Equally important is the observation that caring less does not imply not caring or disaffection. Even powerless youths feel positively about their government, and substantial segments among them feel politically efficacious. There is thus little substantiation here for the various theories of mass society that people low in feelings of personal control also feel unattached or hostile to the larger environment and low in feelings of political control.[16]

In general, then, the three hypotheses were confirmed: Internals are politically more involved, provided they see government as relevant to their lives. This holds particularly for two of the three involvement dimensions, the cognitive and the affect ones. In the behavioral area, greater involvement prevailed only with respect to the more demanding and influence-exerting activities. On all three dimensions, relevance of government made no difference for Externals. A sense of powerlessness apparently inhibits the capacity and/or willingness to become politically involved. The findings also suggest that without the imposition of controls internality in and of itself often increases an individual's propensity to become politically involved. This leads to the conclusion that Rotter's concept of locus-of-control as modified by Seeman offers a persuasive explanation for differences in individual involvement patterns.

Discussion

In demonstrating the relationship of a psychological disposition, such as locus-of-control, to political involvement, we do not wish to create the impression that variations in political orientations are exclusively or even predominantly determined by personality factors. Much of what people do or don't do is only tangentially related to the kind of personalities they have but rather "is dictated by the hard realities of the environment in which they have to cope and the options which are available to them." [17] But the options they notice and the ones they fail to notice, the options they choose and the ones they by-pass are partially determined by an individual's personality. It is the concept of *partial* determination which is important.

We suggest that only select personality dispositions are likely to function as such partial determinants of political involvement, an individual's feelings of personal competence being one of them. Since political involvement requires the willingness to get engaged, to relate to others, and to try to exert influence over others (including powerful others), it seems persuasive that a person's sense of self-worth should play a determining role. Those lacking in this sense presumably would be disinclined to exert themselves politically. In order to test this assumption inquiries should be undertaken to determine whether measures of self-worth other than the Rotter one relate similarly to political involvement.

The central findings emanating from this study clearly indicate that under conditions of control-relevance feelings of personal competence as expressed in the sense of personal control do influence all three dimensions of political involvement. Seeman's modification of Rotter's theory thus constitutes a significant contribution to our understanding of the political involvement-personal control linkage. The evidence on this point is direct and overwhelming: feelings of personal control (internality) have a more substantial as well as a more consistent influence on the political involvement of those for whom politics is salient than for those who have little interest in political affairs and are not aware of government's relevance for their own lives. A person's sense of control acquires political significance to the extent that politics is a salient dimension of his psychological environment.

References

1. Julian B. Rotter, "External Control and Internal Control," *Psychology Today* 5 (June 1971): 42ff.
2. Melvin Seeman, "Alienation, Membership, and Political Knowledge: A Comparative Study," *Public Opinion Quarterly* 30 (Fall 1966): 355.
3. Melvin Seeman, "Powerlessness and Knowledge: A Comparative Study of Alienation and Learning," *Sociometry* 30 (June 1967): 111.
4. Pearl Gore and J. Rotter, "A Personality Correlate of Social Action," *Journal of Personality* 31 (March 1963): 62.
5. Participation was voluntary but no student refused.
6. Jerald C. Bachman, *Youth in Transition,* Vol. 1 (Ann Arbor: Institute for Social Research, 1969): 76–77.
7. The three groups were: students scoring very high in externality (8–14; n = 75); an in-between group (5–7; n = 149); and one scoring very low (0–4; n = 110). Group One was labelled Externals; Group Three, Internals. A median split produced similar results but seemed unnecessarily arbitrary because a very large group obtained the same numerical score.
8. The information questions asking for the names of five very prominent living federal office holders, are from Bachman, *Youth in Transition,* Vol. 2: 155–156.
9. *Ibid.*: 150–151.
10. Several additional relevance questions were asked but yielded similar results.
11. Data on sex, age, and socioeconomic status are reported only in cases where these differences are affected in the findings.
12. Although even on these five items relevance of government had the predicted effect on Internals, i.e., they disapproved less of some of the activities than did Externals.
13. Letter writing may well be a high effort activity for some but it need not always be motivated by a desire to obtain rewards; nor does it have the same force and impact as the activity of a group or a personal visit to a bureaucrat.
14. The high cynical segment contains 40 percent high Externals—21 percent high Internals. In this context, it must be noted that the whole sample is relatively low in cynicism—a finding well known from the political socialization literature; children are seldom true political cynics.
15. The Faith in People Scale correlated −.35 (p<.001) with Externality.
16. This study was undertaken prior to Watergate. A study currently underway by the author

shows much greater political cynicism among Internals and Externals. The general relationship, however, is maintained, i.e., Internals are less cynical than Externals.
17. Roberta S. Sigel, *Learning About Politics* (New York: Random House, 1970): 237.

TO THE STUDENT: A COMMENTARY

Watching politics in contemporary America means keeping your eye on a lot of things. There are the politicians and what they say and do. There are the policies derived from what officials do. And, among many other things, there are the actions you and your fellow citizens take in response to politics. But of late there has been something else to look at, and that is what citizens such as yourself think and feel about politics, government, and your role in all of that.

A new political industry has emerged in the last few decades, one comprised of people who make a living out of taking the public pulse on a variety of issues. That industry is public opinion polling; those engaged in it are the pollsters. They purport to describe—by interviewing cross-sections of Americans—what we believe about our political institutions, our stands on issues, what we like and don't like about political policies and events, who we are likely to vote for, and how we feel about things now and in the future. The reports of the pollsters pop up in several places—in the speeches of politicians, in news columns, on radio and television, in your textbooks, and even in daily conversation. It sometimes seems as if pollsters talk as much about us and what is good for us as do the politicians.

Politicians (or should we call them "polliticians") pay attention to what pollsters say. Rare is the politician in national life who does not monitor poll results regularly, even hiring people to go out and take public opinion soundings. Presidents are no exception. President Lyndon Johnson carried slips of paper in his pocket bearing the results of polls measuring his popularity. Pressed to prove a point he would whip out a pollster's report showing Americans approved of his presidential performance, hence he could not be wrong. As poll results became more negative, fewer paper slips lined his pockets. President Richard Nixon had one of his aides specialize in keeping up with poll results, even making sure that any poll taken—national, state, or local—contain questions rating Nixon's performance. He too found the polls less intriguing as they reported declining popularity.

As David Gergen reports in "A Crisis of Confidence?" President Jimmy Carter grew worried about citizens' responses to politics and government, at least in part, as a result of his personal pollster's memorandum on the subject. It was not the first time Carter heeded his pollster, Pat Caddell. In 1976 Carter fought for the presidential nomination against two prominent Democrats, as well as a host of other contenders. One was considered "liberal," U.S. Representative Morris Udall, the other "conservative," U.S. Senator Henry Jackson. Caddell's opinion soundings detected that matters of political ideology—liberal versus conservative—were scarcely the key concerns of Americans in 1976. Instead they wanted leaders they could trust, leaders who would correct the tendencies of "the Washington Establishment" to mire them down in wars (such as Vietnam) and scandals (such as that of Watergate, which drove Richard Nixon from the presidency). So Carter positioned himself as the "anti-Washington" candidate, promising he could be trusted, that Washington and not the American people had failed, and this country should have a government "as good as its people."

David Gergen notes that Caddell's 1979 memorandum was a key item in provoking President Carter's thoughts about the crisis of confidence. Gergen's summary of Caddell's findings is succinct: Americans were pessimistic about the nation's future, their own personal fortunes, and their ability to influence the course of political events. Results of other polls, notes Gergen, also indicate Americans' declining political confidence.

At this point in Gergen's article, however, a problem arises for you as a political watcher. There are polls and there are polls, pollsters and pollsters. The polls don't always agree in findings, the pollsters in their interpretations. Gergen's comparisons of the results of polls by two reputable pollsters—Louis Harris and George Gallup—on the confidence question is a case in point. Note that Harris reports confidence in such institutions as the military, the U.S. Supreme Court, and organized religion hovering in the 20–30 percent range; Gallup reports a range of 45–65 percent.

Or, consider some evidence on the question of Americans' political confidence not reviewed by Gergen. Writing in the October/November 1979 issue of *Public Opinion,* political scientist Warren Miller reported the results of several decades of polls conducted by the Center for Political Studies, University of Michigan. Miller, then president of the American Political Science Association, argued that to spy a crisis of confidence in poll data was to misread the public pulse. To be sure there had been a decline in citizens' trust in government for two decades since the 1950s, but in recent years (1976–1978) the decline had leveled off. And, since 1952 Center studies reported no appreciable change in "internal efficacy," that is, the degree that citizens feel they can cope with new political events and issues—this in spite of Vietnam, Watergate, and economic woes. Moreover, the Center's measures of "external efficacy" (tapping how much citizens believe politicians care about what "people like me think") give scant credence to the claim of a crisis of confidence. In so far as our beliefs about whether government responds to our needs, Center studies indicate Americans thought government more responsive in the early years of the Carter administration than it had been under his predecessor, President Gerald Ford. Finally, citizens' sense of civic duty—that they should vote in elections—was higher in 1978 than 1952.

Why such differences? There are many reasons. One is that different pollsters employ differing techniques in selecting which people to interview, which people to represent all citizens' responses to politics. For another, pollsters use different questions in soliciting information. (These aspects of polls you will read about in chapter 12.) And, it is not easy to know the state of mind of someone responding to a poll on a given day—what he or she knows about politics and what is going on, what political commitments a person has, and what personal anxieties and conflicts one bears. Commitments, for instance, are clearly important. Gergen's article takes little note of how Democrats versus Republicans respond to politics. Warren Miller's analysis, however, finds that in the first two years of the Carter administration there was a notable increase in political/personal confidence among Democrats, a distinct decline among Republicans—the first time in a decade that an incumbent President's fellow partisans showed a marked increase in their confidence in government. Given the fact that nationwide the proportion of Americans who consider themselves Democrats is substantially greater than those identifying as Republicans, the President might have claimed in 1979 that confidence was growing, not declining!

Claims about a crisis of confidence in citizens' responses to politics must take two aspects into account. First, there is the communitywide rise and fall in confidence. In polls this appears as the average responses of all citizens portrayed in percentages who say, for example, that it makes any difference who gets elected or that people have any say in what government does (note the tables presented by Gergen on these matters). A second key aspect involves not what Americans on the average think but what *you* think. On what does that depend? Do you act politically as you are personally? Does your personality predestine your politics? These are important questions and students of politics differ in their answers. Some political scientists, for example, admit that people's personalities influence their politics in little ways, but that other factors—your social class, age, sex, religion, race, party loyalties learned early in life—are far more important than the ideosyncratic psyches of you and your friends. Not all scholars or journalists agree. To be sure, they counter, the social and political attributes of a person are significant, but it is leadership that shapes the responses of the masses to politics. The options politicians offer, the programs they advocate, the appeals they make—these provoke your responses to politics. That view is reflected in Gergen's discussion of the Carter issue. In this view personality is relevant to one's politics, but a relatively minor, not overriding consideration.

Specialists in the study of political psychology take the role of personality in politics seriously. A few get carried away and reduce all politics to a reflection of different psyches. Most are more modest in their claims. Roberta Sigel typifies this temperate view. "We do not wish," she writes in what you have just read, "to create the impression that variations in political orientations are exclusively or even predominantly determined by personality factors." Hard realities and available options are crucial too. Your confidence will, in part, wax or wane in politics depending upon what government gives and takes away. But the options you notice, Sigel says, and the ones you fail to notice, those you choose and those you bypass are partially determined by your personality as well: "It is the concept of *partial* determination which is important."

But surely personalities are highly complex and differ a great deal from one another—yours from Bill Rivers, Dan Nimmo, Roberta Sigel. How can unique personalities be meaningfully compared, at least so as to establish any sound relationships of personality to politics? One way, which Sigel uses, is to describe personalities on the kinds of traits people have. The *trait* approach permits researchers to classify people with similar traits into differing personality *types*. Once done it is relatively easy to ask if differing personality types differ in politics.

The trait Sigel focuses upon to typify personalities is that of locus-of-control. As she notes, some people locate the control over their lives in themselves. They are Internals. Others believe outside forces control their futures. They are Externals. Consider the following little test. It consists of sample items from an early version of a questionnaire tapping internality/externality devised by Julian Rotter. You recall that Sigel cites Rotter's contributions to the study of locus-of-control. You can discover for yourself your inclinations for internal or external control by simply adding the choices you make on each side.

I MORE STRONGLY BELIEVE THAT

Promotions are earned through hard work and persistence.	*or*	Making a lot of money is largely a matter of getting the right breaks.
When I am right I can convince others.	*or*	It is silly to think one can really change another person's basic attitudes.
In my case the grades I make are the results of my own efforts, luck has little or nothing to do with it.	*or*	Sometimes I feel that I have little to do with the grades I get.
Getting along with people is a skill that must be practiced.	*or*	It is almost impossible to figure out how to please some people.
I am the master of my fate.	*or*	A great deal that happens to me is probably a matter of chance.

There are more items to the full test but by now you have the idea.

Sigel's argument is straightforward: if politics is relevant to people, Internals will be more politically involved—for they see themselves controlling their political destinies—than will Externals. Internals will be more interested and better informed about politics, more active in politics, and have better feelings about government. To test these propositions Sigel followed an approach typical in studies of political psychology. She obtained a sample of people (in this instance high school students), interviewed them, and had them fill out questionnaires measuring internality/externality, political knowledge, activity, and feelings about government.

Not everything turned out as expected. As anticipated, among people who find government relevant, Internals are more politically knowledgeable than Externals. Moreover, Internals are less cynical about politics and more apt to believe they can accomplish something in politics (have higher political efficacy, the quality referred to in David Gergen's article) than are Externals. But, surprisingly, Internals are scarcely more likely to turn to political activity than are Externals when faced with a government policy deemed harmful. Sigel explains this anomaly. Pay close attention to her view for it provides clues to some of the difficulties involved in trying to contrast two ways of taking part in politics—the kinds of passive politics most Americans engage in and the active participation that requires considerably more effort (something we hope you are willing to undertake but most Americans are not).

What things does Sigel say to you? For one, what you know, feel, and do about government may be influenced by how much control you believe you have over your own life. That is especially so if politics is important and relevant to you. What you are as a person (i.e., personality) makes a difference. You are not merely destined to respond to political options in fixed ways conditioned by your social class, age, sex, or some other attribute.

All this says something about the alleged crisis of confidence in citizens' responses to politics. For whatever reasons, political and nonpolitical, perhaps people feel a loss of control over their lives. To that degree we may suffer a declining political confidence, particularly if politics is important to us. But there is another side to this argument. Not only does what you do in politics depend in part upon what you are personally, what you *think* can flow from what you *do* in politics. Much of democratic theory emphasizes this point: that people should take part in politics as a way of experiencing and coping with the options that promote the development of an open, mature personality.

Four decades ago philosopher John Dewey told a conference of teachers that "the keynote of democracy as a way of life may be expressed . . . as the necessity for the participation of every human being in formation of the values that regulate the living of men together." That, he said, "is necessary from the standpoint of both the general social welfare and the full development of human beings as individuals." The hidden message in Sigel's research may be that *through* politics we all have a better chance of becoming Internals, of asserting a personal locus-of-control over our destinies and, thereby, making (Gergen's phrase) the "crisis of confidence quietly forgotten."

More information regarding the crisis of confidence can be found in a revealing confrontation between a President's pollster and a noted social scientist:

Patrick H. Caddell, "Crisis of Confidence: I—Trapped in a Downward Spiral," *Public Opinion* 2 (October/November 1979): 2–8, 60

Warren E. Miller, "Crisis of Confidence: II—Misreading the Public Pulse," *Public Opinion* 2 (October/November 1979): 9–15, 60

The problems associated with using polls and opinion surveys to draw conclusions about citizens' responses to politics—and the possibilities as well—are covered by a free-lance writer and two political scientists respectively in:

Michael Wheeler, *Lies, Damn Lies and Statistics*

Herbert F. Weisberg and Bruce D. Bown, *An Introduction to Survey Research and Data Analysis*

A pollster provides an interesting account of the political consequences of various groups trying to assert control over their destinies, and a political scientist explores in depth the relation of locus-of-control and political efficacy:

Louis Harris, *The Anguish of Change*

Stanley Renshon, *Psychological Needs and Political Behavior*

3 Taking Part in Voting: Why, Why Not?

INTRODUCTION

That citizens' responses to politics in America constitute a crisis of confidence—whether measured in opinion polls or through political psychology tests—is an open question. That is the burden of what you learned in chapter 2. That there is one respect in which citizens seem not to respond to politics at all is more clear. Put simply, most Americans do not vote. Almost one-half of those qualified to do so have not voted in recent presidential elections, only around 40 percent do so in congressional races, and turnout rates in many statewide and local contests fare even worse. Both journalists and political scientists have pondered the reasons behind this alleged voter apathy for years. They have also remarked upon the consequences of low voting rates for American democracy. This chapter introduces you to the conclusions of such concerned reflection.

Curtis Gans brings a useful mixture of expertise to his consideration of "The Empty Ballot Box." He has considerable experience in elections, including that as campaign director for Eugene McCarthy's 1968 presidential campaign. Gans has been deeply involved in party politics as testified to by his service on the Democratic National Policy Council. The journalistic craft has also been part of his life for he has published articles in *Atlantic, Washington Monthly,* the *Washington Post, Nation,* and the *New Republic.* Finally, his service as director of the Committee for the Study of the American Electorate has furnished him with considerable insight into why Americans do and do not vote.

In the selection that follows Curtis Gans first describes the magnitude of nonvoting in American elections. Then he reviews a few of the political consequences of not voting. This leads him to try to account for why people don't vote. His principal concern is that citizens have lost "hope" in the democratic process, a loss he attributes to a variety of underlying trends. He concludes by calling for a "fundamental reexamination of the structure and tenets of American politics." As you read his piece think about how it relates to what David Gergen wrote in "A Crisis of Confidence?" Do both authors see the same illness in American democracy? Does Gans provide a prescription or merely a diagnosis?

Research in political science presents a lengthy list of factors associated with not voting. These include overly restrictive legal requirements; citizens' lack of social, educational, and economic resources that prompt people to vote; negative feelings about government and politicians; and the scheduling of too many elections for too many positions too often. Relatively few political scientists ask yet another question, that is, what are nonvoters like and what would the electorate look like if they chose to vote? One who does look at the characteristics of nonvoters is William Maddox. His "The Changing American Nonvoter, 1952–1978" charts the traits of nonvoters over a quarter of a century. He endeavors ultimately to describe *types* of nonvoters. As you ponder his analysis consider carefully what would be the results for American politics if one or more of his types of nonvoters were to begin taking part in American elections in a more active fashion. That is, instead of asking Gans' question about what happens if people don't vote, ask what would occur if those who normally don't do.

Bill Maddox is associate professor of political science at Central Florida University. He has contributed scholarly articles to various political science journals since receiving his Ph.D. degree in 1978 at the University of Tennessee. He is particularly interested in political psychology and how children learn about politics as well as in voting behavior. His studies include why voters split their tickets or vote straight party ballots, the sources of political party coalitions, and childrens' views of the presidency. Considered along with Gans' arguments, Maddox's provide a useful picture of "the other half," i.e., citizens who don't take part in electoral politics.

THE EMPTY BALLOT BOX

Curtis B. Gans

Edited and reprinted from Public Opinion *1* (*September/October 1978*): 54–57.

Consider just a small slice of history. Early in 1963, President John F. Kennedy established a special bipartisan presidential commission on registration and voting participation in the United States.

He did so, in part, because he was appalled that the level of American voter turnout in the presidential election of 1960 and the congressional elections of 1962 was substantially lower than the turnout rate of most other Western nations. Kennedy wanted to do something about the incongruity he saw—that the greatest democracy in the world had almost the least political involvement of its citizen-electorate of any democracy in the world.

One week after the young President's untimely death and after six months of intense deliberation, the commission emerged with a series of recommendations aimed at increasing the country's voter turnout. Among its major findings, the commission urged the abolition of literacy tests and poll tax as prerequisites for voting; the removal of voting barriers to full voting participation by Blacks and other minorities;

enfranchisement of youth between the ages of eighteen to twenty-one; absentee registration and voting; liberalization of state and local residency requirements; and simplified registration, including the use of outreach programs and postcards.

The commission's report had a profound impact on American political thought. Its ideas became the conventional political wisdom for remedying low political participation and in the fifteen years since the report was first published, almost every major commission recommendation has become registration law.

The only problem, however, was that like the surgeon whose operation was a fantastic success with the single exception that the patient died, the commission-inspired reforms did not yield the expected results.

In 1960, 63.8 percent of the eligible electorate cast their ballots for president. In 1976, only 54.4 percent went to the polls. In 1962, 46.3 percent of the American electorate voted in the congressional elections of that year. In 1974, the percentage of eligible voters who went to the polls for a congressional election had dropped to 38.2. *After a decade and a half of electoral reform, the level of voter turnout in the United States has fallen below that of every other democracy in the world, with the single exception of Botswana!*

Fifteen Million Dropouts

The central and perhaps the greatest single problem of the American polity today is not the direction of the nation with respect to any single area of public policy, but rather the degree to which the vital underpinnings of American democracy are being eroded. The legitimacy of a democratic leadership and the health of the democratic process depend squarely on the informed and active participation of the electorate. Yet the level of political participation is now sinking and the decline seems irreversible.

Neither the parameters nor the import of these trends should be underestimated:

- During the last ten years, fully 15 million Americans who were once regular voters have dropped out of the political process.
- Nearly 70 million eligible Americans failed to vote in the 1976 presidential election; more than 100 million eschewed the ballot box in the congressional election of 1974.
- Fewer than 28 percent of Jimmy Carter's fellow citizens voted for him in the presidential election of 1976; Brendan Byrne became governor of New Jersey with a "mandate" of less than 15 percent of New Jersey's eligible voters; Mayor Koch was the "choice" of less than 12 percent of New York City's electorate; Senator Henry Jackson "won" the 1976 New York presidential primary with less than 6 percent of the total vote.

More than half of America's nonparticipants are chronic nonvoters—people who have never or hardly ever voted, whose families have never voted and who are poorer, less educated and less involved participants in American society. But a growing number of Americans are dropping out of the political process—many of whom are the educated, white collar professionals who were once regular participants—and a growing number of young people are failing to enter as political participants. Both of these trends constitute a major national concern, for there is the very real danger that the habit of good citizenship—of civic virtue, if you will, that has been so intrinsic and necessary a part of the American voluntary democratic process—will atrophy and die and that government of the people, for the people and by the people will become government of the few, by the few and for the few.

Threat to the Body Politic

There is, of course, no foreordained optimal level of political participation, and American democracy has survived and even prospered—at least in this century—despite rates of voting participation lower than many other democracies. (Participation levels in nineteenth century America were substantially higher, albeit with a more limited electorate.) But the continuing and sharp decline in the level of voting and citizen involvement cannot help but adversely affect the health of the American body politic.

•   To the extent that fewer and fewer Americans bother to vote, the ability of organized minorities, special interests and single-issue zealots to polarize American politics and influence the course of public policy will be enhanced. In the 1978 primaries, low turnout allowed right-wing militants to unseat moderate Clifford Case in New Jersey and permitted Republican crossovers and anti-abortion and anti-environmental activists to defeat Democratic party designee Donald M. Fraser in Minnesota.

•   To the extent that American political participation dwindles and the business of politics becomes increasingly the province of organized interest groups, the ability of the political system to produce public policy in the interest of society as a whole declines correspondingly. Public employees, for instance, who constitute one-sixth of the employed adult population and whose turnout rate is normally quite high, might well have a disproportionate influence on the outcome of elections in a diminishing electorate and consequently have undue influence on the course of public policy with regard to such issues as civil service reform or government reorganization.

•   To the extent that citizen interest in, and involvement with, the political process continues to wane and political institutions—especially parties—continue to atrophy, there is a greater likelihood that politics will be dominated by professional media manipulators beholden to no one and that national leadership can emerge which is unknown to the electorate and potentially unstable, demagogic and even authoritarian. The nation is indeed fortunate that whatever his other failings might be, President James Earl Carter is a man of decency, for it was well into his presidency before people stopped asking the question, "Jimmy Who?"

* * *

Identifying the problem of declining political participation, understanding its ramifications, even demonstrating its importance to the welfare of American democracy is not, however, equivalent to finding the way to reverse this trend. This is one area of social inquiry in which exploration for probable cause does not yield a political remedy.

Some of the reasons for a decline in voting are obvious. The sharpest decline in participation among those who had previously considered themselves Democrats occurred between 1964 and 1972—or at precisely the time when the war in Vietnam was dividing Democrats against each other and when pro-war and anti-war factions were taking turns capturing control of their party to the exclusion and hostility of their opponents. Similarly, the sharpest drop in Republican turnout occurred between the congressional elections of 1970 and 1974—or precisely when Watergate made many who had hitherto been Republicans embarrassed to be so identified. The enfranchisement of youth between the ages of eighteen to twenty-one, a larger voter pool with a lower than average turnout rate, also helped in a minor way to depress the national turnout averages. But these events, now history, offer no wisdom to explain or reverse the continuing decline in voting nor to change what sociologist Harold Mendelsohn has termed the present "American anomie."

The will to vote is in essence religious. It rests on the belief that despite the overwhelming majority of elections that are not decided by one vote, each individual's vote will contribute to a general will that will yield honorable leadership, wise policy and sufficient checks on the excesses of power. It is precisely this faith that has been shattered.

As almost all recent survey research has indicated, there has been for more than a decade a high level of cynicism about whether government can address any of the public's perceived needs, a large degree of mistrust of the integrity and competence of public officials and the efficacy of political institutions, and a growing feeling of personal impotence that afflicts not only non-voters but voters as well. It is likely that voting participation will continue to decline until these attitudes are substantially altered and a modicum of that intangible called "hope" is restored to the political process. This, in turn, will not be accomplished by simply acknowledging the sins of the past and replacing the "bad" old officeholders with "good" new ones. More fundamental questions need to be addressed.

The Answer May Depend on the Question

Once the Pandora's box is opened, the questions come tumbling out:

- To what extent have reforms undertaken in Congress, in the two political parties and in the conduct and financing of elections, enhanced or inhibited participation?
- To what extent do modern techniques of identifying a candidate's supporters and pulling only those individuals to the polls contribute to declining participation?
- To what extent has the change in the legislative officeholder from state or national citizen to dispenser of services reduced the competitiveness that sustains voter interest?
- To what extent has the federal government, as a dispenser of services and jobs, undercut the traditional role of the political party and made voter mobilization efforts more difficult?
- To what extent has the practice of districting in favor of one party reduced turnout?
- To what extent is the fact that the United States is the only democracy in the world which does not have a state-run system of universal voter enrollment a contributing cause?

As important as each of these questions may be, there are, I believe, four broader and related questions that are of even greater relevance to the future revitalization of American democracy. They are:

1. The Question of Scale—In survey after survey during the past several years, the American public has responded strongly and negatively to the word "big," especially when followed by the words "government," "business" and "labor." There is without question increasing public uncertainty about issues grown too complex and a growing public helplessness and impotence in the face of the institutions grown too large.

Greater federal authority may well be needed to cope with such issues as energy conservation and a stagflation economy, but leadership can no longer afford to give only lip service to decentralization. It must begin a serious exploration of the instrumentalities needed for the devolution of power and administrative authority of both public and private institutions.

2. The Question of Television—There have been two sets of televised presidential debates—the first in 1960 at the high-water mark for voting in the past three decades and the second in 1976 at the recent low point in voter turnout. In between, voting and political participation have declined sharply and steadily while television has assumed a growing centrality in the lives of Americans.

It would be too facile to ascribe a cause-and-effect relationship between these two phenomena, but there are many questions about the relationship between television, society, and politics that need to be asked. Specifically:

- Has one of the by-products of the television age been the erosion of community political and social institutions and the relative atomization of American society?
- Has the essentially protected position of the three networks enhanced the trend toward larger institutions and greater centralization?
- While creating a public with a greater body of shared knowledge and information, has not television also enhanced public confusion by providing a surfeit of information without distinguishing between that which is important and that which is not? Or put another way, has television, in speeding up the present, robbed American politics of a necessary sense of the historically important?
- Has one political impact of television been to create a demand for candidates who have charm and charisma without due regard for character and competence?
- Is it not also true, as public opinion specialist Irving Crespi among others has suggested, that television has transformed American politics by creating a new breed of campaign technicians—the media image manipulators—who are guns for hire, allying themselves temporarily with one politician and vitiating the role of political parties in selecting nominees and in delivering votes as well as political programs and services?
- Has not television's approach to the coverage of politics been to emphasize the competition involved rather than the stakes of that competition, leaving the citizen as an uninvolved spectator at a horse race rather than an involved participant in a decision that might affect at least some aspect of his life?

These, of course, hardly exhaust the serious questions that can and should be asked about the relationship between television and American politics, but they should suffice to indicate that a serious and critical examination of that relationship is long overdue.

3. The Question of Political Parties—The American system of two heterogeneous parties has served the nation well, but there is mounting evidence that it is, at least for the present, in trouble. The traditional roles of the parties in mobilizing the electorate, finding and training leadership, providing information, dispensing jobs and services have been—to a larger extent than is healthy—supplanted by television, by government and casework, by direct mail specialists, and the new breed of independent television packagers. But what may, in the long run, be more important is the decline in the role of the parties in defining public choice, channelling public debate and creating programmatic alternatives for legislative and governmental action.

For four decades since the advent of the New Deal, the political options were clear:

- The Democratic party was the party of the New Deal and its progeny, the Fair Deal, New Frontier and Great Society. It was the party of the welfare state and the common man, of the economics of John Maynard Keynes and the foreign policy of Dean Acheson. It was the party of labor, the minorities, the big city machines, the small farmers and the liberal intellectuals. It was the party of expansive hope.
- Against the cacaphony of competing interests, the Republican party was the party of the common interest. Against the corruption of the big city machine, the Republican party was the party of moral probity. Against the allure of unreasoned hope, the Republican party was the party of classical economics and political restraint.

The public has every confidence that in voting Democratic or Republican, it was making a meaningful choice and that those choices would be reflected in the public policy decisions made by their candidates once in office.

That certitude broke down in the 1960s.

A concerted drive by an ideologically rigid and politically reactionary right wing for control of the sinews of the Republican party and a flaccid response by legitimate conservatives left the Republicans an atrophied remnant of their former selves. It also left the real debate on central issues of public policy—for and against the war in Vietnam, for and against détente, for jobs or for controlling the despoliation of the environment, for unlimited or restricted growth—to be conducted mainly within the Democratic party rather than between the parties. The fact that these debates were never resolved left the Democratic party ridden with conflict, without a clear sense of direction and without the ability to pull itself together for the delivery of a political program.

Faced with one party that was fast becoming ideologically irrelevant and the other bloated beyond meaning and capacity to contribute to the public good, it is little wonder that the average citizen saw no choice and no good reason to vote.

The 1960s also left the nation with a Republican party controlled at its bottom by ideological zealots and at its top—to a lesser extent—by corporate giants, and a Democratic party, over whose policies and leadership the trade union movement in general and the AFL-CIO in particular exercised a continuing veto. This, in turn, left no political base for the largest single element in the American population—the unorganized but educated white collar and professional middle class, precisely the group in society that is dropping out of political participation. Which is all to say that high on the national political agenda is the need for a definition and perhaps a realignment of the American party system.

4. The Question of Belief—If what propels people to the polls—beyond family upbringing, high school training and concepts of civic duty—is some belief that they might contribute to the direction of their country, one of the salient features of this age is the degree to which neither American liberalism nor American conservatism has provided meaningful choices within the political marketplace.

The public no longer believes in the unlimited cornucopia of resources and moneys that traditional liberals still insist is there, but it also is unwilling to give up dreams of greater equity that many conservatives are anxious to shatter. The public no longer believes there is a program for every problem, but it is not willing to dispense with efforts to make the quality of American life better. In short, a large number of Americans no longer identify with either the New Deal liberalism that is at the core of the Democratic party or the Goldwater conservatism that seems to motivate an increasing number of Republicans.

Perhaps nowhere was the dearth of new and relevant thought more evident than in the recent debate in Congress between liberals and conservatives over national energy policy. Liberals, claiming to represent consumers, fought to hold the line on energy prices, as if somehow they believed that the age of cheap energy might last forever. Conservatives, on the other hand, shilled for big business, urging financial incentives for increased production as if they believed that producing more oil and gas now would somehow address the reality that there may well not be any oil and gas in the near future. Throughout the debate, the overriding national and world interest in a policy of conservation was a political orphan.

Unless American liberalism and conservatism begin to put their respective intellectual houses in order and offer the public choices relevant to the times, it is likely that increasing numbers of American citizens will forget their family upbringing, civic training and sense of patriotic duty and sit out ensuing elections.

It is said that the only certainties in this world are death and taxes. It is, however, a virtual certainty that unless a fundamental reexamination of the structure and tenets of American politics is undertaken soon, the 1978 elections will see fewer voters go to the polls than did in 1974, fewer will vote in 1980 than in 1976, and the erosion of the vital underpinnings of American democracy will continue and, perhaps, sadly accelerate.

THE CHANGING AMERICAN NONVOTER, 1952–1978

William S. Maddox

Edited from an unpublished paper delivered at the annual meeting of the Southern Political Science Association, Gatlinburg, Tenn., November, 1979.

The low level of voting turnout in the United States has long been a topic of discussion for journalists, civic leaders, and social scientists. Comparison with other democratic systems usually leaves the United States somewhere near the bottom of the ranks in voter turnout. The slow decline of turnout in national elections of recent years added to the concern about our citizen's participation. This research report does not claim to discover the ultimate causes of nonvoting. The aim here is to survey the correlates of turnout from 1952 to 1978, present a parsimonious description of the major factors that distinguish voters from nonvoters, and suggest one way (among many potential ways) of understanding the collection of nonvoters in our system.

Research Design

The data for this study of turnout are the University of Michigan National Election Studies from 1952 through 1978. These election studies all contain some measure of reported turnout. Although the reported level of turnout is always higher than the actual vote for that year, we use as the dependent variable the reported turnout, at the risk of measuring an attitude toward voting rather than voting itself. We suspect that the turnout questions on these surveys represent a response similar to those found for the civic duty questions, which deal primarily with voting and are strongly related to the turnout question.

What factors could be related to turnout (or reported turnout)? Milbrath's [1] summary of participation research suggests a variety of explanations of voting as does Reiter.[2] Here we begin with seven categories of independent variables and work toward eliminating those which do not significantly distinguish between voters and nonvoters. Furthermore, we include several components within some categories; the ultimate aim is to use only the most useful measures. The seven categories are as follows (specific operational definitions are available on request):

1. *Social position,* represented by a scale reflecting college education, age over 35, above median income, white collar occupation, and home ownership.
2. *Personality,* combining where available all questions from the personal trust and personal control scales, found elsewhere to be measuring a general personality factor.[3]
3. *Partisan attitudes,* including perception of party differences (net likes and dislikes), affect toward both parties (sum of all likes minus sum of all dislikes for both parties) and strength of party identification.
4. *Candidate attitudes,* including perception of candidate differences and affect toward both candidates, measured the same as for the parties. Presidential candidates are used except in midterm years where open-ended questions about Congressional candidates are available. Additionally, similar measures using feeling thermometer scales since 1966 are presented for comparison.
5. *Issue extremity.* We first created for each year four issue scales: economic action by the government, foreign involvement, civil rights, and social issues (when available). We then summed the absolute values of those issue scales, so that a person received a high score if he expressed more extreme positions across several different types of issues.
6. *Political involvement,* a more general attitude than usually measured by students of political participation; an earlier analysis suggested that political interest, information, and aspects of political efficacy should be considered as a single factor.[4] Media use was sporadically related to this factor but is not considered here.
7. *Political trust,* measured by the five standard political trust questions plus the "officials don't care" question which cluster together consistently across time.[5] Because blacks were systematically excluded from voting during the earlier years and because race is so strongly associated with many of the independent variables, we base this analysis only on whites.

Findings

Table 7 presents Pearson correlations between reported voter turnout and several measures of independent variables among whites only from 1952 through 1978. Social position is consistently related to turnout across all years, with a slight tendency to be more related in midterm election years. Although personality differences may reflect simply another aspect of social position, the personality scale is moderately correlated with turnout years in most years when it is available. Turnout is also positively correlated with all measures of partisanship: perception of differences, general affect toward the parties, and strength of identification. Similarly, affect toward candidates and perception of candidate differences are both correlated with turnout, although in some years the correlations are low. Extreme positions across types of issues seldom demonstrate any association with turnout across this time period. Our examination of correlations between positions on the four types of issues and voter turnout (not reported here) also found no consistent relationship across time. (This finding, of course, does not preclude the possibility that extreme positions on one specific issue, such as Vietnam in the 1970s or civil rights in the 1960s, could be related to turnout.) Our measures of general political orientations indicate that political involvement, not surprisingly, is positively correlated with turnout with only slight differences across election years. Political trust, however, which has declined in recent years as turnout has, shows no such relationship.

At the bottom of Table 7, we present the correlations between turnout and measures of partisan and candidate attitudes derived from the feeling thermometer scales used in later years. Although responses to specific candidates may stimulate or depress

TABLE 7 Pearson Correlations Between Reported Turnout and Independent Variables, 1952–1978 (Whites Only)

	1952	1954	1956	1958	1960	1962	1964	1966	1968	1970	1972	1974	1976	1978
n =	1453	1022	1610	1643	1636	1175	1291	1138	1194	1398	1946	2249	2106	2016
Independent Variables														
Social position	.24	.21	.23	.28	.19	.14	.24	.31	.28	.36	.29	.33	.33	.31
Personality	.08 [a]	N.A.	.18 [b]	.16	.14	N.A.	.13	.16	.24	.19	.14	.30	.26	N.A.
Perception of party differences	.17	.16	.20	.18	.17	N.A.	.16	.15	.17	N.A.	.12 [c]	N.A.	.16	.19
Strength of party identification	.14	.29	.17	.20	.17	.21	.17	.18	.18	.06	.21	.05	.20	.25
Affect toward parties	.23	N.A.	.24	.27	.22	N.A.	.19	N.A.	.24	N.A.	.23 [c]	N.A.	.25	.25
Perception of candidate differences	.21	N.A.	.12	.25	.21	N.A.	.14	N.A.	.16	N.A.	.15 [c]	.10	.15	.23
Affect toward candidates	.22	N.A.	.22	.24	.21	N.A.	.15	N.A.	.24	N.A.	.26 [c]	.10	.25	.28
Issue extremity	.08	.06	.14	.13	.15	.02	.06	.14	.06	.08	.03 [c]	.10	.17	.12
Involvement	.25	N.A.	.28	.34	.29	.35	.24	.29	.25	.28	.30	.04	.33	.25
Political trust	.13	N.A.	.18	.08	.27	N.A.	.10	.05	.13	.05	.13	.09	.11	.02
Feeling thermometer items:														
Party difference								.07	.09	.07	.09 [c]	.05	.08	.14
Party affect								.04	.03	.13	.06 [c]	.17	.17	.10
Candidate difference									.11	.05	.07 [c]	.04	.06	.06
Candidate affect									.01	.16	.10 [c]	.18	.10	.04

[a] n = 476
[b] n = 518
[c] n = 996

82

TABLE 8   Correlations Between Feeling Thermometer Measure and Open-Ended Questions

	1966	1968	1972	1976	1978
Party differences	−.060	.294	.159	.261	.365
Party affect	N.A.	−.045	−.051	−.113	.095
Candidate differences	N.A.	.261	.438	.429	−.067
Candidate affect	N.A.	−.004	−.143	−.125	.028

turnout, the thermometer measures do not relate to turnout as well as more detailed likes and dislikes questions do when they are available. Table 8, which presents the correlations between feeling thermometer questions and comparable open-ended questions, suggests that the feeling thermometer questions with regard to party differences and candidate differences are related in most years and probably could be used as substitute measures if necessary. When both kinds of questions are present, however, in every case from 1966 to 1978, the open-ended measure is more highly correlated with turnout than is the thermometer question.

This evidence indicates that, of the original seven categories, only issue extremity and political trust are unrelated to turnout and can be discarded. All of the party and candidate measures are related to turnout and are also likely to be interrelated. Furthermore, they may be related to involvement, since most require respondent interest and information. Table 9 presents the intercorrelations of involvement, party measures, and candidate attitudes. Given the independence of party identification strength from both involvement and other party measures, we chose it to represent party attachment. Similarly, although candidate affect is slightly more related to turnout, candidate differences is a measure more distinct from involvement; we use it for the remainder of the analysis. Thus we now can compare the relative importance of five variables for distinguishing between voters and nonvoters: social standing, personality, partisan strength, perceived candidate differences, and political involvement.

Discriminant analysis is a technique which helps us to describe which variables best distinguish between the members of two or more groups. Because it is designed, in part, for dichotomous dependent variables, it is more appropriate than other types of analysis.[6] Reiter's recent work uses a similar approach but he analyzes only presidential elections since 1960 and uses nineteen independent variables to provide discriminant functions only slightly more distinguishing than those presented below with only five scales.[7] The results of discriminant analyses for each election year survey are summarized in Table 10.

TABLE 9   Intercorrelations of Party Differences (PD), Party Affect (PA), Candidate Affect (CA), Candidate Differences (CD), Strength of Identification (IDS), and Involvement (INV)

	1952	1954	1956	1958	1960	1962	1964	1966	1968	1970	1972	1974	1976	1978
PD-PA	.59	X	.72	.66	.70	X	.66	.06	.57	.00	.55	.01	.63	.66
PD-IDS	.27	.22	.32	.33	.29	X	.31	.23	.25	.07	.29	.19	.30	.32
PA-IDS	.10	X	.26	.24	.22	X	.24	.04	.15	.08	.20	.04	.19	.28
CD-CA	.57	X	.57	.73	.62	X	.61	X	.58	.18	.40	.98	.48	.78
PA-INV	.40	X	.34	.36	.35	X	.39	.11	.34	.11	.30	.02	.42	.34
CA-INV	.38	X	.40	.42	.42	X	.36	X	.34	.04	.31	.02	.40	.37
PD-INV	.23	X	.25	.24	.21	X	.27	.35	.18	.01	.16	.13	.26	.17
CD-INV	.27	X	.28	.38	.29	X	.24	X	.21	.04	.09	.02	.17	.27
IDS-INV	.08	X	.11	.18	.12	.18	.15	.10	.03	.06	.02	.05	.14	.09

TABLE 10   Discriminant Analyses Between Reported Voters and Nonvoters (Whites Only), 1952–1978

	1952	1954	1956	1958	1960	1962	1964	1966	1968	1970	1972	1974	1976	1978
n =	476 *	1022	518 *	1643	1636	1175	1291	1138	1194	1398	996 *	2249	2105	2016
Social standing	.485	.614	.380	.432	.336	.134	.567	.591	.496	.723	.513	.664	.464	.559
Personality	.082	N.A.	.257	.182	.121	N.A.	.115	.085	.337	.164	.146	.580	.273	N.A.
Partisan strength	.220	.819	.378	.331	.375	.423	.402	.392	.397	.031	.415	.011	.337	.478
Candidate differences	.314	N.A.	.064	.278	.320	N.A.	.222	N.A.	.178	.105	.136	.230	.157	.339
Involvement	.610	N.A.	.583	.509	.570	.814	.417	.479	.364	.410	.575	.108	.448	.290

* Reduced sample size for some years because some questions were asked only of sub-samples.

Social standing and involvement are the variables which most consistently distinguish between voters and nonvoters across these three decades. They are also moderately correlated with each other. If there is any change in the relative strength of the two over time, it is that social standing remains a major discriminator (except in the 1962 survey) while involvement tends to vary more in its importance, with slightly less impact in recent years than in the first decade of studies. Presidential and midterm differences are not extreme. Involvement is a better distinguishing factor in four of seven presidential years while social standing is a better distinguishing factor in three of five midterm years present in the analysis.

The importance of the other factors for distinguishing between voters and nonvoters is more varied, although measurement difficulties could account for some of this variation. Personality does distinguish between the groups in some years, even with social standing controlled through the discriminant technique. Although personality probably is not a major motivation to vote or not, it may act as a strong secondary reinforcement of either social standing or involvement. Strength of partisanship does help to distinguish between the two groups in most years; the impact of partisanship is most consistent in the decade of the 1960s but also emerges as a very clear distinction between voters and nonvoters in the 1978 study. Finally, our measure of perceived candidate differences varies across time as a distinguishing factor; it is important in the presidential years of 1952, 1960, and 1964. The high coefficients in midterm years are in 1958 and 1978, both reflecting availability of open-ended questions about Congressional candidates.

In summary, social standing and political involvement distinguish between voters and nonvoters in the most consistent fashion across time. The other variables, personality, partisan strength, and candidate differences, demonstrate lesser and more varying impact on the distinction between the two groups. These results suggest that a person's social standing, which represents, in part, his involvement and stake in American society as well as his progress through the life cycle, and his political involvement, which reflects feelings of effectiveness, awareness, and interest in politics, are both important contextual variables within which the person decides to vote or not. Personality variables may reinforce or contradict those general tendencies which social or political involvement present. Attitudes toward the parties or candidates also could reinforce or contradict the basic tendencies each person has toward participation in elections. In other words, a search for *the* best single predictor of turnout is and should be doomed to failure. Psychologists often used the word "overdetermined" to indicate that most behavior flows from a variety of contextual conditions and motivations. Similarly, voting or nonvoting is a reflection of many factors operating simultaneously. For different types of people, different motivations or conditions may be more important. The results here indicate that social standing and involvement may be "first among equals" in that they alone appear to be crucial in all years. The other three variables probably play a secondary but still important role in the decision to vote.

A Typological Suggestion

How can we make use of these findings to better understand and describe the nonvoter? One approach is to offer a typological description of nonvoters, using the 1976 election study as a sample case. Given the consistent distinctions between voters and nonvoters according to social position and political involvement, it is reasonable to begin with those two measures when we want to describe the nonvoters in any election year. If we dichotomize both the involvement and social standing scales at the midpoint for each one and then crosstabulate the two, we find four basic types of people: those low in both social position and involvement (44% reported nonvoting) those high in both (only 8% did not vote), and two "mixed" types, the highly involved who lack social position (24% nonvoting) and the high in social standing who are uninvolved (23% nonvoting). The reported turnout of these groups meets our expectations. A better way to approach the explanation of nonvoting, however, may be to begin with nonvoters. Who are the nonvoters in terms of these basic variables? Table 11 presents some evidence. 61.8% of reported nonvoters in 1976 are those who lack both social standing and political involvement which are crucial to participation. We can offer a plausible and simple explanation of their nonvoting: they lacked both social and political involvement which would lead to voting. Another 14.8% were politically involved but lacked social involvement; their position in society or in the life cycle did not reinforce their attitudes, which were favorable to participation. 16%

TABLE 11 A Typological Analysis of Nonvoters in 1976

Type	Social Position (low = 0,1,2) (high = 3,4,5)	Political Involvement (low = 0,1,2) (high = 3,4,5)	Proportion of Nonvoters (n = 579)
Group 1	low	low	61.8%
Group 2	low	high	14.8
Group 3	high	low	16.0
Group 4	high	high	7.4
			100.0%

Type	Proportion Who Scored Low on		
	Strength of Partisanship (0,1, or 2)	Perceived Candidate Differences (0 or 1)	Personality (0 through 3)
Group 1	52.9%	45.4%	69.2%
Group 2	36.7	37.2	43.6
Group 3	43.3	48.6	51.3
Group 4	54.1	43.5	29.4

were in the opposite situation; although their social standing was conducive to voting, their political involvement was too low to stimulate turnout. Finally, only 7.4% of the nonvoters in 1976 "should" have voted according to their social and political involvement.

We should not ignore other factors, however. They may reinforce our initial conclusions or offer evidence as to why some people did not behave as expected from our typological analysis. In the lower part of Table 11, we present evidence as to how each type of person responded to the other three factors. We find that those in the largest category of nonvoters generally were reinforced by other factors besides social and political involvement. 69% of them, in fact, also scored low on the personality scale and about half expressed few strong partisan or candidate attitudes. The second group's sense of political involvement is reflected in the small proportions who scored low on the measures of party strength and perceived candidate differences. In other words, their low *social standing* is the only one of the five variables which is consistent with their nonvoting. The third group, all of whom were high in social position but lacked political involvement, were about evenly split in terms of low versus high scores on the personality and candidate differences scales. For some, the fact that high social standing is not translated into the usual political involvement may reflect personality attitudes. For about as many, the fact that they perceived few differences between the candidates probably reinforced (or contributed to) their low political involvement and their lack of incentive to vote. Finally, we can examine the attitudes of the 7.4% of nonvoters who should have voted, given their social and political involvement. For over half of them, lack of attachment to political parties is a reasonable explanation. For over 40%, lack of perceived candidate differences also contributed to lack of motivation. Few of this high social standing, politically involved group demonstrated personality orientations which would have discouraged turnout.

To summarize, based on two primary variables and three secondary ones, we can offer the following description of nonvoters in 1976:

62% lacked both social incentives and political involvement. Most of these also lacked personality traits conducive to involvement or voting. About half also lacked partisan attachment and about half saw virtually no differences between presidential candidates.

15% were politically involved but lacked social incentives. Most were not only politically involved but also expressed personality traits conducive to involvement and saw differences between the parties and candidates.

16% were in a social position which should be conducive to participation but lacked political involvement or supportive personality traits. About half saw few candidate differences; 43% also lacked partisan attachment.

7% were both socially and politically involved, in other words, possessed characteristics which should have led them to vote. In addition, most of them had reinforcing personality characteristics. About half of these, however, lacked partisan attachment and 44% saw few candidate differences.

We can construct a similar description of the nonvoters in each election year. Such a typal description may be more informative in regard to changes in the nonvoter group over time and presidential-midterm year differences than the correlations and discriminant analyses presented in this paper. Such a typological approach rests heavily on the reliability of our survey questions and on the admittedly arbitrary cut-off points used to dichotomize each scale. (In 1976, at least, shifting the dichotomy cut-off point by one point in either direction made very little difference in the overall distribution of types, given the correlation between social standing and involvement. Whether this would be true in other years, we do not know.) If we are looking for a reasonable description of nonvoters over time, however, we may have to take such chances. The ultimate value of any political analysis is not determined by the intermediate steps which we use to reach it; it is determined by the ability of the final results to help us understand political behavior.

References

1. Lester W. Milbrath and M. L. Goel, *Political Participation: How and Why Do People Get Involved in Politics?* (Chicago: Rand McNally, 1977).
2. Howard L. Reiter, "Why is Turnout Down?" *Public Opinion Quarterly* 43 (Fall 1979): 297–311.
3. William S. Maddox, "The Psychological Foundations of Citizenship." Paper presented at the Annual Meeting of the Midwest Political Science Association, Chicago, April 1979.
4. *Ibid.*
5. *Ibid.*
6. John Aldrich and Charles F. Cnudde, "Probing the Bounds of Conventional Wisdom: A Comparison of Regression, Probit, and Discriminant Analysis," *American Journal of Political Science* 19 (November 1975): 571–608.
7. Reiter, "Why is Turnout Down?" *op cit.*

TO THE STUDENT: A COMMENTARY

Since this commentary is directed at students and you are reading it, chances are you are enrolled in a college or university course. That sets you off from most Americans who, as yet, still do not go to college. It also sets you off in another way, namely, as an electoral being. The likelihood is that since you are receiving education beyond high school you will become a voter rather than a nonvoter, at least in presidential elections. Approximately three-fourths of citizens who continue their education beyond high school vote in presidential elections. Those receiving college degrees vote in even higher proportions. There are a couple of reasons for this. One is that people who enter college generally come from social and economic backgrounds that provide greater resources and incentives to vote. Another is that being in college heightens political awareness, thus motivating more people to vote.

If you are probably going to be a voter anyway, or already are, why bother reading about nonvoters? The articles by Curtis Gans and Bill Maddox give you the answer. To begin with, as Gans notes, citizens who once were regular voters—some with college educations such as yourself—no longer always do so. Fifteen million such regular voters, says Gans, have departed the political process. And, notice that 16 percent of what Maddox identifies as nonvoters are citizens with sufficient social incentives to take part—including education—but are lacking in other qualities associated with voting.

Reflect also upon the four broad reasons Gans provides for the decline in voting among Americans. Each could just as easily touch you as it could those who do not attend college. What of his "question of scale"? Do you feel that America's religious, social, economic, and governmental institutions have become so large, so complex that they are beyond your comprehension and control? If so, you may be a candidate for nonvoting. And you undoubtedly watch television. If Gans is correct, you too may be lulled into politics as a spectator sport, one that tempts you to sit on the sidelines satisfied to have "acquaintance with" rather than "knowledge of" politics (recall that distinction from the prologue to this book?). Moreover, the erosion of political parties that Gans discusses affects your life as much as anyone else. If neither Democratic nor Republican party offers relevant, meaningful alternatives, and neither will change the course of events substantially once in office, why bother to choose between their candidates? Finally, we know from a variety of opinion surveys (some of them reported in chapter 2) that what Gans calls the "question of belief" touches people of all social strata, educational levels, incomes, etc. If doubt and a lack of faith promote nonvoting (and 23 percent of all Maddox's nonvoters shared personal characteristics associated with declining beliefs in political choices), then no manner of education alone will guarantee a person will be a voter.

But assume you continue to differ from most Americans and keep on voting. Why then worry about "the other half"? For Gans the answer is simple, i.e., the consequences of an empty ballot box are so severe that they shape the lives of everyone, voters and nonvoters alike. Gans worries about three results of low voting rates—the increased ability of special interests to have their way at the expense of the general welfare, a narrowing focus in policy making, and a potentially "unstable, demagogic and even authoritarian" brand of national leadership. You will have the opportunity to explore each of these possible consequences in detail in chapters to come. Chapter 6, for instance, asks you to think about the politics of special interests; chapter 9 provides thoughts about policy making; and, chapter 7 discusses the "professional media manipulators" that worry Gans. For the moment, however, ponder if Gans' concerns are real and why.

Not everyone, for instance, agrees with Gans that voter apathy is a critical threat to American democracy. Writing almost three decades ago a sociologist and leading student of voting, Bernard Berelson, offered a counter argument to the civic textbook notion that high levels of voting are good beyond question.[1] Berelson drew a distinction between what democracy, in theory, requires of individual citizens and what it requires of the political community as a whole. To be sure, in a democracy citizens are expected to be knowledgable and informed about politics, should cast votes on the basis of issues and principles, and should behave in rational ways. But, wrote Berelson, studies of voting in America don't find many citizens with such admirable qualities. Most know little about public affairs, do not get involved or vote, ignore issues, and respond in emotional ways. Can democracy survive such a citizenry? Berelson thought it could. He argued that not *all* citizens need be ideal democrats, only some: "What seems to be required of the electorate as a whole is a *distribution* of qualities along important dimensions. We need some people who are active in a certain respect, others in the middle, and still others passive."[2] Berelson went on to argue that too much involvement on the part of too many citizens might lead to "rigid fanaticism," a splintering of political parties, instability, and critical cleavages in society.

Berelson's view became controversial and was the basis for heated debates among political scientists in the 1960s advocating or opposing reforms of the political establishment and of their own discipline. Gans would probably not accept it. Or, if he did, he might argue that the "distribution of qualities" of which Berelson speaks is so out of balance that the very splintering and rigid fanaticism that Berelson decries has, in fact, taken place—not among political parties but among special interests. As both watcher of politics and voter, such a difference in views about what is good for democracy is vital to you. It raises a question, i.e., what would our politics look like if more people actually did vote?

Maddox's "The Changing American Nonvoter, 1952–1978" should have provided you with some evidence for speculation. Maddox employs the standard format for reporting research alluded to in our prologue. Unlike Gans who presents his views with dramatic structure—statement of crisis, threat to the body politic, alternative senarius, potential Armageddon, etc.—Maddox adheres to scientific form. His problem statement is straightforward, i.e., to survey the correlates of voting and nonvoting so as to distinguish voters from nonvoters. His research design involves use of an extensive data base in fourteen nationwide surveys of citizens covering 1952–1978. He neatly identifies seven sets of independent variables that he intends to correlate with a dichotomous dependent variable. Using two statistical techniques, correlation and discriminant analysis, he identifies social standing and political involvement as the key factors that distinguish voters and nonvoters.

Independent variable, dependent variable, dichotomous variable, correlation, discriminant analysis—some of these terms you learned in the commentary in chapter 2, others you did not. Let us review them for you briefly. Recall that a variable is any factor or quality that varies from one object to another, as for example the weight or height of a person, or the amount of pizza one eats. Should someone say to you, "Don't eat that pizza or you'll get fat," the pizza amount you eat serves as an example of an independent variable, your increased weight the dependent variable. A dichotomous variable is of a one-or-the-other quality, black or white. Voter/nonvoter is a clear example. In a given election you are one or the other, not both. Remember that correlation is a statistical procedure for measuring the degree of association between variables, just as Milton Rokeach did in the selection you read in chapter 2. The Pearson correlations Maddox refers to are precisely the measures you learned about earlier. They vary from $+1.00$ to -1.00. Finally, as Maddox states, discriminant analysis is simply a technique used to identify which independent variables best distinguish between members of the dichotomous groups—in this case voters from nonvoters. The measures of Maddox's discriminant analysis appear for each independent variable (social standing, personality, partisan strength, candidate differences, and involvement) in Table 10 for each election year. The higher each coefficient in the table—such as .664 for social standing in 1974—the more the independent variable in question discriminates between voters and nonvoters.

The burden of Maddox's argument is that two sets of independent variables, or attributes, best distinguish people who vote from those who do not. One is *social standing,* a term that refers to a citizen's amount of education, age, income, occupation, and home ownership. Simply put, a person with a college education who is over thirty-five, who makes more money than half of other citizens, has a white collar job, and owns a home is a voter. Those falling outside those categories are less likely to vote. The second variable that separates voters and nonvoters is *political involvement,* i.e., people with high political interest, information, and efficacy are likely voters.

Maddox defines such sets of variables as social standing or political involvement through the use of *scales.* A scale is a set of statistically interrelated indicators. You know, for example, that on some days when the temperature is freezing, whether 32° Fahrenheit or 0° Celsius as the radio disc jockey informs you, you are comfortable. But let a wind come up and you feel much colder. By combining a temperature measure and a measure of wind speed it is possible to indicate to you a sense of how cold you will feel when you step outside your door. The measures, in sum, can be related to form a scale. This is what Maddox has done, for example, in combining levels of education, age, income, occupation, and home ownership to form a social position (or standing) scale.

Note that it is by making use of his scales that Maddox moves to a final analysis, that is, he develops a typology of nonvoters. Comparing and contrasting people of high and low social standing, high and low political involvement, he generates four types of nonvoters. Then, examining how the nonvoters in each of these types look with respect to other characteristics Maddox is able to say what kinds of people do not vote.

What, then, do you think the electorate would look like if the 62 percent of nonvoters without social incentives, political involvement, and partisan attachment did vote? Here are people who see no difference in candidates. How would their votes influence who becomes President? Or, consider the problem of how to stimulate people to vote. What of the 15 percent who have all qualities for voting except social incentives? Would an improved economy bring them into the electorate? And since they do see differences in candidates, what would that mean? Other questions could be raised in light of the Maddox typology. As you return to his article, pay particular heed to his closing remark. He states that the ultimate value of any political analysis lies in whether it helps you understand political behavior. As a political watcher take time now to think back. How would you compare the analyses you have read thus far on the basis of that criterion? Do journalistic analyses help you more than scientific ones, are they about even in value, or what? And, as you move through the remaining chapters of this volume, keep Maddox's utterance in front of you. Your skills of watching politics will improve as you do.

A variety of works have appeared concerned directly and indirectly with the question of who votes and why or why not. For the views of, respectively, a political strategist and an experienced journalist consult:

Frederick G. Dutton, *Changing Sources of Power*
Samuel Lubell, *The Hidden Crisis in American Politics*

And four brief analyses by political scientists that you may fine especially interesting are:

Everett Carll Ladd, Jr., *Where Have All the Voters Gone?*
Louis M. Seagull, *Youth and Change in American Politics*
William C. Mitchell, *Why Vote?*
Raymond E. Wolfinger and Steven J. Rosestone, *Who Votes?*

References

1. Bernard R. Berelson, "Democratic Practice and Democratic Theory," in Bernard R. Berelson, Paul F. Lazarsfeld, and William N. McPhee, *Voting* (Chicago: University of Chicago Press, 1954): 305–323.
2. Ibid., 314.

4 The (Un?)Changing American Voter

INTRODUCTION

In watching politics it is not sufficient merely to know who votes and why they choose to do so. Equally intriguing is how citizens vote. The careers of politicians depend upon the way people vote. Before elections journalists puzzle over how the electorate will vote; afterward they ponder the implications of voters' decisions. And social scientists search for patterns of voting, the factors that produce them, and what those patterns mean for the future of democratic institutions.

In ancient Greece citizens declared their voting preferences by dropping colored pebbles into urns. The Greek word for pebble is *psēphos*. Hence, the technical term for the study of voting and elections is *psephology*. In this chapter we invite you to reflect upon two representative selections of psephology that will add to your skills as a watcher of American voters, the modern day equivalent of people pitching pebbles.

Politicians, journalists, social scientists, and political buffs have practiced psephology in this country for a long time. But the study of voting has become systematic and sophisticated only in recent decades. In several respects the pioneering study came in 1940. It investigated how people in Erie County, Ohio, felt about the presidential contest between the incumbent, Democratic Franklin D. Roosevelt, and the challenger, Republican Wendell Wilkie. *Life* magazine, a highly popular picture weekly of the pretelevision era, and *Fortune,* a business magazine, jointly sponsored the study with the Office of Radio Research of Columbia University. Erie County, thought the researchers, was fairly representative of the whole nation and thus would be ideal for the study. Investigators interviewed a representative cross section of Erie County residents each month from May to the election. *Life* published results of the study as a major news story in its edition that appeared a week before the presidential contest (a 136-page magazine crammed with pictures and stories that sold for ten cents; what can you buy for one thin dime today?).

Four years following the Erie County study a book-length report of its findings appeared under the title of *The People's Choice.* It is now regarded as a classic. There have been many studies undertaken since then, and since 1952 there have been major studies based upon nationwide surveys in each presidential and congressional election year. The information derived from these studies provides psephologists with a rich body of data for speculating about voting trends in America. A key trend identified in the 1950s and early 1960s was the tendency of American voters to vote their party loyalties and to view candidates, issues, and campaign events through partisan lenses. Four of every five voters thought of themselves as Democrats or Republicans and frequently voted accordingly.

But since the mid-1960s there have been hints that the American voter is changing. Higher proportions of citizens designate themselves independent of party, split their tickets when they go to the polls, and appear to be influenced by factors that transcend party loyalties such as important issues, the qualities of the candidates, and the portrayal of the campaign in the mass media. Psephologists sought to chart these changes and it was not without coincidence that a prize winning study of new trends appeared in 1976 with the title *The Changing American Voter*.

Yet, are voters changing all that much? Is their behavior fairly predictable or fickle? Many an ambitious politician might sign a devilish pact to know the answers to such questions. In appraising "Jimmy Carter's Problem" Richard M. Scammon and Ben J. Wattenberg take a look at what is happening in contemporary American politics and, two years before the 1980 presidential election which is now history, assess the fortunes of a President seeking reelection. You met Ben Wattenberg in chapter 1 as he commented upon what the shape of American politics might be like in the 1980s. His coauthor, Richard M. Scammon, is a lifelong psephologist. His memory is packed with facts about the history and trends of voting in electoral districts not only in America, but throughout the world. He once directed the U.S. Bureau of the Census, and now directs the Elections Research Center in Washington, D.C., which publishes a series of statistical studies of American voting including *America at the Polls* and *America Votes*. In 1970 he and Wattenberg published *The Real Majority*, an insight into American politics that became the bible of many politicians for a decade.

Play a game as you read about Jimmy Carter's alleged problem. First, try to place yourself back in 1978. As a watcher of politics do you think that the analysis makes sense for something written at that time? Then move forward to 1980, the time when this book is being written and still prior to the presidential election. Does the Scammon and Wattenberg thesis ring true for then? Finally, with the advantages of hindsight, do you think the outcome of the 1980 election bore out the Scammon-Wattenberg argument or contradicted it?

Robert Axelrod is a political scientist who has been interested in psephology and related matters for a long time. While still a graduate student at Yale University he published an article in a leading academic journal confirming the view that there is no well-defined ideology shared by people that assists them in making sense of political issues. In that piece he formulated a means of analyzing the results of polls and opinion surveys, a bit of invention he undertakes again in exploring "Where the Votes Come From" for you. Born in Chicago in 1943, he received his B.A. at the University of Chicago in 1964, his Ph.D., with distinction, from Yale in 1969. He has taught at the University of California, Berkeley, and the University of Michigan.

In reading Axelrod's "Where the Votes Come From" bear a few things in mind. For one, remember he is trying to identify which groups regularly support each of our two major political parties in elections, which do not. Hence, he has something to say to you about the (un?)changing American voter. Second, in some respects his analysis parallels what Scammon and Watterberg say. Look for that. Finally, Axelrod's article was originally published in 1972 and covered presidential elections only until 1968. Since then he has published brief analyses of the 1972 and 1976 presidential voting coalitions. We have added those to the article to assist you in appraising the relevance of his analysis over even a longer period.

JIMMY CARTER'S PROBLEM

RICHARD SCAMMON AND BEN J. WATTENBERG

Edited and reprinted from Public Opinion 1 (*March/April 1978*): 3–8.

It is the thesis of this piece that the nature and implementation of President Carter's victory in 1976 has within it the seeds of a very great problem for him as he moves now into the second year of his term and begins, inevitably, to look ahead to his own 1980 reelection prospects.

Much of the recent talk has focused on the possibility of Carter becoming a "one-term President," on "his need for victories," the alleged ineptitude of his Georgia staff, the alienation of specific groups because of specific reasons, his attempt to "do too much," and so on. But missing from the discussion so far have been certain structural and ideological factors which may ultimately prove more troublesome to Mr. Carter than—as they say in the polling business—"all of the above."

Mr. Carter's problems are, at once, familiar and national ones, and in a more intense key, regional and peculiar ones: He won by capturing the votes of centrist switchers; he is in trouble, and may get into deeper trouble if he is perceived to be moving from the center toward the left. In his case, these not-so-unusual presidential afflictions are magnified by Carter's remarkable showing in the South in 1976.

Accordingly, it may be useful to look at that Southern regional situation first— critically important in and of itself—because it sheds light on the broader issue as well.

I

Why did Carter win in 1976?

It is, of course, customary after a close election for almost every group to claim that it was their specific group, their hard work, their support that "elected" the winner. When the winner in question is the President of the United States, such claims are made with particular vigor.

The aftermath of President Carter's victory has been no exception. Blacks have claimed the credit—although Gallup data showed that Carter actually got a slightly lesser proportion of the black vote than did McGovern in 1972 or Humphrey in 1968. Jews have claimed the credit, although their voting percentages for Carter—73 percent according to an NBC election-day poll—were actually slightly less than in so-called "normal" years (it being understood that within the election observing trade, "normal" years have become rare enough to be called "abnormal"). Labor has claimed the credit with somewhat greater justification: They "came back" from a 1972 Republican vote to go solidly with Carter—but at a rate not really greater than pre-1972 years—and they provided him with massive financial and organizational help.

In a sense, they are *all* correct. Carter could not have won *without* their support. But that is the very nature of a close election. A close election is close. (You may quote that.) When it gets close enough our psephological favorite, the Maltese-Americans, can also claim credit for victory.

But saying "you couldn't have won *without* us" is not quite the same as saying "you won *because* of us." It may be said that the latter claim can properly be made by a group that not only provides a margin of difference, but votes *away from traditional patterns* to provide the margin of difference.

A simple analysis of recent presidential elections shows that there is one most obvious major group of voters who can lay claim to that formula for 1976. That grouping is "The South."

As the data show [see Table 12], in recent years "The South" had been trending steadily away from the Democrats in presidential elections—until 1976.

TABLE 12 Democratic Percentage of Southern* Vote in Presidential Elections, 1960–1976

1960	50.5
1964	49.5
1968	30.9
1972	28.9
but . . .	
1976	54.1 (!)

* Eleven states of the Confederacy.

This trend has also been reflected in the electoral vote count [see Table 13].

TABLE 13   Electoral Votes Won by Democratic Presidential Candidate in the South,* 1960–1976

1960	81
1964	81
1968	25
1972	0
but . . .	
1976	118 (!)

* Eleven states of the Confederacy.

There is another way of putting the 1976 Southern story: *Carter ran best in that area of the country where recent Democratic presidential candidates had been running worst.* That was the great paradox of the 1976 election.

There is a sub-tabulation available that is of particular relevance. The 1976 break with voting patterns in the South occurred almost exclusively among *white* Southerners. It was the sharpest break in that group in three decades. [Figure 1 presents] a trend line for Southern white Protestants voting Democratic in recent presidential years, showing a dramatic decline—and a dramatic revival in 1976.

FIGURE 1

Southern White Protestants:
Percentage Point Deviation from the National Democratic
Presidential Vote, 1936–1976

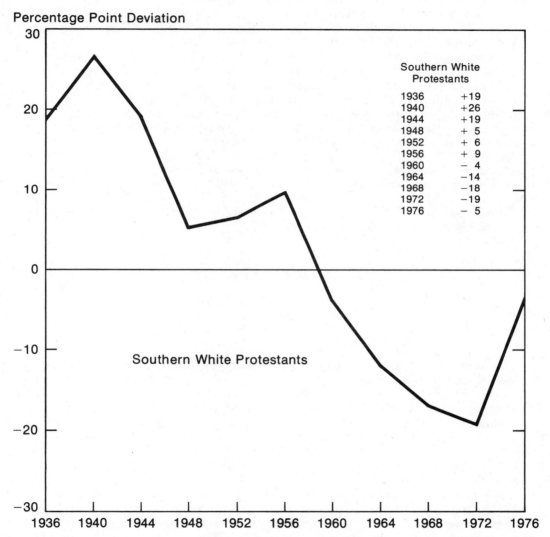

Percentage Point Deviation

Southern White Protestants	
1936	+19
1940	+26
1944	+19
1948	+ 5
1952	+ 6
1956	+ 9
1960	− 4
1964	−14
1968	−18
1972	−19
1976	− 5

Southern White Protestants

Source: Data from the following American Institute of Public Opinion surveys: *1936,* 72, 104, 150, 177; *1940,* 208, 209, 215, 219, 248; *1944,* 328, 329, 336, 337; *1948,* 430, 431, 432, 433; *1952,* 506, 507, 508, 509; *1956,* 572, 573, 574, 576; *1960,* 635, 636, 637, 638; *1964,* 697, 699, 701, 702; *1968,* 769, 770, 771, 773; *1972,* 857, 858, 859, 860; *1976,* 959, 960, 961, 962.

Note: This chart was constructed by Professor Everett Ladd and has been used in the past in his book, *Transformations of the American Party System.* Ladd determines the "percentage point deviation" by first calculating the national vote for each presidential candidate and then comparing it with the vote of a subgroup (here, Southern whites). Both the national and subgroup voting tallies are derived from Gallup surveys taken just before and after the presidential election.

The percentage of Southern blacks voting Democratic has been much higher than Southern whites—but it remained constant in 1976.

The big change came among white Southerners. Had they not switched to Carter in large numbers in 1976 he would not have won. If those switchers do not—for any reason— vote for him in 1980, it is unlikely that he will win again.

White Southerners. Aside from the fact that about half voted for Carter, enabling him to capture the South, what else do we know about them?

We know that despite all of the talk about the "New South"—a term which has a cicada-like rhythm in American politics—white Southerners are still more conserva- tive than most voters in America. Pollster Lou Harris reported in a release last sum- mer: "The South is easily the most conservative part of the country."

If white Southerners were the hinge of the Carter victory, and if white Southerners are more conservative than most American voters, it behooves us to ask: Was Jimmy Carter the more conservative of the presidential candidates in 1976?

The answer is no. Notwithstanding Carter's basic traditionalism (religious, ex-naval officer, small town, moral, businessman, and so on), Ford was generally seen as more conservative by the voters. A nationwide Harris poll taken in early September 1976 asked:

"How would you describe the political philosophy of (Gerald Ford, Jimmy Carter)— conservative, middle of the road, liberal or radical?"

And this was the clear response:

	Ford	Carter
Political Philosophy	%	%
Conservative	36	17
Middle of the road	36	31
Liberal	5	26
Radical	3	4
Not sure	20	22

The most conservative part of the country voted for the more liberal candidate.

Well, then, why did so many white Southerners vote for Carter? Obviously, because he was a Southerner—and in spite of their ideological leanings. Southerners felt, with good reason, that the idea that "a Southerner couldn't be elected President" was an idea whose time had come—and gone. And so, millions of white Southerners, who in other years would likely vote for the more conservative candidate, voted for the Southern candidate.

With all that extra help, Carter managed to carry the South narrowly. Slightly more than half of the white Southerners still voted *against* him. But that was better by far than any recent Democratic candidate had done, as the tabulations above show.

So: looking to the future, we can say that if a relatively few Southern conservatives perceive Carter as a liberal in 1980 and vote conservative instead of Southern Carter could be in serious trouble.

II

There may be a recent analogue to this tale of cross-rippling electoral tides, and it is an analogue that should be of great interest to Carter strategists.

In 1960, John F. Kennedy also won a close election when a large bloc of voters abandoned ideological and/or party-oriented behavior to vote along the axis of an external factor. The "externality" then was not that "a *Southerner* couldn't be elected President," but that "a *Catholic* couldn't be elected President." And millions of Catholics, who would normally have voted Republican, switched to vote for Jack Kennedy in a successful attempt to smash that outrageous religious axiom of our politics.

The big question, in both the Kennedy and the Carter situations, and for election pundits generally, is this: Having once voted on an externality—Catholicism or Southernism—is a voter likely to vote that way again *once his point has been proved?* Would Catholics keep voting for a Catholic for President, against their ideological bent, even after it had been demonstrated that a Catholic *could* be elected President? Will Southerners have to prove a point about the South, again, after they proved it once in 1976?

Of course, we don't know the answer to the Southern question yet, but we have an idea about the Catholic question. John Kennedy, tragically, did not live to run for reelection in 1964. But since 1964, many Catholics have run for either President or Vice President in general elections and primaries: William Miller, Eugene McCarthy, Robert Kennedy, Edmund Muskie, Thomas Eagleton, Sargent Shriver, Jerry Brown—to name a few. *In no instance is there evidence that Catholicism became a major voting issue.*

It is as if the external issue, once settled, disappears, much as Prohibition, child labor, and free coinage of silver disappeared as issues once they were resolved.

Let us assume that the Catholic-Kennedy situation is indeed analogous to the Southern-Carter situation. With Southernism no longer a factor (as Catholicism is no longer a factor), President Carter would have to compete in 1980 along only the normal modes of voter reaction. These include: incumbency, personality, state of the nation, state of the world, record in office—*and ideology.*

Question: Under such circumstances, could Carter do well in the still-conservative white South? Surely he *could*. If the country is at peace and inflation rates are low, unemployment rates are low, and economic growth rates are high, Carter would not only carry the South, he'd sweep the nation. On the other hand, if you change the "lows" for "high" and the "high" for "lows," he might not carry Plains. But in a mixed and mottled real-world situation so common in recent years, the critical question is this: Is Carter *likely* to do as well as he needs to in the white South?

Well, he would have a good shot at it so long as he is not perceived to be wholly out of touch with mainstream Southern ideology (which remains more conservative than that of the rest of the nation).

So far—if one accepts the reportage of President Carter's administration—he has managed to maintain and even strengthen his image as a moderate. Enormous publicity is generated when black leaders denounce Carter for not spending enough. He wins more plaudits when he still says he will balance the budget. He denies federal aid for abortion. He promises the new welfare program will not hike welfare costs. He is attacked by organized labor for a variety of slights. He makes a tough-minded, vigorous defense of human rights and tough SALT proposals. And, as a result, public opinion polls show that fewer Americans regard Carter as "a liberal" than when he was elected.

On the other hand—less often reported, or less stressed for their political impact—have been a series of other acts that would, or should, or likely will, persuade more and more people that there is a "liberal" in the White House. ("Liberal," remember, is what liberal Morris Udall described in 1976 as a "worry word" when he asked the political press to please describe him as a "progressive.")

Many moderates and even more conservatives, viewing political developments through their own prisms, have noted with dismay: that Carter has signed the Panama treaties, that his welfare program ended up calling for substantially more spending, that he axed the B-1, that he condemns America's fear of communism as "inordinate" (neglecting to describe the ordinate parameter of such fear, which leads him to ask for a $10 billion increase in the defense budget), that he has taken mini-steps to recognize Cuba and Vietnam, that his energy program is widely assailed as pro-environmental and anti-production, that he backs down on SALT and human rights, that he deals the Soviets back into the Middle East, that it has become increasingly apparent that his budget will not come close to balance, that he goes public with Ralph Nader for a Consumer Protection Agency, that he allows his administration to be characterized as pro-quotas, and so on.

It could be said that these two lists are not a bad mix. Many voters' views would conform with some items in Group A and some in Group B.

But the key tactical question is this one: How vulnerable would President Carter be in his home region if he can readily be depicted as pro-Panama "giveaway," pro-quotas, pro-welfare, anti-growth, pro-Cuba, and so on. Not to put too fine a point on it, how would you like to carry that record into the South in 1980 running against a candidate who disagreed with all those positions—and perhaps had his own Southern credentials as well? (Several names come to mind.)

Well, some will say, what Carter may lose in the conservative South, he will more than make up in the liberal non-South.

But there is no liberal non-South. There is no clearer datum in modern American politics. Remember: It was Ford, not Carter, who carried the nation outside of the old confederacy, in both popular and electoral votes. And even if there were a liberal non-South, that's not how or why Carter won in 1976. Carter carried what he did outside of the South for the same reason he was able to carry the South: his opponents tried, but were not quite able to tag him as "Southern-Fried McGovern." Carter thus regained many Democratic "switchers," those voters who went to Nixon in 1972 because they found the perceived hyper-liberalism of the McGovernites unpalatable, indeed repugnant. Who were those switchers? Union men and women, Catholics, ethnics, Jews, "inner city peripherals," suburbanites and on and on. Many, many voters of all stripes; voters able in many instances to identify with a traditional muscular, bread-and-butter, pocketbook liberalism—but wholly against anything perceived as "far out."

Looking ahead to 1980, then, it can be postulated that much of what has been advanced here about Southern votes may be wholly applicable to the non-South, albeit in lower intensity and without the special minus (from Carter's point of view) of possibly no longer having his "Southerness" as quite so potent an issue.

Public opinion polls are clear: quotas, Panama, environmentalism, Russians-in-the-Middle-East are not the issues that endear the non-Southern non-liberals to the Democratic Party or its candidate, even if he is President.

III

As this is written President Carter has served just a year of his first term. The issues of today will not necessarily be the issues of 1980. He has plenty of time to shift course gently, almost imperceptibly, if he feels politically threatened in the South or any-where else for that matter.

Indeed, that may prove to be exactly what Carter tries to do—all quite properly within the general presidential rubric of "doing what's best for the country." (After all, one of his jobs is to represent the voters, isn't it?) But there is still this question: Will he be able to make such a shift even if he wants to?

To think about that question, one must look at the nature of the presidential appointments—to those men and women who generate presidential policies and who inevitably shape the presidential image.

At the cabinet level one gets a sense of a political outlook that is, at once, technocra-tic and slightly left-of-center—which is about proper for a Democratic administration.

But quite a different picture emerges when one examines the sub-cabinet and sub sub-cabinet appointments. Perhaps unwittingly, perhaps wittingly, it is not moderate technocrats who most prominently populate these slots. Ideologues live there—idealogues from every one of the activist movements of the last decade. Environmen-talists, consumerists, civil rights and women's activists, veterans of the peace move-ment have moved en masse from their ginger groups to large federal offices control-ling massive budgets and armies of bureaucrats. A recent *Fortune* article named *sixty* high-level appointments made from activist groups; beneath them are a small army of their cohorts. And Senator McGovern, after a list of the Carter State Department appointees was completed late in 1976 remarked that those were the same people *he* would have picked. Senator Jackson did not make a similar statement. Columnist John Roche recently quoted a high-level State Department official saying, "I voted for Carter to get rid of Kissinger, and I got McGovern."

(This story is told: A young woman executive, formerly with the Sierra Club, now with the Department of the Interior at a salary about five times higher than the $10,000 per year she previously made, has suggested that all former Movement-niks tithe 10 percent of their salaries to their previous organizations! Imagine the public reaction if in an earlier administration a businessman recruited to government service suggested tithing back to Exxon!)

It is not the purpose of this short article either to praise or condemn the attitudes and views of those remnants of the Movement who now hold high federal office. Nor is the purpose here to suggest that all the ex-activists-now-in-government are reacting the same way to their present high eminence. Some are of the opinion that they work for the elected executive and should represent his views, some feel that ideology reigns and that it is their job to seek an outlet for their ideology.

Still, agree with them or disagree with them, a great many of these once-young ex-activists can be said to represent a general point of view. We can say several things about that point of view. It tends to be activist about the proper role of the federal government. It is often anti-establishment: anti-business, anti-defense, anti-labor to name a few. In the age-old argument, it tends to stress equality somewhat more than liberty. It tends to be somewhat ashamed of America's role in shaping the modern world. It has a know-it-all elitist quality, probably reinforced by President Carter's insistence that all he did was hire the best people with the most merit—apparently without considering just what substantive policies these apparatchiks would be meritorious at initiating. It is a point of view not only well to the left on the American political spectrum but well to the left in the Democratic Party. It takes positions that, as perceived, tend to be "out of sync" with mainstream American attitudes—which re-main opposed to quotas, a lower defense posture, ecology-over-growth, and so on.

The President apparently feels that his activists, to use the old Washington phrase, are "on tap not on top." The theory is that the moderates can balance the activists, and one may speculate that is the reason President Carter appointed at the top rung men of moderate reputations—the Schlesingers, Strausses, Lances, Vances, and Schultzes. Ideally, these senior moderates could channel the energies and ideas of the activists into courses sympathetic to the President's own views and synergistic to his political interests.

Well, maybe. We shall see. But many veteran bureaucracy-watchers are dubious. This dubiety stems from several sources. First, in Washington, if you ever have a choice of choosing the cabinet or the sub-cabinet, pick the latter. The men and women whose names are pre-fixed with "Sec." spend a great deal of time testifying, traveling and giving speeches. Their underlings tend to make policy. Bureaucrats sense that more ideas bubble up than trickle down. Second, winning half the battles isn't nearly enough. As the bubbling-up process ensues, some—most—ideas and rhetoric (and a candidate can get hung on a phrase as well as a program) that are not in keeping with the President's views are surely screened out. No matter. Some are not. If and as they become policy or doctrine, the President must live with them and defend them—all over the country. The hardliners may win on an I.L.O. decision. Fine. But down in the ranks someone wrote a sentence for the President's Notre Dame speech about the "inordinate fear of Communism," and that may be a subject of attack even if the attackers approve of the I.L.O. position.

As this is written, President Carter is on the griddle for a number of policies that seem clearly to derive from the New Politics bias of his government-by-sub-cabinet apparatchik.

—True to that bias, his energy program was heralded as an ecology program. "The age of abundance is over," crowed the environmentalists after its promulgation last spring. True to that bias, a score and more dams were axed. In each instance, the Congress thought otherwise.

—True to that bias, ideological environmentalists within the government have recently sought to apply American ecological standards to export goods, irrespective, apparently, of the wishes of the buying countries and with scant regard for the economic chaos that might be generated in America.

—True to that bias, the government's *amicus* brief on Bakke was open to interpretation as pro-quota or at least not anti-quota: "Minority-sensitive" is the new obfuscatory phrase. The President will be politically lucky if the Nixon-dominated Court goes against his brief, bails him out, thereby mooting the issue. If it does not oblige, the President can look forward to a campaign where he is described as Jimmy Quoter.

—True to that bias, Carter seemingly dealt the Soviets a plum in the Middle East, managing in a stroke to politically unite those sympathetic to Israel with those unsympathetic to the Soviets. It was only Anwar Sadat's bold effort that was able to rectify the error.

—True to that bias, early indications show a SALT treaty destined to cause an historic Senate confrontation.

Are these chance occurrences? Will the pattern of a leftward tilt continue? Does it represent the views of "the real Carter"? Is the GOP wise enough, and unified enough, to capitalize on it? If this pattern is perceived in the Washington political community but not around the country, will a ripple effect spread the perception? Credibly? Can Carter control his apparatchiks if he wants to? Has he already begun to try? Do his State of the Union and budget messages already presage that attempt? Will his I'll-never-tell-a-lie personality, which a majority of Americans still trust according to the polls, be enough to override these problems?

In all truth, no one knows. It is a situation without precedent. The last time the Democrats took the White House from the Republicans a very different cast of characters took over. JFK's New Frontiersmen were described as "pragmatic" and "tough." They were men very much from the center of the political spectrum.

Today it is different. The Democratic Party now has a large and militant flapping left wing, nurtured by activists who are veterans of a decade-and-a-half of civil rights, anti-war, environmental, consumerist, and feminist causes. In a party that is slightly to the left of the people on most issues, the activists are to the left of the party and the apparatchiks are often to the left of the activists. They are part of the Carter coalition, they have moved into government and no one knows what their long-range effect will be. It is fair to ask, however, "upon what meat doth this our Caesar feed?"

The circumstance being a new one, it is fair to speculate about it. How much political indigestion have the activists caused Carter so far? Considerable, the authors feel. What will happen in the future? Our speculations vary only in degree, not in kind. Mr. Scammon thinks Mr. Carter will not lose control of his government, and a majority of the apparatchiks in question will be co-opted. Mr. Wattenberg acknowledges that possibility, sees some evidence of it, hopes to see more, but remains somewhat more concerned: for him there is a recurring image of the President as the Sorcerer's Apprentice, trying desperately and honorably to gain control of what proves to be uncontrollable.

WHERE THE VOTES COME FROM

ROBERT AXELROD

Edited and reprinted from American Political Science Review 66 (*March 1972*): 11–20; 68 (*June 1974*): 717–720; and 72 (*June 1978*): 622–624.

Where do the Democrats get their votes from? Where do the Republicans get *their* votes from? Because of the great interest of scholars, politicians, and the public in the changing shape of electoral politics in America, these questions have been asked over and over.

Surprisingly enough, even professional politicians have only a rough and ready idea of how their own national coalitions are formed. For example, many do not know whether Blacks contribute more or less than union members to the vote totals of the Democratic party. As another example, we may ask whether the common wisdom is really correct that the Republicans do worse than the Democrats among the young and the poor. Questions such as these require measurement of groups and their voting behavior. Measuring where the parties have been and where they are now is the first step toward a sophisticated analysis of where they are going.

This paper has two purposes. The first is analytic—to specify the components of a group's contribution to a party's electoral coalition. The second is empirical—to measure the actual magnitudes of the contributions that have been made by selected groups in each of the last five presidential elections.

The Meaning of a Contribution to a Coalition

What does it mean to ask how large a contribution a group makes to the electoral total of a party? Clearly, a large group can contribute more votes to a party than can a small group. It is also true that a group with a high turnout can contribute more votes than a slightly larger group with a lower turnout. And yet it is also true that a relatively small group with a poor turnout can contribute votes to a party quite out of proportion to its size if the group loyally gives overwhelming support to that party. Thus measurement of the contribution of a group to a party's total vote must depend on three factors: the size of the group, its turnout, and its loyalty to the given party.

Each of these three components of a group's contribution is important. Much confusion arises in political discussions about how the parties build their coalitions because no one of these components tells the whole story. Only when all three components are taken into account can the actual contribution of a group be fully determined.

Fortunately, the three components of size, turnout, and loyalty can be fitted together in a rather simple way to determine a group's contribution to a party's vote total. The formula is:

$$\text{Contribution} = \frac{(\text{Size}) \times (\text{Turnout}) \times (\text{Loyalty})}{(\text{National Turnout}) \times (\text{National Loyalty})}$$

This formula says that if you multiply the size, turnout, and loyalty of a given group, and divide the result by the product of the national turnout and national loyalty, you get the magnitude of the contribution of that group to the electoral coalition of the party. The *size* of a group is the proportion of all adults of voting age who are members of that group. The *turnout* of a group is the proportion that voted in a given election. The *loyalty* of a group to a certain party is simply the proportion of the votes of that group which are cast for that party. The *national turnout* is the proportion of all adults who vote, and *national loyalty* is the proportion of all votes that go to the given party. Finally, the *contribution* of a group to the electoral coalition of a party equals the proportion of all the party's votes that come from members of that group.

The value of this formula is that it specifies how the three components can be combined to form the total contribution of a given group. It allows us to study contributions of a group over time, to determine how the contribution is attained in terms of the separate components, and to compare the contribution of one group to that of another.

Since any combination of groups may be chosen for analysis, the groups will typically overlap. A comparison can still be made between the overlapping groups in terms of their separate contributions, size, turnout and loyalty, but these factors cannot be added together directly. For example, in 1968 the poor (i.e., families with incomes less than $3000 per year) contributed 12 per cent of the Democratic votes, while the Blacks contributed 19 per cent. The contribution of the group consisting of those who are poor or Black (or both) can be determined by adding the separate contributions and subtracting the contribution of the overlapping group, namely the poor Blacks. Since the poor Blacks contributed 5 per cent of the Democratic votes, the contribution of those who were poor or Black (or both) was 12% + 19% − 5% = 26%. A similar procedure applies to measuring the *size* of the group which is the union of two overlapping groups.

It should be clear that the term "contribution" as it is being used in this study refers to the proportion of a party's total votes that is provided by a given group. It does not tell how the votes were gathered or even whether the group membership provides a reference point for its members. For example, it does not measure a group's contribution in terms of money, policy, or organizational strength. It simply counts what ultimately matters in elections, namely votes.

The Coalition Members

Since the New Deal there has been a generally accepted answer to the question of where the Democrats get their votes. The answer is that the Democrats are a coalition of diverse overlapping minorities: the poor, Blacks, union members, Catholics and Jews, Southerners, and city dwellers. In the last few years it has been suggested that, at least for presidential elections, the Southerners may have left the Democratic coalition while the young people have entered it.

The Republicans are a different matter. It is possible to think of the Republicans also as a coalition of minorities such as the rich and the people of Anglo-Saxon descent. But the Republican party itself tries to avoid this sort of formulation in favor of the view that Republicans appeal to the nonminorities, while the Democrats appeal to the minorities. In these terms, the Republicans can be thought of as a coalition of the nonpoor. Whites, nonunion families, Protestants, Northerners, and those outside the central cities.

The Republican groups are larger in size than the corresponding Democratic groups, and they generally have a higher turnout, but size and turnout are only two of the components of a group's contribution to a party's coalition. The Democrats' relative advantage is in the third component, namely partisan support, because the pro-Democratic minorities generally give a higher percentage of their votes to the Democrats than the corresponding nonminorities give to the Republicans.

To measure the magnitude of the three components and the total contribution of each group to its party's electoral coalition, a combination of survey data and election returns can be used. The election returns show the total national loyalty each party received, and they can be also used in conjunction with census data to estimate the national turnout. A survey based upon a carefully drawn national sample can be used to measure the components for each of the separate groups. Fortunately, the Survey Research Center of the University of Michigan has conducted such a national survey for every presidential election since 1952, so comparable data for the last five presidential elections are now available. Income, race, union membership, religion and place of residence, being relatively objective criteria, present few of the problems associated with measuring attitudes. There are still problems in determining how a person actually voted, even if the person is reinterviewed after the election as these respondents were. Some of them evidently reported that they had voted when in fact they did not, and a small percentage reported that they voted for the winner when the actually voted for the loser. The raw survey data have been adjusted with the use of national election data to compensate for these two types of error. The numbers will still contain some random sampling error, but most of them are probably within three or four percent of their true value.

The Democrats.   Table 14 gives the data for the Democratic coalition in terms of the selected groups. Along the top of the table is written the formula for a group's contribution to a party, and within each block of the table are listed the different groups by year. Directly under the block for loyalty is a block which shows how a group's loyalty differs from the national loyalty.

1. *The Poor.* The poor are defined to be those with an annual family income less than $3000. Column 1 of Table 14 shows that the contribution of the poor to the Democratic coalition has fallen dramatically: from 28 per cent of Democratic votes in 1952 to only 12 per cent in 1968. The main reason their contribution has fallen is that their size has shrunk over these years, from 36 per cent of the total adult population to 16 per cent (column 7). This decrease in the "poor" is partly due to the fact that $3000 per year is a more restrictive definition for the 1960's than it is for the 1950's because of inflation. Much of the decrease, however, is due to gains in real income. Since their turnout has been steady but low at about 45 per cent (Column 13), and their loyalty (Column 19) has been about 45 per cent Democratic (except in 1964), the decrease in the contribution of the poor to the Democrats is due almost solely to the dwindling size of this group.

The curious fact about the voting pattern of the poor is that, contrary to popular belief, they are not distinctly loyal to the Democrats. Column 19 shows that only in 1964 did they give the Democrats a majority of their votes, and Column 27 shows that to within a few percentage points, their vote generally divides the same as does the entire nation's vote. In brief, the poor are *not* part of the Democratic coalition. The working class may be loyal, but the poor are not.

2. *The Blacks.* The Blacks are another story altogether. Their contribution has grown substantially from 5–7 per cent in 1952–1960 to 12 per cent in 1964 and 19 per cent in 1968 (Column 2). This increase in their contribution to the total Democratic vote is not due to an increase in the number of the Blacks, since their size has been almost constant at about 10 per cent of the population throughout this period (Column 8). It is their turnout that has increased dramatically, nearly doubling between 1952 and 1968. The biggest jumps came in 1960 and 1964 as Blacks began to exercise their franchise in greater numbers, not only in the South but throughout the nation. The Blacks have always been very loyal to the Democrats (Column 20), especially in relation to voting patterns of other groups (Column 28). Curiously enough, this over-whelming loyalty of the Blacks was present in 1952, but not in Stevenson's second effort or in Kennedy's campaign. It returned to and exceeded its previous high level in the campaigns of Johnson and Humphrey. Only in 1968, however, did high loyalty and moderately good turnout combine to produce a Black contribution to the Democrats that was strikingly larger than their population percentage. Of course, the low national loyalty to the Democrats in 1968 also helped account for the high percentage of all Democratic votes that were contributed by Blacks in that year.

3. *The Unions.* Union members and their families provide yet a different story. They contributed more than a third of all Democratic votes in the 1950's, but in the 1960's their contribution fell slightly to a still very respectable figure of 28 per cent (Column 3). This large contribution arises because about a quarter of all adults are in union families (Column 9), they have a turnout close to the national average (Column 15 versus Column 25), and they consistently vote more Democratic than the nation as a whole (Column 29). The gradual decline of the union contribution to the Democratic party is due to a slight decline in their relative size (Column 9) and a large drop in their loyalty in 1968 (Column 21).

TABLE 14 The Democratic Coalition, 1952–1968

	Percentage Contribution						=	(Size						×	Turnout						×	Loyalty)						÷ (NT×NL)	
Year	P	B	U	C	S	CC		P	B	U	C	S	CC		P	B	U	C	S	CC		P	B	U	C	S	CC	NT	NL
1952	28	7	38	41	20	21		36	10	27	26	28	16		46	23	66	76	35	68		47	83	59	57	55	51	63	44.4
1956	19	5	36	38	23	19		25	9	26	25	29	14		40	23	64	72	39	63		47	68	55	53	52	55	60	42.0
1960	16	7	31	47	27	19		23	10	25	25	34	13		46	31	60	74	50	74		48	72	66	82	52	65	64	49.7
1964	15	12	32	36	21	15		19	11	23	26	28	12		45	42	69	72	49	65		69	99	80	75	58	74	63	61.1
1968	12	19	28	40	24	14		16	11	24	26	31	10		44	51	61	68	53	63		44	92	51	61	39	58	62	42.7
Column	1	2	3	4	5	6		7	8	9	10	11	12		13	14	15	16	17	18		19	20	21	22	23	24	25	26

Percentage Deviation in Loyalty to Democrats

Year	P	B	U	C	S	CC
1952	+ 2	+38	+14	+12	+10	+ 6
1956	+ 5	+26	+13	+11	+10	+13
1960	− 2	+22	+16	+32	+ 2	+15
1964	+ 8	+38	+19	+14	− 3	+13
1968	+ 1	+49	+ 8	+18	− 4	+15
Column	27	28	29	30	31	32

P poor (income under $3,000/yr.)
B Black (and other nonwhite)
U union member (or union member in family)
C Catholic (and other non-Protestant)
S South (including border states)
CC central cities (of 12 largest metropolitan areas)
NT National turnout
BL National loyalty to Democrats

A comparison of the Black contribution and the union contribution is revealing, provided one bears in mind that people in both groups vote the way they do for many reasons other than their race and union membership. In 1960 the union voters contributed more than four times as many votes to the Democrats as the Blacks did, but by 1968 the unions contributed only one and a half times as many votes as the Blacks (Column 3 versus Column 2). So until recently the voters from union families made a much, much larger contribution than the Blacks, and they still make a significantly greater contribution.

4. *The Catholics.* The Catholics have formed a large and reliable segment of the Democratic coalition. They have always provided more than a third of the Democratic votes (Column 4), even though they are only a quarter of the population (Column 10). Part of the reason is their exceptionally high turnout (Column 16). The other part of the reason is their steadfast loyalty (Column 22) which has always been more than 10 per cent greater than that of the population as a whole (Column 30). Included in the Democratic coalition with the Catholics are the Jews, whose numbers are small, but whose turnout and loyalty have consistently been very high.

Of course a special year for the Catholics was 1960, when John Kennedy was the Democratic nominee. In that year the Catholics gave more than four-fifths of their vote to the Democrats (Column 22), thereby providing nearly half of all the votes the Democrats got in 1960 (Column 4).

5. *The Southerners.* The South, including the border states, offers something of a surprise. Voters from this region have provided roughly one-fourth of all Democratic votes (Column 5). The size of the group has held steady (Column 11), while the turnout has increased since 1956 (Column 17), partly because of the increased turnout of the Blacks in the South. The surprise is that overall, Southerners have not been exceptionally loyal to the Democrats since 1956 (Column 23). In the Eisenhower elections they split their vote down the middle, and since then have voted within a few percentage points of the national Democratic average (Column 31).

It appears from these figures that the South is moving away from the Democrats. The Southerners were about 10 per cent more pro-Democratic than the nation as a whole in the 1952 and 1956 elections, but only 2 per cent more in 1960; in 1964 and 1968 they voted 3 per cent and 4 per cent *less* Democratic than the country as a whole did (Column 31). This trend has occurred despite the counter-trend of Black Southerners, who are very loyal Democrats, to increase their turnout in those same years. The Democratic loss is not necessarily the Republican gain, for in 1968 a third of the White Southern votes went to Wallace (not shown in the table), accounting for slightly more than half of all Wallace's votes.

6. *The Central Cities.* Only about 10 per cent of the nation's population now lives in the central cities of the dozen largest metropolitan areas, a figure that has been falling slowly since 1952 (Column 12). Central city dwellers used to have a slightly better than average turnout (Column 18), and since 1956 they have been 13 per cent to 15 per cent more Democratic than the nation as a whole (Column 32). These trends make the central cities an important but slowly decreasing part of the Democratic coalition, having provided about 20 per cent of the Democratic votes in the 1950's and about 15 per cent of the Democratic votes in the last two elections (Column 6).

A person may, of course, belong to more than one of these overlapping groups. For this reason the contributions and sizes of the groups listed on Table 14 can add up to more than 100 per cent. Some of the Democratic groups overlap more or less than would be expected from their sizes alone. Thus, for instance, the Blacks constitute a higher proportion of the population of the South than of the North, while on the other hand, the Blacks represent a lower proportion of Catholics than they do of Protestants. Typically, the overlap of two given Democratic groups has a higher loyalty than the average of the loyalties of the two given groups. For example, in 1968, Catholic union members had a loyalty of 65 per cent which is actually greater than the loyalty of either the Catholics (61 per cent) or the union members (51 per cent).

Some people belong to none of the six overlapping groups listed on Table 14. Actually about one-fifth to one-fourth of the adult population is neither poor, Black, unionized, Catholic, Southern, nor in central cities. This residual group tends to vote Republican, as would be expected, and in fact votes about twenty per cent more Republican than the nation as a whole.

One could go on almost indefinitely examining the partisan support provided by people with different attributes. But one additional group merits particular attention: that is the young. Those between 21 and 29 years of age are about 18 per cent of the voting age population, yet they provide only about 14 per cent of all Democratic votes. There are two reasons for this curious fact. First, the young have a turnout record about 15 per cent below the national average. Second, the young are simply not loyal to the Democrats. In fact, in four of the last five presidential elections the young have given the Democrats the same proportion of their vote (within 3 per cent) as has the whole country. In 1968 the young with their weak party loyalties, were slightly pro-Wallace compared to the nation as a whole. So like the poor, the young have not been part of the loyal Democratic coalition. Now that the 18 to 21 year olds have been enfranchised, the size of the under-30 group will increase. Their turnout is likely to remain below average, but it is uncertain whether their pattern of not being loyal to either major party will continue.

The Republicans.   The Republican coalition can be thought of as consisting of the overlapping majorities that are the precise complements of the minorities that describe the Democratic coalition. This makes the Republican coalition a combination of the nonpoor, Whites, nonunion families, Protestants, Northerners, and those outside the central cities. Virtually everyone is in at least one of these overlapping groups, and most people are in four or five of them.

Most of the facts about how these groups contribute to the Republican party follow directly from what has already been said about how their complements contribute to the Democratic party. For example, the fact that the poor are no more loyal to the Democrats than is the nation as a whole implies that the nonpoor cannot be especially loyal to the Republicans. Because of these relationships we can discuss only a few of the more salient facts and let Table 15 tell the rest of the story of how the Republican coalition is put together.

1. *The Nonpoor.* Those with incomes greater than $3000 have contributed an increasing proportion of all Republican votes since 1952 (Table 15, Column 1), mainly because more and more people have crossed this line over the years (Column 7). But as was just pointed out, the nonpoor do not deviate much from the national average in their loyalty to the Republicans (Column 27).

2. *The Whites.* Virtually all Republican votes come from Whites (Column 2). Even in 1960 when a quarter of the Black vote went to Nixon, 97 per cent of Nixon's votes came from Whites, while in 1968, 99 per cent of Nixon's votes came from Whites. Whites are about 90 per cent of the population (Column 8) and they vote 1 per cent to 3 per cent more Republican than the nation as a whole (Column 28). This is just the

obverse of the statement that the Blacks, who are about 10 per cent of the population, vote heavily Democratic.

3. *The Nonunion Families.* Nonunion families have voted 5 per cent or 6 per cent more Republican than the nation as a whole from 1952 to 1964 (Column 29). This figure takes on real importance when combined with the fact that three-quarters of all adults are in families without a union member (Column 9).

4. *The Protestants.* The Protestants are also about three-quarters of the population (Column 10), and have usually voted about 5 per cent more Republican than the nation as a whole (Column 30). The special year of course, was 1960 when a Catholic candidate opposed a Protestant for President and 90 per cent of the Republican votes came from Protestants (Column 4).

5. *The Northerners.* The Northerners have an unusually high turnout (Column 17), relative to the turnout in the South. When it comes to loyalty, however, the Northerners have never been more than 3 per cent pro-Republican in these five presidential elections, and twice have not been pro-Republican at all (Column 31).

6. *Outside the Central Cities.* Those living outside the central cities of the twelve largest metropolitan areas have slowly increased from about 85 per cent of the total population in the 1950's to 90 per cent in 1968 (Column 12). Their turnout, however, is only about average, and their loyalty is only slightly more Republican than the nation as a whole (Column 32), partly because they are so close to equaling the whole nation.

The Party Coalitions

The most obvious fact about American party coalitions is that they are very loose. They are loose first in the sense that most group loyalties are not total. Except for Blacks, none of the twelve groups that have been examined in the Tables ever gave more than 80 per cent of their votes to one party. Second, the coalitions are loose in the sense that group loyalties are not constant from one election to the next. Finally, when a group's loyalty shifts it is as likely to shift in response to a national trend as it is for reasons specific to the group. Indeed, again with the exception of Blacks, each of the groups usually divided their votes no more than 15 per cent differently than did the nation as a whole.

The data from Table 14 and Table 15 do not point to an election in these years which suddenly shifted the nature of the coalitions and then set the pattern for the elections to follow. The gradual shifts have been in different factors for different groups: loyalty of the South, size of the poor and central cities dwellers, and both turnout and loyalty of the Blacks. There have also been dramatic short-term shifts, for instance by the Catholics.

The data on party identification provide another point of view about what has been happening to the party system. In each year the respondents were asked, "Generally speaking, do you usually think of yourself as a Republican, a Democrat, an Independent, or what?" The results in Table 16 show that the party identification has remained almost stable since 1952. Neither major party has gained strength, and the Democrats still have a considerable edge over the Republicans. A new factor in 1968 was an increase in the number of Independents to 29 per cent of the national sample. This increase is not due solely to the appeal of George Wallace, because fully 28 per cent of those who did not vote for Wallace thought of themselves as Independents in 1968.

TABLE 15 The Republican Coalition, 1952–1968

Year	Percentage Contribution						=	(Size						×	Turnout						×	Loyalty)						÷ (NT×NL)	
	NP	W	NU	P	N	NCC		NP	W	NU	P	N	NCC		NP	W	NU	P	N	NCC		NP	W	NU	P	N	NCC	NT	NL
1952	75	99	79	75	87	84		64	90	73	74	72	84		72	67	61	58	73	61		56	57	61	61	57	57	63	55.1
1956	84	98	78	75	84	89		75	91	74	75	71	86		67	64	58	56	69	60		59	59	63	62	60	60	60	57.4
1960	83	97	84	90	75	90		77	90	75	75	66	87		70	68	65	61	71	63		50	51	55	63	50	52	64	49.5
1964	89	100	87	80	76	91		81	89	77	74	72	88		67	66	61	60	68	63		40	42	45	44	38	40	63	38.5
1968	90	99	81	80	80	92		84	89	76	74	69	90		65	63	62	60	66	62		44	47	46	49	47	45	62	43.4
Column	1	2	3	4	5	6		7	8	9	10	11	12		13	14	15	16	17	18		19	20	21	22	23	24	25	26

Percentage Deviation in Loyalty to Republicans

Year	NP	W	NU	P	N	NCC
1952	+1	+2	+6	+6	+6	+2
1956	+1	+1	+5	+4	+2	+2
1960	0	+1	+5	+13	0	+2
1964	+1	+3	+6	+5	-1	+1
1968	0	+3	+2	+5	+3	+1
Column	27	28	29	30	31	32

NP nonpoor (income over $3,000/yr.)
W White
NU nonunion
P Protestant
N Northern (excluding border states)
NCC not in central cities of 12 largest metropolitan areas
NT National turnout
NL National loyalty to Republicans

TABLE 16   Percentage of Party Identification, 1952–68

Party	Democrat	Independent	Republican
1952	47	22	27
1956	44	24	29
1960	46	23	27
1964	51	23	24
1968	44	29	25

(Note: Several per cent "apolitical" and "don't know" in each year
are not shown.)

The third-party coalition put together by Wallace can be measured just as the coalitions of the other two parties have been. In 1968 Wallace received 14 per cent of the national vote. The only one of the twelve groups that gave him a great deal more than this was the South (including the border states) which had a loyalty to Wallace of 28 per cent. The Catholics gave Wallace only 9 per cent of their vote, the central city dwellers 8 per cent, and the non-Whites a mere 1 per cent. The other categories did not have much of a net impact. The poor gave him 16 per cent of their vote, compared to 13 per cent from the nonpoor; the union families gave him 15 per cent, compared to 13 per cent from the nonunion families; and the young gave him 18 per cent, compared to the 13 per cent from those 30 and older.

All in all, there have been and still are significant differences in the electoral coalitions of the two major parties, despite Wallace's claim that there isn't a dime worth of difference in what they stand for. Race, union membership, religion and place of residence still matter. The Democrats usually get major contributions of votes from the Blacks, the union members, the Catholics and those in central cities. The Republicans usually have slightly greater appeal for the Whites, the nonunion families, the Protestants, and those outside the central cities. The poor and the young, however, divided their votes just about the same way as did the nation as a whole and were not really part of any party's electoral coalition.

Some Strategic Considerations

There is little a party can do to increase the size of a demographic group, but there is much it can do to try to increase its turnout and loyalty. A major consideration for a party in deciding whether to appeal to a given group is what might be called the group's "elasticity of response." The question is not whether a group will be receptive to an appeal, but whether a greater or lesser appeal will make much difference in the behavior of the members of the group. From a strategic point of view, the problem is to use scarce resources in the best way, presumably to maximize the chances of victory. If a group has a nearly constant response, independent of the intensiveness of the appeal to it, there is little sense in devoting many resources to that group. But if a group's response is sensitive to the magnitude of the efforts to appeal to it, then a party would do well to devote scarce resources to increase this appeal.

A good example of how a group can respond to a particular appeal is provided by the Catholics. In 1960, the Democrats nominated a Catholic for President, and the proportion of the Catholic vote that went to the Democrats went up almost 30 per cent from 53 per cent in the previous election to 82 per cent. In the same four year period the nation as a whole increased its loyalty to the Democrats by only 8 per cent. Thus the Catholics' response to the appeal of a Catholic candidate was highly elastic. Unfortunately for the Democrats, it was also elastic in the other direction as well. In the next two presidential elections, when Protestants were again nominated, the deviation in loyalty of the Catholics to the Democrats fell back almost to its previous levels (Table 14, column 3).

Another approach is for a party to direct some of its resources to increase the turnout of a group, through such means as a registration drive. If loyalty is to be increased, voters must be converted from another party, but if turnout is to be increased, they need only be mobilized. The mobilization strategy has the disadvantage that a newly mobilized voter who votes for the party is only half as valuable as a voter who is newly converted from the other party of a two-party system. The mobilization strategy has the further disadvantage that the newly mobilized voter may not vote for the intended party. Mobilization is sometimes relatively inexpensive, however, and it can often be accomplished without antagonizing other groups in the coalitions. The ideal opportunity for a mobilization strategy by a party arises when a group has high loyalty combined with low turnout. Such has been the case with the Blacks, and the Democrats have acted accordingly. If there is new evidence that the young will depart from their previous pattern of behavior and start to be loyal to a given party, that party would be wise to use a mobilization strategy aimed at the young.

Other problems can also be analyzed with the strategic equation. If an appeal to a group increases its loyalty by a given amount, how much can the loyalty of the other voters decrease before the break-even point is reached? If the turnout of a given group is increased by a given amount, how much does this increase a party's percentage of the national vote? Finally, a generalized form of the strategic equation can be used to analyze similar questions involving the partitioning of the population into more than two nonoverlapping groups.

This essay has described how the contributions that different groups make to a party's total strength can be specified. It has also shown how these contributions can be broken down into their three components—size, turnout, and loyalty. Through the examples of selected groups, the actual magnitude of these contributions and their components for each of the last five presidential elections have been presented and discussed with the hope that measuring these previous coalitions can be helpful in the task of understanding what may come next. I leave that greater task to others, whether they be scholars, politicians, or voters.

1972 Update

Before looking at the coalitions themselves there are two well known facts about the 1972 election that bear repeating. The first is that it really *was* a landslide, with the Democrats getting only 37.5 per cent of the votes to the Republicans' 60.7 per cent. The second basic fact is that the turnout was the lowest in at least twenty years, with only 56 per cent of the adults of voting age actually voting.

More interesting than these overall facts is what happened to the "traditional" coalitions of the two major parties. Let us consider the Democrats first (Table 17). The Democrats are often thought of as a coalition of diverse overlapping minorities: the poor, Blacks, union families, Catholics and Jews, Southerners, and city dwellers. In 1972 this combination suffered serious defections. The Blacks and central cities remained highly loyal in both absolute and relative terms (col. 20, 24, 28 and 32). In

TABLE 17 The Democratic Coalition, 1952–1972

Year	Percentage Contribution						=	(Size						×	Turnout						×	Loyalty)						÷	(NT×NL)	
	P	B	U	C	S	CC		P	B	U	C	S	CC		P	B	U	C	S	CC		P	B	U	C	S	CC		NT	NL
1952	28	7	38	41	20	21		36	10	27	26	28	16		46	23	66	76	35	68		47	83	59	57	55	51		63	44.4
1956	19	5	36	38	23	19		25	9	26	25	29	14		40	23	64	72	39	63		47	68	55	53	52	55		60	42.0
1960	16	7	31	47	27	19		23	10	25	25	34	13		46	31	60	74	50	74		48	72	66	82	52	65		64	49.7
1964	15	12	32	36	21	15		19	11	23	26	28	12		45	42	69	72	49	65		69	99	80	75	58	74		63	61.1
1968	12	19	28	40	24	14		16	11	24	26	31	10		44	51	61	68	53	63		44	92	51	61	39	58		62	42.7
1972	10	22	32	34	25	14		12	11	25	25	34	8		37	47	58	65	44	60		45	86	45	43	36	61		56	37.5
Column	1	2	3	4	5	6		7	8	9	10	11	12		13	14	15	16	17	18		19	20	21	22	23	24		25	26

Percentage Deviation in Loyalty to Democrats

Year	P	B	U	C	S	CC
1952	+ 2	+38	+14	+12	+10	+ 6
1956	+ 5	+26	+13	+11	+10	+13
1960	− 2	+22	+16	+32	+ 2	+15
1964	+ 8	+38	+19	+14	− 3	+13
1968	+ 1	+49	+ 8	+18	− 4	+15
1972	+ 8	+49	+ 8	+ 6	− 2	+24
Column	27	28	29	30	31	32

P poor (income under $3,000/yr.)
B Black (and other nonwhite)
U union member (or union member in family)
C Catholic (and other non-Protestant)
S South (including border states)
CC central cities (of 12 largest metropolitan areas)
NT National turnout
NL National loyalty to Democrats

TABLE 18 The Republican Coalition, 1952–1972

Year	Percentage Contribution						=	(Size						×	Turnout						×	Loyalty)						÷	(NT × NL)	
	NP	W	NU	P	N	NCC		NP	W	NU	P	N	NCC		NP	W	NU	P	N	NCC		NP	W	NU	P	N	NCC		NT	NL
1952	75	99	79	75	87	84		64	90	73	74	72	84		72	67	61	58	73	61		56	57	61	61	57	57		63	55.1
1956	84	98	78	75	84	89		75	91	74	75	71	86		67	64	58	56	69	60		59	59	63	62	60	60		60	57.4
1960	83	97	84	90	75	90		77	90	75	75	66	87		70	68	65	61	71	63		50	51	55	63	50	52		64	49.5
1964	89	100	87	80	76	91		81	89	77	74	72	88		67	66	61	60	68	63		40	42	45	44	38	40		63	38.5
1968	90	99	81	80	80	92		84	89	76	74	69	90		65	63	62	60	66	62		44	47	46	49	47	45		62	43.4
1972	93	98	77	74	73	95		88	89	75	75	66	92		58	57	55	52	62	55		61	66	63	64	60	63		56	60.7
Column	1	2	3	4	5	6		7	8	9	10	11	12		13	14	15	16	17	18		19	20	21	22	23	24		25	26

Percentage Deviation in Loyalty to Republicans

Year	NP	W	NU	P	N	NCC
1952	+1	+2	+6	+6	+6	+2
1956	+1	+1	+5	+4	+2	+2
1960	0	+1	+5	+13	0	+2
1964	+1	+3	+6	+5	-1	+1
1968	0	+3	+2	+5	+3	+1
1972	+1	+5	+3	+3	-1	+2
Column	27	28	29	30	31	32

NP nonpoor (income over $3,000/yr.)
W White
NU nonunion
P Protestant
N Northern (excluding border states)
NCC not in central cities of 12 largest metropolitan areas
NT National turnout
NL National loyalty to Republicans

113

contrast, although the poor, the unions and the Catholics were each six to eight points more loyal to the Democrats than the nation as a whole (col. 27, 29 and 30), all three of these groups gave less than half of their votes to the Democrats (col. 19, 21 and 22). The South was not even relatively pro-Democratic in 1972 (col. 23 and 31). Looking at it another way, the contribution of the Blacks has continued to grow until in 1972 they accounted for 22 per cent of all Democratic votes (col. 2). Nevertheless, both the union and the Catholic contributions to the Democrats (col. 3 and 4) were substantially larger than the Black contribution due to the much larger size of these two groups (col. 9 and 10).

The Republicans did well among all six of their traditional coalition groups with sixty per cent or more of the vote of the nonpoor, the Whites, the nonunions, the Protestants, the Northerners, and those outside the central cities (Table 18, col. 19–24). But even more impressive is that the Republicans received a majority of the votes from the complements of four of these groups, namely the poor, the unions, the Catholics and the Southerners, as we have seen in examining the traditional Democratic supporting groups.

The young, who were previously not part of anyone's coalition, made a large contribution to the Democratic coalition in 1972. In each previous election since 1952 people under thirty years of age accounted for only 13 per cent to 15 per cent of the Democratic votes, but in 1972 they accounted for fully 32 per cent of the Democratic votes. There are three reasons for this dramatic increase. First, their size went up from 18 per cent to 28 per cent of the adults of voting age principally due to the lowering of the voting age, but also due to the baby boom. Second, their turnout went up relative to the nation as a whole from 15 per cent below average to 9 per cent below average. Third, their loyalty which had never been more than 3 per cent pro-Democratic since 1952 went up in 1972 to 12 per cent pro-Democratic.

The future of the electoral coalitions cannot be predicted with certainty, but several important shifts which have taken place in recent years can now be seen more clearly. The members of union families used to be 13 per cent to 19 per cent pro-Democratic but since 1968 they have been only 8 per cent pro-Democratic (Table 14, col. 29). The South, which used to be 10 per cent pro-Democratic, has continued the pattern started in 1960 of voting within a few percentage points of the nation as a whole (Table 14, col. 31). To offset these losses the Democrats can at least be pleased that the young in 1972 have finally made a large contribution to their electoral coalition.

1976 Update

Analyses of the contributions of particular groups to a party's electoral coalition have long been a mainstay of both scholarship and strategy. In recent years, this kind of calculation has also become a vehicle for the assertion of claims of political merit. Black leaders who remind Carter of the contribution of black voters to his victory are the latest of these claimants.

Two well-known facts about the 1976 election are worth elaborating before we look at the coalitions themselves. The first is that the election was close. Only 2.1 percent of the popular vote separated Carter from Ford. This is quite a contrast from only four years before when Nixon's lead over McGovern was 23.2 percent. The second basic fact is that the turnout was very low: only 54 percent of the voting-age population voted, the lowest turnout in the seven elections analyzed. Especially significant in this regard is that only 41 percent of those under thirty voted.

TABLE 19 The Democratic Coalition, 1952–1976

Year	Percentage Contribution =						(Size ×						Turnout ×						Loyalty)						÷ (NT×NL)	
	P	B	U	C	S	CC	P	B	U	C	S	CC	P	B	U	C	S	CC	P	B	U	C	S	CC	NT	NL
1952	28	7	38	41	20	21	36	10	27	26	28	16	46	23	66	76	35	68	47	83	59	57	55	51	63	44.4
1956	19	5	36	38	23	19	25	9	26	25	29	14	40	23	64	72	39	63	47	68	55	53	52	55	60	42.0
1960	16	7	31	47	27	19	23	10	25	25	23	13	46	31	60	74	50	74	48	72	66	82	52	65	64	49.7
1964	15	12	32	36	21	15	19	11	23	26	28	12	45	42	69	72	49	65	69	99	80	75	58	74	63	61.1
1968	12	19	28	40	24	14	16	11	24	26	31	10	44	51	61	68	53	63	44	92	51	61	39	58	62	42.7
1972	10	22	32	43	25	14	12	11	25	31	34	8	37	47	58	65	44	60	45	86	45	45	36	61	56	37.5
1976	7	16	33	35	36	11	9	11	23	30	32	8	32	44	62	55	57	58	67	88	63	57	53	61	54	50.1
Column	1	2	3	4	5	6	7	8	9	10	11	12	13	14	15	16	17	18	19	20	21	22	23	24	25	26

Percentage Deviation in Loyalty to Democrats

Year	P	B	U	C	S	CC
1952	+ 2	+38	+14	+12	+10	+ 6
1956	+ 5	+26	+13	+11	+10	+13
1960	− 2	+22	+16	+32	+ 2	+15
1964	+ 8	+38	+19	+14	− 3	+13
1968	+ 1	+49	+ 8	+18	− 4	+15
1972	+ 8	+49	+ 8	+ 8	− 2	+24
1976	+17	+38	+13	+ 7	+ 3	+10
Column	27	28	29	30	31	32

P poor (income under $3,000/yr.)
B Black (and other nonwhite)
U union member (or union member in family)
C Catholic (and other non-Protestant)
S South (including border states)
CC central cities (of 12 largest metropolitan areas)
NT National turnout
NL National loyalty to Democrats

For the Democrats, the New Deal coalition made a comeback in 1976. For the first time since the Johnson landslide of 1964, the Democrats got a majority of the votes from each of the six diverse minorities which make up their traditional coalition: the poor, blacks, union families, Catholics, southerners, and city dwellers (Table 19, columns 19–24). The blacks have continued their pattern of very high loyalty, in this year giving 88 percent of their vote to the Democrats (col. 20), but with a turnout of only 44 percent (col. 14). Thus with 11 percent of the population (col. 8), they contributed 16 percent of Carter's vote (col. 2). Union families and Catholics (and other non-Protestants) provide an interesting contrast to the blacks. Both of these groups provided more than twice as many votes to the Democrats as did the blacks. They voted 13 and 7 percent respectively more Democratic than the nation as a whole (col. 29 and 30), they had comparatively good turnout (col. 15 and 16), and most importantly they were more than twice as numerous as the blacks to begin with (col. 9 and 10). Finally, there is the South, including the border states. Surprisingly, the South gave only 53 percent of its votes to Carter (col. 23). This can be understood as the combination of the trend since 1960 whereby the South is moving away from its loyalty to the Democrats (col. 31), and the immediate appeal of a Democratic candidate from the South.

The Republicans have experienced a dramatic comedown since 1972, when they attracted 60 percent or more among all six of their traditional coalition groups: the nonpoor, whites, nonunion families, Protestants, northerners, and those living outside the central cities. In 1976 they got no more than 53 percent from any of these groups, and failed to get even a majority of the loyalty of the nonpoor, northerners, and noncity dwellers.

One lesson from the 1976 election is that even when the Democrats can put together all of the elements of their traditional coalition, the election can be very close. The experience of the Democrats after running a Catholic candidate in 1960 shows that the gains in Catholic deviation in loyalty may not be lasting. The same may apply in the South after Carter. If the Democrats lose the South again, or if they lose the enthusiasm of the blacks or the loyalty of any of their other traditional groups, they will be in trouble. This could easily happen despite their large and steady lead in party identification.

TO THE STUDENT: A COMMENTARY

Among the qualities that separate the seasoned political observer from the novice is the ability to interpret each political event within the larger context of enduring, more transcendent patterns. This differs from the now-ism we spoke to you about in the prologue. Now-ism is jumping to conclusions, seeing each event as establishing a unique trend. What you might think of as "contextual interpretation" involves taking the event and looking at what it shares with other happenings rather than treating it as unique or in isolation. Suppose you make decent grades, say a grade point average of 3.0 or above. If you are a now-ist, then an unusually bad mark in a course might alarm you, forcing you to lose confidence in your abilities and leading you to believe that the GPA will start dropping precipitously. But considered within the context of both your

GPA and other things in your life, the disappointing grade is just that, i.e., disappointing and not devastating.

Scammon, Wattenberg, Axelrod—each is a seasoned political watcher. Scammon and Wattenberg employ what we and Gerald Grant labeled in our prologue as a Type III journalistic approach. They have an underlying theory about why people vote as they do and they view "Jimmy Carter's Problem" within that context. Axelrod, a political scientist, has a theory about how the coalitions that comprise political parties come about. He interprets the outcomes of presidential elections within that context.

Scammon and Wattenberg are explicit. What won for Jimmy Carter in 1976 might undo him in 1980. What won for him? "Structural and ideological factors," they say. By structural, you will note, they mean something very close to what Axelrod suggests by coalition. Simply put, various groups—by giving their votes more to one presidential candidate or the other—help shape the structure of the election's outcome, the winning coalition for a political party. So, for Scammon, Wattenberg, and Axelrod it is important to know how groups vote—not only in a single election but in the historical context of several elections.

For Scammon and Wattenberg a key group contributing to Carter's 1976 victory was the South. In presidential elections immediately preceding 1976 that region had been drifting away from the Democratic party. Carter brought it back. Accordingly, his success in 1980 would depend upon his holding the South.

Does Axelrod agree? Consider his analysis. Although his lengthy formula and tables of elaborate statistics seem formidable on first blush, they are not. The formula is simply a device that indicates how important the votes of a segment of the population are to the total number of votes a political party receives in an election. Axelrod explains the logic behind his formula and makes the calculations for you, then reports the findings in tables that—with but a little study—are easy to understand. He confines his attention to only a few groups: poor and nonpoor, blacks and whites, religious groups, regional groups (lo and behold, the South!), etc.

Who then are Democrats, who Republicans? Both parties are coalitions of minorities, says Axelrod. (Scammon and Wattenberg believe the same thing, even jestingly throwing in the Maltese-Americans.) This view is scarcely new. Old political salts have preached it for years. Conventional wisdom aligns the poor, blacks, union members, Catholics and Jews, southerners, and city dwellers with the Democrats. That same wisdom puts the nonpoor, whites, nonunion families, Protestants, northerners, and people residing outside central cities with the Republicans.

But, to paraphrase an utterance made famous by Walter Cronkite, is that the way it is? Axelrod answers that question. Some of his findings, and the rationale behind them, may surprise you. "The poor are *not* part of the Democratic coalition," he writes. "The working class may be loyal, but the poor are not." And, look closely at what he says about a group not placed in either party by conventional wisdom, the young. Persons in your age group have been loyal members of neither party's coalition. And, ask yourself this (especially in light of what you were thinking about in chapter 3), why do the young vote so little, a record of 15 percent *below* the national average?

Axelrod concludes with a point you probably know from personal experience: there is considerable looseness in the coalitions of the two parties. As a member of various groups included in Axelrod's analysis you know that many of your fellow members don't vote the same way you do. At best, group tendencies are just that, tendencies; they do not apply to every person. So if you are a Catholic that votes

Republican or a Protestant Democrat, don't count yourself an oddball, but don't dismiss Axelrod's arguments either. Tendencies are not absolutes, or permanent. Group loyalties may shift from one party to another between elections.

This brings us back to Scammon and Wattenberg, 1976 and 1980, and Jimmy Carter's future but now past problem. Examine Axelrod's 1976 update. Note especially the last paragraph. Remember what Scammon and Wattenberg say about Carter and the South, Kennedy and Catholics in 1960. The arguments—published in both cases in 1978 but prepared independently—are almost identical. Both the journalistic and scientific analysis—when put in the same historical and structural context— conclude the same thing; i.e., the Democrats to win in 1980 must hold the South.

As this commentary is being written the presidential election of 1980 is still almost six months away. Neither Democrats nor Republicans have selected a nominee. But at this writing the odds are strong that both parties will nominate candidates with considerable appeal in the South—Jimmy Carter and Ronald Reagan. Do what Bill Rivers and Dan Nimmo cannot do, take advantage of the fact that you *know* who won the 1980 presidential election. Exercise your skills as a political watcher—what *did* happen to the South? Did it stay with the Democrats and, if so, did it comprise a cricial factor in their victory—or did it stay and did the Democrats still lose? Or did the South defect and, if so, did it seal defeat for the Democrats, victory for the Republicans? Or did the Democrats still win? Or, did the South's votes make any difference at all?

But Scammon and Wattenberg say another factor is at work in Jimmy Carter's problem, one that Axelrod does not consider but that you must as you puzzle over the outcome of 1980. That is the ideological factor. Scammon and Wattenberg argue that Carter won in 1976 because voters thought him a "centerist," i.e., neither too conservative nor too liberal. Scammon and Wattenberg outline a scenario posing a dilemma for Jimmy Carter, namely, remain centerist or become known as a "liberal in the White House." Writing in early 1978 they thought Carter might go either way, but given the soft underbelly of liberal sentiment among the "apparatchiks," or subcabinet levels of the Carter administration, they hint at a "leftward tilt." A little nowism creeps in. Carter's responses to the Iranian crisis of 1979–1980, the Soviet invasion of Afghanistan, the economic problems of 1980—all may have formed popular perceptions that righted the leftward tilt of the ideological boat. Again you have the advantage. Did Carter remain the centerist candidate for President in 1980, challenged by Reagan on the right, John Anderson on the left? Or did something else happen?

Pebble watching. A worthy undertaking. And fun. Scammon and Wattenberg are good at it, so is Axelrod. In fact, Scammon and Wattenberg coined the term, "pebble watching," in one of the books you can turn to for added information on the American voter:

Richard Scammon and Ben J. Wattenberg, *The Real Majority*

E. John Bucci, *What Really Decides an Election: The Six Factors*

William A. Rusher, "The Failure of the GOP as an Alternative Party," in Seymour Lipset, ed., *Emerging Coalitions in American Politics*

And here are three works by political scientists that speak to the points in this chapter:

Richard L. Rubin, *Party Dynamics: The Democratic Coalition and the Politics of Change*

David B. Hill and Norman R. Luttbeg, *Trends in American Electoral Behavior*

Norman H. Nie, Sidney Verba, and John R. Petrocik, *The Changing American Voter* (read the enlarged, 1979 edition)

PART 2 VIEWING THE POWERS THAT BE

5 Who's Running Our Nation?

INTRODUCTION

On October 18, 1961, a newspaper in Charleston, South Carolina, published an unusual editorial. *The News & Courier* argued that to understand the United States it was essential to know about the Establishment. The newspaper went on to say that most citizens don't realize the Establishment exists, yet "it affects the nation's policies in almost every area." What is the Establishment? According to *The News & Courier* the term refers to "those people in finance, business, and the professions, largely from the Northeast, who hold the principal measure of power and influence in this country irrespective of what administration occupies the White House." In government matters it produces "a bland bi-partisan approach to national politics."

The News & Courier was not alone in believing that America is governed by an Establishment. Four years before the newspaper's editorial a noted sociologist, C. Wright Mills, published a controversial book entitled *The Power Elite*. Members of that elite, he wrote, occupy positions from which they make decisions of major consequences. So important are their positions that even their failure to make decisions affects our lives. And what are these positions? They are the key slots that rule big corporations, run government, and direct the military. In these positions center power, wealth, and celebrity.

Speculating that political power is centered in a small group of Americans is one thing. But to call it Establishment or power elite, proving that it exists and who the members of it are, is another matter. For more than a quarter of a century many journalists and social scientists have debated where political power resides in America, asking in effect who *really* governs America? The debaters argue many points. Who, for example, makes up the Establishment—elected political leaders, corporate moguls, labor union bosses, intellectuals, technocrats? Is it all of the above, none of the above, or some combination? If a combination, is the alliance of elitists a fixed, tightly bound unit or a shifting, loose coalition that changes depending upon the stakes at a given moment? Can someone like yourself become part of the Establishment, or are you destined to be an outsider?

The two selections you are about to read—indeed all of the articles in the five chapters of Part II—address such questions, either directly or indirectly. First enters Kirkpatrick Sale with "Power Shift." In its editorial in 1961 *The News & Courier* made one point clear, that is, "Southerners have no place in the Establishment." Kirkpatrick Sale thinks things have changed. Power, he argues, has shifted from a northeastern-based Establishment to the "Southern Rim." We now have a contest between yankees and cowboys (but not the major league baseball team versus the professional football team).

Sale has been a professional writer for more than twenty years. He has been an editor of the *New Leader,* a foreign correspondent for the *San Francisco Chronicle* and the *Chicago Tribune,* and a lecturer in history at the University of Ghana. He became an editor of the *New York Times Magazine* in 1965, worked there for more than three years, then turned to writing and lecturing. In 1975 he published *Power Shift,* a book whose subtitle tells its thesis, *The Rise of the Southern Rim and Its Challenge to the Eastern Establishment.* The selection before you is the introductory chapter of that book.

"Power Elites," by Thomas R. Dye, Eugene R. DeClerq, and John W. Pickering follows next. The article was first published in a professional journal under the title "Concentration, Specialization, and Interlocking Among Institutional Elites." The editor of that journal wrote at the time that reviewers who had read the manuscript "were quite enthusiastic about it." The editor was apparently also enthusiastic for he made the article the first, or lead, piece of the June 1973 issue of his journal. Many scholars covet such an honor. Being the lead article for a social scientist is something akin to a journalist's making page one with a bylined story.

Dye, DeClerq, and Pickering don't talk much about the educational elite in their article. Had they chosen to do so, Tom Dye would be numbered a member. Since completing his Ph.D. at the University of Pennsylvania in 1961, Dye has been one of the most productive and successful political scientists in the country. His research interest has centered upon comparing the institutions and policies of state governments, an interest giving rise to a number of scholarly articles and books. The latter include *Politics, Economics and the Public: Policy Outcomes in the American States* (1966); *The Politics of Equality* (1971); and *Understanding Public Policy* (1972). But he has not limited himself to writing research monographs. His text *Politics in States and Communities,* published in 1969, was widely adopted. And, he is coauthor of two introductory texts in American politics and government. He is thus in the unique position of competing with himself for a share of the textbook market, perhaps silent testimony to the institutional elites thesis.

In the spring of 1972 Dye conducted a graduate seminar at Florida State University, "Research on Power and Elites." Gene DeClerq, who later joined the faculty at George Washington University, and John Pickering, who went to the faculty at Memphis State University, were two of the graduate students enrolled in that seminar. They helped collect and code biographical data for over 5,000 leaders of American institutions. Out of that seminar came Pickering's dissertation, "The Concentration of Power and Authority in the American Political System," yet another book by Dye, *Who's Running America* (1976), and the jointly written article that follows.

In reading "Power Shift" ask yourself several questions. How persuasive is Sale's argument and, most importantly, are you satisfied with the evidence he produces? Is he basing his thesis on sound historical and social information, or is the piece too facile, glib, and based upon his impressions? How would you relate what he has to say to what you learned about the role of the South in electoral politics (chapter 4)? Does Sale's view help explain why Jimmy Carter won in 1976 and the outcome of the 1980 presidential election?

Then compare "Power Shift" to "Power Elites." Again ask about the strength of argument and supporting evidence. Do Dye, DeClerq, and Pickering draw correct conclusions from their mountain of data? Do they account for, or even take into account, the yankee-cowboy schism in the Establishment?

POWER SHIFT

Kirkpatrick Sale

Edited and reprinted from Kirkpatrick Sale, Power Shift: The Rise of the Southern Rim and Its Challenge to the Eastern Establishment *(New York: Vintage Books/Random House, 1975): 3–15.*

In the Oval Office of the White House, shortly before two o'clock on March 13, 1973, Richard Nixon is nearing the end of a long and rambling conversation with his counsel, John Dean, about ways to deflect the growing Watergate scandals that are just beginning to threaten his Administration. On Capitol Hill, L. Patrick Gray, Nixon's nominee to be head of the Federal Bureau of Investigation, is continuing his testimony to the Senate Judiciary Committee, before whom he has already disclosed damaging secrets that point suspicions directly to the White House; the day before, Nixon issued a proclamation denying permission for his staff members to appear before the various Senate committees, pulling a blanket of "executive privilege" hard around him to withstand the increasingly bitter winds of Watergate. The President is now feeling himself very much the beleaguered hero under attack from a cruel press and a manipulated public, and angrily declares at one point, "Nobody is a friend of ours," later on reflecting more plaintively, "It will remain a crisis among the upper intellectual types, the soft heads, our own, too—Republicans—and the Democrats and the rest." Dean, shrewd to detect and reflect the mood of his superior, soon joins in and begins berating with him "the press ... the intellectuals," claiming they would never believe the Watergate burglars were acting alone, "they would have to paint it into something more sinister, more involved, part of a general plan." The President nods, seems to grow morose, and then bursts out with the idea that has been troubling him all along:

"On and on and on. No, I tell you this, it is the last gasp of our hardest opponents. They've just got to have something to squeal about it."

Dean, ever the second banana, begins to chime in, "It is the only thing they have to squeal—" but Nixon, warming to his subject now, won't be interrupted.

"They are going to lie around and squeal. They are having a hard time now. They got the hell kicked out of them in the elections." Then just to make sure Dean appreciates the full dimensions of who this enemy is, Nixon enlarges: "There is a lot of Watergate around in this town, not so much our opponents, even the media, but the basic thing is the Establishment. The Establishment is dying, and so they've got to show that despite the successes we have had in foreign policy and in the election, they've got to show that it is just wrong, just because of this. They are trying to use this as the whole thing."

The basic thing is the Establishment.

Extraordinary. This is a President of the United States talking, and in the normal taxonomy of this country a President is regarded as a key part, if not the very center, of any "Establishment"—yet here is a President who plainly sees himself outside the Establishment, and, more than that, an *enemy* of that Establishment. Clearly, then, Richard Nixon is changing the usual definitions, is in fact pointing to a new conception of what the Establishment is and what its position has become in mid-century America, a conception which he no doubt had never fully articulated but which his highly developed political antennae told him was nonetheless quite real. For Nixon, the Establishment is a distant and a foreign world, the world of New York and Boston and Newport and Grosse Pointe and Winnetka, the world of great wealth, high culture, nurtured traditions, industrial power, and political aristocracies, the world of "the soft heads" and "the media," the "liberal elite" and the "impudent snobs"—"the enemy." Nixon sees himself as standing apart from all of this, obviously a newcomer, an outsider, a challenger, representative of a newer breed of people who, no matter how many deals they make with this Establishment, no matter how many times they rub shoulders with it, will never be a part of that world, for they come from a new place and they hold different values and they serve variant causes. Nixon understands, if only primitively, that there is in fact a new configuration of forces in America. to which he and his Presidency are joined, that stands in opposition to the traditional Establishment and is therefore a new component to be reckoned with in the equations of national power.

Looked at in its broadest terms, the modern Establishment in America enjoyed a virtually undiminished influence from the time of its consolidation after the Civil War right down to the beginning of World War II, roughly the whole seventy-year period from 1870 to 1940. In practically every aspect of life, this country was dominated by a nexus of industrial, financial, political, academic, and cultural centers based in the Northeast, stretching from Chicago to New York, from Boston to Philadelphia, and associated with the names of Mellon, Carnegie, Rockefeller, Morgan, Ford, McCormick, Vanderbilt, and the like. It was this nexus that influenced the selection of Presidential candidates (between 1869 and 1945 only two Presidents were born outside of the Northeast), that controlled the houses of Congress, that determined American foreign policy, that set the economic priorities and directions, that more or less created the cultural and moral standards, that determined who were to be the powerful and the powerless. And such provincial areas as *did* manage to grow up at the same time—the San Francisco Bay Area, say, with its "upstart" A. P. Giannini, founder of the Bank of America, or New Orleans, prosperous through the Mississippi River traffic—were largely contained in their remoter regions and allowed to exert very little economic or political influence on a national scale.

All that began to change with the advent of World War II and its new technologies and priorities. Slowly there grew up a rival nexus, based in the Southern and Western parts of the country that stand in geographical—and to a large degree cultural, economic, and political—opposition to the Northeast, specifically in the *Southern Rim,* the broad band of America that stretches from Southern California through the

Southwest and Texas, into the Deep South and down to Florida. Here a truly competitive power base took shape, built upon the unsurpassed population migrations that began to draw millions and millions of people from the older and colder sections of the Northeast to the younger and sunnier sections of the South and Southwest ... upon an authentic economic revolution that created the giant new postwar industries of defense, aerospace, technology, electronics, agribusiness, and oil-and-gas extraction, all of which were based primarily in the Southern Rim and which grew to rival and in some cases surpass the older industries of the Northeast ... upon the enormous growth of the federal government and its unprecedented accumulation of wealth, the great part of which went to develop and sustain the new areas and the new government-dependent industries, the new ports and new inland transportation systems, the new military and aerospace bases and the new water and irrigation systems ... upon the political development of the Southern Rim and its growing influence in almost all national party organizations of whatever stripe, its decisive role in the selection of candidates of both major parties, its control over the major committees and much of the inner workings of Congress, and ultimately, from 1963 to 1974, its occupancy of the Presidency itself. Over the last thirty years, this rival nexus, moving on to the national stage and mounting a head-on challenge to the traditional Establishment, has quite simply shifted the balance of power in America away from the Northeast and toward the Southern Rim.

That this is not some arcane geographical games-playing or a form of paranoia born in Richard Nixon's mind is easy enough to demonstrate. The evidence is abundant and rather wonderfully diverse, manifested, for example, in the takeover of the Republican Party by the new and generally conservative forces from the Southern Rim—Barry Goldwater, Ronald Reagan, Nixon himself—and the consequent displacement of Northeastern liberals, at least for the long decade between 1964 and 1974 ... in the assaults by Southern Rim tycoons, Clint Murchison, James Ling, Nelson Bunker Hunt, Howard Hughes, and many colorful others, upon the citadels of Wall Street and the giants of Northeastern industry ... in the shift of major-league sports franchises out of the Northeast to the South and West, and the creation of six new professional leagues by entrepreneurs of that era ... in the succession to power in the tight and potent world of the U.S. Congress of such men, over the years, as Allen Ellender, Sam Rayburn, Richard Russell, James Eastland, Wright Patman, Wilbur Mills, Chet Holifield, John Stennis, Sam Ervin, Carl Albert, John Rhodes, Howard Baker, Joseph Montoya, every one of them from the Southern Rim ... in the emergence of new official stock exchanges in places like Miami and Los Angeles, flourishing at a time when the New York exchanges are floundering ... in the extraordinary rise and growth of new cities like Anaheim, San Diego, Phoenix, Albuquerque, Dallas, Houston, Memphis, Jackson, Atlanta, Jacksonville, Orlando, stretching right across the southern part of the country, cities which have grown from sleepy cowtowns and frontier outposts into major commercial centers, among the most thriving in the land ... in the relocation of organized crime activities out of the wizened world of the Northeast to the newly hospitable centers of Los Angeles, Las Vegas, Phoenix, New Orleans, Hot Springs, Miami Beach ... in the extraordinary investment of $55 million by H. Ross Perot, the Texas computer executive, who single-handedly kept the stock brokerages from collapsing in 1971 ... in the rise within the Democratic Party of figures like George Wallace, Jerry Brown, Lloyd Bentsen, Fred Harris, Jimmy Carter, Robert Strauss, Terry Sanford, Reubin Askew, all of them from the Southern Rim and all among the new figures reshaping that party

. . . in the flight of thousands of businesses and hundreds of major corporations out of the big cities of the Northeast into the aggressive new cities of the Southern Rim, draining the Northeast of at least forty of *Fortune*'s top-ranked industrial firms in just the last ten years . . . in the development of serious cultural centers in such places as Los Angeles, Houston, Atlanta, and Miami, each with enterprises to rival those of New York's and to meet or surpass those of most of the rest of the Northeast . . . in the rising personal incomes of the people in the Southern Rim states which have been growing steadily while there has been a decline in the Northeast, and in the last decade the growth rates of the leading sunbelt metropolitan areas have been twice as high as in the leading coldbelt areas . . . and in such small facts as that the West Coast plans to build its own Statue of Liberty . . . that the Federal Reserve Board has established its first new bank in thirty-three years in Miami, Florida . . . that the national headquarters of the American Contract Bridge League is in Memphis . . . that Bergdorf Goodman, the fancy Fifth Avenue department store in New York, is owned by Carter Hawley Hale Stores of Los Angeles . . . and that Hebrew-National Kosher Foods, Inc., the most famous name in all of New York's delicatessen culture, is owned by the Riviana Foods of Houston, Texas. . . . And that's only a start.

And the Northeast under this kind of siege? Well, it has not disappeared, nor does it give any signs of doing so: the very fact that Nixon is no longer in that Oval Office and that he has been replaced by a man from Michigan is evidence enough that considerable power still resides in the Northeast. But one can see plainly that the Establishment is *declining,* and even a Presidential coup cannot disguise that reality. The large urban centers are all decaying and losing population, some like Newark and Buffalo and Detroit and Gary turning into outright sinkholes. . . . The riches of the Northeast are flowing to other sections of the country, producing "a pronounced shift of income" over the next fifteen years toward the Southern and Western regions, according to the Census Bureau, with particularly rapid growths for manufacturing operations in the South and below-average rates for "nearly every major industry in the Middle Atlantic region . . . for the next two decades." . . . The textile firms of New York have picked up and headed for the South, the car makers of Detroit have gone into a disastrous decline, the dairy farms of New England have been deserted and left to lie fallow. . . . The railroad systems have deteriorated so rapidly, with nine major lines in bankruptcy by 1975 and others to follow, that the whole transportation infrastructure of the Northeast is facing collapse and the regional economy is seriously jeopardized. . . . The industrial importance of the Northeast is rapidly diminishing, according to the business-oriented Conference Board, citing figures to show that industries there accounted for 70 percent of all value added in manufacturing as recently as the late 1940s but "by 1971 this share declined to 51 percent" and was dropping with every passing year. . . . The old money markets are no longer capable of supplying the capital needs of the Northeast or of the nation, and the brokerage houses that once served as the glittering jewels of Wall Street have been so badly tarnished that they are going under at the rate of more than fifty a year. . . . And in almost every sphere the conventional stability and dominance of the Establishment is deteriorating. It is surely too soon to say from all of this, as Nixon tells it to Dean, that "the Establishment is dying," but just as surely that hyperbole is pointing toward a truth."

The idea of a "Southern Rim" in American economic and political life is not mere capriciousness, a paranoid's invention. There is a reality to this area, a climatic, historical, and cultural cohesiveness, that serves to set this broad band off from the rest of the country in many ways.

The most obvious unity to the Southern Rim is climatic, and a look at any of those weather maps that the newspapers print helps to show why. No matter what the time of year, there will probably be a dotted line running across the map from around the tip of North Carolina in the East, on out through Memphis and Oklahoma City, swerving down a bit to Albuquerque, and then up through southern Nevada and on to San Francisco. In the winter this is normally the 60-degree line—temperatures south of it running from 60 degrees on up, north of it below 60 degrees—and in the summer it is usually the 80-degree demarcation. It will vary, of course, weather being what it is, but it is remarkable how consistently the temperature line cuts this same pattern.

This seems as appropriate a way as any to start to define the Southern Rim, since it is to a great degree the climate that has given it its spectacular growth. In the area below this line are to be found all of the tropical and semitropical regions of the United States: the Florida beaches, the Deep South savannas, the Louisiana lowlands, the Texas and Oklahoma plains, the Southwestern deserts, the palmy California coast. Here is the zone in which the average annual temperature is above 60 degrees, the average maximum temperature is 74 degrees; there are between 250 and 350 days of sunshine a year, and frost, if it should come, does not descend before November. This is, in short, America's sunbelt.

But there is more than climatic unity to this area. There is also a rough populational cohesion as well, for before the modern migrations this area had a fairly uniform pattern of settlement, the movement sweeping almost due west from the South, spreading a human substratum from the Carolinas to California. The earliest migrations in the eighteenth and nineteenth centuries moved almost exclusively westward from the East Coast, one broad wave sweeping southwest through Georgia and Alabama to the Gulf Coast and on up the Rio Grande, another moving due west through the Tennessee, Arkansas, the Red River valleys across the Texas plains and up against the Rockies. By the early twentieth century both of these waves had tapered off roughly in eastern New Mexico, but then came two final movements that completed the settlements, one pouring down into Florida from the Deep South states from the early 1920s on, and the other, made famous by the Okies, moving westward over the Rockies and into Southern California and the Central Valley in the later 1920s and 1930s. By the time of World War II the entire Rim area enjoyed an unusual homogeneity for "melting-pot America": it was marked not only by Southern—and overwhelmingly Southern *white*—settlement, but by the comparative absence of foreign-born immigration. And even the modern influx, though perhaps a half of it has come from the Northeast, has not changed this fixed character appreciably.

Partly as a result of these migration characteristics, partly as a result of the common heritage they imply, the Southern Rim is also marked by a rough cultural unity. The entire area encompasses almost all the regions that have historically been the principal battlegrounds of the American frontier, from the Tennessee of Davy Crockett to the Texas of Sam Houston to the Arizona of Wyatt Earp, with all that this heritage implies (which, for Frederick Jackson Turner, for example, means "perennial rebirth . . . fluidity of American life . . . new opportunities . . . simplicity . . . primitive existence . . . the meeting point between savagery and civilization"). It also encompasses almost precisely the area unique in this country for its economic dependence upon slave and subservient labor (black, brown, or red), not only the famous plantations of the South and their successors, but the ranches of Texas and the Southwest and the fruit farms of California and Florida. The region includes all of the states of the Southern Confederacy (except Virginia), plus the two territories with greatest Confederate sympathy (Oklahoma and New Mexico), and that implies a cultural heritage that of course goes far beyond the simply military. Finally, the entire region from the Carolina coast to eastern New Mexico and from Oklahoma to Florida is the heartland of the Southern Baptist Convention and its offshoots—it is the most populous church today in every state from North Carolina to Texas—and there are additional strong Baptist representations in Arizona and Southern California as well.

Taken altogether, these characteristics of the Southern Rim define a remarkably consistent geographical area. It hardly seems an accident, in fact, that there is indeed a cartographical line that sets off this area almost precisely: the boundary line which runs along the northern edges of North Carolina, Tennessee, Arkansas, Oklahoma, New Mexico, and Arizona, or, generally, the 37th parallel. Extend this line through Nevada and California to the Pacific, with just the slightest swing upward to embrace San Francisco, and the demarcation is complete. The land south of that line takes in all of thirteen states—North and South Carolina, Georgia, Florida, Tennessee, Alabama, Mississippi, Arkansas, Louisiana, Oklahoma, Texas, New Mexico, and Arizona—and the southern and by far the most populous parts of two more states, Nevada and California. This is the Southern Rim.

Now, traditionalists will have noted that this neat demarcation by the 37th parallel creates some divergences from normal geographical constructs. On the eastern end, for example, it excludes the state of Virginia, despite the fact that it was a part, an important part, of the Confederacy and that in its northern half it has experienced much of the same rapid growth that the true Rim areas have. Still, Virginia is simply different in its basic climate and most of its agriculture from the pattern of the Southern Rim; its historical migrations have been either due west, through the Appalachians into Kentucky and West Virginia, or dead north along the coastlines; and its population growths of recent years have almost all taken place in the Washington environs as part of a suburban belt that relates to Maryland and the North far more than to Norfolk and the South. On the western end, the Rim demarcation includes the mid-California region from the Bay Area on south—despite the fact that San Francisco was an old-line center of wealth, with pretensions to "old aristocracy" and the like, and though much ink has been expended trying to make a dividing line between Los Angeles and the Bay Area. The reason is simple enough: climatologically, topographically, and geologically, this region has much more in common with the south than in contrast to it (the real dividing line in California is not the Tehachapi Mountains but the Mokelumne River), and the area around San Francisco to the south (San Mateo, Santa Clara, and Alameda counties, for example) has been every bit as explosive a growth region as the southern part of the state and shares all its contemporary characteristics. Similarly, the southern tip of Nevada is included in the territory cut by the 37th parallel, again an area that just happens to be of a piece with its southern rather than its northern neighbors: it is related by geography through the Colorado River system to Arizona and Southern California, by its midcentury patterns of growth to the spectacular boom cities like Phoenix and Los Angeles, and by its economy and culture—especially Las Vegas—to the rich world of Southern California, where most of its players come from.

The region that stands in opposition to this Southern Rim should be accorded some definition as well. The Northeast, as used here, encompasses the entire quadrant east of the Mississippi and north of the Mason-Dixon line (and its rough extension west-ward), taking in the fourteen states of New England and the Great Lakes: Maine, New Hampshire, Vermont, Massachusetts, Rhode Island, Connecticut, New York, New Jersey, Pennsylvania, Ohio, Michigan, Indiana, Wisconsin, and Illinois. This region, too, enjoys a certain cohesion, of climate, geography, culture, settlement, and history, but above all of economics and demography: this is the traditional manufacturing belt of America, the area that since the middle of the nineteenth century has been charac-terized by a band of heavy industry virtually unbroken from Chicago to Boston; and it is the land of the megalopolis, the vast urban clusters that show up on a population map as a mass of black circles again stretching almost without interval from Chicago along the Great Lakes on to Philadelphia and New York and up to Boston. There are some, to be sure, who would like to divide this quadrant in half, creating some sort of "Midwest" that begins around the Pennsylvania-Ohio border—but there is, alas, no evidence whatsoever that there are real distinctions between the two regions.

There is a broadly metaphorical but rather apt way of describing these rival power bases, the one of the Northeast and the other of the Southern Rim, as the *yankees* and the *cowboys*. Taken loosely, that is meant to suggest the traditional, staid, old-time, button-down, Ivy-League, tight-lipped, patrician, New England-rooted WASP culture on the one hand, and the aggressive, flamboyant, restless, swaggering, newfangled, open-collar, can-do, Southern-rooted Baptist culture of the Southern Rim on the other; on the one hand, let us say, the type represented by David Rockefeller, Charles Percy, Edmund Muskie, James Reston, Kingman Brewster, John Lindsay, Richard Lugar, Henry Ford, Sol Linowitz, Bill Buckley, and Stephen Sondheim, and on the other the type personified by Bebe Rebozo, George Wallace, Lyndon Johnson, Billy Graham, Frank Irwin, C. Arnholt Smith, H. L. Hunt, Strom Thurmond, Sam Yorty, John Wayne, and Johnny Cash.

The terms are meant only in the loosest and most symbolic way, of course—flamboyant operators can be found in the Northeast, staid blue-bloods in the Southern Rim—but it is interesting that they even have an appropriate heritage in this very context. "Cowboy" was the epithet used by the Wall Street people who first ran up against some of the newly powerful Texas entrepreneurs, broad-rimmed hats and tooled-leather boots and all, when they started throwing their weight around in East-ern financial circles in the late 1950s and early 1960s—during the fierce battle, for example, between the Texas millionaires Clint Murchison and Sid Richardson and Pennsylvania's patrician Allen Kirby for control of the Allegheny Corporation and the New York Central Railroad in 1961. "Yankee," the invective which goes back to the days of the Civil War to describe Northerners in general, was naturally the word with which the newcomers responded, at least back home in the boardrooms and bars.

Slowly these words began to have a kind of currency, in financial circles at any rate, and then during the 1960s they came to be used by the New Left—particularly by the theoretician Carl Oglesby—in its attempt to understand and describe the workings of the "power structure" of America. From there they moved gradually into academic and journalistic circles—economist Kenneth Boulding, for example, used "the cowboy economy" to describe the period of rapacious growth after World War II, political writer Milton Viorst analyzed the Northeast as "the Yankee's America," scholar Wil-liam Domhoff described a "Jewish-Cowboy" financial group behind the Democratic Party. It is doubtful if Richard Nixon ever thought of the world in precisely these terms, as ably as they would have served him, but it just may be that his successor does:

shortly after becoming President, Gerald Ford announced that, in settling the economic problems of America, he was not going to "act in cowboy fashion."

Let those simple terms, then, stand for the complicated process that Richard Nixon barely conceptualized that mid-March day in the Oval Office. What he was groping toward, what those labels help to delineate, is an understanding of the emergence of a counterforce based in the cowboy sunbelt states capable of challenging the traditional hegemony of the yankee Northeast, and the unmistakable and irreversible shift of power, for the first time in a century, away from the Eastern Establishment and toward the Southern Rim.

This power shift is more than a passing phenomenon; it is a way of comprehending modern America. An understanding of its sweep and pattern helps to make sense out of the recent past, from World War II to the Vietnam War, from the Kennedy assassination to Watergate, from the rise of Richard Nixon to his resignation. It helps to make order out of the tangled present, to explain the energy crisis and the price of food, the economic chaos of the mid-1970s, the accession to power of Nelson Rockefeller, the kinds of Presidential candidates coming forth for the next election. And it helps to illuminate the foreseeable future, to suggest the regions that may be benefited, the interests that may be served, the causes that may triumph, not just in the next few years but for as long as this competition will pertain.

POWER ELITES

Thomas R. Dye, Eugene R. DeClerq, and John W. Pickering

Edited and reprinted from Social Science Quarterly, *54 (June 1973): 8–28.*

The study of institutional leadership is an important responsibility of social science. We are aware, of course, that the potential for power which is lodged in great institutions is not always exercised by the leadership. There are innumerable formal and informal restraints on the exercise of their legal authority. Yet as Mills observes: "No one can be truly powerful unless he has access to the command of major institutions, for it is over these institutional means of power that the truly powerful are, in the first instance, powerful."[1] Berle writes:

> Power is invariably organized and transmitted through institutions. Top power holders must work through existing institutions. There is no other way of exercising power—unless it is limited to the range of the power holder's fist or his gun.[2]

And Mills provides a highly literate and compelling argument about the relationship between power and institutional authority when he writes:

> If we took the one hundred most powerful men in America, the one hundred wealthiest, and the one hundred most celebrated away from the institutional positions they now occupy, away from their resources of men and women and money, away from the media of mass

communication that are now focused upon them—then they would be powerless and poor and uncelebrated. For power is not of a man. Wealth does not center in the person of the wealthy. Celebrity is not inherent in any personality. To be celebrated, to be wealthy, to have power, requires access to major institutions, for the institutional positions men occupy determine in large part their chances to have and to hold these valued experiences.[3]

This paper examines top institutional leadership in both the public and private sectors of society—industry; communications, transportation, and utilities; banking; insurance; law; civic and cultural affairs; government; foundations; education; the military; personal wealth; and political finance. The purposes are to develop a systematic definition of a national, institutional elite; to measure the concentration of authority in top institutional positions; to examine the extent of interlocking and specialization among institutional elites, and to describe the pattern of recruitment to top institutional positions.

Is there a convergence of power at the "top" of the institutional structure in America, with a single group of individuals, recruited primarily from industry and finance, who occupy top positions in industry, finance, education, government, foundations, civic and cultural affairs, and the military? Or are there separate institutions, with elites in each sector of society having little or no overlap in authority and many separate channels of recruitment? Social scientists have differed over this important question and at least two varieties of leadership models can be identified. A *convergence model* implies that a relatively small group of individuals exercises authority in a wide variety of institutions—forming what has been called a "power elite." In contrast, a *polyarchial model* implies that different groups of individuals exercise power in different sectors of society, and acquire power in separate ways.

The convergence model is derived from the familiar literature on power. Mills argues that: "The leading men in each of the three domains of power—the warlords, the corporation chieftains, and political directorate—tend to come together, to form the power elite of America."[4] According to Mills, leadership in America constitutes "an intricate set of overlapping cliques." And Hunter, in his study of *Top Leadership, U.S.A.*, concludes "Out of several hundred persons named from all sources, between one hundred and two hundred were consistently chosen as top leaders and considered by all informants to be of national policy-making stature."[5] The notion of interlocking directorates has widespread currency in the power elite literature. Kolko writes that: "Interlocking directorates, whereby a director of one corporation also sits on the board of one or more other corporations, are a key device for concentrating corporate power. . . ."[6] The convergence model also implies that top leaders in all sectors of society—including government, education, civic and cultural affairs, and politics—are recruited primarily from business and finance.

In contrast, other writers have implied a polyarchial leadership structure, with different sets of leaders in different sectors of society with little or no overlap, except perhaps by elected officials responsible to the general public. According to this view, leadership is exercised in large measure by "specialists" who limit their participation to a narrow range of societal decisions. These specialists are recruited through separate channels—they are not drawn exclusively from business and finance. Generally, writers on polyarchy have praised the dispersion of authority in American society. Dahl writes: "The theory and practice of American pluralism tends to assume, as I see it, that the existence of multiple centers of power, none of which is wholly sovereign, will help (may indeed be necessary) to tame power, to secure the consent of all, and to settle conflicts peacefully." [7] But despite the theoretical (and ideological) importance of the question of convergence versus polyarchy in the leadership structure, there has been very little *systematic* research on the concentration of authority or the extent of interlocking among top institutional elites.

Identifying Institutional Elites

Before we can examine interlocking and specialization among elites, we must first devise an operational meaning for our concept of institutional elite. In general, our goal is to identify *those individuals in the United States who occupy formal positions of authority in those institutions which control over half the nation's total resources.* This involves the identification of the minimum number of institutions in each sector of American society which control 50 percent of the resources of that sector, and the further identification of the individuals who hold positions of authority in these institutions. For purposes of analysis, we can divide society into 12 sectors: Industry, Transportation-Utilities-Communications, Banking, Insurance, Education, Law, Civic and Cultural Associations, Foundations, Government, the Military, Personal Wealth, and Political Finance. Authority is defined as legal power to direct, manage, and guide programs, policies, and activities of the institutions operating in each sector of society. Control is defined as formal legal authority over some proportion of the total resources in the various sectors of societies. Except where otherwise noted, the time for our data on institutional control and occupancy of formal positions is 1970.

In each of the corporate sectors—industry, utilities-transportation-communications, banking, and insurance—the institutions were ranked by the size of their assets, and then assets were cumulated moving from the top of the ranking down until roughly 50 percent of the assets in each sector were included. Table 20 lists all institutions included in this study and the sources from which data about them were obtained. In the field of law, positions of authority were defined as senior partners in the 20 most prestigious New York law firms. In civic and cultural affairs, positions of authority were defined as the presidents, chairmen and members of the boards of trustees, directors, or governors of recognized national civic and cultural organizations. In the sector of private foundations, positions of authority were defined as presidents and boards of trustees of the 12 largest private foundations which control nearly 40 percent of all foundation assets in the nation. In the educational sector, positions of authority are defined as the presidents and boards of trustees of the 12 wealthiest and most prestigious private universities which control over half of all private endowment funds in the nation. In the sectors of personal wealth and political finance, we turn from institutional authority to personal control over resources: control positions in personal wealth were defined as those 66 individuals who are reported to own more than $150 million in personal wealth; control positions in political finance were defined as those individuals reported to have contributed more than $20,000 in the 1968 presidential campaign. In the military sector, positions of authority were defined as the secretaries, undersecretaries, and assistant secretaries of the Army, Navy, and Air Force, the Joint Chiefs of Staff, and all of the four-star generals and admirals serving in the Army, Navy, Air Force, and Marines. In the governmental sector, positions of authority were defined as: president, vice-president, all secretaries, undersecretaries, and assistant secretaries of executive departments, the chairman and ranking minority member of each congressional standing committee, Supreme

Court justices, presidential advisors, ambassadors-at-large, the Council of Economic Advisors, and the Federal Reserve Board.

Any effort to operationalize a concept as broad as a national institutional elite is bound to generate discussion over the inclusion or exclusion of specific sectors, institutions, or positions. (Why law, but not medicine? Why not religious institutions, or labor unions? Why not governors or mayors of big cities?) *Systematic* research on national elites is still very exploratory, and there are no explicit guidelines. Our choices involve many subjective judgments. But let us see what we can learn about concentration, specialization, and interlocking using the definition above; perhaps other researchers can improve upon our attempt to operationalize this elusive notion of a national institutional elite. In the analysis to follow, we will present findings for both our aggregate institutional elite, and for specific sectors of that elite. Findings for specific sectors will be free of whatever bias which might exist in the aggregate elite, owing to our judgments about the inclusion or exclusion of specific sectors.

TABLE 20   Rankings of Top Institutions by Value of Assets by Sector, 1970

Rank	Name	Assets (B$)	Cumulative Percent	Rank	Name	Assets (B$)	Cumulative Percent
1.	Industry: Industrial Corporations						
01	Standard Oil (N.J.)	19.2	3.4	38	Gulf & West. Ind.	2.2	34.1
02	General Motors	14.2	5.8	39	Monsanto	2.1	34.5
03	Texaco	9.9	7.6	40	Firestone	2.1	34.8
04	Ford Motor	9.9	9.3	41	International Paper	2.0	35.2
05	Gulf Oil	8.7	10.8	42	Honeywell	2.0	35.5
06	I.B.M.	8.5	12.3	43	American Brands	2.0	35.9
07	Mobil Oil	7.9	13.7	44	Armco Steel	2.0	36.2
08	G.T. & E.	7.7	15.0	45	Getty Oil	1.9	36.6
09	I.T. & T.	6.7	16.2	46	Litton Industries	1.9	36.9
10	Standard Oil (Calif.)	6.6	17.3	47	R. J. Reynolds	1.9	37.2
11	U.S. Steel	6.3	18.4	48	Xerox	1.9	37.6
12	General Elec.	6.3	19.5	49	Procter & Gamble	1.9	37.9
13	Std. Oil (Ind.)	5.4	20.5	50	Reynolds Metals	1.8	38.2
14	Chrysler	4.8	21.3	51	Republic Steel	1.8	38.5
15	Shell Oil	4.6	22.1	52	Caterpillar Tractor	1.8	38.8
16	Atlantic Richfield	4.4	22.9	53	Weyerhaeuser	1.8	39.2
17	Tenneco	4.3	23.6	54	Anaconda	1.8	39.5
18	Western Elec.	3.7	24.3	55	McDonnell Douglas	1.8	39.8
19	E. I. DuPont	3.6	24.9	56	Std. Oil (Ohio)	1.7	40.1
20	Union Carbide	3.6	25.5	57	Kennecott Copper	1.7	40.4
21	Westinghouse Elec.	3.4	26.1	58	Georgia-Pacific	1.7	40.7
22	Bethlehem Steel	3.3	26.7	59	Rapid-American	1.7	41.0
23	Phillips Petroleum	3.1	27.2	60	Nat'l. Cash Reg.	1.6	41.2
24	Eastman Kodak	3.0	27.8	61	Singer	1.6	41.5
25	Continental Oil	3.0	28.3	62	Kaiser Aluminum	1.6	41.8
26	Goodyear	3.0	28.8	63	Celanese	1.6	42.1
27	R.C.A.	2.9	29.3	64	Allied Chemical	1.6	42.4
28	Dow Chemical	2.8	29.8	65	W. R. Grace	1.6	42.6
29	Sun Oil	2.8	30.3	66	National Steel	1.6	42.9
30	Alcoa	2.6	30.8	67	United Aircraft	1.5	43.2
31	Boeing	2.6	31.2	68	Continental Cars	1.5	43.4
32	Ling-Temco-Vought	2.6	31.7	69	N. American Rockwell	1.5	43.7
33	Occidental	2.6	32.1	70	Lykes-Youngstown	1.5	44.0
34	Union Oil of Cal.	2.5	32.6	71	Deere	1.5	44.2
35	Boise Cascade	2.3	33.0	72	Minn. Mining & Mfg.	1.5	44.5
36	International Harv.	2.2	33.3	73	American Can	1.5	44.8
37	Cities Service	2.2	33.7	74	Burroughs	1.4	45.0

TABLE 20 (*continued*)

Rank	Name	Assets (B$)	Cumulative Percent	Rank	Name	Assets (B$)	Cumulative Percent
75	Sperry Rand	1.4	45.2	88	International Util.	1.2	48.2
76	Burlington Industries	1.4	45.5	89	American Std.	1.2	48.4
77	Inland Steel	1.4	45.7	90	Philip Morris	1.2	48.6
78	General Foods	1.4	46.0	91	Greyhound	1.2	48.9
79	Marathon Oil	1.3	46.2	92	Borden	1.2	49.1
80	Signal Companies	1.3	46.4	93	U.S. Plywood Papers	1.2	49.3
81	Avco	1.3	46.7	94	City Investing	1.2	49.5
82	Owens-Illinois	1.3	46.9	95	Amerada Hess	1.1	49.7
83	Uniroyal	1.3	47.1	96	Olin	1.1	49.9
84	B. F. Goodrich	1.3	47.3	97	General Dynamics	1.1	50.1
85	Control Data	1.3	47.6	98	United Brands	1.1	50.3
86	PPG Industries	1.3	47.8	99	TRW	1.1	50.4
87	Ill. Central Ind.	1.3	48.0	100	American Metal Climax	1.1	50.6
						290.1	

Total Number of Manufacturing Corps. = 202,920
Total Manufacturing Assets in U.S. = 572.9 B$

2. Banking: Commercial Banking Companies

Rank	Name	Assets (B$)	Cumulative Percent	Rank	Name	Assets (B$)	Cumulative Percent
01	Bank America	29.7	5.2	27	PNB (Philadelphia)	2.6	40.4
02	First Nat'l. City Corp.	25.8	9.6	28	Seattle—1st Nat'l. Bk.	2.5	40.9
03	Chase Manhattan	24.5	13.9	29	Girard Co. (Phila.)	2.5	41.3
04	Mfrs. Hanover	12.7	16.1	30	Wachovia (Win. Sal.)	2.3	41.7
05	J. P. Morgan	12.1	18.2	31	Detroit Bank & Tr.	2.3	42.1
06	Western Bancorp.	11.4	20.2	32	First Wisconsin	2.2	42.5
07	Chemical N.Y. Corp.	11.1	22.1	33	Nat'l. Bk. of N. Amer.	2.2	42.9
08	Bankers Trust	9.9	23.8	34	Mfrs. Nat'l. Bk.	2.2	43.2
09	Conill Corp.	9.0	25.4	35	Nortrust (Chicago)	2.1	43.6
10	Security Pacific	8.0	26.8	36	First Nat'l., Dallas	2.1	44.0
11	First Chicago Corp.	8.0	28.1	37	Harris Trust	2.1	44.3
12	Marine Midland	7.6	29.5	38	Pittsburgh Nat'l.	2.0	44.7
13	Charter New York	6.3	30.6	39	Lincoln First	2.0	45.0
14	Wells Fargo	6.2	31.6	40	Bank of Calif. (S.F.)	2.0	45.4
15	Crocker Nat'l.	6.0	32.7	41	Valley Nat'l.	1.9	45.7
16	Mellon Nat'l. B&T	5.7	33.7	42	Citizens & S. Nat'l. (Atlanta)	1.9	46.0
17	Nat'l. Bk. of Detroit	5.2	34.6	43	U.S. Bancorp. (Port.)	1.8	46.3
18	First Nat'l. Boston	4.7	35.4	44	BancOhio	1.8	46.7
19	First Bank (Minn.)	4.4	36.1	45	Shawmut (Bos.)	1.7	47.0
20	N. W. Bancorp.	4.3	36.9	46	NCNB (Charlotte)	1.7	47.2
21	Franklin N.Y.	3.5	37.5	47	Fidelity Penn. (Phila.)	1.7	47.5
22	First Pennsylvania	3.3	38.1	48	Nat'l. City (Cleve.)	1.6	47.8
23	Bank of New York	3.1	38.6	49	Marine BkCorp. (Seattle)	1.5	48.1
24	Unionamerica	2.7	39.1	50	Commonwealth (Det.)	1.5	48.3
25	Cleveland Trust	2.6	39.5				
26	Rep. Nat'l. Bk. of Dallas	2.6	40.0			278.6	

Total Number of Banks in U.S. = 13,511
Total Banking Assets in U.S. = 576.3 B$

3. Service: Transportation, Utilities, and Communications Companies

Rank	Name	Assets (B$)	Cumulative Percent	Rank	Name	Assets (B$)	Cumulative Percent
01	Am. Tel. & Tel.	49.6	19.0	16	UAL	2.2	38.1
02	Penn. Central	6.9	21.6	17	Gen. Public Utilities	2.1	38.9
03	Consolidated Edison	4.4	23.3	18	Philadelphia Electric	2.1	39.7
04	Pacific Gas & Elec.	4.3	25.0	19	Columbia Gas System	2.1	40.5
05	Commonwealth Edison	3.4	26.3	20	Consumers Power	2.0	41.3
06	American Elec.	3.2	27.5	21	Detroit Edison	2.0	42.1
07	Southern Cal. Edison	3.2	28.7	22	El Paso Natural Gas	1.9	42.8
08	Southern Co.	3.1	29.9	23	Pan Am. World Airway	1.8	43.5
09	Southern Pacific	3.1	31.1	24	Virginia Elec. & Power	1.8	44.2
10	Burlington Northern	2.9	32.2	25	Duke Power	1.9	44.9
11	Norfolk & W. Ry.	2.8	33.3	26	Texas Eastern Trans.	1.8	45.6
12	Union Pacific	2.8	34.4	27	Middle South Utilities	1.7	46.2
13	Chesapeake & Ohio Ry.	2.7	35.4	28	Pennzoil United	1.7	46.9
14	Publ. Ser. El. & Gas	2.6	36.4	29	Texas Utilities	1.7	47.5
15	Santa Fe Industries	2.3	37.3	30	American Natural Gas	1.7	48.2

TABLE 20 (*continued*)

Rank	Name	Assets (B$)	Cumulative Percent	Rank	Name	Assets (B$)	Cumulative Percent
31	Niagara Mohawk Power	1.6	48.8	33	American Airlines	1.5	50.0
32	Southern Ry.	1.6	49.4			31.4	

Total Number of Comps. = 67,311
Total Assets of Trans. & Service Industries = 261.0 B$

4. Insurance: Life Insurance Companies

Rank	Name	Assets (B$)	Cumulative Percent	Rank	Name	Assets (B$)	Cumulative Percent
01	Prudential Ins. Co.	29.1	14.0	11	Mutual Life of N.Y.	3.7	59.4
02	Metropolitan Life	27.9	27.5	12	New England Mut. Life	3.5	61.1
03	Equitable Life	14.4	34.4	13	Connecticut Mutual	2.8	62.5
04	New York Life	10.7	39.6	14	Mutual Benefit Life	2.6	63.7
05	John Hancock	10.0	44.4	15	Penn. Mutual Life	2.4	64.9
06	Aetna Life	7.2	47.9	16	Tchrs. Ins. & Ann.	2.3	66.0
07	Northwestern Mut.	6.1	50.8	17	Lincoln Nat'l. Life	2.3	67.1
08	Connecticut Gen. Life	5.1	53.3	18	Bankers Life	2.0	68.1
09	Travelers Ins. Co.	4.7	55.6				
10	Mass. Mutual Life	4.3	57.6			141.1	

Total Number of Life Ins. Cos. = 1,790
Total Life Ins. Assets in U.S. = 207.3 B$

5. Law: Wall Street Law Firms

01 Sherman, Sterling, and Wright	11 Breed, Abbott, & Morgan
02 Cravath, Swaine, and Moore	12 Winthrop, Stimson, Putnam, & Roberts
03 White and Case	13 Cadwalader, Wickersham, & Taft
04 Dewey, Ballantine, Bushby, Palmer & Wood	14 Willkie, Owen, Farr, Gallagher, & Walton
05 Simpson, Thacher, & Bartlett	15 Donovan, Leisure, Newton, Irvine
06 Davis, Polk, Wardell, Sunderland & Kiendl	16 Lord, Day, & Lord
07 Milbank, Tweed, Hope, & Hadley	17 Dwight, Royall, Harris, Koegel, & Caskey
08 Cahill, Gordon, Reindel, and Ohl	18 Mudge, Stern, Baldwin, Todd
09 Sullivan & Cromwell	19 Kelley, Drye, Newhall, & Maginnes
10 Chadbourne, Parke, Whiteside, & Wolff	20 Cleary, Gottlieb, Friendly, & Hamilton

6. Civic Affairs: Civic and Cultural Organizations (No Ranking)

Metropolitan Museum of Art	Museum of Modern Art
JKF Center for Performing Arts	American Red Cross
National Gallery of Art	Metropolitan Opera Guild
Smithsonian Institution	National Association of Manufacturers
Council on Foreign Relations	Council on Economic Development
Brookings Institution	National Industrial Board
American Assembly	

Rank	Name	Assets (B$)	Cumulative Percent	Rank	Name	Assets (B$)	Cumulative Percent
7.	Foundations						
01	Ford Foundation	2.902	14.6	07	Mott Foundation	.371	30.9
02	Lilly Endowment	.778	18.5	08	Pew Memorial Trust	.367	32.7
03	Rockefeller Found.	.757	22.3	09	Hartford Foundation	.342	34.4
04	Duke Endowment	.510	24.9	10	Alfred P. Sloan Found.	.303	36.0
05	Kresge Foundation	.433	27.0	11	Carnegie Corp. of N.Y.	.277	37.4
06	Kellogg Foundation	.393	29.0	12	Mellon Foundation	.240	38.6
						7.673	

Total Number of Foundations = 6,745
Total Assets of U.S. Foundations = 19.9 B$

8. Government: Federal Governmental Officials (No Ranking)
President and Vice-President of the United States
Secretaries, Undersecretaries, and Assistant Secretaries of Cabinet Departments
Presidential Advisors, Ambassadors-at-Large, Council of Economic Advisors Members, and Federal Reserve Board Members
Congressional Leaders including the Speaker of the House and President Pro Tem of the Senate, Committee Chairmen and Ranking Minority Members, and Congressional party leaders
Supreme Court Justices

TABLE 20 (*continued*)

Rank	Name	Endowment (B$)	Cumulative Percent	Rank	Name	Endowment (B$)	Cumulative Percent
\multicolumn{8}{} 9. Education: Privately Endowed Colleges and Universities							
01	Harvard	1.013	18.5	07	Cornell	.163	44.0
02	Yale	.358	25.0	08	Northwestern	.135	46.5
03	Chicago	.275	30.0	09	Princeton	.134	48.9
04	Stanford	.223	34.1	10	Johns Hopkins	.112	51.0
05	Columbia	.201	37.7	11	Pennsylvania	.095	52.7
06	M.I.T.	.184	41.1	12	Dartmouth	.091	54.4
						2.984	

Number of Institutions = 107
Total Endowment Funds = 5.488 B$

10. Military: Secretaries, Undersecretaries, Assistant Secretaries of the Army, Navy, and Air Force, the Joint Chiefs of Staff, and Generals and Admirals (No Ranking.)
   Army, Secretaries, Undersecretaries, Assistant Secretaries
   Navy, Secretaries, Undersecretaries, Assistant Secretaries
   Air Force, Secretaries, Undersecretaries, Assistant Secretaries
   Chairman of Joint Chiefs of Staff
   Chief of Staff, Army
   Chief of Naval Operations
   Chief of Staff, Navy
   Commandant of the Marine Corps
   Generals, Army
   Generals, Air Force
   Admirals, Navy
   Generals, Marine Corps

Rank (est.)	Name	Rank (est.)	Name
\multicolumn{4}{} 11. Wealth: Americans with Personal Wealth in Excess of $150 million			
01	J. Paul Getty (oil)	34	Nelson Rockefeller
02	Howard Hughes (Hughes Tool)	35	Winthrop Rockefeller
03	H. L. Hunt (oil)	36	C. S. May (Mellon)
04	Edwin H. Land (Polaroid)	37	Richard Mellon Scaife (Mellon)
05	Daniel K. Ludwig (shipping)	38	DeWitt Wallace (*Reader's Digest*)
06	Alisa Mellon Bruce	39	Mrs. C. Payson (Joan Whitney)
07	Paul Mellon	40	John Hay Whitney
08	Richard King Mellon	41	J. S. Abercrombie (oil, iron)
09	N. Bunker Hunt (oil)	42	W. Benton (*Encyclopedia Britannica*)
10	John D. MacArthur (Insurance)	43	J. Blaustein (Standard Oil of Indiana)
11	William L. McKnight (3M)	44	C. Carlson (inventor of zerography)
12	S. Mott (General Motors)	45	E. J. Daly (World Airways)
13	R. E. (Bob) Smith (oil)	46	Clarence Dillon (banking)
14	Howard F. Ahmanson (banking)	47	Doris Duke (tobacco)
15	Charles Allen, Jr. (banking)	48	L. DuPont Copeland
16	Mrs. W. Van Alan Clark (Avon)	49	H. B. DuPont
17	T. Dorrance, Jr. (Campbell Soup)	50	Benson Ford
18	Mrs. A. I. DuPont (DuPont)	51	Mrs. W. Ford, II
19	C. W. Engelhard, Jr. (mining)	52	William C. Ford
20	S. M. Fairchild (Fairchild Camera, I.B.M.)	53	Helen Clay Frick (steel)
21	Leon Hess (oil)	54	W. T. Grant (variety stores)
22	W. R. Hewlett (Hewlett-Packard)	55	Bob Hope (entertainment)
23	D. Packard (Hewlett-Packard)	56	A. A. Houghton, Jr. (Corning Glass)
24	Amory Houghton (Corning Glass)	57	J. S. Johnson (Johnson & Johnson)
25	Joseph P. Kennedy (banking)	58	Peter Kiewit (construction)
26	Eli Lilly (Lilly & Co.)	59	A. P. Kirby (Woolworth)
27	F. E. Mars (Mars Candy)	60	J. S. McDonnell, Jr. (aircraft)
28	S. I. Newhouse (newspapers)	61	Mrs. Lester J. Norris
29	Marjorie Post (General Foods)	62	E. C. Robins (drugs)
30	Mrs. J. Mauze (Abby Rockefeller)	63	W. C. Stone (insurance)
31	David Rockefeller	64	Mrs. A. H. Sulzberger (*Times*)
32	John D. Rockefeller, III	65	S. M. Taper (financial)
33	Laurance Rockefeller	66	R. W. Woodruff (Coca-Cola)

TABLE 20 (*continued*)

12.   Political Finance: Contributors to 1968 Presidential Campaign
      Reported contributors of $20,000 or more in the 1968 presidential campaign constituted our top group in
      political finance. The data are reported by Herbert Alexander in *Financing the 1968 Election*. The 424
      individuals reporting contributions of $20,000 or more donated a total of over $12 million—41 percent of
      all individual contributions received by both political parties and campaign committees.

The Concentration of Authority

Forty-one hundred individuals—less than two one-hundredths of one percent of the population—control roughly half of the nation's resources. These 4,100 individuals occupy 5,400 positions of formal authority in 12 sectors of society. These individuals, taken collectively, control half of the nation's industrial assets, half of all assets in communication, transportation, and utilities, half of all banking assets, two-thirds of all insurance assets; they control nearly 40 percent of all the assets of private foundations, half of all private university endowments; they control the most prestigious civic and cultural organizations; they occupy key federal governmental positions in the executive, legislative, and judicial branches; they occupy all of the top command positions in the Army, Navy, Air Force and Marines; they hold the largest accumulations of personal wealth; and they make the largest contributions to political campaign finances.

These aggregate figures—roughly 4,000 individuals in 5,000 positions—are themselves important indicators of concentration of authority and control in American society. Of course, these figures are the direct product of our specific definition of the universe of top institutional positions. Yet these aggregate statistics provide us, for the first time, with an explicit, quantitative estimate of concentration of authority and control in America.

Interlocking and Specialization in Positions of Authority

About 40 percent of all top *positions* are interlocked with other top positions (see Table 21). However, the vast majority of *individuals* who occupy positions of authority in America are "specialists"—that is, individuals who hold only one position in a top-

TABLE 21   Overlap in Top Institutional Positions

	Number Top Institutional Positions	Percent of Total Positions	Number of Individuals in Top Positions	Percent of Total Individuals
Total	5,432	100.0	4,101	100.0
Specialized	3,294	60.6	3,297	80.4
Interlocked	2,138	39.4	804	19.6
Number of Interlocks:				
Two	1,026	18.9	513	12.5
Three	552	10.2	184	4.5
Four	260	4.8	65	1.6
Five	105	1.9	21	0.5
Six	48	0.9	8	0.2
Seven or more	147	2.7	13	0.3

ranked institution at any given time. Only 20 percent of the individuals in top positions hold more than one position.

The reason why 40 percent of the *positions* are interlocked, but only 20 percent of *individuals* hold more than one position, is that some individuals hold three or more positions. The multiple interlockers are indeed men of considerable stature, as the following list indicates:

David Rockefeller. Chairman and Chief Executive Officer, Chase Manhattan Bank. He is a director or trustee of the Rockefeller Foundation, Museum of Modern Art, Harvard University, University of Chicago, Council of Foreign Relations. He is also a Director or Chase International Investment Corporation, Morningside Heights, Inc., Rockefeller Center, Inc., Downtown Lower Manhattan Association. He is a centi-millionaire and a heavy political contributor.

Richard King Mellon. Chairman of the Board of Mellon National Bank and Trust Company; President, Mellon and Sons, director of the Aluminum Company of America, General Motors Corporation, Gulf Oil Corporation, Koppers Company, Pennsylvania Company, and the Pennsylvania Railroad. He is a centi-millionaire. He is a lieutenant general in the Reserves, a trustee of the Carnegie Institute of Technology, the Mellon Institute, and the University of Pittsburgh.

Crawford H. Greenewalt. Chairman of the Board of Directors E. I. duPont de Nemours; a director of the Equitable Trust Company, Boeing Aircraft Corporation, Christiana Securities Company, and Morgan Guaranty Trust Company; a trustee of Massachusetts Institute of Technology, Wilmington General Hospital, Philadelphia Academy of Natural Sciences, Philadelphia Orchestra Association, American Museum of Natural History, Carnegie Institute of Technology, and the Smithsonian Institution.

Arthur A. Houghton. President and Chairman of the Board of Directors of Corning Glass Works; a director of Steuben Glass Company, Erie-Lakawanna Railroad Company, New York Life Insurance Company, and the United States Steel Corporation; a trustee of the Corning Museum of Glass, J. Pierpont Morgan Library, Philharmonic Symphony Society of New York, Fund for the Advancement of Education, Lincoln Center of Performing Arts, Cooper Union, Metropolitan Museum of Art, New York Public Library, Rockefeller Foundation, and Institute for Contemporary Art of Boston. He is a centi-millionaire.

Amory Houghton. Chairman of the Board of First National Bank of New York City (First National City Corporation); a director of Metropolitan Life Insurance Co., Dow Corning Corporation, Pittsburgh Corning Corporation, Boy Scouts of America, Eisenhower College. He is a former Ambassador to France, and a trustee of the International Chamber of Commerce. He is a centi-millionaire.

Stewart R. Mott. Son of Charles S. Mott, former President and Director of General Motors Corporation, former Chairman of the Board of U.S. Sugar Corporation, and former mayor of Flint, Michigan. He is a director of: Michigan National Bank, U.S. Sugar Corporation, Combo Industries, Rubin Realty, Planned Parenthood, Center for the Study of Democratic Institutions, National Committee for an Effective Congress, and the Urban League. He is a centi-millionaire, and a large political finance contributor.

Grayson L. Kirk. President and trustee of Columbia University. He is Director of Mobil Oil Co., IBM Corporation, Nation-Wide Securities Co., Dividend Shares, Inc., Consolidated Edison Co., Greenwich Savings Bank, Morningside Heights, Inc., and for Carnegie Foundation. He is also Bryce Professor of History and International Relations at Columbia University.

James Stillman Rockefeller. Former Chairman and current director of First National City Bank of New York; a director of the International Banking Corporation, National City Foundation,

First New York Corporation, First National City Trust Company, Mercantile Bank of Canada, National City Realty Corporation, Kimberly-Clark Corporation, Northern Pacific Railway Company, National Cash Register Company, Pan-American World Airways, and Monsanto Company.

C. Douglas Dillon. Chairman of the Board of Dillon, Read & Co., Inc., member of New York Stock Exchange, and Director of Chase Manhattan Bank. He was formerly Secretary of Treasury, and Undersecretary of State. He is a trustee of Metropolitan Museum of Art, Brookings Institution, The American Assembly, and Harvard University. He is a large political contributor, and his wife is a trustee of the Museum of Modern Art.

Cyrus R. Vance. Senior Partner, Simpson, Thatcher & Bartlett. He is a director of Pan-American World Airways, Aetna Life Insurance Co., IBM Corporation, Council of Foreign Relations, American Red Cross, University of Chicago, and the Rockefeller Foundation. He was formerly Secretary of the Army, and Undersecretary of Defense. He was Chief U.S. Negotiator at the Paris Peace Talks on Vietnam under President Lyndon Johnson.

G. Keith Funston. Former President of the New York Stock Exchange. He is Chairman of the Board of Olin Mathieson Corporation, a director of Illinois Central Industries, Chemical Bank of New York, IBM Corporation, Metropolitan Life Insurance Co., Ford Motor Co., Republic Steel Corporation, AVCO Corporation, and National Aviation Corporation. He is a trustee of Trinity College and a director of the American Cancer Society. He was Chairman of the War Production Board during World War II.

Harold Holmes Helm. Chairman of the Board of Chemical Bank of New York. He is a Director of Equitable Life Assurance Co., McDonald Douglas Aircraft Corporation, Uniroyal, Western Electric, Bethlehem Steel, Colgate-Palmolive Co., F. W. Woolworth Co., Cumm Engine Co., and Lord and Taylor. He is a trustee of Princeton University, National Industrial Conference Board, and the Woodrow Wilson Foundation.

H.L. Romnes. Chairman of the Board and Chief Executive Officer, American Telephone and Telegraph Company. He is a director of United States Steel Corporation, Chemical Bank of New York, Colgate-Palmolive Co., Cities Service Co., Mutual Life Insurance and Co. He is also active at the national level in the United Negro College Fund, the Urban League, and the Salvation Army. He is a trustee of M.I.T., the National Safety Council, and the Committee on Economic Development.

Henry Ford, II. Chairman and Chief Executive Officer, Ford Motor Company. He is a Director of General Foods Corporation and a trustee of the Ford Foundation. His brother, Benson Ford, is also a director of Ford Motor Company and the Ford Foundation, as well as a director of the American Safety Council and United Community Funds of America. Another brother, William Clay Ford, is President of the Detroit Lions Professional Football Club and a director of the Girl Scouts of America, Thomas A. Edison Foundation, and the Henry Ford Hospital. These Fords are centi-millionaires and heavy political contributors.

Richard S. Perkin. President and Chairman of Board of Perkin-Elmer Corporation. He is a director of Ford Motor Co., International Telephone and Telegraph, New York Life Insurance, Consolidated Edison, Southern Pacific Railroad, Aetna Life Insurance, New England Telephone Co., U.S. Trust Co. of New York. He is a trustee of Metropolitan Museum of Art, American Museum of Natural History and Pratt Institute.

Robert V. Roosa. Partner, Brown Brothers, Harriman & Co. (investments). He is a director of American Express Co., Anaconda Copper Co., and Texaco. He is a trustee of the Rockefeller Foundation, The Rye County Day School, Council on Foreign Relations, and the National Bureau of Economic Research. He was formerly Undersecretary of the Treasury. He holds an earned Ph.D. from the University of Michigan.

Arthur H. Dean. Senior Partner, Sullivan and Cromwell; Chairman of the U.S. Delegation on Nuclear Test Ban Treaty, chief U.S. negotiator of the Korean Armistice Agreement; a director of American Metal Climax, American Bank Note Company, National Union Electric Corporation, El Paso Natural Gas Company, Crown Zellerbach Corporation, Campbell Soup Company, Northwest Production Corporation, Lazard Fund, Inc., and the Bank of New York; a trustee of New York Hospital, Cornell Medical Center, Cornell Medical College, Cornell University, the Carnegie Foundation, and the Council on Foreign Relations.

Thomas S. Gates. Chairman of the Board and Chief Executive Officer, Morgan Guaranty Trust Co. (J. P. Morgan, New York). He is a director of General Electric Co., Bethlehem Steel Corporation, Scott Paper Co., Campbell Soup Co., Insurance Co. of North America, Cities Service Co., Smith Kline and French (Pharmaceuticals). He is a trustee of the University of Pennsylvania. He has served as Secretary of the Navy and Secretary of Defense.

Ellmore C. Patterson. President, J. P. Morgan & Co. He is a director of Atlantic Richfield Co., Canadian Life Assurance Co., International Nickel, Atcheson, Topeka and Santa Fe Railroad, Warner Patterson Co. He is a trustee of the Alfred P. Sloan Foundation, the Carnegie Endowment for International Peace, and the University of Chicago.

Albert L. Williams. Chairman of the Board of Directors of the International Business Machines Corp. (IBM). He is a director of General Motors Corporation, Mobil Oil Corporation, First National City Bank of New York, General Foods Corporation. He is a trustee of the Alfred P. Sloan Foundation.

Leslie B. Worthington. Former President, United States Steel Corporation, and a current director. He is also a director of Mellon National Bank and Trust Co., TRW, Inc., American Standard, Greyhound Corporation, Westinghouse Air Brake Co., and the Pittsburgh Pirates. He is a trustee of the University of Illinois and the University of Pittsburgh.

These 21 individuals comprised our top group of "interlockers" in 1970—individuals occupying six or more positions of authority in top-ranked institutions. By any criteria whatsoever, these individuals must be judged important figures in America. The fact that men of this caliber emerged at the top of our investigation of positional overlap lends some face validity to the assertion that interlocking is a source of authority and power in society. However, despite the impressive concentration of interlocking authority in this top group, it should be remembered that most of the universe of 4,100 top position-holders were "specialists."

The Pattern of Interlock

Let us turn now to an examination of the pattern of interlocking among the various sectors of society. Table 22 shows (1) the number of control positions in each sector identified in our study; (2) the number of positions in each sector which are "specialized" (occupied by an individual who holds no other position identified in our study); and (3) the number of positions which are "interlocked" (occupied by an individual who holds other key positions identified in this study).

There is proportionately greater interlocking among individuals listed as centi-millionaires than those listed in any other sector; control of personal wealth is clearly linked with occupancy of top positions in the leading institutions of society. Bank directors are also likely to hold more than one key position in society. The tendency of bank directors to interlock with other institutions in society—particularly industrial corporations—may result from the practice of banks of placing their officers on the

TABLE 22   Specialization and Interlocking in Top Institutional Positions by Sector

	Indus-try	Comm. and Util.	Bank-ing	Insur-ance	Law	Civic Assoc.	Founda-tions	Govt.	Educa-tion	Wealth	Pol. Finance	Mili-tary
Number of Positions	1,534	476	1,184	368	176	392	121	227	656	66	173	59
Number of Positions "Specialized"	920	284	583	215	150	224	57	183	440	18	124	59
Number of Positions "Interlocked"	614	192	601	153	26	168	64	44	216	48	49	0
Percent of Positions "Interlocked"	40.4	40.3	50.8	41.6	14.8	42.9	52.9	19.4	32.9	72.7	28.3	0.0

141

boards of corporations which are heavily indebted to them. A majority of the directors of the major foundations are also men who hold key positions elsewhere. Many of the leaders of civic and cultural organizations are also interlocked into other key positions, but not a majority of them. There is greater interlocking in the corporate sector—industry; transportation, utilities, and communications; and insurance—than in law, education, the military, or government. Even so, overlap in the corporate sector is not as common as widely believed; only 40 percent of the top positions in industry are interlocked with other top positions in our study. Interlocking in transportation, communications, and utilities is only 43 percent, and interlocking in insurance only 42 percent.

Senior partners in top Wall Street law firms are *not* interlocked in directorships of major corporations and banks. Indeed, for the most part, top lawyers appear to be "specialists." Of course, they may exercise great influence over their corporate and financial clients, but they do not, by and large, accept positions on corporate or financial boards. Military leaders are *not* interlocked with the corporate sector of society or with any other sector. Not one of the military officers or civilian officials in the Army, Navy or Air Force held any other concurrent position in our study. All were "specialists." Of course, this reflects the special regulations which govern military leaders and prevent them from holding concurrent positions outside of their military commands. Finally, it is important to note that government leadership is *not* extensively interlocked in top positions in other sectors of society. Only 18.6 percent of our 227 top government officials held any other top positions in our study.

We also examined interlocked positions in each sector to see what sectors they were linked with. In other words, we examined the *pattern* of inter-sector interlocking, as well as the total number of positions which were interlocked in each sector. To the extent that government leadership interlocked at all, it is *not* interlocked with the corporate world. There were no high government officials holding top positions in anything other than civic and cultural and educational institutions. This clearly reflects the prevailing ethos that individuals should give up positions in the corporate world as a prerequisite to high government office.

Top political contributors are not necessarily key institutional leaders. Only 28 percent of the largest contributors were identified as directors of our leading institutions. Only one of the top contributors in the 1968 presidential election became a *top* government official in 1970: David Packard, Deputy Secretary of Defense, a centi-millionaire and formerly President of Hewlett-Packard Company and a former Director of National Airlines, Pacific Gas and Electric, Systems Development Corporation, and former trustee of Stanford University. (However, other top contributors did accept government positions of lesser rank. J. William Middendorf, II, Ambassador to the Netherlands; John C. Pritzlaff, Ambassador to Malta; Fred J. Russell, Deputy Director of Emergency Preparedness.)

Multiple Positions of Authority over Time

Let us pursue the notion of overlap a bit further. How many positions of authority in all types of institutions have top leaders *ever held* in their lifetime? We can answer this question by examining the biographies of the individuals occupying top positions in our study. We carefully reviewed the biographies of our top position-holders to see how many authoritative positions—president, director, trustee, etc.—were *ever held* by these men at any time in their life. The record of leadership of an average top official turned out to be truly impressive. Each top leader held an average of 10.7 authoritative positions in his lifetime!

These are not merely previous posts, offices, or occupations, but *top positions* as presidents or directors of corporations, banks, or insurance companies; trustee or directors of colleges, universities, foundations, museums, civic and cultural organizations; partnerships in law firms or investment firms; and so forth. Of course, these positions are not all in *top-ranked* institutions. But it is clear that top leaders occupy a number of authoritative positions in their lifetime.

This impressive record of position-holding is found among leaders in all sectors of society except the military. Table 23 shows the average number of authoritative positions ever held by top leaders in each sector of society. Leaders in law and government have held somewhat fewer top positions in their lifetime than leaders in the corporate world, but nonetheless their record of leadership experience was impressive. Only in the military sector do we find a narrowness in leadership experience. Most military leaders came "up through the ranks"; only the civilian department heads had any previous leadership experience outside of the military. Generals have benefited from command experience at lower levels, but they have not held high positions in business, or served as trustees of universities, or foundations, or cultural and civic associations. These military leaders have been "specialists" all of their life.

The tradition of public service is very much alive among our top institutional leaders. Most of them reported one or more public service appointments during their lifetime; the average number of public service jobs for each member of our top group was 1.4. These appointments included everything from Ambassador, U.N. delegate, and Presidential Commission member, to city planning council, school board, and state and local study commissions of various kinds. Fewer than five percent of these public service positions were elective. Top governmental leaders, political contributors, and civic and cultural organization trustees had better records of public service than leaders of the corporate world.

As we might expect, corporate directorships are common among top leaders in industry, communications and utilities, and banking. It is common for these men to have held four or more directorships in their lifetime. The centi-millionaires and top political contributors also have held a number of corporate directorships. In contrast, top government officials have not held many such directorships. Their experience in authoritative positions is derived mainly from public service, and to a lesser extent from educational and civic organizations. Top lawyers have held fewer corporate directorships than any other top group except our high government officials. The top political contributors appear to divide their interest between corporate directorships and public service positions.

The Source of Top Leadership

How did the people at the top get there? Certainly we cannot provide a complete picture of the recruitment process in all sectors of society. But we can learn whether the top leadership is recruited from a single sector, or whether the top leadership in each sector is recruited from that same sector. Specifically, we can ascertain whether or not the business and financial sectors provide the top leadership for education, government, foundations, and civic and cultural affairs.

TABLE 23 Authoritative Positions Ever Held by Individuals Currently Occupying Top Institutional Positions

	Indus-try	Comm. and Util.	Bank-ing	Insur-ance	Law	Civic Assoc.	Founda-tions	Govt.	Educa-tion	Wealth	Pol. Finance	Mili-tary
Average Number of Authoritative Positions Ever Held	9.9	12.2	10.7	11.6	9.0	11.7	11.1	7.1	10.9	11.5	12.3	0.9
Average Number of Authoritative Positions Ever Held in Each Sector:												
Industry	4.0	4.5	4.1	2.8	1.5	2.2	2.0	0.7	2.3	3.5	3.0	0.1
Banking	1.1	1.6	1.7	1.7	0.7	1.0	1.0	0.3	1.0	1.0	0.9	0.1
Insurance	0.4	0.8	0.5	1.4	0.2	0.2	0.2	0.0	0.3	0.3	0.2	0.1
Law	0.2	0.2	0.1	0.3	1.4	0.4	0.3	0.4	0.3	0.0	0.2	0.0
Civic Assoc.	1.6	2.2	2.0	2.1	2.3	3.0	2.6	1.1	2.3	2.8	2.8	0.1
Foundations	0.5	0.6	0.7	0.6	0.7	0.8	1.7	1.4	1.0	1.5	0.8	0.0
Education	1.0	1.2	1.0	1.5	0.9	1.4	1.6	1.0	2.0	0.9	0.9	0.3
Average Number of Public Service Positions Ever Held	1.0	1.0	0.6	1.4	1.3	2.6	1.7	3.1	1.7	1.5	3.5	0.6

Biographical information on individuals occupying positions of authority in top institutions in each sector of society reveals that there are many separate paths to authority. However, corporate industry supplied a disproportionate share of the top leadership in every sector except law, government, and the military. Needless to say, these exceptions are significant.

Table 24 shows the principal lifetime occupational activity—"the primary recruitment sector"—of individuals at the top of each sector of society. Categorizing individuals by their principal activity in life depended largely on their own designation of principal occupation in *Who's Who*. It turns out that the industrial sector supplied a majority of the occupants of top positions in industry (78.9 percent); transportation, communications, and utilities (62.2 percent), and banking (67.9 percent). The industrial sector also supplied the largest portion of the leadership in insurance (46.0 percent), foundations (36.2 percent), and even education (36.7 percent) and civic affairs (27.9 percent). But the corporate world is not the only source of top leadership. The corporate world did not supply any significant portion of the top leadership in government or law. Top leaders in government are recruited primarily from the legal profession (56.1 percent); some have based their careers in government itself (16.7 percent) and education (10.6 percent). This finding is important. Government and law apparently provide independent channels of recruitment to high office. We have already seen that governmental authority is not interlocked with corporate authority in terms of "horizontal" positional overlap. Now we see that high position in the corporate world is not a prerequisite to high public office; there is not much "vertical" overlap between the corporate and governmental sectors.

The military sector provides still another independent channel of recruitment to top leadership positions. Top military officers are recruited through the military itself. The only military leaders recruited from outside the military are the top civil officials of the Defense Department; they are recruited from industry, law, banking, and government.

Some Thoughts on the Concentration of Authority in America

There can be no doubt that the institutional structure of American society concentrates great authority in a relatively small number of positions. The fact that formal legal authority over half the nation's resources is concentrated in fifty-five hundred positions is a commentary on the extent of centralization in American life. Even though this statistic is in part a product of our definition of institutional sectors, nonetheless, it provides an explicit, quantitative indicator of extensive concentration.

At first glance, this concentration of formal institutional authority lends support to the convergence model of national elites. It is certainly true that an infinitesimal proportion of the population—two one-hundredth of one percent—occupy positions of authority over roughly half of the nation's resources. Indeed, if we accept the contention of Mills, Berle, and others, that power and institutional authority are closely related, we must accept the view that *power* in America is highly concentrated. The only alternative is to argue that findings about institutional authority have little relevance to the study of power, that men at the top of the institutional structure are heavily constrained in their exercise of formal authority, that conflict and competition characterize their interactions rather than concensus and cohesion, that men in au-

TABLE 24 Recruitment to Top Institutional Positions in Percents

Primary Sector from which Individuals in Control Positions Were Recruited	Industry	Comm. and Util.	Banking	Insurance	Law	Civic Assoc.	Foundations	Govt.	Education	Wealth	Pol. Finance	Military	Total
	(N=365)	(N=127)	(N=361)	(N=272)	(N=76)	(N=211)	(N=58)	(N=166)	(N=207)	(N=46)	(N=60)	(N=46)	
Industry	78.9	62.2	67.9	46.0	1.3	30.9	37.2	9.3	36.7	78.3	56.7	4.4	50.7
Banking	9.0	20.2	22.5	15.8	0.0	17.1	11.4	3.0	13.5	17.4	20.7	0.0	13.9
Insurance	1.2	3.9	3.3	19.9	0.0	2.4	0.0	0.0	2.9	4.3	10.3	0.0	4.8
Law	5.5	7.1	5.0	11.0	96.1	16.1	14.1	53.5	18.8	0.0	0.0	6.5	14.7
Civic Assoc.	0.0	0.0	0.0	0.0	0.0	0.0	0.0	0.0	0.0	0.0	0.0	0.0	0.0
Foundations	0.0	0.0	0.0	0.0	0.0	0.0	0.0	0.0	0.0	0.0	0.0	0.0	0.0
Government	1.7	0.8	0.3	1.5	2.6	11.4	7.2	16.7	6.8	0.0	0.0	4.4	4.9
Education	3.3	4.1	0.8	5.1	0.0	10.0	21.0	10.6	9.2	0.0	0.0	2.1	5.3
Wealth	0.0	0.0	0.0	0.0	0.0	0.0	0.0	0.0	0.0	0.0	0.0	0.0	0.0
Pol. Finance	0.0	0.0	0.0	0.0	0.0	0.0	0.0	0.0	0.0	0.0	0.0	0.0	0.0
Military	0.0	0.8	0.0	0.0	0.0	0.0	0.0	0.0	1.4	0.0	0.0	82.6	2.1
Artists, Writers, etc.	0.0	0.0	0.0	0.0	0.0	6.2	0.0	0.0	1.4	0.0	0.0	0.0	0.8
Labor	0.0	0.0	0.0	0.0	0.0	0.5	0.0	0.0	0.0	0.0	0.0	0.0	0.1
Other	0.4	0.9	0.2	0.7	0.0	5.9	9.1	6.9	9.3	0.0	12.3	0.0	2.7
	100.0	100.0	100.0	100.0	100.0	100.0	100.0	100.0	100.0	100.0	100.0	100.0	100.0

thority are held responsible for their actions by stockholders, unions, governments, competing institutions, and the public in general.

Yet despite institutional concentration of authority, there is evidence of considerable specialization among elites. Eighty percent of the individuals identified as occupying top institutional positions are "specialists." This is certainly evidence of polyarchy in the national leadership structure. There is little or no overlap between the corporate, governmental, and military sectors of society, as Mills implied. If it is true that there is a convergence of power at the top of the institutional structure, it is *not* by means of interlocking positions. Of course, convergence may result from *interaction* among specialized elites (formal, institutional contacts; informal association; recognized commonalities of interest, etc.), rather than interlocking directorates; but the notion of interlocking directorates can be put to rest.

The case for convergence can be strengthened if one *defines* the top power-holders as those individuals who are multiple "interlockers." In other words, the multiple interlockers become, by definition, the "power-holders." This is one way to give operational meaning to a concept—the power elite—which is exceedingly vague and elusive in the literature. Our biographical information on the highest interlockers certainly does not contradict the assertion that these men are powerful figures in America. But there is considerable circularity in this line of reasoning: the elite is defined as the high interlockers, and then the elite is found to be highly interlocked. Unless we have additional information showing that the high interlockers actually influence decisions in institutions more than the specialists, we cannot infer that the interlockers are the power elite.

The record of leadership experience of top institutional elites lends some substance to the view that *over a lifetime* the same individuals will occupy many high positions in different sectors in society. Thus, the convergence model is strengthened if we consider "vertical" overlap rather than "horizontal" overlap. But even the pattern of vertical overlap suggests some specialization in experience—government officials tended to hold previous positions in government and civic affairs, while corporate officials tended to hold previous positions in industry.

Perhaps the best evidence of polyarchy in our findings is the existence of separate, independent recruitment channels to top institutional leadership. Corporate industry supplied a major share of the leadership in many sectors, but *not* in government, law, and the military. These sectors provided independent paths to authority. Clearly, an individual can acquire high position in America without any prior experience in industry or finance. Of course, it may be that individuals pursuing careers in government, law, or the military must establish good relationships with industrial and financial elites (we have shown that these elites constitute the bulk of the large political campaign contributors). But there is a clear separation of career paths among our men in authority.

Thus, our findings do not all fall neatly into either the convergence or polyarchial leadership models. There is both concentration and specialization in the nation's institutional elite structure. And, of course, all of these findings about institutional elites are subject to the charge that institutional authority is not the equivalent of power—that findings about formal institutional positions are only tangential to more important questions about competition, access, interaction, responsibility, and accountability. Our data do not really permit any inferences about interaction, communication, informal association or mutuality of interest, among our institutional elites. But we believe that debate over the concentration of power in America will be better informed by continuing attempts to systematically define institutional elites, to measure the real extent of interlocking and specialization, and to examine the actual paths of recruitment to top institutional positions.

References

1. C. Wright Mills, *The Power Elite* (New York: Oxford University Press, 1959): 9.
2. Adolph A. Berle, *Power* (New York: Harcourt, Brace and World, 1967): 92.
3. Mills, *The Power Elite*, 10–11.
4. Mills, *The Power Elite*, 9.
5. Floyd Hunter, *Top Leadership, U.S.A.* (Chapel Hill: University of North Carolina Press, 1959): 176.
6. Gabriel Kolko, *Wealth and Power in America* (New York: Frederick A. Praeger, 1962): 57.
7. Robert A. Dahl, *Pluralist Democracy in the United States* (Chicago: Rand McNally, 1967): 24.

TO THE STUDENT: A COMMENTARY

Question: is America ruled by the Establishment, if so what is it like? The authors of "Power Shift" and of "Power Elites" address this common question, but with sharply contrasting styles, evidence, and conclusions. Take style first. The journalistic-scientific approaches to watching politics are marked in this chapter. Remember in our commentary to you in the prologue that we noted the tendency of journalists—be they beat, investigative, or interpretative reporters—to employ a dramatic format. Their narratives highlight actors (agents) doing things (acts) in settings (scenes) by various means (agencies) for various reasons (purposes). The five elements in this dramatic pentad emerge in the accounts of interpretative journalists, such as Kirkpatrick Sale, as the who, what, when, where, how, and why of the story. By contrast, a scientific format is impersonal, consisting of the statement of a problem, the design of the research, methods used, analysis, findings, and conclusions.

Sale's narrative is indeed dramatic. He focuses the points he wants to make about an abstract Establishment by recreating a scene in the Oval Office of the White House in 1973: the President and his counsel engage in intense conversation, motives bared. Sale uses that conversation as the vehicle for introducing the Establishment. The President's views serve as a dramatic theme running throughout "Power Shift," i.e., the anomaly of a President being "outside" the Establishment. How could this be so? Sale narrates the how and why. Relying upon impressions garnered from a vast amount of reading, talking with people, and personal experience Sale tells the story of the emergence of the *Southern Rim*. It is the story of financial tycoons, political upstarts and barons, vibrant cities, and wealth, wealth, wealth. With a little work Sale's account could almost become a screenplay for *Dallas*, television's widely watched and discussed prime-time soap opera of the 1979–1980 season.

But Sale's drama is not only of birth, pulsating life, and emergence. It is also of failing health, decline, and death. Says Richard Nixon, "the Establishment is dying." It is the Northeastern Establishment, a fading political center under siege by the Southern Rim. Drama thrives on conflict. Sale provides it—the contest of yankees and cowboys. "Power Shift," in authentic melodramatic fashion, is actually "power struggle."

And, in authentic scientific style, "Power Elites" is a restrained presentation. This is not to say dull. Tom Dye and his colleagues offer a nontechnical article, well organized and written, not bogged down in sophisticated statistical formulae and tests. There are lengthy tables, but they do not intrude; indeed they add to the account. The thesis remains clear: "There can be no doubt that the institutional structure of American society concentrates great authority in a relatively small number of positions."

Dispassionate style aside, however, the authors of "Power Elites" are dealing with a hot potato, a conflict less dramatic than yankees versus cowboys but no less intense to some of the combatants. For decades students of American politics—principally political scientists and sociologists—have debated the question of who governs America. The controversy occupies space in scholarly journals, monographs, and even introductory textbooks. Dye, DeClerq, and Pickering fuel the fire of this heated exchange, but do not put it out.

Employing a scientific format Dye and his coworkers provide a statement of their research problem that lays out the contrasting poles of the scholarly dispute. On the one hand are believers in a *convergence model.* They contend that "a relatively small group of individuals exercises authority in a wide variety of institutions." Opposed to this thought are the advocates of a *polyarchial model,* i.e., "different groups of individuals exercise power in different sectors of society, and acquire power in separate ways." Reenter, momentarily, Kirkpatrick Sale. Where do you think he would line up in this dispute? Could it be that he would argue that the convergence view must yield to the polyarchial? In short, has the tightly knit yankee Establishment been penetrated by cowboys?

But in the convergence-polyarchial debate, how can we know who has the better argument? Dye, DeClerq, and Pickering propose to find out by discovering who are in the nation's "institutional elite." This is a slippery notion. It can be defined in many ways. One is to say that all persons who occupy decision-making positions of importance in key institutions comprise the elite. But who are they? Have you read the novel, or seen the movie, *One Flew Over the Cuckoo's Nest?* The story revolves about the daily lives of patients and staff members of a mental hospital. Who runs that institution? Surely the staff members—doctors, nurses, orderlies, etc.—and not the patients. But the arrival of Randle Patrick McMurphy as a patient produces a power struggle. Patients begin to usurp the institutional elite. No longer is it clear who is in, who is out of, the power elite.

There are other ways to try to learn who's in charge or "who's running this show." You can, for instance, sniff around and ask people who *really* make the decisions. Or, you can study specific decisions and try to ferret out who made them. In short, there are many ways to identify elites, but none foolproof. If you doubt that, just try to list the people who run your college or university. How do you know they do?

We stress this point to you because it is important, both to evaluating Sale's evidence and that of Dye and his coworkers. How we define an Establishment or elite goes a long way toward saying who comprises it. Sale takes it for granted that financial wizards, corporate directors, national politicians and all the others he lists by name are members of either yankee or cowboy Establishments. He does not prove they make the key, vital, "real" decisions, he simply assumes it. When he cites evidence it is not to test or prove his thesis, but to illustrate it. Dye, DeClerq, and Pickering also make an assumption—but with explicit scientific caution. They opt for a positional definition of institutional elites: *"those individuals in the United States who occupy formal positions of authority in those institutions which control over half the nation's total resources."* This is what scientists call an "operational" definition. That is, the scientist defines something through the way it can be measured. Temperature can be defined by how it is measured—in degrees on Fahrenheit or Celsius scales, a foot is 12 inches, etc. Hence, by the operation of finding first, what institutions control over half the nation's total resources, and second, who occupies formal positions in them, Dye and his students defined America's institutional elite.

A bold contention emerges: 4,100 persons control half of the nation's resources! Dye, DeClerq, and Pickering not only tell you the number, they list the names of the key members of the institutional elite. Read their listing. Compare it to the names Sale mentions. Do you find overlaps? Dye and his colleagues note that most of the 4,100 members of the elite are "specialists" but still there is a concentration of authority among 21 persons in the "top group." Ask yourself if the "Top Twenty-One" are yankees or cowboys. Whether your general thought is that yankees or cowboys rule, or the institutional elite is best described as convergent or polyarchial, at least the degree of concentration must impress you. Moreover, add the fact that each top leader occupied about 11 positions of authority in his lifetime and you become more impressed!

Impressive as the evidence is, the authors of "Power Elites" suspend judgment on the validity of the convergence model. And well they should. With specialization among elites, no overlap in the membership of most positions, and multiple avenues for reaching positions, the case for polyarchy strengthens. And, if Kirkpatrick Sale is correct, the yankee-cowboy cleavage makes convergence remote.

But think again. Could it be that the cowboys are on the ascendancy? Will they replace the yankees? Will the Southern Rim become a new concentrated Establishment? Cowboy Jimmy Carter squared off against cowboy Ronald Reagan in the 1980 presidential election. Did the fact of such a shootout mean both major political parties were under cowboy, not yankee, control? Was the independent candidacy of John Anderson a reflection of yankee decline? These are things to think about as you assess the merits of what you can learn from "Power Shift" and "Power Elites."

But does it matter who governs? A colleague teaching an introductory course in American government told a story. He had taken great pains to prepare a lecture on political leadership in America. He carefully laid out for his class the contrast between elitist (convergence) and pluralist (polyarchy) ways of looking at who rules. After 50 minutes of "inspired" presentation, he asked for questions. One student bearing a puzzled expression raised her hand. Upon being recognized she simply said, "So what?"

There may be the rub. We can speculate with Sale or conduct research with Dye and others about who governs. But so what? What are the implications of having yankees or cowboys at the helm or in the saddle; of having a concentrated or pluralist elite? And, if we don't like what we find, what do we do about it? Ask "so what?" but do so as an informed watcher of politics. Views of journalists can assist that watching. Among those with views on who governs America, a few excellent books include:

Richard H. Rovere, *The American Establishment*
Douglass Cater, *Power in Washington*
Kirkpatrick Sale, *Power Shift*

And, from social scientists:

C. Wright Mills, *The Power Elite*
David T. Bazelon, *Power in America*
G. William Domhoff, *Who Rules America?*
G. William Domhoff, *The Powers That Be*
Thomas Dye, *Who's Running America?*
Arnold Rose, *The Power Structure*

6 Is the Party Over?

INTRODUCTION

We invited you at the close of chapter 5 to speculate about whether yankees or cowboys control our nation's two major political parties. Some political observers argue that it makes no real difference one way or the other, for political parties can no longer be numbered among the powers that be. Once potent mobilizers of power, recruiters of candidates for office, organizers of the electorate, and makers of policies, the Democratic and Republican parties are now but shells of their former selves. Their societal role has been sapped from all sides: special interest groups select candidates, sponsor them, fund them, elect them; professional political campaigners sell themselves to candidates, ignore parties in conducting campaigns, and make elected public officials virtually independent of party ties; and voters ignore party labels more and more in reaching their choices, focusing instead upon narrowly defined yet highly emotional issues and the stands candidates take on them. In short, say critics of the nation's politics, the party's over.

The Party's Over, in fact, was the title of a major work in political journalism written by the author of the next article you will read, "Parties in Trouble." David Broder is a highly respected national political correspondent of the *Washington Post.* Broder has watched politics on the national level from a variety of professional perspectives— once as correspondent of the *New York Times,* as a nationally syndicated columnist, as winner of a Pulitzer Prize, and as associate editor of the *Post.* In his book he reviewed the key role political parties have played in the history of our republic, diagnosed the ills of the current party system, and suggested prospects for the future. He argued in that work in 1972 that "the governmental system is not working because the political parties are not working."

Seven years later in "Parties in Trouble" Broder echoes his earlier theme. The focus turns to special interest politics and single issue politics. Broder writes well and you will have no problems understanding either his argument or the notions he uses to explain it. He clearly identifies what he believes to be the new powers that be and the threat to American politics he thinks they pose. Read his contribution carefully and consider what he is saying in light of all the things you have learned from other textbooks about what political parties are like (and in light of your experience in party politics if you have been so fortunate to take part). Do you agree with his premise that things will continue to get worse before improving, that ultimately we will need to "reinvent political parties"?

Not every political observer thinks the party's over, but a large number recognize that major changes are taking place in party politics. Prior to the 1980 presidential election political scientist William Schneider speculated that we might be reaching a watershed year in party politics. That he should employ the watershed metaphor says something about where he stands, for a watershed, so says the dictionary, is a ridge of high land dividing two areas that are drained by different river systems. As you peruse Schneider's analysis ask yourself if (1) Republicans and Democrats constitute different river systems draining American politics, and (2) if it is possible that each party has, in effect, spouted two river systems within it. Will the future of American politics witness the confluence of streams from formerly different systems and, if so, what erosion of American politics might this too imply?

William Schneider is senior research fellow, Hoover Institution, Stanford. Actually Schneider doubles in brass, being not only a political scientist but also a political consultant. He has consulted for the *Los Angeles Times* and was public opinion columnist for *Politics Today.* That now defunct magazine published articles—based upon the findings of scientific research—in a format paralleling that of many popular magazines. Since "1980—A Watershed Year?" was first published in *Politics Today* you will undoubtedly find the style of the article less rigid in format and more breezy than that of many of the scholarly articles you have read in this volume. Perhaps this will offer added evidence of what Gerald Grant argued in our prologue; that is, the approaches of the Type III, interpretative journalist and the social scientist verge ever nearer on one another. Does this mean a vanishing watershed between journalism and social science in political watching?

PARTIES IN TROUBLE

David S. Broder

Edited and reprinted from Today, May 11, 1979, 10–11.

Some call them special interest groups. Some call them single-interest groups. Whatever the name, it is agreed that they are a shame. "Strident and self-righteous," as one Senator terms them, the single-issue groups are accused of fragmenting the political consensus, whipsawing conscientious public officials with non-negotiable demands, and generally playing havoc with responsible government and politics.

But if single-cause groups are an evil, they are a necessary evil. In fact, rather than hoping that they can be curbed, as some members of Congress have proposed, it may be better to let such groups flourish and exasperate politicians as much as possible.

I say this in the belief that American politics has reached the point where it has to get worse before it can get better. Specifically, it must become more painful and difficult for politicians and officeholders. And because single-interest groups are making it more painful and difficult, they are helping create the conditions in which responsible politics and government may be reborn.

Twin Perils

The complaints about single-interest groups are abundant, if sometimes overstated. When Democratic Senator Edward M. Kennedy of Massachusetts declared last October that "the Senate and House are awash in a sea of special interest campaign contributions and special interest lobbying," he was probably mixing dreadnaughts and dories, if apples and oranges do not suit his nautical metaphor.

He cited as evidence the growth in political action committees and in their contributions to congressional campaigns.

It is true that the $76 million reported spent by 1,911 independent, non-party groups in the 1978 elections were records, both in dollars and in numbers or organizations. But many of the largest spenders—the AFL-CIO, the National Conservative Political Action Committee, the American Medical Association, for example—have broad political and policy agendas.

Nevertheless, there are certainly narrow, one-cause groups—the opponents of gun control, most notably, but also some conservation, arms-control and equal rights amendment advocates—that raised and spent substantial sums.

The concern about their influence is not misplaced. Groups like these—or the right-to-life organizations, which depend on volunteer workers rather than dollars for their influence—can effectively threaten officeholders with political retaliation because of stands on a single question.

They have demonstrated a capability—at least in some states and some races—to upset not only individual careers but also powerful party organizations. For example, the Minnesota Democratic Farmer-Labor Party, a rich source of national leadership for the past generation, has been riddled by infighting between pro- and anti-abortion groups.

When admitting the destructive power of single-interest groups, however, it is important to stress that their rise represents the second stage in the demolition of the party system in the United States, not the first.

The first stage came in the 1950s and 1960s, when ambitious office-seekers found that they could bypass the party and win office from the courthouse to the White House on their own. Now, in the 1970s, issue-concerned citizens are applying the same lesson—not to gain office but to force their policy views on the government. Like the candidates, they are bypassing the party structure and "taking their case directly to the people."

The result is that independent, autonomous officeholders are confronting independent, autonomous interest groups in a kind of unmediated power struggle that leaves the national interest in shreds and helps persuade voters to express their dissatisfaction in the most dramatic way possible—by not voting.

What is not generally perceived is that single-issue groups and single-shot candidates are twin perils to responsible politics and government. In reality, the Gun Owners of America Campaign Committee is no more narrow or selfish in its aims than was the Carter-for-President Committee. The League of Conservation Voters is fundamentally no different in this respect than the Committee for the Re-election of the President. One has the single interest of seeing a certain policy adopted, the other of having a certain candidate elected.

That is an alien notion, I know. But it may be more easily understood by following a short historical trail to see how we arrived at this point in our politics.

Breaking Patterns

In the innocent days of the 1940s or 1950s, what would a young man eager for public office do? In most places, he would decide first whether he felt more comfortable as a Democrat or Republican, and then present himself to a party screening or slating committee.

After examining his credentials, the party elders might offer him their support for supervisor or sheriff, for prothonotary or (at a different level) president. But they also might say, "Doubtless you are all the things you claim, but we already have a good candidate for Senator, so why don't you run for clerk this year and we'll see how you do in that job." In that way, the party maintained its members loyalties and fresh ambitions were channeled into useful roles.

The young man, of course, understood that he had acquired certain advantages and taken on certain obligations upon being embraced by the party.

His campaign costs would be met in whole or part by the party, which collected contributions from supportive citizens and interest groups. Party precinct workers would push his candidacy as they made the rounds. He would be cloaked with a label, Democrat or Republican, which had broad significance for voters, so that even if they did not know him, they would know he was (or was not) "their kind of candidate."

At the same time, the young man knew that he was no longer a free agent. He had acquired obligations to help promote his party and win votes for his ticket-mates, whatever he thought of their individual merits. A degree of loyalty was expected. His disagreements with party leaders would be expressed privately or, if publicly, in muted tones. When they needed help, he would be available.

He also knew that when the party was popular, he might benefit from the "coat-tails" of its leaders, and when the party lost the public's confidence, he might be booted out of office—no matter how conscientiously he had done his own job for his constituents.

That is roughly the way the game was played for most of American history in most places in this country.

But after World War II, the pattern changed. It changed because certain smart fellows discovered that they could achieve their ambitions without going through all this rigamarole. Senator Kennedy's brother John probably was not the first, but he was an important trend-setter.

When he returned to Boston from Navy service, Governor Maurice Tobin and Democratic Party elders invited the 29-year-old novice to go on the ticket for lieutenant governor. It was a flattering offer, but one Kennedy could refuse. His goal was the House of Representatives, and he plunged into a 10-man primary without asking anyone's permission. While his father pulled strings to mollify some of the old-guard politicians, Kennedy and his young friends put together the organization of political amateurs and volunteers that won the campaign.

It worked for him not only in that first House race, but in later campaigns for the Senate and his presidency—and he was not alone.

Jerry Ford did the same thing in Grand Rapids, taking a House nomination away from a Republican incumbent. Richard Nixon launched his career in California with the same sort of volunteer effort. Jimmy Carter followed the pattern in Georgia.

They and their counterparts made a number of discoveries. They found that volunteers worked harder and were more persuasive in campaigns, than patronage-oriented "soldiers" of the old political machines.

They found that interest groups preferred to give money directly to candidates rather than through the party. They found that people of means who would never have "dirtied their hands" with party politics would contribute to a candidate who had a tasteful cocktail party or after-theater reception. Later, with the development of direct-mail techniques, people like Barry Goldwater, George Wallace, and George McGovern found that the wallets of thousands of less affluent citizens could also be tapped to finance individual candidacies.

The new candidates then discovered more powerful ways of communicating with the voters. Radio and television ads, telephone banks, and computerized, targeted mailings carried much more impact than the slate-cards precinct captains used to hand out at the polls.

They discovered—or intensified the use of—an old trick: door to door personal campaigning. If they were willing to spend enough time with the voters themselves before a primary, they found, they could beat the organization-backed candidate.

So individuals eager for public office no longer "submit" themselves to a party screening process. They organize to capture a nomination with a full-time, extended primary campaign, and then they announce, as the most recent product of that process announced to his party on the evening he captured its nomination: "My name is Jimmy Carter, and I am running for President of the United States.

Party of One

In office, these new-style politicians behave with an independence appropriate to their manner of acquiring office. They are under no obligation to anyone—and certainly not to others who claim to be "leaders" of their party. This independence of House members has made the job of lining up votes for Democratic legislation far more difficult than it used to be. Those legislators do not feel their fate rests with the voters' judgment on their party, but on them as individuals, and they vote as best suits their individual interests.

Elected executives are no different. Cleveland Mayor Dennis Kucinich ran against the party "establishment" and carried his policy differences with the Democratic city council to the point of forcing his city into bankruptcy. Newbreed governors from West Virginia's Jay Rockefeller to Illinois' Jim Thompson to California's Jerry Brown have been at odds with their legislatures as often as Carter has with Congress.

What really has developed is a system of independent, autonomous candidates and officeholders, each with a political and governmental agenda of his own—a political party of one.

And now those officeholders are raising a cry of alarm about the invasion of their turf by independent, autonomous issue groups.

"Single-issue politics," says Democratic Senator John Culver of Iowa, "has, in my judgment, disturbing implications for the nature and quality of political representation in this country."

"Increasingly, he says, "splinter lobbies are forcing upon elected officials and candidates . . . loyalty tests on wide ranges of peripheral matters. . . . We have vocal, vehement, and well-orchestrated lobbies on abortion, consumer agencies, gun control, labor law reform, and a host of other subjects," each judging the officeholder not on his overall record but "by a single litmus test of ideological purity."

More and more, officeholders are demanding protection from what one of them has called the "issues extortionists." They are asking why there is nothing to provide some defense against this crossfire of non-negotiable, special-interest demands.

The blunt answer is that they themselves helped destroy the one institution that historically filled that function—the political party. The officeholders are now being victimized by people who have borrowed their own campaign techniques to use against them.

In the old system, the parties served to screen the demands of interest groups as well as to regulate the ambitions of candidates. All groups were invited to present their proposals at platform time, but all understood that platform-writing, like ticket-balancing, was a matter of compromise and tradeoff. Individual goals were likely to be subordinated to the overall aim of maintaining the party in power.

The Vigueries

In the last 10 years, however, the issue constituencies, witnessing the success of candidates who bypassed the party, decided they could do the same thing. If your aim was to clean up the rivers, you did not have to establish that as a priority with the Democratic or Republican platform committees. You could form the League of Conservation Voters and run campaigns against "the dirty dozen." So it went if you wanted to ban guns or protect guns, stop abortions or make them more available.

Like the candidates, these groups discovered the effectiveness of organizations built on the disciplined enthusiasm of volunteers. They learned that door-to-door canvassing and church or shopping center leaflets can have tremendous impact when targeted for or against particular candidates.

And they learned even better than the candidate organizations of the 1950s and 1960s how to use computerized direct-mail techniques. It is the ability of these groups to generate mail and money, literally at the push of a button, to support or oppose a particular legislative issue or candidate that makes officeholders most upset.

Richard Viguerie, the owner of the most active direct-mail company, has become, in an astonishingly short time, a political power in his own right. He did his first right-to-work mailing in 1969 and his first anti-abortion mailing two years later. But it is only since 1975, he says, that he had begun to "focus in on special-interest clients," and his success so far guarantees an expansion of the technique.

Most of the recent complaints about single-issue groups have come from Democratic liberals. But Anne Wexler, the Carter White House aide who has given several thoughtful speeches about the problems that single-interest groups create for presidential leadership, has been honest enough to admit that she is herself the product of an important single-interest movement, one that was warmly applauded at the time by Democratic liberals.

That movement—Wexler's home ground—was the Vietnam peace movement, which mobilized around that one issue so effectively that it drove a President from office. What worked for the peace movement is now working for the right-to-life movement and other single-cause groups.

Therapeutic Value

For lawmakers subjected to the computerized power of single-interest groups, it can be a frightening experience. Suddenly their offices are flooded with mail warning that unless they vote a particular way on an approaching issue, "we will defeat you next time you run." Suddenly their campaign organizations pick up reports of the district being flooded with disparaging letters—not by their opponent but by some organization they never knew was there.

The politicians' plea for protection, however, must be scrutinized with care. There are important constitutional rights involved here; the right to petition the government applies equally to organizations with computer mailing techniques as without.

Moreover, there is a therapeutic value in letting the politicians experience the dangers of the kind of politics we have today—a primal struggle for control among single-shot candidates and single-interest groups.

To be sure, it is a brutal, ugly kind of politics, and it is helping turn off the American people in massive numbers. The people are not issue ideologues. They are not candidate fanatics. They are what they have always been—reasonably broad-minded, practical, and progressive.

What they hear in the last 10 days of a campaign, whenever they turn on a radio or TV set, is a babble of voices saying "vote for me, vote for me, vote for me." What they read, whenever they open their mail, are injunctions to "vote for this, vote for that." Being sensible, most of them are covering their ears against the din, shutting their eyes to all the commands, and tuning out this self-serving racket by turning away from the polls.

What is missing from our politics is the mechanism which once helped organize those voter choices in a sensible fashion, which channeled the individual ambitions of eager aspirants and the conflicting claims of various interest groups into a coherent ticket and platform. That agency was the political party, and it is in a shambles today.

The destruction of the political parties began with the individual office-seekers, and it is they who keep the parties weak today.

They loved free-lance, individualistic politics—until the techniques of free-lance, individualistic politics were turned against them. Now they are saying that something dangerous has been unleashed. They are right—but about 20 years late in their discovery.

The first reaction among officeholders was to try in 1978 to curb the influence of single-interest groups by reducing the amount of money their political-action committees could contribute to congressional campaigns. Their second ploy—sure to be repeated this year—was an attempt to expand taxpayer financing of individual campaigns beyond the presidential level to House and Senate contests.

But before any curbs are put on the role of single-issue groups and before any more public funds are given to single-shot candidates, it seems reasonable to expect officeholders to demonstrate that they are prepared to sacrifice some of their own precious autonomy.

It really has to be one way or the other. If individual candidates are to be allowed to play their own games for their own ends, with blithe disregard of the effects on the governmental and political system, then single-interest groups are not to be denied the same destructive freedom. If single-issue groups are to be brought back within the constraints of party politics, then the candidates must, too.

The tests of their seriousness about reconstructing the party system are very clear:

• Are they prepared to submit their own credentials to serious screening by party leaders, or will they continue to insist on their absolute right to pursue any office any time the desire strikes them? Will they continue to legislate increasing numbers of primaries, thereby adding to the incentive for full-time candidates to bypass the party endorsement process, or will they cut back on that destructive change in the nominating system?

• As nominees, are they prepared to campaign as members of a party ticket, rather than set up a private political organization of their own? Are they prepared to defend the record of their party, or just their own work on behalf of their own constituents?

• Are they prepared to raise money for their party and partake of the party treasury, or will they keep all the funds they can gather for themselves? Will they channel public campaign subsidies through the political parties, rather than giving them to individual campaign committees, as is the case now?

• Will they accept a responsibility to cooperate with the leaders of their own party—both legislative and executive—in carrying out the party program? Or will they insist that they are free agents on every vote, responsible only to their own conscience and constituents?

My guess is that few candidates or officeholders are ready to sacrifice their own freedom of action to rehabilitate their party. But it may be that when more of them have been bullied by single-issue lobbyists, threatened by single-interest mailings, and beaten by single-interest machines, they will perceive their need for the protections political parties once offered against these ideological buccaneers.

Franklin's Choice

There is no way to put the genie of single-issues groups back in the bottle. But they are not new to our politics. From the anti-Masons of the 1830s to the anti-saloon leagues of the 1920s, such groups have flourished. In a pluralistic society, with a constitutional guarantee of freedom of speech and association, they have an inevitable and proper role to play.

What is different now is that the political parties are not strong enough to play their equally essential role. As Anthony King, the British journalist and political scientist has observed, the threat to American government is not partisanship but hyperpluralism. Political parties function to build coalitions, but in today's politics, to use King's phrase, "they are only coalitions of sand."

The lesson the officeholders have to learn was stated at the beginning of the republic by Benjamin Franklin: Either they hang together or they hang separately.

Give them a few more years of the rigors of single-shot candidacies and single-issue movements, and even the dullest politicians will discover the need to reinvent political parties.

1980—A WATERSHED YEAR?

WILLIAM SCHNEIDER

Edited and reprinted from Politics Today 7 (*January/February 1980*): 26–32.

By election day 1980, Independents may well be the largest political party in this country. A trend toward increasing independence and diminishing partisanship has been going on for the last quarter-century. According to the widely respected surveys conducted every two years by the University of Michigan's Center for Political Studies, 75 percent of the American electorate identified themselves with a political party in 1952. By 1978, that figure was down to 60 percent—39 percent Democrats and 21 percent Republicans. And in that year there were just about as many Independents as Democrats.

Also on election day 1980, the two parties may well present the country with the most pronounced and evenly matched ideological confrontation of any election in nearly 50 years. Edward Kennedy and Ronald Reagan, the early leaders in the polls and with party leaders, would certainly defy the common voter belief—and complaint—that there is usually no difference between the candidates. But unlike past choices with a difference (Johnson-Goldwater or Nixon-McGovern), both Kennedy and Reagan are able to project an ideological identity. And neither is isolated on the political fringe. A contest between them would be a clear-cut clash between a liberal and a conservative with broad legitimacy in their respective parties.

Even if such factors as Chappaquiddick or Reagan's age short-circuit the confrontation, the prospect of weakened parties putting on a strengthened ideological battle strikes an intriguing note. It suggests that the U.S. could be on the verge of a significant sorting-out of disparate political trends. Those trends have reflected and intensified the nation's uncertainties. Their resolution could greatly clarify the nation's direction.

Virtually all the candidates seem to sense a shift in the political winds. Howard Baker speaks of "a sea change." Kennedy refers to "a watershed period." Jerry Brown expects "some kind of political realignment." John Connally says, "This will be the most important election in this century." Whatever the outcome of the predicted change, it is possible now to discern the forces that created it. The style of American politics, the structure of the parties and the stimulus of the Independents have each played a critical role.

One new force that has had a large impact on our politics is mass marketing. An important reason for the decline of partisanship is that our present style of campaigning is no longer very partisan. Partisan campaigns seek to mobilize supporters around highly divisive issues—class conflict, religious animosity, racial antagonism, ideological polarization and the like. Each "party system" in American history was founded on conflict over great issues of principle. Federalists opposed Jeffersonian Democrats over the question of whether the infant republic should side with England or France during the Revolutionary Wars in Europe. Republicans opposed Democrats over the great issues of the Civil War. In the 1880s, the Democrats became identified with rural Populism and the Republicans with urban industrial capitalism. Our current party system had its birth in the 1930s, when the Democrats became the party of organized labor and New Deal social welfare policies. In each case, a sense of "us" versus "them" served to solidify party loyalty.

This conflict-oriented style of politics is very different from the modern "mass-marketing" style. That style is to appeal to all voters as potential supporters, not just to the party's base. Candidates are sold to the electorate by means of nondivisive issues—peace, prosperity, competence, leadership—that appeal to the broadest range of voters without necessarily excluding anyone. Conflict, the very basis of partisanship, is avoided at all costs. Instead, the techniques of advertising and promotion are used to persuade voters that a candidate is the best man.

Mass marketing is not a style of politics that generates much enthusiasm. Turnout in twentieth-century American elections has been consistently lower than turnout in the nineteenth century, when the partisan style predominated and voters had a more intense sense of conflict. Mass marketing also does very little to create or sustain party loyalty.

This is not to say that recent politics has been devoid of conflict. Conflict was what the sixties were all about. But the conflicts of the 1960s were different in two important respects. First, they were primarily over social and cultural, not class, issues. Divisions over race, the Vietnam War and radicalism tended to cut across class lines. By the late 1960s, there were discernible left and right factions in the middle class (McCarthy, Goldwater) and in the working class (Humphrey, Wallace). Second, the conflicts of the 1960s also cut across party lines. Many of the sharpest ideological conflicts were within the parties or outside them, rather than between them. Liberals and conservatives of the 1960s often criticized the traditional parties for being irrelevant to the burning issues of the day. The net impact was to reduce the intensity of partisanship, rather than invigorate it.

Consider the Democrats. The great conflicts over race and Vietnam were fought out mostly among warring factions within the Democratic party. The center wing of the party consisted of the "regular" Democrats, led in the 1960s by Lyndon Johnson and Hubert Humphrey. The regulars stood in a direct line of descent from Franklin Roosevelt through Harry Truman and John F. Kennedy. This party establishment stood for the social welfare liberalism of the New Deal, the anti-Communist interventionism of the cold war and the racial liberalism of the civil rights era.

The commitment of the Democratic party to racial liberalism represented a courageous—and costly—decision by the party regulars (Kennedy, Johnson and Humphrey) to end the party's historic evasion of the issue out of deference to its southern wing. That brought the first challenge to the party establishment. It came from the right, as George C. Wallace ran against Johnson in the 1964 primaries and carried the politics of racial backlash from South to North.

Then, in 1968, the New Politics movement emerged with the antiwar candidacy of Eugene J. McCarthy. In 1968, neither the center nor the right competed in the Democratic primaries. The left won the primaries, the right ran an independent campaign, and the regulars, who controlled the convention, nominated Hubert Humphrey, who proceeded to lose the election in November. In 1972, all three factions competed in the primaries, the left led by George McGovern, the right by Wallace, and the regulars by Humphrey. This time the left controlled the convention. They nominated McGovern, who then proceeded to lose the election in November.

The basic logic of party conflict during this period was not the left against the right, but the left and the right against the center. The Wallace voters opposed the regulars' commitment to civil rights and the McCarthy/McGovern voters opposed the regulars' commitment to military interventionism. But in both cases, their anti-Establishment appeal was limited by their ideological appeal. Many voters said they agreed with a lot of what George Wallace thought was wrong with the country, but they could never vote for him because he was a racist. And many voters said they sympathized with George McGovern's criticisms of the country, but they could never vote for him because he was a radical.

What Jimmy Carter did was to separate the protest from the ideology. Like McGovern and Wallace before him, Carter was not a regular. But he was not a racist nor a radical, either. Carter's protest against Washington—the symbol of the regulars, the Establishment and the system—was a rare phenomenon in American politics: a protest movement of the center. The Wallace and McGovern criticisms of the government often came across as criticisms of the country, and so they communicated a sense of ugliness and pessimism that many Americans refused to endorse. Carter's remarkable achievement was to create a protest of good feeling. His love-and-decency message, the religious symbolism and the optimism of his campaign, turned the anti-Establishment mood into something positive and reassuring.

Carter took on and defeated the party's right, center and left factions one at a time, each on its own turf: Wallace in Florida, centrist Henry Jackson in Pennsylvania and leftish Morris Udall in Wisconsin. And his victory, therefore, did not represent a victory for any faction. Indeed, in the later primaries, when the liberals and the regulars made an effort to gang up against Carter, their combined votes were enough to defeat him in several states. What those primaries demonstrated is that Carter lacks a secure base within the Democratic party.

If the Democrats have been divided, left, right and center, so have the Republicans. Since World War II three factions have emerged: the Republican party of Wall Street, the Republican party of Main Street and the Republican party of Easy Street. But whereas the dominant cleavage within the Democratic party has historically been North versus South, Republican conflicts have followed an East/West axis.

Wall Street is the eastern wing of the party. It is the Republican party of Thomas E. Dewey and Wendell Willkie, of Dwight Eisenhower and Henry Cabot Lodge, and, for the past 15 years, of Nelson Rockefeller. In a usage that must be hopelessly confusing to Marxists, the Wall Street Republicans are usually considered to be the left wing of the party, for indeed big business learned to accommodate to and even prosper under the economic management policies of the New Deal.

Main Street is the midwestern wing of the party, the center of the Republican party both geographically and ideologically. Main Street Republicans are rural and small-town dwellers, small businessmen and professionals, the party of decent, honest, God-fearing and tight-fisted men. The Republican party of Main Street is the Republican party of Robert Taft and Everett Dirksen, of Arthur Vandenberg and of his political protege, Gerald Ford.

Easy Street, the Republican party of the nouveau riche, is an altogether new phenomenon. It appeared quite suddenly in the suburbs and boomtowns of the Sunbelt, an area that had not in the past been a significant center of Republican strength. Easy Street Republicans include Barry Goldwater, John Connally, Jesse Helms, Strom Thurmond, Ronald Reagan and S. I. Hayakawa. Historically, the South and the Southwest were areas of conservative Democratic strength. Therefore it is not surprising that this new Republican right held a special appeal for former Democrats. All the figures just listed, except Goldwater, were once Democrats.

In 1964, Barry Goldwater challenged and defeated the eastern wing of the party, led by Nelson Rockefeller. Many centrist Republicans, such as Senator Dirksen, were willing to go along with the Goldwater nomination, though without great enthusiasm. Richard Nixon won the nomination in 1968 as a party centrist against challenges from Ronald Reagan on the right and Nelson Rockefeller on the left.

In 1976 the Republican campaign pitted the right against the left and center of the party. The reconciliation of the GOP left and center in the face of the external threat from the right could not have been better symbolized than by the Main Street/Wall Street alliance between Gerald Ford and Nelson Rockefeller. Reagan also showed an acute awareness of the factional structure of the Republican party when he offered the vice-presidential position on his ticket to a bona fide eastern liberal, Sen. Richard Schweiker of Pennsylvania. But in the end, the liberal Republicans stuck with Ford, the candidate who, while not of their persuasion, was still closer to them on most of the issues.

So when the smoke of '76 had cleared, the skirmishing among the three factions in each party had not been settled. Nonetheless, there is a good chance that the 1980 election will complete a process of realignment, leaving the parties distinct in terms of social and cultural ideology as well as economic ideology. The two parties have, in fact, been moving apart ideologically for the past 15 years, the Republicans to the right and the Democrats to the left. This likely clarification of party positions comes several years after the most intense period of social and cultural conflict—the late 1960s and the early 1970s. But that is not really surprising. Institutions usually respond slowly to changes in ideology and public opinion, since they have a heavy investment in perpetuating the conflicts of the past.

The first step in the process of party realignment is the elimination of anomalous party factions—liberal Republicans and conservative Democrats. This is well under way. Both factions have diminishing influence in their respective parties. The 1976 contest demonstrated that the focus of conflict within the Republican party has shifted decisively to the right. Liberal Republicans have become an isolated and demoralized force, unable to influence party policy or run a serious presidential candidate of their own. They manage to hang on in a few areas (New England, Oregon) only because of the ability of particularly attractive candidates to draw liberal Democrat and Independent support. But that is becoming more difficult, as liberal Democrats find that they have more attractive candidates in their own party (the defeat of Massachusetts Sen. Edward Brooke) and as liberal Republicans are faced with primary challenges from the right (the defeat of New Jersey Sen. Clifford Case).

In 1978, only 6 percent of Republicans described themselves as liberals in the University of Michigan's national election survey, while a majority, 54 percent, called themselves conservatives. The balance in the Democratic party was much closer—24 percent liberals and 18 percent conservatives. Yet it also seems clear that conservatives are a diminishing influence in the Democratic party. Their position is not quite as forlorn as that of liberal Republicans only because they have somewhat stronger local bases of support.

The heartland of conservative Democratic strength is, of course, the South. Since the New Deal, southern conservatives have been an anomaly in the Democratic party. Franklin Roosevelt tried to purge them in 1938. Bourbon Democrats like Strom Thurmond and Harry F. Byrd led protest movements against the national party's presidential tickets in the 1940s and 1950s. But the decisive break came in the 1960s, when Goldwater and Wallace led massive defections of southern Democrats away from their historic party loyalty. After the national Democratic party became decisively identified with the civil rights movement in the early 1960s, Democratic candidates for President failed to carry the South in 1964, 1968 and 1972. And according to the CBS News/*New York Times* poll taken on the day of the 1976 presidential election, southern white voters failed to support one of their own; that poll showed Ford leading Carter 52 to 48 percent among southern whites.

Republicans have become dominant in presidential politics in the South, competitive in state-level contests and increasingly strong in local and congressional voting. The number of southern Republicans elected to the House of Representatives increased from 11 in 1960 to 21 in 1964, 36 in 1968 and 42 in 1972. The number dipped to 34 in 1976 but rose again to 38 in 1978. The old guard of conservative southern Democrats in the Senate is gradually dying off and being replaced by younger moderate Democrats and by Republicans.

Conservative Democrats have an even more difficult time outside the South. Occasionally they win on the basis of protest votes, but, as in the case of the "cop candidates" like former Philadelphia Mayor Frank Rizzo, they usually have tense relations with party regulars. In Massachusetts, Governor Edward J. King, who rode the tax revolt to power, has been repeatedly thwarted by a massively hostile and uncooperative Democratic majority in the legislature. The future of conservative Democrats, whether southerners or the occasional Sam Yortys and Frank Rizzos, does not seem bright.

The second part of the realignment process is the reconciliation between the moderate and ideological factions within each party—i.e., between regular and New Politics Democrats, and between moderate and conservative Republicans. That process also seems well under way. For one thing, liberal and conservative activists have tended to become the "regulars" in their respective parties. That situation is far different from 1964, when the Goldwater activists saw themselves as opposing the eastern establishment of the Republican party, or 1968, when the McCarthyites fought the Democratic party establishment. To a large extent, New Right Republicans and New Politics Democrats are the establishments of the two parties today.

Moreover, centrists in each party have become more tolerant of and agreeable to the views of their ideological copartisans. The ideological difference between Carter and Ford in 1976 was certainly greater than the difference between Nixon and Kennedy in 1960. Carter had to prove his acceptability to the Democratic left by proclaiming his total commitment to racial liberalism and his acceptance of a noninterventionist foreign policy. Ford differed with Reagan only on the issue of detente.

Survey data substantiate the fact that Democrats have been moving to the left and Republicans to the right. In *The Changing American Voter*, Norman Nie, Sidney Verba and John Petrocik measured issue attitudes in the American electorate from 1956 through 1973. The number of those holding consistently liberal or consistently conservative views increased during those years while the percentage of "centrists" declined. But among Republicans, the shift was overwhelmingly in a conservative direction. The percentage of strong conservatives doubled from about 17 in 1956 and 1960 to 34 in 1964. This figure fell somewhat in 1968 and 1972 (to 27 and 23 percent), but it remained substantially higher than it had been before 1964. The percentage of liberals hardly changed at all, remaining at about 10 percent of Republican identifiers.

By the same token, the shift was primarily to the left among Democrats. In 1956 and 1960, 15 percent of Democrats were consistently liberal in their issue attitudes, hardly more than the 11–13 percent conservative. The liberal percentage rose to 28 in 1964 and 33 in 1968, then fell slightly to 26 in 1972. The conservative proportion increased only marginally over this period, to 17 percent in 1972.

Edward M. Kennedy symbolizes the merger between the New Politics and regular wings of the Democratic party. Kennedy's base is clearly among liberal Democrats, but he also has substantial appeal to party regulars (party officials, officeholders, labor union activists and ordinary working-class voters). This, it will be recalled, is the same coalition that gave Jerry Brown his margin of victory over Jimmy Carter in the late primaries in 1976. In 1976, Brown was the stopgap leader of a makeshift coalition that would have preferred either Hubert Humphrey or Edward Kennedy. In 1980, the coalition has grown much stronger. If Carter has any base at all, it is among moderate-to-conservative southern Democrats. Carter, of course, may best Kennedy in the fight for the support of party regulars, simply because regularity implies loyalty to the party's leadership. But regulars also want to be on the side of the winners. When Mayor Jane Byrne of Chicago looked at some Illinois poll results and found out from local party leaders that President Carter had almost no support among rank-and-file Democrats, she quickly switched sides and endorsed Senator Kennedy. A Kennedy nomination in 1980 would ratify the merger between liberal and regular Democrats. It would probably also drive most of the remaining conservative southern whites out of the Democratic party once and for all.

A Reagan nomination would have a similar effect on the Republican side. Reagan has worked hard to nullify the charge of extremism that tainted Barry Goldwater in 1964. His views are certainly acceptable to most Republican centrists, if not to party liberals. The leading moderate candidates for the GOP nomination, Howard Baker and George Bush, have been moving noticeably to the right in order to make themselves acceptable to party conservatives. This is particularly true in the area of foreign policy, an old issue of contention between conservative and moderate Republicans. If the moderates are able to deny the nomination to Reagan in 1980, it will probably not be because of his views, but because of his age. If Reagan does win the nomination, it will confirm the shift of the GOP to the right and probably drive the few remaining liberals out of the party once and for all.

Such a realignment might begin the process of reclaiming the Independents, who are now threatening to become the largest group in the electorate. The survey data reveal that there are many issue-oriented voters who have refused so far to identify with a political party. That is one reason why the category of Independents has grown so rapidly in recent years; it is a home for many idealogues.

The proportion of Independents began to climb noticeably in the mid-1960s. Their numbers were swelled by the enfranchisement of 18-to-20-year-olds in 1972, but the trend was under way even before that. Recent party history shows there were some short-term fluctuations in party fortunes in particular election years. Democratic identification shot up in 1964, when Lyndon Johnson swamped Barry Goldwater. Embarrassment over Watergate can be detected in the 1974 figures, when Republican identification declined sharply. Democratic partisanship fell noticeably in 1966, when the reaction against the Great Society set in, and again in 1972, the year of the McGovern debacle. But all of these appear to have been temporary shifts when seen from the perspective of long-term trends. In the long run, both the major parties have been losing support.

But just how independent are all these newly declared Independents? In the standard survey question on party identification, those who call themselves Independents are then asked, "Do you think of yourself as closer to the Republican or to the Democratic party?" Thus, there are three categories of Independents: those who lean toward the Democrats, those who lean toward the Republicans, and the "true" Independents, who lean toward neither party. All three types of Independents are quite young compared with Republicans and Democrats. But there is a strong educational disparity between different types of Independents. Independents who say they lean toward one party or the other are among the best-educated voters in the electorate, while Independents who have no partisan inclination are among the lowest in education.

The annual surveys by the National Opinion Research Center also ask voters to indicate whether their political views are liberal, moderate or conservative. The results are worth looking at. Independents who lean toward the Democrats are the most liberal category in the electorate. They are two-to-one liberal over conservative, which is just about the same as the ideology of strong Democrats. By contrast, Independents who lean Republican are two-to-one conservative over liberal. They are as conservative as weak Republicans, although not quite as overwhelmingly conservative as strong Republicans. The remaining category of Independents, those with no partisan leanings, are preponderantly moderate, or else say that they have never thought about their ideological views. "True" Independents are quite similar to weak Democrats, who are also moderate in orientation.

Thus one can speak of strong Democrats and Independent Democrats as the key liberal constituencies; these two groups totaled 31 percent of the electorate in the 1973–1977 NORC surveys. Independent Republicans join with weak and strong Republicans to form the conservative coalition, which totaled 30 percent of the electorate. The weak Democrats and the "true" Independents are the moderate or "nonideological" groups. Weak Democrats, who comprise fully one-quarter of the electorate, are the critical category. Their traditional partisan disposition is Democratic, but they are not strongly liberal. This is the group that a Democratic nominee must hold on to in order to win the election—and the group that the party risks alienating if it continues to shift to the left.

The most interesting categories are the "Independent leaners." They are young, well educated, and strongly ideological—but they do not identify with a political party. The data show that Independent leaners tend to vote consistently for the party they feel closer to. Indeed, they are often more loyal to the party than weak partisans. But the loyalty of these voters is to their ideology, not to the party; after all, they have decided to call themselves Independents.

Is this a problem? Isn't it healthy to have Independents who vote "for the man, not for the party"? Should anyone care whether we have strong parties dominating our political life?

The principal argument for parties is that they provide continuity of responsibility. In a system of disorganized factionalism, it is difficult or impossible to relate the candidates to past policies or to make any rational calculation of what a candidate is likely to do once he is elected. A President cannot get his program through Congress where there is no sense of party loyalty or discipline. Lobbyists and special interests become particularly powerful when politicians have no stable basis of party support that they can depend on.

Party leaders used to make sure that the parties nominated candidates who were seasoned by party loyalty and tested by years of experience in public office. The system ensured that candidates were, at the very least, "reliable." Often enough the system got out of hand and party leaders chose candidates who were too reliable—i.e., party hacks. But since party leaders' principal interest was in winning, they were usually careful to nominate candidates with at least a modicum of public appeal. Nowadays, public appeal and media effectiveness count for everything, while experience and reliability mean little. The effect on the quality of our officeholders is readily apparent.

Certainly strong parties would do no worse. In any case, we may soon have the opportunity to find out. If it is true that Democrats are more and more likely to nominate strong and consistent liberals and that Republicans are more and more likely to nominate strong and consistent conservatives, the result ought to bring Independent leaners into closer identification with the parties, and therefore breathe some new life into the party system. The greater philosophical conflict that such a realignment would generate would also strengthen party involvement. With such a shift in prospect, it is no wonder that present politicians anticipate that 1980 will be a "watershed year" in our politics.

TO THE STUDENT: A COMMENTARY

He does not call it such but David Broder advocates a doctrine of "party government," or what some scholars label a responsible two-party system. The doctrine of party government holds that the best way to make governing officials responsive and responsible to you and other citizens is by making them dependent upon political parties for their election. Being thus dependent upon the political party, the party can then make officials do its bidding. Failure to toe the party line would result in a loss of party backing for reelection. Since each political party would make clear to you its proposed programs, then you as a voter could make your desires for policies known by voting for a particular party. If that party failed you while in office, you could then "throw the rascals out."

The plan sounds simple enough, but is not all that easy to achieve. Both David Broder and William Schneider give you some reasons for the difficulty. Broder, for instance, presents a brief but clear picture of how things have changed in party politics since the 1940s and 1950s. In that era candidates exchanged loyalties to party for party support. But latter-day Kennedys, Carters, Fords, Nixons, Reagans, and others build their own organizations of professionals and volunteers. They owe little or nothing to party and, hence, once in office are not eager to follow party wishes. In fact, by winning office the candidates often win control over party organizations. Parties are dependent upon candidates, not vice versa. The tail wags the dog.

Yet the candidates still incur obligations—if not to party then to other groups that help elect them. Broder calls these "single-issue groups." Each has an ax to grind. Some have the "single interest of seeing a certain policy adopted," others of "having a certain candidate elected." Through campaign contributions, organized volunteers, hired consultants, and pressures on officials the single-issue groups meld a combination of bucks, vols, pros, and pols that can scarcely be ignored. Those who pay the fiddler, in short, call the tune. The upshot is a fragmented politics closer to what you encountered in chapter 5 as a polyarchial model of power elites than one of convergence.

Single-issue groups, single-shot candidates, single-issue politics—small wonder that Broder thinks the party's over! Parties, he concludes, must be reinvented. Not every writer is so pessimistic. And, in recent years a number of theories about the future of America's political parties have been offered to rebut the "party decomposition" view that the party's over. For instance, pollster Louis Harris thinks that an influx of socially aware groups into the Democratic party may revitalize the party of Thomas Jefferson, Woodrow Wilson, Franklin Roosevelt and John Kennedy. The groups include both "haves," i.e., educated, moderately affluent, middle-class Americans concerned about problems of energy, the environment, and social change; and "have nots"—i.e., the poor, racial minorities, women seeking equal rights, etc. Such a new Democratic majority will force a Republican response, thus bringing that party, too, toward a broader, less special interest-oriented appeal.

Columnist-commentator Kevin Phillips has taken another view—in fact two. Writing in the 1960s—and observing the growth of the Republican party in the Southern Rim and sun-belt states of the West—Phillips spoke glowingly of "an emerging Republican majority." Richard Nixon's ascendancy to the presidency in 1968, he thought, was proof of that thesis. More recently, however, Phillips has had second thoughts. The return of the South to Democrats with Jimmy Carter, continuing failures of Republicans to win congressional majorities, and a host of factors associated with what Phillips regards as technological changes in a "post-industrial society" provoke his double take. Now he writes of "mediacracy"; that is, a government influenced by the mass media rather than parties, special interests, or other power centers.

And, you have already been introduced to the view of Richard Scammon and Ben J. Wattenberg. For Democrats and Republicans to survive and prosper, you recall, they must be neither overly liberal nor conservative in appeal. Candidates who are victorious will be so because of the ability to attract votes among moderates of left, right, and center. The real majority is neither Democrat nor Republican, but moderate.

Now comes William Schneider with his thesis. Consider it. Note that he agrees in some respects with David Broder. He, too, thinks political parties have changed as a result of how candidates go about campaigning. Mass marketing has replaced a conflict-oriented style, he notes. Party loyalties have declined. Parties don't screen candidates, candidates capture parties. One result of all this is that each party has strange and uneasy bed-fellows within it. So among Democrats you find the left, right, and center; among Republicans you have Wall Street, Main Street, and Easy Street.

But, writes Schneider, the presidential election of 1980 might mean the end of such divisions. Party realignment might be the order of the day. If so, each party will eliminate its "anomalous party factions—liberal Republicans and conservative Democrats." Here is where you enter the scene and put your political watching skills to work. You know what happened in 1980. Moreover, you have read in earlier chapters what happened in previous presidential elections. Are there any problems raised by Schneider's analysis for you?

Look, for instance, at what Schneider has to say about "the heartland of conservative Democratic strength, the South." He argues that Democrats are having an increasingly hard time in the South (the Southern Rim?). "Republicans have become dominant in presidential elections in the South," writes Schneider. But wait a minute! How does that square with what you read in chapter 4? Didn't Jimmy Carter—contrary to what Schneider asserts—do well in 1976 in the South? Did the Democrats do as well there in 1980?

Look also at what Schneider says about the Republicans. Did Ronald Reagan's success in seeking the 1980 presidential nomination reflect a victory of Main and Easy Streets over Wall Street? If so where did that leave alignments within the Republican party? Were the anomalous liberal Republicans banished?

And, as you are pondering those questions, look at one other feature of 1980, which Schneider could scarcely have foreseen when he wrote his article prior to the presidential nominations of 1980. That feature was the candidacy of John Anderson as an independent. Where was his support? Was it among liberal Republicans departing the Grand Old Party, pro-Kennedy Democrats unable to abide Southern conservatives, or those Schneider labels "among the best-educated voters in the electorate," Democratic- and Republican-leaning independents?

Schneider's thesis is provocative and well worth your speculation in light of the events of 1980. Broder may think the party's over but Schneider just thinks its changing places. "The Beat Goes On" was a hit pop tune of the 1960s; another pop tune by the same name made it big on the singles charts in 1980. Perhaps the title is prophetic. Despite the readiness of political observers to sound the death knell of our political parties, or see them undergoing an identity change, they may just go on—sometimes winning, sometimes losing; sometimes powerful, sometimes impotent; but always as loose coalitions of diverse, conflicting interests.

As noted, theories about the future of our political parties are in great supply. Those writing with a journalistic bent on the matter include:

David Broder, *The Party's Over*
Kevin Phillips, *The Emerging Republican Majority*
Kevin Phillips, *Mediacracy*
William Rusher, *The Making of the Majority Party*

And the fortunes of our political parties have been assessed frequently by political scientists. Among the works you will find most rewarding are:

Everett Carll Ladd, Jr., and Charles D. Hadley, *Transformations of the American Party System*
William J. Crotty and Gary C. Jacobson, *American Parties in Decline*
E. E. Schnattschneider, *The Semisovereign People*

7 The New Politicos

INTRODUCTION

You have probably seen it. A handsome, greying gentleman assures a young house-wife, or business associate, or luncheon companion that cutting down on caffeine does not mean giving up coffee. The gentleman, actor Robert Young, recommends a popular brand of decaffeinated coffee. It works—the cares, frustrations, and irritations of daily living wash away. There is no mention that Robert Young for years starred as Dr. Marcus Welby in a hit TV show, that his performance was so convincing people wrote letters to him as though he were a physician. But the Young-Welby identification lingers. If Dr. Welby recommends Sanka brand, it must be good.

Yet it is Robert Young, not Marcus Welby, who hucksters the product. Would the TV commercial be even more appealing if Welby were the salesman? Apparently some producers of televised ads think so, at least producers of political spots. It is April, 1980, and the Pennsylvania Democratic presidential primary is but a few days away. On the TV screen actor Carroll O'Connor's easily recognizable features appear. But wait a minute. No, it is not O'Connor but the television character he made famous—Archie Bunker of "All in the Family" and "Archie Bunker's Place." It must be a spot promoting a forthcoming episode, you think. But, no, as Archie Bunker he urges you to vote for Senator Edward Kennedy in the upcoming primary; for Archie like you worries about inflation, interest rates, and the economy.

Such is the world of the "new politicos," or at least one segment of them. Paid, professional specialists in producing television commercials comprise that segment. Along with campaign managers, political consultants, pollsters, speech writers, speech coaches, direct mail specialists, public relations personnel, fundraisers, and many, many others they constitute a new breed of politician. Some watchers of politics argue that these new politicos are an emerging political elite, a cadre of technicians indispensable to electoral victory in a mass mediated age. Others, such as David Broder or William Schneider, view the new politicos as sources of party decomposition and creators of a mass-marketed political style.

171

The two articles in this chapter provide an opportunity for you to learn about the practices and approaches of the new politicos that merchandise candidates on television. The first selection, "The Ford and Carter Commercials They Didn't Dare Run," provides a backstage look at the people who make political TV spots, how they do it, and the tensions that develop among them over how best to market a candidate. In 1976 President Gerald Ford and challenger Jimmy Carter each spent approximately $22 million in their general election campaigns. For Ford almost $8.5 million of that went for TV spending, for Carter approximately $11 million. In the following article Edwin Diamond gives you insights into how all that money was spent.

Edwin Diamond is a close student of the relation between politics, the press, and television. Although a senior lecturer in political science at Massachusetts Institute of Technology, he is a journalist by trade. He is a commentator for the *Washington Post-Newsweek* broadcast group and a senior editor of the *Washington Journalism Review*. He has written two books critical of the notion that television is an all-powerful political force, *The Tin Kazoo* (1975) and *Good News, Bad News* (1978). In 1980 he turned his hand to biography and was coauthor of a psychological study of *Jimmy Carter: An Interpretative Biography*.

Producing TV political commercials is an art form. Like any artistic enterprise it reflects the values, institutions, and rituals of its society. Political scientist James E. Combs argues that the art of TV political advertising is even more; that is, he thinks of "Political Advertising as a Popular Mythmaking Form." His study links political advertising to commercial advertising. He makes clear how many of the goals and practices associated with the latter are the basis for political commercials. As you read his selection pay particular attention to his discussion of the emergence of political advertising and to changes in styles of presentations, "positioning" and image making. Then think back to Diamond's behind-the-scenes glimpse at the Ford and Carter commercials. Does what Combs is saying suggest reasons why those commercials did not air?

Jim Combs teaches political science at Valparaiso University, a position he assumed in 1972. His roots are southern and one of his ancestors was a noted figure in Virginia politics. Combs studied at the University of Tennessee and East Tennessee State University, and received an M.A. in political science from the University of Houston and Ph.D. from the University of Missouri at Columbia. He views life and politics as a series of unfolding dramas, most without a scriptwriter. His books reflect that judgment: *Drama in Life* (1976), *Dimensions of Political Drama* (1980), and *Subliminal Politics* (1980). He is engaged in a book-length study of popular culture and politics, hence the article here.

THE FORD AND CARTER COMMERCIALS THEY DIDN'T DARE RUN

Edwin Diamond

Reprinted from More, 6 *(December 1976): 12–17.*

Jimmy Carter may have won the election, but he lost the campaign. Everyone on Madison Avenue knows that. Even if the more conservative polling figures are used, Carter came close to squandering a 15-point lead. Most media specialists credit the "brilliant" Ford media campaign for making the race close.

But most media specialists have not yet begun to appreciate the fact that the Ford media blitz was more accident than design. The Ford camp fought heavily in the last week because it hadn't pulled itself together early enough to get air time until the very end. And still fewer "experts" realize that the "brilliant" Ford campaign they saw on network television was not necessarily as good as the campaign they didn't see. Throughout the month of October, Ford's Campaign '76 media group headed by Bob Bailey and John Deardourff in Washington, had commissioned a series of six anti-Carter spots. By mid-October, one was already running in most key states—with devastating effectiveness: a 60-second spot featuring man-in-the street interviews with drawling Georgians who quite credibly professed serious doubts about their former Governor's trustworthiness and performance in office.

Meanwhile, on 44th Street in Manhattan, a commercial production house called Winkler Video was finishing tough last-minute anti-Carter ads, some of which were beginning to be aired in the last week of the campaign. One of these, dubbed "Title Crawl" by the Ford media people, was particularly strong. For those of you—and that includes most Americans—who never got to see it, "Title Crawl" opens on a still picture of Jimmy Carter. White type on the black screen is accompanied by a brisk off-camera voice: "Those who know Jimmy Carter best are from Georgia. . . . So we thought you'd like to know. . . ."

Then comes the crawl, or rather march, of Georgia newspapers, white type on black screen: The Savannah, Georgia, *Press* endorses President Ford; the Savannah, Georgia, *News* endorses President Ford; the Albany, Georgia, *Herald* endorses President Ford. . . . The big Atlanta papers aren't there, but how many non-Georgians would catch this? What the TV audience sees is what appears to be more newspapers than most viewers dreamed *existed* in Georgia. One after another, they reeled off their rejection of their native son. The "We thought you'd like to know" line, of course, steals from Exxon's highly visible corporate image ad, the one that shows how much wildlife loves an oil well in the wilderness.

Perhaps the toughest—"I don't like the word 'negative,'" says Deardourff—anti-Carter ad of all was the one nobody saw. It was finished about 10 days before election day. When the storyboard for this particular spot, dubbed "Personal Taxes," came through to Winkler Video, no one had to tell Michael Owen, the man in charge of production, that it required "special handling." "I just kept it separate from the others," Owen recalls. "It was a rough ad."

The spot starts with an excerpt from one of Jimmy Carter's own commercials in which Carter talks about certain tax law inequities that favor the rich and concludes, "That's disgraceful," as the words ACTUAL CARTER COMMERCIAL are superimposed on the picture. Carter continues to talk about tax loopholes for millionaires. Then the picture freezes over Carter's image, and the voice-over states: "The millionaire Carter family took advantage of tax loopholes to reduce their taxable annual income from $135,000 to below that paid by a family of three earning $15,000 a year . . . and *that's* disgraceful."

With all the money and TV time at their disposal, with all the tests apparently showing their spots so effective, why didn't the Ford people air more of the "Title Crawl" and Georgia-man-in-the-streets spots?

The answer, it seems, is that there was not one, but three, Ford media campaigns. Three different "teams" ran the operation at one time or another, calling different signals. And even *within* each team, there was a split between going with "positive" or "negative" advertising. It may be that the Ford people ultimately were seduced—and abandoned—by their own jingle, the upbeat one that talked about "Feelin' Good. . . ."

When the President Ford Committee (PFC) organized its media operations in the fall of 1975, it borrowed a page—but not, mercifully, the book—from the Nixon campaign of 1972. Nixon's CREEP organization had an in-house media operation, known as The November Group, to create, produce, buy the time for and distribute all campaign advertising. The Ford committee set up a similar operation, using staff on leave from Grey Advertising, Leo Burnett, McCann Erickson, J. Walter Thompson and other well known advertising agencies. The Ford in-house operation was known as Campaign '76, Media Communications, Inc., and it was housed on L Street in Washington, just up the road from *The Washington Post*. The chief executive officer was Peter H. Dailey, a Los Angeles adman. Bruce H. Wagner was executive vice president. Winkler Video, in New York, did all the production of the television and radio spots. Dailey-Wagner eventually became known as Team One; two other "teams" were later to take the field for Ford in the campaign.

The Dailey-Wagner team fashioned in Wagner's words, an "assumptive" strategy for Ford. The Ford media campaign would emphasize the strengths of the presidency and of Gerald Ford. The ads would not even mention his opponents in the primaries or in the general elections. "Our plan was to be positive and presidential and to stick with those themes," Wagner says.

If you happened to live in any of the contested primary states, you might have seen, briefly, Campaign '76's "Oval Office" commercials: President Ford listening to aides, smoking his pipe, wearing a vested suit, striding through the White House, gravely ticking off his accomplishments, presiding at Cabinet meetings. The tone was documentary, the colors blue and gold, the storyboards carefully researched to address the concerns that Campaign '76 polling surveys had shown to be on the minds of the electorate. About $1.2 million was spent on the assumptive commercials through May . . . and then the whole "presidential" ad campaign was dumped unceremoniously right before the California primary.

"When it got down to the short strokes before California," Wagner says, "the White House panicked." Wagner diplomatically refuses to say who the panicky people were, although most lists include the names of Bill Carruthers, a White House media adviser, Ron Nessen, the press secretary, and Richard Cheney, the White House chief of staff. Whoever "they" were, "they" did an end run around Campaign '76. "Suddenly a separate loop developed in our advertising," Wagner says. They brought in Jim Jordan of BBDO and Jordan turned out three so-called slice-of-life commercials for Ford which used professional commercial actors and actresses to pose as average citizens. Slices of life went on the air in California only to be yanked off after 48 hours, but they have become instant legends among campaign media watchers; they are probably the most heavy-handed and amateurish campaign spots ever aired by a major candidate ("worse than Mr. Whipple," one media consultant says).

In one "slice," a pretty young actress outside a studio-set "President Ford Headquarters" runs into another pretty young actress emerging from a supermarket with shopping bags. They are apparently meant to impersonate housewives. Actress number one says she is working for the election of President Ford. "Did you know he's cut inflation in half?" she asks. "In half?" exclaims the other woman. "Wow!"

In a second "slice," a father holds up his son to see President Ford, the man who makes us all feel proud again. The actors are clearly in a studio; the Ford footage, just as clearly, comes from news film. The splicing is clumsy; not even the four-year-old son would be fooled on seeing it on television. The third slice-of-life commercial puts two handsome, lean-jawed actors, better cast in Brut ads, in yellow hard hats, then splices together some Ford news film footage so that the hardhats seem to be watching Ford come by their construction site. They talk about how Ford has put working men like them back on the job again.

Michael Owen, the producer who worked on all the Ford spots at Winkler Video says, "Those workers wouldn't convince anyone in a bar in Queens." Robert Winkler, the affable head of Winkler Video, says simply, "They were shitty." Bruce Wagner says, "There was a lot of bad comment about slice-of-life as soon as they got on the air. . . . The audience is smart, admen have to respect it. You can't jerk people around."

Still another "loop" developed in Campaign '76—the first purely negative anti-Reagan spots. "They" commissioned a California-based firm to make a Rhodesia commercial. The commercial quotes a Ronald Reagan line about the hypothetical possibility of sending American troops to Africa. A middle-aged woman talks about how the campaign issues are becoming clearer. She concludes: "Governor Reagan can't start a war. President Reagan can."

The Rhodesia spot got one day's exposure before it was killed because of an outcry from GOP people concerned about splitting the party à la Goldwater. But that was enough for Dailey and Wagner: they both resigned. Campaign '76 shrunk from a staff of around 35 to a five-person holding operation. June, July and half of August went by with the Ford media operation essentially dead in the water.

The Feelin' Good Strategy

The week of the Republican National Convention, Bailey, Deardourff and Eyre came aboard. John Deardourff is a youngish, bright, attractive campaign specialist who usually takes on young, bright, attractive, moderate Republican candidates; his commitments when the President Ford Committee called him included Kit Bond and John Danforth in Missouri, Jim Thompson in Illinois and Pierre DuPont in Delaware. Deardourff spent a week in Vail with Ford and his White House staff after the convention getting to know the candidate. Together with Bob Bailey he developed a Media Planning Document for Ford; the campaign would emphasize two major positive themes—the character and decency of Ford and the progress the country had made since Nixon and Watergate. They were back on the "presidential" track after the California panic. Things were better, the bitterness was gone, Deardourff maintained. The general plan was later sharpened to diminish the amount of actual open campaigning Ford would do. Campaign director Stuart Spencer said he wanted to maximize Ford's good points and minimize his liabilities. He would keep the President off the stump and in the Rose Garden. Mainly Ford would appear in controlled television situations in order to decrease the opportunities for Chevy Chase-isms by Ford—misstatements, mispronunciations, malapropisms and other stumbles and pratfalls. "We faced it," a White House man told me. "Ford is not a great speechmaker. He is not great in news conferences. We had to find a setting in which he was comfortable."

Deardourff and Spencer spent more than half their $21.3 million federally mandated bankroll on a radio/television campaign between October 10 and November 1. This media blitz was aimed at the Big Eight states—such as New York, California and Pennsylvania, with their 228 electoral votes—and at the "second tier" states—like the Carolinas, Virginia, Wisconsin and Oregon.

The media blitz used two types of commercials—national "concepts" shown on network television, and regional spots with specific appeal for different parts of the country. The national concepts were upbeat: their themes were expressed in the Pepsi-Cola-like jingle "I'm feelin' Good About America." When Ford appeared he was always in controlled situations—speaking from Air Force One, for example, or taking softball questions from Joe Garagiola on "The Joe and Jerry Show" shown on state-wide networks in the last week of the campaign. (Joe: "How many leaders have you dealt with, Mr. President?" Jerry: "One hundred and twenty-four leaders of countries around the world, Joe.") The regional ads used local "advocates" to speak for the President—John Connally in Texas, Strom Thurmond in South Carolina, Governor Ray in Iowa.

Deardourff estimates that 75 per cent of the TV ad material was "very positive," some of it to the point of being hazardous to the health of any diabetics who might have been watching.

Well, the ads were extremely good as television—that is, high in production values. Tony Schwartz, for one, admired the Deardourff work; he found it "more current and contemporary than the Rafshoon Carter product. If anyone looked closely, they would have thought Dailey-Wagner were back."

Deardourff, though, did do some tough stuff in the form of twelve "man-in-the-street" sequences. "I want a Georgian for President," a woman says in one of the commercials. "But not Carter."

Still, the Ford people knew the negative ads were achieving results. "The strategy as it took shape," recalls Ford media consultant Phil Angell, "was that during the week of October 18 we ran exclusively on network television those Atlanta man-in-the-street anti-Carter ads. . . . The heavy thrust of these coincided with the last downward spiral of Carter and the upsurge of Ford in the polls." According to Angell, Ford's polling expert Bob Teeter believed that "those commercials were as responsible as anything for narrowing the gap."

But on October 25, one week before the end of the campaign, the Ford media strategists began to withdraw the anti-Carter man-in-the-street spots from the air, and replace them with pro-Ford man-in-the-street spots, pro-Ford mini-documentaries with the "Feelin' Good" jingle and half-hour documentaries produced daily in each state where Ford campaigned—the ones hosted by genial Joe Garagiola.

Why phase out the commercials that seemed to have done so well for Ford? It was all part of a game plan drawn up several weeks earlier, according to John Deardourff and Phil Angell, a game plan they were unwilling to tinker with. "We phased out the anti-Carter material in the final days of the campaign because we wanted to finish the campaign on a totally positive note," Deardourff says. In fact, beginning on Friday of the last weekend of the campaign *all* the anti-Carter man-in-the-street spots were yanked.

Nevertheless, the Ford people had tested and held in reserve two very strong direct (as opposed to man-in-the-street) attacks on Carter that final week. Eight days before the vote, Bob Teeter, Phil Angell and other Ford media aides flew out to a motel in Cleveland where they assembled a small demographically representative "focus group" of potential voters, and screened both negative spots for them, then questioned them about their reaction.

One of the spots, called "Map Zoom," opened with a map of the U.S., zoomed in on the state of Georgia and used the Carter line "What he did for Georgia, he'll do for America" to launch an attack on what Carter *did* do for Georgia—his record as Governor. The Cleveland focus group liked this one, and it appeared in several spot markets in the last week of the campaign.

The other one tested that night in Cleveland—the "Personal Taxes" spot—came closest to a personal attack on the candidate's character. It made a strong case that Carter was a hypocrite for denouncing tax breaks for the rich while his "millionaire" family was growing fat on them.

But according to Ford's media men, this powerful spot that they all found "very effective" was kept off the air not because it was too tough but because the Cleveland focus group that night found it "too confusing." The reason? It was the intricacies of the tax laws, not the complicated structure of a Carter commercial within a Ford commercial, according to Angell, who wrote the spot. Of course, the Ford campaign's predisposition against negative spots—they had certainly been burned by the anti-Reagan Rhodesia spot in the last minutes of the primary campaign—increased the odds against such a strong anti-Carter commercial running, no matter what the Cleveland focus group said.

Asked after the vote whether he regretted the decision to phase out the negative and return to the presidential spots in the final days, Deardourff said, "In an election as close as this there are 50 things you wonder might have made the difference, but if I had to do it over I would have made the same decision." Despite the phenomenal success of the Ford media campaign in making it that close, it could perhaps be said that its obsession with being presidential cost them the presidency.

Two Admen's Two Jimmys

Inside the Carter camp in that frantic final campaign week a decision had to be made not unlike the one the Ford people faced—to run or not to run a series of tough, anti-Ford commercials produced by legendary media guru Tony Schwartz, or to continue running the down-home image advertising that Atlanta adman and longtime Carter confidante Gerald Rafshoon had produced—which had done little to slow the slippage of undecided votes to Ford on the can-you-trust-Carter issue.

"I have a reputation for toughness," the 50-year-old Schwartz concedes, although he likes to think of himself as an all-round media campaign theorist and designer of "deep sell" rather than just "hard sell" political ads. He earned the guru tag working on the team that produced the now notorious anti-Goldwater spot featuring a child counting daisy petals which segues into an apocalyptic nuclear blast countdown, complete with mushroom cloud. The "daisy spot" appeared exactly once in 1964, before protests led the LBJ campaign to kill it overnight.

That was one more time than certain other Schwartz negative classics were allowed to appear. The napalmed baby, for instance—he did that one for George McGovern in 1972. It featured a news clip of a shocked and terrified Vietnamese mother fleeing down a road cradling her scorched child, burnt skin hanging loose from its body like a torn shirt while a jet engine roars on the sound track. The anguish on the mother's face is as searing as the wounds on the child's body. The voice-over—Schwartz's own five-year-old son—asks, "Does a President know that planes drop bombs?" Then the message: Vote McGovern. McGovern's people vetoed it. Schwartz also produced some of the extremely tough Watergate commercials McGovern *did* run in '72, spots that used the words "lying," "dishonesty," "stealing" and "bribery," to the accompaniment of Woodward and Bernstein clippings about the break-in. Schwartz is also capable of doing positive, empathic, symbolic commercials—he's worked for 230 Senate and House campaigns since 1964—but when news leaked in mid-October that Carter media man Gerald Rafshoon had made a pilgrimage to Schwartz's studio in a converted Pentacostal church near Manhattan's Tenth Avenue, the move was interpreted as a sure sign that Rafshoon's Atlanta-based media operation and the campaign strategy he fashioned down there were being abandoned in panic, and that Carter was ready to go for the jugular.

It wasn't quite that simple. In fact, one week after the election, Schwartz and Rafshoon were still sniping at each other in print over who came to whom and why, and over which of the 25 spots Schwartz produced should have been aired and why 10 of them never were.

Oddly enough it was *The New York Times'* media watcher who first brought the two media manipulators together. Joseph Lelyveld was interviewing Rafshoon during one of the Atlantan's trips to New York and suggested a visit to Tony Schwartz's studio. Up until that point, the entire Carter media campaign had been a Rafshoon exclusive.

Jerry Rafshoon and Jimmy Carter were together right from the start, 10 years ago, in that first unsuccessful race for Governor of Georgia. Carter is the first and only political client of Rafshoon's Atlanta-based advertising agency, and Rafshoon has been a member of the inner-circle—the Georgia Mafia. Beginning with the Iowa caucuses and the New Hampshire primary last winter, Rafshoon used a country and western theme in his Carter commercials. He put the candidate in work shirts and had him walk the peanut fields while a guitar picked out a Down Home sound. Technically, he used a lot of movement: jump cuts, marching bands, "honey" shots, cutaways, faces in the crowd. The candidate moved about in the Rafshoon spots, pressing the flesh, kissing cheeks, pulling up peanut roots. "Rafshoon was on a film trip," Tony Schwartz says in retrospect, neither praising nor condemning. In the standard five-minute Rafshoon-produced Carter biography, shown during the primaries and in the general election, the words "love," "home," "family," "land" and "hard work" occur a half-dozen times.

When Rafshoon got Carter off the farm in his commercials, he typically showed him campaigning, speaking in three-quarter profile to an audience or reporters off-camera ("Now listen to me carefully, I'll never tell a lie. I'll never make a misleading statement, I'll never avoid a controversial issue. Watch television, listen to the radio. If I ever do any of those things don't support me . . .").

These twin themes of the Rafshoon spots—on the farm, on the campaign trail—became the basic building blocks of the Carter media campaign. As Rafshoon explained his campaign to *New York Times* reporter Joseph Lelyveld: "It's Jimmy. . . ." The commercials reflected the man.

The man, however, was looking like a loser when Rafshoon went to Tony Schwartz for help. With his wife Reenah doing most of the writing, Schwartz designed 25 commercials. Carter himself twice slipped away in the midst of furious campaign schedules to sit at Tony Schwartz's microphone and look into his cameras.

More than half the commercials Schwartz did for Rafshoon were "positive," or "symbolic" spots. There was Carter dressed up in a "presidential" suit and tie looking into the teleprompter and talking about his hope for America and the need for leadership on the issues. Then there were the symbolic spots: E.G. Marshall's voice over stills of FDR and JFK and then Jimmy Carter, a kind of rendezvous-with-destiny approach to the campaign ("What happens if people ask why we left out LBJ?" Schwartz asked Rafshoon. "We'll tell them we forgot," Rafshoon reportedly replied).

Then finally there were the "negative" commercials—13 of them. Most of them never made it on the air, because Rafshoon rejected them. In one, a New York actor named Michael Fairman, quotes, in biting tones, a Republican Party comment about "necessary unemployment." *Necessary* unemployment, Fairman says feelingly. In a second unused commercial, an off-camera voice ticks off all the Ford "against" positions—against medicare, against job training, against school lunches, against food stamps, against day care. The voice-over asks, "Who'd believe a nice man like Gerald Ford would vote against or oppose all these?"

A third no-show—the one, I suspect, is Schwartz's favorite—is a variation of the "against" commercial. The spot opens on a white sheet of paper titled, RESUME FOR GERALD FORD. The page turns and the resume ticks off all of Ford's "against" positions, once more—a series of 10 or 12 items. Finally, the voice-over says: "Mr. Ford, you can expect to hear from us November 2."

A fourth no-show takes off on the theme of the "two Jimmy Carters." The first Jimmy Carter, seen in black and white, is the flipflopping, fuzzy "fiction" depicted by the Republicans; the other, "real" Jimmy Carter, shown in color, is the leader of principle and vision.

Finally there was a group of highly evocative 30-second and 60-second picture commercials. One picture spot opens on a shot of the Manhattan skyline seen from the river. There are the sounds of the harbor, shots of the bridges, wheeling gulls. The voice-over, Carter's own, asks, "How can anyone say to this great city, Drop Dead?" In a variation, the pictures of Manhattan scenes are accompanied by distinctive cultural sounds of the city—a string quartet, the hint of a salsa, a bongo beat for a millesecond, a hora, Italian music. These Schwartz spots were rejected, too.

The only negative spot the Rafshoon people went so far as to have duplicated for possible airing was, it turned out, the dirtiest of the lot—or the strongest, depending on whose side is commenting. This one opened with newsreel shots of Russian tanks entering Budapest to crush the Hungarian uprising. Dramatic shots of pathetically armed street-fighters overwhelmed by massive Soviet artillery. "Can this President of the United States be ignorant of *this*?" the voice-over asked. "Doesn't he remember Cardinal Mindszenty?"

There is disagreement about why the Schwartz attack commercials did not run in the last two weeks of the Carter campaign. Schwartz says that the "Resume" and the "Nice Man" commercials were pronounced "too strong" by Rafshoon. "They were rejected based on some theory of Rafshoon's grounded in southern politics," he says. "In a one-party system all the fighting goes on within the Democratic party."

Carter's people say they preferred "positive" ads pointing up their man's abilities; they went to Schwartz in the first place, for spots aimed at the undecided voter. The "intimate" style of the accepted spots played to this idea of getting to know the candidate better; the others did not.

Hamilton Jordan, the Carter campaign manager, says, "Schwartz really didn't understand Jimmy." He then changes the subject. Schwartz says, "In politics you're working to win and you have to stress the inabilities of your opponent as well as your man's abilities. . . . Negative is not dirty. You've got to attack. . . . Negative can be surprisingly effective." As for the two Jimmy Carters, Schwartz says, "Since everyone was talking about Carter being fuzzy on the issues, why not deal with it directly?" That, however, is just what the Carter people didn't want to do; they were not going to spend their own money to remind voters of their candidate's alleged flip-flops. (In 1972, the most memorable of the Nixon attack commercials, pictured George McGovern as a two-faced weather vane, adjusting positions to the prevailing winds; this itself was a version of a 1968 attack commercial used by Humphrey.)

Schwartz did not know it at the time, but his desire to mount a more aggressive campaign paralleled a movement within the Carter camp led by Patrick Caddell, the Carter public opinion specialist. According to Caddell, when Carter's lead began eroding in mid-October, he and other advisers went back to the candidate with fresh data indicating that the Nixon pardon issue was "our best issue with the younger voters and independents" who were moving to Ford. "The pardon issue was vetoed by the candidate himself," Caddell told a meeting of the American Association of Political Consultants the Saturday after the election. According to Caddell, Carter didn't want blood spilled all over the floor that late in the game.

According to Schwartz, however, when he asked why the pardon was a forbidden subject, he was told that Caddell had polled people and found that they didn't feel the pardon should be an issue. What Schwartz discovered was that Caddell's polling had consisted of a "closed-end" question, something like "Do you think the pardon of Nixon should be a campaign issue—yes or no." Schwartz, a great believer in research, particularly open-ended polling questions that elicit feelings more complex than "yes" or "no," thinks that if Caddell had asked people how they actually felt about the pardon, many of the verbatim answers ("I just get this feeling there must have been some kind of deal . . ." etc.) could have been translated directly into powerful campaign spots.

How important is the advertising campaign? What if Schwartz's materials had been used? New York fell to Carter without them, but what about New Jersey and Connecticut? What if Deardourff had started earlier? Or used tougher ads? Would more "attack" commercials have helped tilt the balance to Ford in some of the closer states?

I belong in the minority. I still believe in the "old politics" of pocketbook issues, party organization and heredity—kids vote like their parents. But as Bruce Wagner says, "In a close election, where every ounce of effort is magnified, the commercials *must* influence a few per cent of the vote." And on November 2, 1976, a very few per cent *did* make the difference. So perhaps the best answer to the question of how to win a Presidential election is deceptively simple: mix the old politics with the new, turn on the electorate through the media, turn them out through old-fashioned organization.

John Deardourff, it turns out, would agree. When he looks back at his media campaign, he says he would conduct it the same way again, except of course he would like to start earlier. "It almost worked," says Deardourff. "Hell, it *did* work, considering where we were."

POLITICAL ADVERTISING AS A POPULAR MYTHMAKING FORM

James E. Combs

Reprinted from the Journal of American Culture, 2 *(Summer 1979): 331–340.*

Advertising, wrote Daniel Boorstin, was "destined to be the omnipresent, most characteristic, and most remunerative form of American literature. . . . In mid-twentieth-century America the force of the advertising word and image would dwarf the power of other literature."[1] It is common to link the rise and ubiquity of advertising with the advent of a consumer economy and the rise and wide distribution of wealth.[2] Other observers have pointed out that advertising is perhaps the most spectacular form of modern propaganda.[3] The propagandist's job is persuasion of large numbers of people, consequently knowledge of the nature of the mass media, the psychology of mass audiences, and the techniques of "reaching" potential audiences became important. Current advertising periodicals abound with the latest findings in psychological research, accounts of successful advertising campaigns and why they worked, and the most exquisite new technology. Vance Packard's famous *The Hidden Perusaders* recounted the early development of "motivational research" and the ethos of the manipulation and even creation of human desires.[4] However, many researchers have since doubted that advertising has the mass effect that early writers like Packard asserted, and of course advertising people have argued that there is nothing sinister about what they do.[5]

It was perhaps inevitable that the arts of persuasion would spread to areas other than simply selling products. Public relations and publicity firms began to sell organizations, ideas and people. Established economic institutions—automobile, oil and steel companies—began to worry about their "image" and hired public relations experts to shore up public confidence in them. Cultural organizations—religions, universities, charities—began to use advertising and public relations firms for their purposes. Publicity agents helped create the celebrity, someone "who is known for his well-knownness."[6]

In the decades since World War II, the "persuasion industry" has become more prominent in politics. Government agencies spend many millions on public relations.[7] Presidents and other political leaders (and hopefuls) maintain public relations and advertising staffs. Professional firms play an increasingly important role in the conduct of major political campaigns.[8] These professional firms brought with them many of the assumptions and techniques of non-political advertising, but soon learned what was permissible and what worked in political advertising. By the 1970s political advertising could be called an important subform of the popular art form of advertising, certainly recognizably related to commercial and cultural advertising but with some features peculiar to it.

Advertising has been called "the permissible lie."[9] It is true that much advertising makes claims which are only marginally accurate at best. But in a sense that is unimportant. Advertising is an art, and like any other art has its own form and content, traditions and conventions, standards and evaluations. A "good" ad is admired not for its certitude, but for its credibility. Many admakers have genuinely aesthetic values, and judge ads not merely for their success but for their artistry. This is not to say that the world of advertising is not manipulative, pecuniary and even cynical, but to assert that advertising people are often sincere admirers of innovations in the popular art their colleagues create.[10]

Mass advertising takes many forms, but the "art" of advertising creates drama—a pseudo-world of fantasy to which people are transported. Ernest Bormann, relying on Robert Bales' study of the process of "group fantasy," has expanded this notion to larger mass media contexts. When a message is introduced, it may conjure up fantasies among a group which they may talk about and share, "chaining out" among more group members. A shared fantasy has "characters, real or fictitious, playing out a dramatic situation in a setting removed in time and space from the here-and-now transactions of the group." The fantasy may be more real, exciting and dramatic than mundane "real life." Bormann maintains that such "rhetorical visions" are not simply the product of small group talk, but can also be the product of mass media messages—a program, news or advertising.[11] He appears to assume that a media-created fantasy has to be shared by audience discussion, but this is not necessarily the case. Advertising in particular can "transport" or "involve" an individual by appeal to private fantasies through a created drama. An after-shave lotion ad, for example, may appeal to sexual fantasies one may not want to articulate. Indeed, much advertising is directed toward the "mass" (individuals alone) rather than to the "public" (groups).[12] Mass media advertising conjures up private as well as shared fantasies.

The purpose of creating such "fantasy events" is to affect perception and, hopefully, behavior. The advertiser dramatizes things of potential concern to members of an audience. By drawing them into the created fantasy, he may then be able to shape their perceptions and, indirectly, their willingness to "buy." The after-shave lotion ad may draw males into a fantasy world of sexual prowess, and unconsciously "condition" their propensity to purchase Hai Karate. Like other forms of popular art, advertising is designed to entertain; in a sense persuasion is a function of its success as entertainment. If it successfully creates a pseudo-world for members of the mass, if they share the fantasy, then it may be able to affect behavior.

Some observers have noted that, historically, advertising has "persistently played on certain themes despite noticeable changes in decorum, style, and methods of persuasion."[13] The most familiar theme has been the linkage of a particular product, organization or individual with some deep human desire or social value. These desires and values have been termed "zero-order beliefs," those deep desires which stem from existential anxieties of ingrained social values.[14] A more useful term for such beliefs is *myth*. Often unexamined, myths are fundamental things we believe about ourselves and the world, ranging from what we might call the "mythology of the body" to myths about how the world should and does work.[15] At one end of the continuum, we hold myths about our sexuality and immortality to allay fears about impotency and death; at the other, we hold myths about the goodness of democracy and the causes of poverty. These myths are created realities, the reaffirmation of which we seek constantly, through thought and action. We "confirm" our sexuality through clothing, perfume and availability. We "deny death" by dressing "young," using cosmetic aids and taking Geritol. We find information which proves democracy is good, and vote for candidates who understand the causes of poverty as we do. The first kind of myth we may call "primal myths"; the latter, "social myths." Both are manifest in fantasy, and are amenable to manipulation by the fantasies developed by advertisers.

The fantasy dramas of modern advertising are a popular art form which present skits with mythological themes. They dramatize social or primal myths which may be associated with the product. There are a great many of these. Packard, in his chapter entitled "Marketing Eight Hidden Needs," for example, discusses emotional security, reassurance of worth, ego-gratification, creative outlets, love, sense of power, sense of roots and immortality.[16] There are others, and they vary in emphasis from era to era; perhaps archeologists of the 27th century will be able to fathom trends in American culture by looking at changes in their ads. One classic example will illustrate. The famous Listerine ads of the 1920s developed the American habit of using mouthwash (despite the fact that it is apparently useless) by appealing to primal fears. One magazine ad showed an attractive young woman looking alone and anguished. The caption read, "Often a bridesmaid but never a bride." The message described her case as "really a pathetic one." Why? "Like every woman, her primary ambition was to marry." Most of her "set" were married, she was charming and lovely, but "as her birthdays crept gradually toward that tragic thirty-mark, marriage seemed farther from her life than ever." The problem? Halitosis. The solution? Listerine. Thus anxiety about a primary life goal is alleviated. It is unlikely today that such an ad would appeal to *Cosmopolitan* or *Ms.* readers, given changes in the mythology women hold about their life goal; but certainly ads appealing to women still speak to the desire for social acceptance, sexual success and fashionability. The Virginia Slims ads which show elegant, "now" women appeal to mythology as much as did the old Listerine ads.

There are a variety of other mythical themes in commercial advertising. A common tactic is identification, or the presentation of some archetypically "ordinary" or "extraordinary" personage with whom we may identify or who arouses mythological recognition. The ordinary housewife who knows which detergent to use (as her husband does not) is a dramatization of fantasies about competence and power in everyday life. The heroic Western figures of the Marlboro commercials permit subconscious identification with an archetypical motif in American culture. One writer has suggested that ads dramatize a variety of subliminal themes, most of them relating the product to sex. The suppressed appeal of illicit and elegant sex is suggested, and associated with the product by presentation, for instance, of a party scene in which an obviously married young woman considers the "offer" of a handsome lone wolf next to a table with a "triangle" of filled liquor product glasses.[17]

Many observers have noted the presence of magic and divine intervention in advertisements. God-like figures (e.g., "Man from Glad," "Big Wally") suddenly appear and save an everyday situation. The implication is that marriage and the home are preserved by a *deus ex machina* that intervenes to avert a crisis. In other fantasy skits, an authority figure intervenes and introduces a product which solves a problem and increases social prestige. A friend introduces the protagonist to a product which makes her luncheon plates shine and "that's a nice reflection on you." Much the same presentation is made for "body products" (headache remedies, laxatives, vitamins, denture creams and so on); as in traditional magic, the potion overcomes nature in a miraculously short time. (One wag has pointed out the preponderance of body products on the national evening shows, and argued that the primal reality they portray in their fantasy skits is more "real" to the viewer than the fantasy world portrayed on the news.)[18]

Finally, in commercial advertising there is the phenomenon of "positioning." The fantasy theme of the ad involves attempting to "place" the product within a particular group or atmosphere, vis-a-vis other similar competing products. In the past few years, beer industry ads have marketed "light" beers. They have attempted to carve out a share of the market by defining their product as belonging within some particular group or atmosphere. The ads are fantasy skits which create myths about the product and its drinkers. To overcome the impression that light beers were somewhat feminine, Miller has run ads with masculine types—athletes and urbane figures such as Rodney Dangerfield and Mickey Spillane all in male-bonding situations. Slightly to the "left" of this macho world are the Schlitz ads with James Coburn, looking cool and tough, ordering Schlitz Light while people look on. In these, the clientele is more upper-middle class and suburban and includes women. Anheuser-Busch's Natural Light attempts to attract women and younger drinkers.[19] The ads attempt to portray a pleasing mythical group or world (wherein the product is prominent) with the aim of attracting individuals in the mass or groups as consumers. The more ambiguous and inclusive the appeal, the larger the potential market, but the greater the danger of becoming mythically unidentifiable; thus the advertiser may appeal to the fantasies of less inclusive and more identifiable individuals and groups.

Cultural organizations, such as churches, universities and charities, use mythical appeals in their advertising as well. In the contemporary era of intense competition for students, university ads appeal much to the myth of individuality and personal growth. Typical fantasy skits will involve a prospective student "much like you" who receives personal attention and given much curriculum choice in a "growth atmosphere" that is magically educated and transformed into an adult because of the experience. Charities hire Madison Avenue agencies to promote their fundraising campaigns, frequently appealing to our primal fears about death and disease and our sympathy for the afflicted. Typical are scare tactics, tearjerker appeals and romantic death. One anti-drunken-driver campaign included a rock ballad entitled "Janie," which tells of her dreams to write a novel and see Venice; but at the end, the voice-over says solemnly that she never made it to Venice: "Janie died on an endless road in America . . . killed by a lonely man who was drunk out of his mind." "Janie" became a big radio disc jockey show hit, and was followed by TV commercials showing a beautiful young "Janie" running on a beach, fondling her child, vibrantly alive, all ending with a shot of an empty bed.[20] It is difficult to gauge the effect of such an ad, but the appeal to myths is clear. Tony Schwartz, one of the most famous of "hitmen" in the persuasion industry, maintains that appeals to shame can have great impact on behavior. Like the close society of pre-electronic small towns, today's instant mass communications can shame people into stopping undesirable behavior. Schwartz has used the "shame pitch" to convince urban dog owners to curb their dogs, to protect old people from crime and to discourage shoplifters. The dog owner radio spot, for instance, advised us to feel sorry for someone who cannot even train a little dog: "He really should be pitied. You can't tell which end of the leash the master is on."[21]

This discussion does not exhaust the range of mythical appeals which characterize the popular art form of advertising. Indeed, contemporary advertising is perhaps a most sensitive cultural instrument for reflecting (and shaping) American social mythology and trends. Modern advertising, print, visual and audial, has succeeded in developing a fantasy world with its own motifs, logic and purposes. One observer of popular culture has called TV commercials "the sonnet form of the twentieth century."[22] And indeed, the short, tightly drawn messages of primary values found in the best print and TV ads do resemble a sonnet, although the motives behind the two forms are, needless to say, quite different. The imagery draws upon cultural mythology from primary, historical and popular sources. The myths of the rural extended family and the hardboiled detective, for example, survive as strongly in ads as anywhere else. Ads are a form of "bourgeois theater," presenting a cast of characters, settings and images which celebrate (or at least play upon) myths deep in the American psyche. With the disintegration of other institutions into cynicism, alienation or self-defense, advertising is perhaps the last ritual setting that openly affirms mythical values for popular audiences.[23]

II

Political advertising has a long history, but in recent decades has become ubiquitous and increasingly sophisticated. The decline of political parties as the mechanism of candidate selection and the rise of the primary has made mass advertising more important in campaign settings. Many of the "campaign management" experts hired by candidates have come out of commercial advertising and similar professions. It was to be expected, then, that the assumptions and habits which helped to shape the popular art forms of commercial advertising would come to the new political field. Many of the same "pitches" did not work, however, and after several decades of trial-and-error and development, political advertising has become a distinct art form. There are many different types of political advertising, such as Army recruiting campaigns, government-sponsored media campaigns to sell a policy, and "prop art." [24] But let us here limit the discussion to American political campaign television ads.

The most familiar motif is likely the association of the candidate with national political mythology. This includes embracing patriotic and political-cultural values, exploiting the "log cabin" myth, and using war hero symbols. Ads may simply present the candidate as a "talking head" expounding on his commitment to the national "civil religion." [25] Variations on this include the 1972 "Democrats for Nixon" ads in which John Connally talked of Nixon's concern with our mission and character. Perhaps the most artistic and innovative ads with this theme develop a collage of visual and audial images which are more subtle and even subliminal. The Nixon campaign of 1968 ran ads with "voice-overs" of Nixon calmly talking while the camera blended stills first of riots, Vietnam, urban and rural decay, then moving to a "continuing montage of creative and contributing faces" ("They give life to the American Dream"), then finally into a "montage of scenic values" featuring beautiful shots of mountains and oceans concluding with a sunrise. The message was auditory (the same verbal message was used on the radio), but most strikingly visual.[26] The 1976 Carter campaign used a very similar ad. In it, Carter is seen speaking of his "vision for America"; the camera fades to a montage of landscape scenes, culminating in a shot of the heads of Presidents on Mt. Rushmore, followed quickly by a fade-in to Carter's head. The subliminal message is that he will be the fifth head.[27] The combination of flattering and patriotic verbal symbols with equally moving visual symbols in a short "spot" format has become a favorite in professional circles.

Some campaign ads attempt to build myths about the candidate's heroism. This is an ancient campaign practice, dating back at least to the age of Jackson, and including certain recurrent themes.[28] Such efforts combine depictions of both political and cultural heroism, past achievements, personal traits, alleged abilities. The most straightforward are "look at the record" commercials, such as the Nixon spot ads in 1972 which were simply mini-documentaries, filled with a sequence of shots of the President conferring with aides on the way to China, shaking hands with Mao Tse-tung, and delivering the keynote speech at a White House conference. Indeed, in the 1970s political heroism has been increasingly promoted in the ads which resemble "newsreels" or news documentaries. Campaign media managers believe that people are more influenced by TV news coverage than by political ads, so they have made spot ads resemble "news." A favorite motif is to show the candidate in what appears to be a "real life" setting, either quick images of heroic action (as in the Nixon ads mentioned above), or demonstrations of democratic communication. McGovern ran ads which showed him in a factory, coat off and sleeves rolled up, rapping with workers. This *cinéma vérité* style has become a popular format in major campaigns, since it gives the illusion of a desired reality: a political figure talking and listening with ordinary people, a virtue of democratic heroism.[29] Tony Schwartz pioneered the format of recording a candidate's intimate talk to a small group for television use: "A voter wants the candidate to talk *to* him, not *at* him; to use the medium not as a large public *address* system, but rather as a private *undress* system." [30]

One major variant of this style of presentation is the "contrived spontaneity" of the talk show format. The candidate is seen in what appears to be a talk show setting, often with klieg lights, stage furniture and "discussants." The famous "Hillsboro Format" of the 1968 Nixon campaign placed the candidate on a raised stage, standing above but communicating with "average citizens" who sat in a semicircle beneath him. Nixon stood without notes or podium and talked in an informal manner to the participants. The voice-over announced at the beginning, "Recently Richard Nixon talked to a group of _____ citizens." The effect was to create the illusion that we were being let in on an informal session which demonstrated Nixon's openness, grasp of the issues and willingness to talk with ordinary citizens. The visual imagery of him "above" the people but communicating with them, heroically standing as the "man in the circle," was "a triumph of form over content." [31] The fantasy was created and shared by a mass audience that the situation was spontaneous and the candidate heroic.

The other extreme from these "democratic" and "intimate" motifs is the image of omnipotence. In these ads, the candidate is often not even shown, but his potency is displayed. If a candidate cannot display warmth, he can at least display power. When Nelson Rockefeller ran for re-election as Governor of New York, his campaign advertising depicted god-like power. One ad showed a stretch of road as seen from the front of a moving car, the dotted white line whipping by; abruptly, the car stops at sand; turns and the same dotted line is seen whipping by. During this, a voice simply announces that if all the roads Rockefeller had built and fixed were laid together end to end, they would stretch all the way to Hawaii! The impression was of an omnipotent heroic power (who is not shown and thus is remote and invisible) and of the performance of mighty acts.[32] Other ads will portray the candidate more directly as a kind of "Man from Glad" who intervenes in ordinary situations to help out a constituent. In both cases, there is the implication of magical powers.

Many political ads attempt to "position" the political hero in much the same way as the beer ads mentioned above do. The mosaic of symbols and images show the hero as acting in and for a particular political milieu. Issue commercials attempt to associate the candidate with an identifiable segment of the political spectrum. Both real and mythical constituencies are conjured up. A Congressman appeals to the local ethos of his district. Nixon's "forgotten Americans" of 1968, however, were in a large part a "created" constituency, one formed by identifying Nixon with a composite of positions and identifications which transcended real groups; it was an appeal not to groups but to the fantasies of the mass. Positioning in political ads does not only take the form or issue of Left-Right spectral identification; it can also take more subtle mythical forms. Gerald Ford attempted to identify himself in 1976 as "President Ford"; an experienced professional politician positioned within the Establishment "up there." Carter attempted to portray himself as "down there," someone not part of the Establishment.

(He also positioned himself in the murky Center between Udall on the Left and Jackson on the Right.) Ford ads showed heroic presidential action; Carter ads never showed him in Washington, but rather in heroic action out in the country. The Carter ads even utilized the most astounding of all created myths: that he was not even a politician. This positioning as "outside" the political world had been pioneered by Ronald Reagan in his race for the Governorship of California in 1966. The Reagan ads in that race made a virtue of necessity: since he had no professional political experience, he was cast as a "citizen politician" whose political virginity was his chief virtue.[33] This seems to appeal to the old popular myth of the "outsider," the moral individual who enters a situation (e.g., a corrupt frontier town) and "cleans it up."

Many of the fantasy dramas of political campaign advertising speak to primal myths, those deep human desires and fears which are exploited in popular drama and commercial advertising. There has always been the presentation of the candidate as a sex object (Robert Redford's wife in the movie *The Candidate* explains why she thinks he will be successful: "He's got . . . you know . . . the power"). This power can only be implied, never flaunted; but there is little doubt that the handsomeness of a John Kennedy or Jerry Brown appealed to vicarious desires. Much more common are appeals to our fears: security is a primary political symbol. In campaign ads, it tends to come out in fantasy skits which relate personal and familiar well-being (financial, social, mortal, etc.) with the political success of a candidate. Many of these are "attack" ads directed at one's opponent, conjuring up fantasies about the dire consequences which may occur if he wins. An anti-McGovern ad in 1972 showed a construction worker eating lunch on a girder; a voice intones that McGovern's "welfare bill" will make half the country eligible and you'll pay for it; the workingman's face freezes into an incredulous look; fade out.

Undoubtedly the most famous campaign ad to use a primal theme was the "Daisy Girl" ad run by the Democrats in 1964. The spot simply showed a pretty little girl picking daises in a field. She counts petals; as the count reaches ten, the motion is frozen and a countdown is heard, culminating in a shot of a nuclear explosion. President Johnson's voice is heard to say: "These are the stakes, to make a world in which all God's children can live, or to go into the darkness. Either we must love each other or we must die." Senator Goldwater is not even mentioned.[34] The ad evoked that deep familiar fear about the political world "out there" harming one's children. Although "Daisy Girl" and other ads (another showed a little girl eating an ice cream cone while a voice explained that Stronium 90 is a fallout found in milk, and that Goldwater voted against the Nuclear Test Ban Treaty) solidified the fantasy that Goldwater was "irresponsible" and "trigger-happy" with nuclear weapons.

In political advertising, then, we see many of the same mythical themes which were developed in the earlier art form of commercial advertising. It is true that certain norms of American political culture inhibit the blatant use of some commercial themes (such as sexual success). But on the other hand, the logic, much of the style, and the intentions of political advertising resemble its commercial ancestor. Both political and non-political advertising create a fictional fantasy world into which audiences may be transported; both utilize the full range of artistic devices to entertain and persuade; both are selling something, and they freely utilize symbols from our national mythology and primal anxieties as appeals. Both have taken on a "reality" for us to the extent that we accept these fantasy worlds as part of our environment, and they even appear to affect our perceptions of the world, political and otherwise.[35] The fictional world created by advertising resembles very much the definition of the "world of myth" defined by Northrop Frye: ". . . (A)n abstract or purely literary world of fictional and thematic design, unaffected by canons of plausible adaptation to familiar experience. . . . (M)yth is the imitation of actions near or at the conceivable limits of desire."[36]

As a popular art form, then, political advertising has utilized mythical "design" drawn from a variety of sources to evoke or even create a fictional and thematic world of considerable power. To use another term from Frye, politics has become increasingly a "world of total metaphor" in which the use and creation of myth plays a central role. It is a tribute to the artistic skill of the "image merchants" that they understand mythology and the human capacity to believe it so well.

References

1. Daniel Boorstin, *The Americans: The Democratic Experience* (New York: Random House, 1973), p. 137.
2. Vance Packard, *The Hidden Persuaders* (New York: Pocket Books, 1958), pp. 14–5.
3. Jacques Ellul, *Propaganda* (New York: Vintage Books), p. 68.
4. Packard, *passim*.
5. See, for example, the selections in Part V, "Communication in Advertising," in Lee Richardson (ed.) *Dimensions of Communication* (New York: Meredith Corporation, 1969), pp. 275–358.
6. Daniel J. Boorstin, in *The Image: A Guide to Pseudo-events in America* (New York: Harper Colophon, 1964), p. 57.
7. Herbert Schiller, *The Mind Managers* (Boston: Beacon Press, 1973), pp. 47–48.
8. See Dan Nimmo, *The Political Persuaders* (Englewood Cliffs, N.J.: Prentice-Hall, 1970); Robert Agranoff (ed.), *The New Style in Election Campaigns* (Boston: Holbrook Press, 1976); Melvyn H. Bloom, *Public Relations and Presidential Campaigns* (New York: Thomas Y. Crowell, 1973); James M. Perry, *The New Politics* (New York: Clarkson N. Potter, 1968); David Lee Rosenbloom, *The Election Men* (New York: Quadrangle Books, 1973); and the classic work, Stanley Kelley, Jr., *Professional Public Relations and Political Power* (Baltimore: Johns Hopkins University Press, 1966).
9. Samm Sinclair Baker, *Advertising: The Permissible Lie* (Boston: Beacon Press, 1970).
10. See, for instance, David Ogilvy, *Confessions of an Advertising Man* (New York: Atheneum Publishers, 1963); Rosser Reeves, *Reality in Advertising* (New York: Alfred A. Knopf, 1961); Tony Schwartz, *The Responsive Chord* (Garden City, N.Y.: Doubleday Anchor, 1973).
11. Ernest G. Bormann, "Fantasy and Rhetorical Vision: The Rhetorical Criticism of Social Reality," *Quarterly Journal of Speech*, Vol. 58 (1972), pp. 396–407.
12. Herbert Blumer, "The Mass, The Public, and Public Opinion," in Bernard Berelson and Morris Janowitz (eds.) *Reader in Public Opinion and Communication* (New York: The Free Press, 1966), p. 46.
13. Donald McQuade and Robert Atwan, *Popular Writing in America* (New York: Oxford University Press, 1977), p. 3.
14. Daryl J. Bem, *Beliefs, Attitudes, and Human Affairs* (Belmont, Calif.: Wadsworth Publishing Co., 1970), pp. 5–6.
15. See, variously, Ernst Cassirer, *The Philosophy of Symbolic Forms, Vol. II, Mythical Thought* (New Haven: Yale Univ. Press, 1966); Henry A. Murray (ed.) *Myth and Mythmaking* (Boston: Beacon Press, 1960); Northrop Frye, *Anatomy of Criticism* (Princeton: Princeton Univ. Press, 1957); Joseph Campbell, *The Hero With a Thousand Faces* (Cleveland: World Publishing Co., 1956); Susanne K. Langer, *Philosophy in a New Key* (New York: Mentor Books, 1951).
16. Packard, op. cit., pp. 61–70.
17. Wilson Bryan Key, *Subliminal Seduction* (New York: New American Library, 1073), pp. 92–95.

18. Ron Rosenbaum, "The Four Horseman of the Nightly News," *More* (March 1978), pp. 27–29.
19. Nicholas von Hoffman, "The President's Analyst," *Inquiry,* (May 29, 1978), pp. 6–8.
20. Ron Rosenbaum, "Tales of the Hearbreak Biz," *Esquire* (July 1974), pp. 67–73, 155–158.
21. "Shame is the name of media man's game," Chicago *Tribune,* section 1, pp. 11, October 1, 1977, reprinted from *Media Decisions* (September 1977).
22. Marshall Fishwick, course outline, "Popular Culture," Temple University, Spring 1975.
23. Marshall McLuhan, *Understanding Media* (New York: New American Library, 1964), pp. 201–207.
24. Gary Yanker, *Prop Art* (New York: Darien House, Inc., 1972); David Wise, *The Politics of Lying* (New York: Vintage Books, 1973).
25. See Roderick Hart, *The Political Pulpit* (Lafayette, Ind.: Purdue Univ. Press, 1977).
26. Joe McGinniss, *The Selling of the President 1968* (New York: Pocket Books, 1970), pp. 91–95.
27. Joseph Lelyveld, "Ford to Delay Ads on TV Until After First Debate," New York *Times,* September 14, 1976, p. 28.
28. See W.B. Brown, *The People's Choice: The Presidential Image in Campaign Biography* (Baton Rouge: Louisiana State University Press, 1960), pp. 144–145.
29. See "Political Advertising: Making it Look Like News," *Congressional Quarterly,* Vol. 30 (November 4, 1972), pp. 2900–2903.
30. Schwartz, *Responsive Chord,* p. 84.
31. Nimmo, *Political Persuaders,* p. 142.
32. Perry, *The New Politics,* p. 118.
33. Ibid., pp. 24–31.
34. Schwartz, p. 93.
35. This argument has appeared in various forms. See Jules Henry, *Culture Against Man* (New York: Random House, 1963); Nimmo, pp. 181–82; Herbert E. Krugman, "The Impact of Television Advertising: Learning without Involvement," *Public Opinion Quarterly,* Vol. 29 (Fall 1965), pp. 349–56; Marvin Karlins and Herbert I. Abelson, *Persuasion* (New York: Springer Publications, 1970).
36. Frye, *Anatomy of Criticism,* p. 136.

TO THE STUDENT: A COMMENTARY

In all likelihood you had not yet been born. The city of San Francisco in the year of 1946 blossomed with billboards. Each carried the picture of a giant politician. But the politician had no face. A billboard caption read, "Who's Behind the Recall?" Radio messages—there was no TV—wanted to know who was behind "the faceless man."

In 1946 the mayor of San Francisco, Roger Lapham, fought for his political life in a recall election. In short, people wanting him out of office obtained enough signatures on petitions to force a recall election, a referendum on whether Lapham should quit. Lapham was on the defensive, for he faced no opponent as such, just himself. So he hired a group of political professionals, Campaigns, Inc., to help in the election. Campaigns, Inc., was headed by Clem Whitaker and Leone Baxter, two highly skilled, imaginative, and experienced practitioners of political public relations. Why not make the best of a bad situation? they thought. Instead of taking the defensive, go on the attack. The faceless man theme was the attack gimmick they needed. They exploited that theme through political advertising on all available media—billboards, radio, newspapers, etc. The theme left in voters' minds the impression that sinister forces were out to take over the city, forces unnamed, hidden, and up to no good. The gimmick worked. Lapham was not recalled.

The faceless man gimmick was not the first use of political advertising for electoral advantage. Political advertising is as old as the American republic. Posters, campaign buttons, broadsides—all have been around a long time. But the faceless man did represent an early attempt of professional public relations specialists to ply their trade in politics. With the advent of television, political PR and advertising have become increasingly sophisticated. Edwin Diamond and Jim Combs give you a clue as to just how sophisticated.

Let's put televised political advertising into perspective for you. The 1950s ushered in the art. Formats for TV political commercials copied the political practices of radio and of product advertising on television. Radio ads had frequently been little more than the "live" appearances of candidates broadcast on radio—speeches at rallies, public appearances, etc. The candidate was, so to speak, "up front" and visible to TV audiences, just as candidates had been live on radio. The up front format was common to product advertising as well. Radio and TV celebrities talked directly to audiences about household cleansers, dish washing liquids, soups, teas, cigarettes, and a host of other goodies. Arthur Godfrey, a popular entertainer of the era, had an all-morning radio show on the CBS network, most of which consisted of Godfrey's huckstering. When he later became a TV star, he could often be viewed telling audiences what they should purchase. Political celebrities also did up front product advertising on TV. It was quite an event—and controversial—when a former first lady of the land, Eleanor Roosevelt, appeared in TV ads for an oleomargarine.

Typical of the 1950s, up front political advertising on TV was the series of ads on behalf of presidential candidate Dwight Eisenhower, "Eisenhower Answers the Nation." "Ike" Eisenhower would face the camera and respond to a question from an off-camera interviewer: "Mr. Eisenhower, what about the cost of living?" Ike would respond that higher prices were a problem that he and his wife, Mamie, worried about; he would as President see that they came down!

Faces of candidates virtually vanished from the TV screen in the 1960s, but political advertising did not. TV ads often consisted of graphic, animated, and entertaining messages backed by an anonymous narrator's account about the positive qualities of the candidate in question. Such advertising again aped that of commercials for products. A canned tuna, for instance, was depicted as always disappointing an animated figure, "Charlie the Tuna" who was not good enough to be chosen for Starkist. Jim Combs' selection that you just read provides an example typical of televised political advertising of the era—i.e., the Rockefeller ad graphically announcing that the governor of New York had built enough state highways to reach all the way to Hawaii, and back!

The 1970s introduced a variety of formats for political advertising on television. Dramatizations, and what Combs calls *cinéma vérité*, were important. Again product advertising served as a model. Think, for example, how often in the last decade—and this—you have seen commercials with a pair of housewives intensely debating the merits of dishwashing liquids or being "candid" about feminine hygienes. Or, consider baseball "superstar" Pete Rose telling you what to do to "smell like a man." Each format has a functional equivalent in politics. Ed Diamond, for instance, describes to you the "feelin' good" strategy of Gerald Ford's 1976 commercials, especially the "man in the street" sequences. The woman who says "I want a Georgian for President, but not Carter" reads her lines much like the young bride who finds her party glassware is spotted because she has used the wrong product in her automatic dishwasher. Or, Joe Garagiola and Pete Rose are interchangeable, even though former major league catcher Garagiola never reached Rose's superstar status.

Recent elections have spawned a new—and much larger—generation of Whitakers and Baxters. In his discussion of the 1976 presidential ads Diamond names many of them and describes their techniques—Grey Advertising, Leo Burnett, McCann Erickson, J. Walter Thompson, John Deardourff, Robert Bailey, Stuart Spencer, Gerald Rafshoon, Tony Schwartz, and many, many others. These same public relations specialists, often using the same techniques, were active in the 1980 presidential campaigns and will be again in 1984—not to mention their presence in a host of local, statewide, and congressional contests every year.

Reading what these new politicos do and how is fascinating to any serious political watcher. Diamond's narrative is informative, even titillating. But before getting too carried away with Diamond's drama of personalities and techniques, pause to think about two questions implicit in Diamond's—and Combs'—account. First, who counts most in elections today, the candidates or their paid technicians? On the surface the 1976 presidential contest was between Gerald Ford and Jimmy Carter. Behind the scenes we find two sets of PR specialists squaring off against one another, each searching for effective "positioning," "images," and the larger share of the market. Small wonder David Broder in chapter 6 told you political parties are in trouble. But that's not the whole of it, is it? What Jim Combs implies to you in his article is that—at least in product advertising—positioning and image making are important because there is *no substantial difference between competing products*. Advertisers create an artificial difference by (1) positioning a product to capture various segments of the market and (2) projecting images of the product appealing to those segments. Is that what PR technicians are doing in politics, i.e., providing an illusion of differences between competing candidates when there are no differences?

Reflect on this point even more. Diamond notes that Ford really had two marketing strategies. One stressed Ford as "the President," the other that Ford left us "feelin' good." And, Diamond says there were, for Jimmy Carter, two admen, hence, "two Jimmys." In short, depending upon who gets the upper hand among a candidate's coterie of PR advisers, the office seeker may become any one of a number of possible things. And if nobody gets the upper hand, perhaps no clear, consistent image of the candidate emerges. One is many things, hence nothing. Where does this leave you, both as watcher of politics and as a citizen trying to make an informed judgment in selecting your officials?

This raises a second set of problems you might ponder. How effective is televised political advertising? When it comes to influencing how people vote, political and communication scientists are uncertain. The general thought is that political ads probably do not determine directly how people vote, but they may influence what voters believe candidates are like. Much seems to depend upon what voters seek when they watch TV ads—advice, general information, stands on issues, perhaps just something to talk about with friends, or simply entertainment. In short, how people interpret what they receive from political ads may well have more to do with advertising's effectiveness than all of the niceties of positive versus negative ads, image making and positioning, etc. that Diamond and Combs so capably explain.

But Combs suggests another possible effect of political advertising. Political ads create myths. That is, they build pictures in our heads about what politicians are like, what they can do, what politics is like, and what can be accomplished by being a part of it all. If political advertising creates the illusion that a choice between Jimmy Carter and Ronald Reagan is no more meaningful than one between One-A-Day and Geritol, then indeed political parties, even voting, may be over. Whether such indirect effects, i.e., myths about politics, rather than direct effects—changing votes—are the results of what new politicos do, we cannot say. It is a problem political watchers—you and we—must start taking seriously.

As you start taking such questions seriously, you will find works by both political journalists and scientists useful. Of the following works, the first three are by journalists and the remainder by political scientists:

James M. Perry, *The New Politics*

Joe McGinniss, *The Selling of the President 1968*

Betsy Strom, "Political Advertising: Candidates Put Their Best Faces Forward." *Madison Avenue* 22 (March 1980): 18–28

David Lee Rosenbloom, *The Election Men*

Dan Nimmo, *The Political Persuaders*

Thomas E. Patterson and Robert D. McClure, *The Unseeing Eye*

Thomas E. Patterson, *The Mass Media Election*

8 Watching Power You Can't See?

INTRODUCTION

It is difficult—but as you saw in chapter 5, not impossible—to identify power elites, either by geographic region or by institutional position. And, it is not too hard to find out whose the single-issue interests are that threaten political parties. Persons we can label new politicos you have just observed. But there are some wielders of power in American politics not so easily detected. They are more hidden from our view, partly because you might not think of them as politically powerful. Yet they are. This chapter will assist you in uncovering them and watching what they do.

In "Power and the Knowledge Industry" political columnist and commentator Kevin Phillips points at a power complex that should be of particular interest to you. It consists of people in what he calls the knowledge industry, especially teachers and bureaucrats. As a client of that industry you may be essential to its survival. Read Phillips' argument carefully and compare what you observe as a college student with what he thinks he sees.

When Kevin Phillips was serving as the special assistant to the Attorney General of the United States in 1969, he published a book he had worked on earlier—*The Emerging Republican Majority*. Appearing as it did in the first year of Richard Nixon's presidency—and considering Nixon's reelection by a massive margin in 1972—Phillips' book seemed to harken the wave of the future. As you know, events intervened and the heralded Republican majority did not emerge. Phillips left the Nixon Administration in its earliest years and became a syndicated columnist in 1970. Articles and columns have poured forth from his typewriter ever since. In 1976 he published *Mediacracy: American Parties and Politics in the Communications Age*. As we noted in chapter 6, Phillips there turns his back on his earlier thesis about the Republican majority and speaks instead of the power of the mass media. One element in that power is the knowledge industry, the subject of the following article.

The knowledge industry can be thought of as a complex of what political scientist Mark Nadel calls private governments in his "The Hidden Dimension of Public Policy." At first blush Nadel's selection appears lengthy, at least when compared to some of the other articles in this volume, especially that by Kevin Phillips. Don't be discouraged by that. Nadel writes clearly and you will have no difficulty grasping the basic point, a point too often overlooked by political watchers. That point is that a large number of policies that influence what you do in your life are made not by elected governing bodies—say the President or Congress—or by people appointed to what you normally think of as "government" positions (say bureaucrats or judges). Rather, people in private, nongovernmental positions make key policies. The question is, how do we hold them accountable to those of us who obey those policies?

Mark Nadel has devoted a great deal of his research and writing to an area vital to you—the formation and adoption of legislation to protect consumers. In 1971 he published *The Politics of Consumer Protection*, a study growing out of interests he had as a graduate student at Johns Hopkins University (where he completed his Ph.D. in 1970). His added interests in economic policy and regulation gave rise to his reflections about the role major economic institutions, such as business corporations, play in making policies. Compare what he has to say about that subject with what Phillips argues about the knowledge industry. Where are their points of view about the same, where do they differ?

POWER AND THE KNOWLEDGE INDUSTRY

KEVIN PHILLIPS

Edited and reprinted from "A Matter of Privilege." Harpers (*January 1977*): 95–97.

Ancient Sparta was a military state. John Calvin's Geneva was a religious state. Mid-nineteenth-century England was Europe's first industrial state, and the contemporary United States is the world's first media state.

No, this isn't another attempt to blame the woes of the world on a secret cabal of Manhattan journalists. American economic and social change is brought about by the various means of communicating information and ideas—not just the words of communicators, but the paper flow of bureaucrats, the unbelievable new information systems of minicomputer technology, the voluminous output of scientists and social scientists, the influence of law and public regulation, the shapes and sounds of art.

A neo-Marxian conservative, as *National Review* once thought to libel me, might offer this explanation. As of the 1970s, 30 to 40 percent of the U.S. gross national product is accounted for by the production, consumption, and dissemination of knowledge. Not alfalfa, calico, rolling stock, or petroleum products—*knowledge*. The media in question may be government memos, school instruction, newspapers, television, foundation studies, legal briefs, computers, scientific evaluations, phonograph records, rock concerts, movies, paintings, statistical analyses, or architects' blueprints. Collectively, they have created a revolution as profound as the mid-nineteenth-century upheaval when manufacturing—now increasingly subordinated by the knowledge economy—moved ahead of agriculture.

Wait a minute, you say. Most members of the U.S. knowledge community, being middle-class or upper-middle-class, deny that they belong to a new elite, waving their overdrawn bank statements to prove that no new caste has emerged to match the industrial-era Rockefellers, Carnegies, et al. Perhaps. But let's look beyond periodic lamentations over the meager earnings of artists, teachers, and poets.

It's not necessary to demonstrate that teachers and bureaucrats now earn salaries *above* the national average. They do, and an increasingly well-paid bureaucracy is a characteristic of the media state, but the larger economic dimension of change is even more compelling. Consider two artists in very different circumstances—Pablo Picasso and Wolfgang Amadeus Mozart. The latter, working before the industrial revolution, hopped from petty ducal court to petty princely court, churning out four or five compositions a month for barely enough money to get by on. If it's Tuesday, this must be Saxony-Anhalt. Picasso, on the other hand, was lucky enough to survive into the media era. After the blue and pink periods of his younger days, Picasso died in a green period. His estate, swollen by the value of 800 of his own pictures, came to almost $1 billion. In one study of Picasso, the English critic John Berger noted that after World War II, Picasso bought a house in the South of France merely by turning out a still life. "Whatever he wishes to own," Berger observed, "he can acquire by drawing it."

To paraphrase Marshall McLuhan, the media are increasingly the money. Picasso's situation is unusual, but not a fluke. From record sales and box-office receipts, a pop star like Elton John grosses about $50 million a year. With the sale of movie rights, a best-selling author like Peter Benchley can make $10 million to $20 million out of a book like *Jaws*. Famous musicians and conductors are getting rich from record royalties. Well-known journalists increasingly constitute a financial as well as intellectual elite. Great crises can be grist for media conglomerate profits—Watergate was worth millions to the Washington Post Company. And in the bull market of the 1960s, the knowledge revolution was strongly affecting corporate finance. Half of the hot new stocks on Wall Street had such prefixes as data-, tele-, techni-, or compu-.

What's more, a parallel trend is taking shape in political finance. In the 1976 Presidential race, for example, corporate money was largely squeezed out. In contrast, the power of the new knowledge-economy organizations is increasing. The National Education Association and other fast-growing public-employee unions are wielding unprecedented dollars and clout. In Ohio, one unhappy local candidate went so far as to argue—and his theme deserves attention—that media endorsements are so powerful and important as to amount to a corporate contribution. And with individual fat cats limited in what they can contribute to a candidate, rock stars are becoming the new kingmakers—*they* can stage a concert, and raise $100,000 in small contributions for a politician in a single night. Back in November 1975, Phil Walden of Capricorn Records arranged a concert for Jimmy Carter that staffers admit saved the Georgian's campaign. Without those proceeds, Carter might have had to quit. Now the artist Jamie Wyeth is developing a new angle—painting a picture to serve as a door prize for a fund-raising event. Apparently, this also slips through a campaign law aimed at older forms of monied power.

The fact is that older forms of monied power are losing ground. Gone are the days when great landlords or aristocrats were the nation's major political patrons. Timber interests, railroads, and power companies no longer call many political shots except in a few small Western states. DuPont is losing Delaware. Wise politicians now look for patronage from the knowledge institutions—news media, universities, research institutions, and foundations. Consider the post-officeholding vocations of such conservatives as Richard Nixon, Spiro Agnew, Ronald Reagan, and James Schlesinger: they're commentators, authors, foundation organizers, and think-tank officials. Before long, we'll be adding would-be columnist Henry Kissinger to the list.

American law is changing, too, shifting as it always has to reflect major realignments of economic power. Take, for example, the recent flurry of propaganda about the public's "right to know" coupled with media invocation of a First Amendment "free press" spirit going back to the Founding Fathers. In reality, though, it's difficult to invoke Thomas Jefferson or James Madison on behalf of the new legal rights claimed by the knowledge industry, because judicial interpretation of the First Amendment is only a matter of the last half-century. Today's media power would have been absolutely unrecognizable to the architects of the Constitution. And the situation is getting worse. Like past emerging economic concentrations, the communications industry is busily trying to expand a segment of the Bill of Rights (in this case, the First Amendment) to fight off regulation. To some scholars, the news media have become "the last stronghold of laissez-faire," and justly so. The public interest has virtually no legal status or access.

Anglo-American law has always accorded privileges to power. Centuries ago, "benefit of clergy" summed up the special legal status (and privilege) of churchmen. During the nineteenth and early twentieth centuries, the wealthy enjoyed manifest legal privileges, from multiple enfranchisement to exemption from military conscription. As middle-class power grew, increasingly firm legal privilege surrounded the relationship of doctor and patient and that of lawyer and client. Now, as a result of the knowledge revolution, we are seeing the emergence of a *new* privileged class. In recent years, journalists have pretty well completed the legal fortifications around their right to refuse to divulge confidential sources. And a case in a California federal court last spring extended a kindred privilege to professors and researchers. In his unprecedented opinion, U.S. District Court Judge Charles B. Renfrew ruled:

> Society has a profound interest in the research of its scholars, work which has a unique potential to facilitate change through knowledge. . . . Compelled disclosure of confidential information would without question severely stifle research into questions of public policy, the very subject in which the public interest is greatest.

From all these perspectives, the knowledge revolution and the emergence of "the media" (in the broader sense) has caused a major upheaval in U.S. society. Places like the East Side of Manhattan and Back Bay, Boston, once the conservative residential strongholds of a conservative economic elite, are now the liberal strongholds of a liberal economic elite. Steel executives, railroaders, and cocoa brokers have been displaced by foundation executives, urban planners, and communications specialists. From Palo Alto to Princeton, scores of university towns have likewise changed their socioeconomic stripes.

As for the direct political impact of the news media, that hardly needs comment after the disturbing media-oriented nature of the 1976 Presidential campaign. Allegations of liberal ideological bias have been supplemented (or even superseded) by explanations of how the news media operate to trivialize debate. Media events have themselves emerged as the most important events of a national campaign. Meanwhile, the withering of the political parties has become increasingly apparent, and why not? After all, mass parties as we have known them were creatures of the early nineteenth-century industrial era, and there is no reason why they should serve a continuing role in the knowledge-revolution era, what with the information, mobilization, and welfare functions of the old party system so greatly usurped by the communications media and government bureaucracy.

After attending an Aspen Institute-Berlin conference this September in which American, British, and German participants discussed many of these points with little agreement, it seems to me that only we Americans are far enough into the sociopolitical upheaval of the knowledge revolution to really appreciate its consequences. I have used the term *mediacracy* to try to describe the change, but this word seems to run afoul of objections to its Agnewesque implications of a coterie of manipulators.

That's too bad, because there *is* an increasingly important media aristocracy in the United States, and the national news media *do* serve as a dissemination system and linchpin of sorts for the views of the so-called Eastern Establishment of think tanks, councils, universities, foundations, and kindred institutions. But, unfortunately, one finds an overall reluctance to discuss the emerging new set of vested interests as such. In this respect, of course, the major media and their allies differ very little from previous economic power elites. They deplore analysis and arguments that seek to strip away their philosophic mystique and present their bare self-interest, just as the Goliaths of American manufacturing disliked the arguments of Oliver Wendell Holmes and Charles Beard, men who sought to show the way in which American law reflected and evolved with economic interest. Today, "free press" is often as unthinking an industry war cry as "free enterprise" was in the long-ago days of constitutional furor over basic state economic regulation.

Back in the days when the Morgans, Rockefellers, and Carnegies were trying to portray their assorted trusts, holding companies, and watered-stock pyramids as living embodiments of the philosophy of the Founding Fathers, they did not shut off press discussion. Granted that the giants of business controlled a fair amount of the press (and awed a good bit more), there were still muckrakers ready and able to challenge them. It may be harder to challenge the knowledge-revolution elite, since the best-known muckrakers are themselves part and parcel of that interest group. After all, if we had to wait for the oil industry to open the pages of petroleum corporate journals to critical analysis of the depletion allowance, it would have been a long wait. And because the vast national scale of communications no longer permits much competitive new entry into the mass-media marketplace, any debate will have to occur largely in the existing context.

Unfortunately, and without suggesting that "the media" are a monolith, there is something dangerous in the unprecedented situation where an increasingly dominant economic interest group controls the means of its own scrutiny. Yet that is substantially the case today. If, as seems likely, the knowledge revolution is to be as powerful a force as the industrial revolution, and the rise of capitalism before it, we could do with a good bit more serious inquiry and a good bit less knowledge-industry protectiveness and First Amendment breast-beating.

THE HIDDEN DIMENSION OF PUBLIC POLICY

Mark V. Nadel

Edited and reprinted from Journal of Politics 37 *(February 1975): 2–34.*

Public policy, like obscenity, is usually defined in practice by Justice Potter Stewart's maxim: "I don't know how to define it, but I know it when I see it." On a superficial level, most definitions are in basic agreement and differences are primarily semantic. Overcoming the diversity of more specific definitions, the new Policy Studies Organization defines policy as "actual and potential government programs and actions designed to cope with various social problems."[1] More specifically, Robert Salisbury's definition states: "Public policy consists in authoritative or sanctioned decisions by governmental actors. It refers to the 'substance' of what government does and is to be distinguished from the processes by which decisions are made. Policy here means the outcomes or outputs of governmental processes."[2]

Common to these and most other definitions of public policy is the broad notion that public policy is what government does. What differences there are in definitions involve policy—the question of defining that "what" in what government does. It is widely assumed that by definition public policy is *government* policy. The present analysis is intended to examine and challenge that assumption.

The Boundary between Public and Private

The equation of public policy with government policy would be on firmer ground if there were a clear distinction between governmental (public) organizations and non-governmental (private) organizations. The line between public and private organizations has not been exact. Indeed, that organizational boundary line has long been questioned by a number of scholars.[3] This question is both paradoxical and indicative of the need to expand the meaning of "public" in the concept "public policy."

In an early discussion of the subject, for example, Charles Merriam pointed out that the "lines between 'public' and 'private' are not absolutes, but . . . there are zones of cooperation and cohesion in the common cause and on a common basis in many fields of human action."[4] Merriam, however, argued that a line between public and private existed although he did not posit firm criteria for public functions other than some consideration of the common good.

Attempting a major formulation of the problem, Robert A. Dahl and Charles E. Lindblom go farther than Merriam and dismiss the sharp public-private distinction as being foolishly rigid, unrealistic, and unnecessarily limiting of the real choices at hand. They demonstrate that the situation is more accurately conceived as a continuum on which organizations display varying degrees of public and private function. On this continuum, which shows some of the choices available between government ownership and private enterprise, the possibilities run from "an enterprise operated as an ordinary government department such as the post office" to "a hypothetical small proprietorship subject only to common law" on the private end. Various types of enterprise in the middle of the Dahl and Lindblom continuum, like subsidized corporations, the TVA, and government contracts, point out the fuzziness of the public-private boundary (and, they argue, its lack of utility).[5]

Probably because they are the largest and most pervasive entities that are popularly regarded as "private," much discussion of the private-public boundary question concerns corporations. Increasingly, the public character of the large corporation is acknowledged. For example, Dahl argues that large corporations are political entities and asserts that "it is a delusion to consider [the great corporation] a *private* enterprise. General Motors is as much a public enterprise as the U. S. Post Office." [6] But surely there are some differences—particularly in law and public conception. The question is whether there are inherent and substantial differences in function. Gordon Tullock addresses this very question:

> What then, is the difference between a government and a corporation? The answer to this question is simply that we have grown accustomed to calling one particular type of collective organization a government. Characteristically, there is one collective apparatus in society that is more powerful than any other and that can, if it comes to a battle, win over others. This apparatus we call the government. It should be emphasized, however, that the difference between this organization and a general contract is less than one might suppose. [7]

Thus, scholars in a variety of fields have come to regard the distinction between public and private, between governmental and nongovernmental as rather tenuous and artificial—particularly with regard to the management of large-scale economic enterprise. This blurring of boundaries between public and private organizations and functions has several aspects. First, the extensive co-operation between governmental and nongovernmental bodies makes it difficult to know where one ends and the other begins. The defense procurement policies instituted by Secretary of Defense Robert S. McNamara are an extreme but good example. Weapons systems were developed through the coequal co-operation of the Pentagon and "private" industry. [8] The provision of government-sponsored job training programs by private industry through the old Job Corps is another example. Morton Grodzins has shown that the interconnectedness of public and private may be even greater at the local than at the national level. In many small localities private businesses and associations perform a variety of planning and service functions in co-operation with or instead of local government agencies. [9] Also, new forms of enterprise have evolved which themselves straddle whatever distinctions may exist between governmental and nongovernmental. Comsat and Amtrak are two prominent examples.

A second feature of boundary blurring is the impact and nature of actions taken by private entities on their own. Thus, Dahl argues that large corporations are political systems:

> By its decisions, the large corporation may:
> Cause death, injury, disease, and severe physical pain, e.g., by decisions resulting in pollution, poor design, inadequate quality control, plant safety, working conditions, etc.;
> Impose severe deprivations of income, well being, and effective personal freedom, e.g., by decisions on hiring and firing, employment practices, plant location, etc.;
> Exercise influence, power, control, and even coercion over employees, customers, suppliers, and others by manipulating expectations of rewards and deprivations, e.g., by advertising, propaganda, promotions, and demotions, not to mention possible illegal practices. [10]

A third aspect of the boundary problem was extensively analyzed in studies by Grant McConnell [11] and Theodore J. Lowi. [12] Both studies are critical of the direct policy-making role played by private interests. This policy-making role is based on the delegation of governmental functions by the government to private groups—groups that are essentially unaccountable to many of those affected by the policy decisions they make. In the present context the essential point about these critiques is that the phenomenon they attack is not so much a usurpation of a policy-making role by private interests as a voluntary delegation of that function by the government. While this aspect of the boundary problem is closely related to the other two aspects, it is distinct in that it emphasizes the utilization of private organizations to perform explicitly governmental functions.

Although Lowi and McConnell explicitly deal with the co-optation of governmental functions by private entities, the ultimate conception of *public* in public policy is substantially unchanged. The co-optation is both a process and a policy. It is a process in that it is an ongoing method of creating policy outputs, one in which the official governmental input is consistently intertwined with the private input. More important, the co-optation itself is a result of explicit government policies ceding to private entities certain functions that had been or reasonably could be performed by the government. It is this initial governmental policy of voluntary co-optation which is the problem. The resultant outputs are considered public policy because of that initial series of decisions and because of the ongoing policy process. Thus the thrust of their analyses questions the legitimacy of that process. But in both cases public policy is still defined ultimately as the policies of government—even when government has allowed itself to be usurped.

A final aspect of the blurring of the public-private boundary is more fundamental and more controversial than the others: the alleged dominance of private elites in public life. Since a good many articles and books have been devoted both to positing and criticizing this proposition, it would be redundant and beyond our present purpose to rehash that debate. Suffice it to say that the power elite model holds that effective power in communities is actually held by a ruling class rather than by elected officials responsible to a widely dispersed plurality of interests. The elite is neither conspiratorial nor completely cohesive but does have a nexus of interests to which the formal government normally responds. The actual positive policy outputs thus emanate from the government although the decisions behind those policies are reached by the elite acting with and through the government. The power elite model, then, is also part of the orthodoxy in defining public policy. Power elite theorists part company with the pluralists in the analysis of the policy-making *process;* the argument is over the degree of concentration of influence on government as policy-maker—but they both see the government as the only source of formal public policy outputs.

It can be seen that we are left with a major paradox. On the one hand, it is readily acknowledged that in many instances no clear distinction can be drawn between governmental and nongovernmental organizations. But on the other hand, public policy is viewed as emanating exclusively from the government. But how can the latter definition be useful when, in many instances, it is not clear what is a government? The answer must be that the prevalent definitional equation of public policy with government policy is therefore limited and unrealistic. An alternative and preferable strategy would be to analyze the nature of public policy and to determine who makes it. One potential utilization of such a strategy can be seen if we consider the expanded and innovative analysis of the role of private elites that was posited by Peter Bachrach and Morton S. Baratz.[13] According to their conception, the power of elites to influence policy should not be measured solely by their positive actions toward their objectives, which lead to victory in a controversy, but also by their ability to keep that controversy from surfacing in the first place. Achieving a "nondecision" in an area where Participant X has an interest in maintaining the status quo is as much a demonstration of influence as if Mr. X had fought in a public controversy and won.

Therefore, there is a basic utility to looking at nondecisions. A major reason for difficulty in utilizing the nondecision concept is that Bachrach and Baratz as well as their critics all ultimately view the matter from the perspective of formal governmental institutions. That is, Bachrach and Baratz view nondecisions as issues on which the political structure of the community begs off because of anticipated reactions from the nongovernmental power structure. So the result is a nondecision by government. This conception leaves the analyst with the task of trying to study a nonevent—something which can be an exercise in metaphysics. But the conceptual trouble arises only insofar as one attempts to study the influence of powerful private interests on the formal government, and such a study leaves aside the crucial consideration that the nondecision is only a nondecision by the government (whether or not it is a conscious suppression of an issue). Decisions on the issue (or nonissue if you please) may still be made by nongovernmental bodies. Thus there are decisions and cumulatively there is a policy—policy which I will argue may be public policy in many instances. For example, air pollution may be a nonissue in a community. When no governmental regulation exists, the decisions as to air quality are left to the polluter. In a large city with many polluters, no one in fact makes the decision. The resultant policy about pollution is established by the "tyranny of small decisions." But in a single industry town, or region, real and visible decisions about pollution levels are in fact being made unilaterally.[14]

Let us recap the analysis of the role of private organizations in policy-making. We have proceeded from the participation of private organizations in governmental policy-making to the co-optation or delegation of policy-making functions to private organization and finally to a monopoly of policy-making functions by private organizations in the face of governmental noninvolvement (via nondecision) in a policy area. The subject is shown graphically in Table 25.

It is readily acknowledged that policy outputs on the left end of the continuum constitute "public policy" regardless of the participation of private groups and regardless of the blurred lines between public and private organizations. Indeed this understanding is inherent in the conceptual orientation and in the actual role of government. As noted before, even in the case of co-optation it is ultimately the government that makes the positive decision to allow co-optation and it is the government that defines the permissible range of alternatives to its (private) delegated decision-makers.

As we get to the right end of the continuum, however, the situation becomes more debatable. Who is making policy and what is the nature of that policy (if any)? Fundamental to the discussion of the nondecision question is whether government officials make an identifiable decision to stay out of an issue-area. That question can readily be bypassed and can be transformed into an inquiry about who does make the decisions relating to the policy area. The nature of such decisions is fundamentally different from those reached through all the other mixtures of public and private policy-making participation. Even in the case of co-optation, authority ultimately is traceable to the government and a specifiable boundary of decisions is discernible. Where the government is completely uninvolved, no such delegation of authority is present and no boundaries are set. The question then becomes: "Is the resultant set of decisions 'public policy'?" The answer often must be in the affirmative if we view public policy

TABLE 25 Range of Nongovernmental Group Involvement in Public Policy-Making

Noninvolvement in Public Policy-Making ← → Monopoly of Public Policy-Making

Type of Group

Nonpolitical groups (social fraternal, etc.)	Interest groups	Large scale government contractors	Delegated power recipients (Farm Bureau, medical and bar associations)	Local elites and some corporations
Neutrality	Influence	Intervention	Co-optation	Nondecision and direct policy-making

Type of Involvement

more comprehensively than has hitherto been the case. The distinction is demonstrated in Figures 2 and 3. In highly simplified form, Figure 2 represents the prevalent model of the policy-making process. The influence of various groups is filtered through the government. Most scholarly debate concerns the relative weight of influence of the various groups and elites and the process by which their influence is transmitted through the government. The present argument, however, is that the realities of policy-making by some nongovernmental groups necessitate a broader view of the policy process, represented by Figure 3. In this conception most interests contribute to public policy through government, but some interests are able to make public policy directly. To establish the validity of that rather unorthodox assertion it is first necessary to explore the essential components of public policy.

FIGURE 2
Policy-Making Process Transmitted through the Government

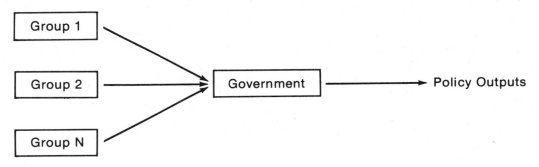

FIGURE 3
Policy-Making by Some Nongovernmental Groups

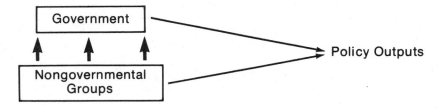

The Components of Public Policy

Since so many definitions of public policy are based on David Easton's work—or at least have his framework implicit in them—it is appropriate to examine his definition of public policy and its conceptual relationship to government. Easton writes that a policy "consists of a web of decisions and actions that allocates values." [15] Since political science, however, is concerned with the authoritative allocation of values for a society, not all policies are within the purview of the discipline. The scope is limited to policies that are authoritative allocations of values. Thus a public policy is implicitly defined as an authoritative value allocation for society. Or, in another formulation, public policy is seen as the outputs of the political system—outputs that are produced by the authorities in the political system. Furthermore, inherent in the nature of authoritative outputs is that members of the system "consider or are compelled to accept [them] as binding."[16]

We can readily accept the Eastonian components of public policy: authority, bindingness, and allocation of values for society. To these we would add another requirement—intent. Like bindingness, intent is actually implicit in any definition that equates public policy with government policy. There is no question that the authorities formulate policy outputs (although not necessarily *outcomes*) with deliberate intent. To establish the validity of the concept of nongovernmental public policy-makers, it is necessary to make explicit the intent of such policy. Without fulfilling the criterion of intent, private group actions with public consequences would simply be nothing more than transactions that incidentally affect society. Of course, unintentional policies may also have a significant impact on society, but we are concerned here with public policy rather than with all public effects. In this way we are adhering to a more conservative and rigorous concept of public policy than one that would include all significant social effects.

To sum up, a public policy is an allocation of values that is authoritative, binding, and intentional. The question is whether these criteria must be limited to the outputs of the formal government.

Allocation of Values

Allocation of values is a relatively simple concept. Gabriel Almond and G. Bingham Powell define allocations in the political system as the distribution of "goods, services, honors, statuses and opportunities."[17] Although they distinguish between allocations and extractions, for our purposes it is more convenient to consider extractions simply as the allocations of costs. With this comprehensive view, subsidies, taxes, a military draft, public offices (both substantive and honorary), welfare, medical care, education, and many other values may all be policy outputs—values that are allocated by the political system.

Easton cautions that the proper scope of political science (and, implicitly, public policy) includes not all allocations, since this would be hopelessly universal, but only those that are authoritative and that are society-wide. He notes the variety of organizations and institutions whose members accede to their authority—churches, employers, and so on. Yet the policies of such organizations are not public policies because they are not authoritative for the whole of society. While Easton acknowledges that many government policies apply only to some people or regions within a society, he argues that this differential effect is distinct from the similarly limited effect of private group policies because government policies are considered to be authoritative by all members of society. We will deal with the question of authority below. At this stage, the important point is that a public policy must be an allocation of values but that allocation need not apply equally to the whole society. Indeed, it may even have a very narrow scope of application as long as it is authoritative.

Authority and Bindingness

In Easton's formal system the authorities are, by definition, the government, and he is very clear and explicit on the role of the government in making public policy (rendering outputs). It is a completely exclusive role by definition: "Fundamental to the present conceptualization of outputs is the idea that they consist of a stream of activities flowing from the authorities in a system. It is the fact that they are produced by the authorities that distinguishes them as outputs."[18] As for the political role and power of nonauthorities, he acknowledges that they may engage in activities that "may flow into the environment" such as large scale political strikes, and they may even dominate the formal authorities. Nonetheless, Easton asserts that "the politico-economic elite making the decisions involved in this behavior are not to be considered as producing political outputs in my sense of the term." Such an expansion of the conception of outputs, he asserts, would make the study of outputs "equivalent to the examination of all political behavior."[19] It is precisely this formulation that is contrary to the present analysis. While it is no doubt useful in Easton's model of the political system, it is, nonetheless, needlessly limiting in selectively examining the formation and content of public policy per se. Indeed, when we move from the identity of the authorities to what the authorities do, we see that the case is less clear for equating public policy with government policy.

The function of authorities in a political system is to produce outputs—to make public policy. As we have seen, Easton argues that the authorities are the exclusive producers of outputs. The source, however, is not the only characteristic of outputs. Inherent in the character of authoritative outputs is that they are binding. Citizens must conform their behavior as specified by the particular output—pay taxes, pay the minimum wage, and the like. Easton distinguishes between "authoritative" and "associated" outputs on the basis of the binding character of the former. Associated outputs may also emanate from the authorities in a political system, but they are not binding. What consequences they have result only from their being associated with authoritative outputs. Such associated outputs include legislation introduced but not enacted, various policy proposals and the informal and/or sub-rosa granting of favors. But because they are not binding and formal they are not authoritative outputs. Easton concedes that such outputs may border on being binding but maintains that there is a discernible boundary line although he is not specific on what it is. It is also not quite clear whether associated outputs constitute public policy, but if they do it must be because they are linked to *binding* authoritative outputs.

Nearly all definitions of public policy include its binding nature. Like the definition of public, however, that binding nature is usually conceived of as stemming from the government—from the *binder*. Thus public policy is binding because it stems from the government. We are told by Easton and others, however, that a distinguishing characteristic of government is that it makes binding policy. We are left with the circular conclusion that outputs are binding only because they are governmental, and they are governmental because they are binding. If, however, we view the "bindingness" of policy from the perspective of the affected citizens—the "bindees"—we can start constructing a more comprehensive and realistic view of policy. From this perspective a policy is authoritative for society if it is binding—regardless of the source of the policy.

The essence of binding policy is the absence of effective choice by the affected party. A's policy is binding on B if B must conform his behavior to the dictates of A's policy regardless of B's own preferences in the matter. A policy may be binding through two situations. First it may be enforced by sanctions after the fact. For example, I file an income tax return and pay taxes even though I do not want to because the policy-maker (in this case the federal government) will punish me if I do not. I can act in a way contrary to the binding policy, but it is irrational for me to do so because I would then be punished. We can call this type "sanction bindingness." In the second type of situation, I do not even have the option of resisting the binding policy. Once I am sentenced to jail, my freedom is eliminated, and by physical coercion the state does with me what it will, in accord with its binding policy. Physical coercion and violence are not the only implements of this kind of binding policy. All that is required is removing from the bindee all options of resistance. For example, I do not have the option of not paying income taxes which have already been withheld from the paycheck. The government, acting through my employer, has removed that option. This kind of bindingness we can call "situational bindingness" because the total situation is controlled.

The question now is whether nongovernmental entities can employ either or both of these kinds of binding policies. The answer is clearly "yes." For example, the New York Stock Exchange may punish individual violators of Exchange regulations by prohibiting member firms from employing them for a specified period of time. Just as in government, a corporation may thus cause an individual to act against his own preferences or face the more unpleasant alternative of a severe deprivation of material and status values—a sanction little different in effect from a judicially imposed fine. Of course the sanctions of a corporation are unlikely to be physical, but the economic sanctions represent a coercive force as powerful as a judicially imposed fine or an attachment of wages or assets by a governmental unit.

The second kind of binding policy, situational bindingness, is even more pervasive as an element of nongovernmental policy-making. This bindingness largely includes many externalities of corporations. Environmental degradation is probably the most obvious and pervasive example of situational bindingness. For example, the citizens of Gary, Indiana, suffer a binding deprivation of health and aesthetic values due to the air pollution emanating from the plants of United States Steel. Now, they may consider this a worthwhile trade-off for employment and prosperity, but they are nonetheless bound by the policy outputs (pollution) of the industry. Similarly, all citizens of large urban areas suffer the binding policy outputs of automobile pollution. The point to be emphasized is that pollution, to continue the example, does not simply occur as a spontaneous act of God. It is, rather, the result of identifiable decisions made by corporate officials in the first instance. It is, in short, a policy made by those officials.

In one sense, this formulation of bindingness as authoritative outputs is congruent with Easton's own conception of authority since he notes that society has a variety of authority relationships. Easton, however, differentiates between nongovernmental authority figures and those that he calls the authorities. As we have seen, this distinction leads to an automatic equation of public policy with government policy. The problem is that such a scheme arbitrarily excludes authority figures who are functionally equivalent to "the authorities." Furthermore, it is not always clear just who are "the authorities" in a political system. When we say that a member of the school board in Sheboygan, Wisconsin, is part of "the authorities" but the president of General Motors is not, we cannot go very far in understanding political behavior or public policy.

It can be readily conceded that nongovernmental public policy, while authoritative, need not be legitimate. That is a different question. Easton and most other scholars regard legitimacy as an adjunct to government and an important element of governmental power. The belief in the "rightness" of the authorities' role as policy-makers enables the authorities to rule with a minimum of coercion. Privately made public policies may prevail even though citizens do not regard them as legitimately made. Citizens may be unable or unwilling to change those policies or upset the position of the policy-makers. Thus, one useful distinction between government pub-lic policy and nongovernment private policy may be that of legitimacy.

It should not be assumed, however, that legitimacy offers an automatic or mutually exclusive distinction between government and nongovernment policy. The relation-ship between the government and groups which have authority over their members may be such that those groups' legitimacy is positively accepted by the government. For example, when a state government delegates professional licensing power to local bar or medical associations the authority of those groups over their members is, in effect, no different from the authority and legitimacy of the state in comparable circumstances. Similarly, when federal legislation provides for a union shop, then the union is also an authoritative and legitimate allocator of values—particularly in indus-tries like construction where hiring is done through union officials. As with gov-ernmental laws that apply differentially by region and person, such private uses of authority also are considered to be legal and binding for all who fit into whatever categories are prescribed.

Intent

In assessing the question of intent, we can start with the situational binding policy of pollution. We need not go as far as Ralph Nader, who labels environmental degrada-tion as "chemical warfare," to appreciate pollution as a binding public policy. It may be objected that corporations do not produce pollution as a primary goal and that such externalities are certainly not intended—at least not as a goal. Cigarette companies do not market their product in order to produce lung cancer, and steel manufacturers do not produce steel in order to produce pollution. However, while some binding exter-nalities do not constitute policy, others do. These externalities constitute binding policy when the social risk of the externality becomes known to the decision-makers. Once the danger of the transaction or production process becomes known, someone must decide on how much danger to allow and how to assess the costs of preventing the danger. When an explicit government policy exists on the subject (for example, the National Environmental Policy Act) the government is the effective policy-maker. In the absence of government public policy, however, corporate officials themselves decide on the cost they find acceptable to prevent negative consequences. They decide on the allocation of negative values to the total number of affected citizens. In doing so, they make public policy. Even if they do not intend negative externalities as their goal, they do intend them as an allowable cost to be assessed on society. In the intended allowance of risk, the corporation policy-makers are acting in the same fashion and with the same consequences as government policy-makers who also allow for a certain level of risk in regulatory measures. The results are all public policy; the only difference is in who makes the public policy.

A good example is the automobile industry. Prior to the National Traffic and Motor Vehicle Safety Act of 1966, the question of automobile safety was largely left to the unilateral discretion of the automobile manufacturers. Their policy was that only minimal expenditures would go to automobile safety and that even such low-cost devices as effective restraint systems and collapsible steering columns would not be provided. Such policies were made even in the face of abundant evidence that these devices would save a significant proportion of the 50,000 lives lost annually in crashes.[20] As a result of new government policy, such devices were eventually mandated. It is an empty exercise in formality to say that the corporate decisions about automobile safety were not public policy while the government's decisions were public policy. In both cases, the decisions had binding consequences for most citizens. Returning to the question of intent, in deciding on vehicle-safety requirements and other regulations, government officials do not intend that a certain number of people should die or be injured but that a certain risk is acceptable. Nonetheless, it is universally conceded that the policy is intentional. In the same sense, the cost calculations of auto makers and other corporate officials who make these decisions also constitute intentional public policy.

Nongovernmental Public Policy

To say that private entities may make public policy is not enough. As a proposition it goes no further than simply arguing the inadequacy of prevailing definitions of public policy. Just as with governmental public policy it is necessary to differentiate among different types of policy. Therefore, a typology of privately made public policy is formulated here for three reasons: first, it further demonstrates the character of such policies as public policies; second, it differentiates between different types of such policies; finally, it allows comparisons between policy-makers and political systems.

The first category is labeled "resource transfer," and it includes all binding allocations of costs and benefits. The second category is "regulatory." Regulation involves control over personal conduct. The third category, constituent policy, includes policies that affect the procedures by which societal decisions are made. While this category may appear to be a policy process rather than a substantive policy output, its conception hinges on a time dimension. At the time a constituent policy (for example, reapportionment) is formulated, it is a policy output. Once in force it clearly becomes a part of the policy-making process. Furthermore, such constituent policy outputs are conceived here as the political equivalent of resource transfers. Rather than material resources, constituent policy involves transfers of political power resources. Just as with material resources, they are valued not only for their own sake but for what they can be converted into.

A series of brief examples can make the nature of privately made public policy and its categorization clearer. Because of their predominant position as nongovernmental makers of public policy, the examples focus on large corporations.

Resource Transfer

In terms of the impact on citizens, the most pervasive form of corporation-made public policy involves resource transfer—the extraction and allocation of material values. By the same token, this category is predominant in government policy. This fact can be seen by simply looking at the extent of government taxation—an activity that directly affects more citizens than any other. Indeed, taxation by private industry is the major mode of private resource transfer. The concept of taxation by private organization is not a novel one. Thurmond Arnold noted that "taxation by industrial organizations is a pleasanter way of paying tribute than taxation by government." [21] Arnold argued sarcastically that the distinction was a convenient myth.

> No one observed the obvious fact that in terms of total income of an individual it made no difference whether his money went for prices or taxes. Men believed there was a difference

because prices were automatically regulated by the laws of supply and demand. If any great corporate organization charged too much, in the long run it would be forced out of business by other corporations which did not charge so much. This might not be true if the corporation had a monopoly but our antitrust laws protected us from anything like that. . . .

Arnold viewed the entire pricing and investment structure of industry as "taxation." We need not go as far as that to appreciate some industry practices as a form of taxation. The very purpose of corporations is to effect resource transfers by procuring, producing, and distributing goods and services. Yet only a small proportion of these transactions (and their externalities) constitutes public policy. The distinction lies in the degree of control that a particular corporation exercises over its transactions and can be most readily seen in the form of taxation by administered prices.

Administered pricing is a major form of corporate resource transfer policy. Rather than setting prices as a reaction to competitive pressures expressed through the "law" of supply and demand, some corporations in highly concentrated industries are able to exercise considerable (although not unlimited) discretion in setting their own prices. This kind of situation, which results from a market wherein a few competing producers predominate, was described by Gardiner Means:

> (1) Prices tend to be administered, and not sensitive to short-run changes in demand and supply. (2) Competing producers tend to set the same prices or maintain the same price differentials over considerable periods of time. (3) There is apt to be one producer who is looked to as the leader in making price changes. (4) Prices tend to be set in terms of long-run considerations and not in terms of the short-run variations in demand and supply factors which dominate prices set by competition.[22]

A Senate antitrust subcommittee concluded that administered pricing was the general situation in the steel industry. Despite wide fluctuations of demand over time, steel prices rose steadily through the 1950s. The situation contrasts sharply with the price of scrap metal where the selling market is composed of many small firms. In the steel industry, United States Steel is the price leader, and the other companies have historically matched its price rises to the penny. As Gardiner Means points out, the setting of administered prices is not an unlimited power. United States Steel cannot set prices at *any* level it chooses. There are vaguely defined lower and upper limits. But, as Means says, "the price leader in steel operates within an area of pricing discretion such that within a significant range it can set one price rather than another."[23] In this situation, the price leader is engaging in the same kind of pricing power as that exercised by a governmental agency in a regulated industry. There, too, the power is not unlimited but rather is utilized within reasonable lower and upper limits. In both cases a binding resource transfer is effected by a public policy-maker. The public policy role of the administered price leader was implied in the statement of United States Steel Chairman Roger Blough before the Senate Antitrust Subcommittee when he stated, "I commend to the thoughtful consideration of this committee the question of whether or not our price action was responsible and in the public interest."[24] While there is considerable disagreement as to whether administered prices lead to excessive or exorbitant profits, the point remains that such a system consists of unilateral price setting in a regulated price structure. Just as the CAB makes public policy when it sets airline fares, so too does United States Steel when it sets steel prices.

Given the impact of steel prices on automobiles, artificially high steel price hikes represent a nationwide regressive tax (particularly when coupled with a "voluntary" steel import agreement reached with Japan in 1972).

Another major type of resource transfer is in the form of investment. While most investment decisions are conditioned by considerations of risk and potential return, there is considerable latitude for discretion within those broad parameters. It is within the bounds of that discretion that public policy-making occurs. The major forms of investment as policy-making involve the financing of major projects by banks and insurance companies through the extension of credit, the placement and removal of major corporate installations, and large-scale property development. These decisions have had a particularly significant effect in major cities whose viability has been damaged as major corporations pull out, locate in the suburbs, and channel their investments away from central-city areas. Nor is this impact confined to urban ghettos. Unilateral decisions by large private land-development corporations have a profound impact on community life in suburban and rural areas.

It should not be thought that the effects of corporation-made public policy are necessarily malevolent. Corporate "charity," which is a frequent mode of resource transfer policy, includes support of the arts, grants to educational institutes, programs for ameliorating inner-city conditions, and a variety of other such subsidies. They are all essentially public policy in that the individual corporation (or group of corporations acting jointly) unilaterally decides on allocation of societal resources for public purposes. Whether the federal government or Gulf Oil formulates and pays for a minority training program, the process still involves public policy. This was certainly true during the Johnson administration when private corporations received government contracts to run Job Corps centers, and it is no less true when corporations perform the same function unilaterally.

Regulatory Policy

A widespread type of private regulatory policy is the regulatory framework established by manufacturers or parent corporations in their relationships with retail distributors or franchise holders. This practice is particularly pervasive in the automobile industry. Until the passage of the Automobile Dealers Day in Court Act (1956), auto manufacturers had complete control over their dealers and could terminate their franchises at will. Exhibiting one of the classically posited requirements of a state, the manufacturers even had their own judicial system for adjudicating disputes between dealers and manufacturers. Naturally, the manufacturers usually prevailed in those disputes—a problem which led to the passage of the 1956 legislation. Nonetheless the auto manufacturers still have control over their dealers, and according to the representative of one large dealers association the 1956 legislation has done little to affect the regulatory power of the manufacturers. Indeed, the distributive system of automobiles is still in the form of a controlled regulatory framework. The heart of the system is the manufacturers' ability to control dealer entry through the granting of nonexclusive franchises. In controlling entry into the retail end of the business, the auto manufacturers function like such entry controlling regulatory commissions as the FCC and the ICC. Similarly, the manufacturers place a series of continuing requirements on franchised dealers once entry is granted. These include requirements that only certain replacement parts supplied by the manufacturer be used, minimum sales quotas, and the providing of highly detailed financial information. Furthermore, as is the case with some industries regulated by government, franchisees can not sell their franchise except to an approved buyer. If the manufacturer has any financial interest in the dealership (an increasing trend), the manufacturer gets voting control of the dealer. This situation is unique among sellers of high volume "big ticket" items such as major appliances. If we make the reasonable assumption that the retail selling of cars is a business distinct from their manufacture, the automobile manufacturers are thus in the position of controlling entry and otherwise regulating another entire industry. This practice is normally, and correctly, thought of as a public policy formulated by government. In this case, however the "government" is an automobile manufacturer.

Private regulation also extends beyond situations that are analogous to government economic regulation. It is a process of social control that includes sanctions to affect individual behavior and can be similar to the highly coercive use of police power by the state. For instance, the early struggle to unionize the coal mines and other basic industries saw the utilization of private police and even private armies to control workers.

Private regulative policy also involves all those activities that promote or adversely affect individual welfare—binding allocations *or deprivations* of such values as life, health, and pleasure. They include food and drug regulation, occupational safety, pollution control, and so forth.

Let us take the case of pollution control. It is clearly public policy when a government requires installation of various pollution abatement devices either in industry or automobiles. It is also public regulatory policy when an industry unilaterally decides to install or *not to install* such devices—precisely what happened in the automobile industry. There was not even the problem of a "non-decision"; The Big Three plus American Motors formulated a public policy of not developing and installing pollution abatement devices. In 1955, the four auto manufacturers agreed to a cross-licensing arrangement on antipollution devices. As later adduced by a federal grand jury, the arrangement consisted of agreements not to publicize competitively any solution to the problem of automobile emissions; to adopt a uniform date for the announcement of the discovery of any control device; and to install such devices only on an agreed date. The industry enjoyed a virtual monopoly of policy-making until 1964 when California approved four emission control devices and, in accord with a previous California law, required the installation of qualifying devices on all 1966 cars sold in the state. Although the Automobile Manufacturers Association in February 1964 had stated that the devices would be ready for the 1967 model year, the grand jury found that the auto companies in fact already had developed devices at the time the AMA resolution was issued. In any event, the automobile manufacturers managed to comply with the California requirement in 1966, all their previous protestations notwithstanding. Nonetheless, their conspiracy resulted in the lack of any voluntary development and installation of antipollution devices between 1954 and 1967. As the Antitrust Division noted in its summary of the grand jury investigation, the evidence proved:

> the existence of an industry wide agreement and conspiracy among the auto manufacturers, through AMA, not to compete in the research, development, manufacture and installation of motor vehicle air pollution control devices for the purposes of achieving interminable delays, or at least delays as long as possible. The cross-licensing agreement was used as a cover and focal point of the conspiracy.[25]

The case was eventually settled by a consent decree.

Just as the Clean Air Act of 1970 was a public policy placing maximum limits on polluting automobile emissions, the 1955 agreement among the automobile manufacturers was a public policy in the opposite direction. The only difference is that the former was a policy of the federal government, while the latter was a policy of private governments. They both, however, were public regulatory policies.

Constituent Policy

Constituent policy is more procedurally oriented than the other two policy types. It involves the setting of the structure and procedures of formal governance in a society. For example, the United States Consitution is our basic constituent policy and the Federal Election Campaign Act of 1971 is a more recent example. It might, therefore, be thought that this kind of policy can only be associated with public governments. Such a supposition, however, is more of a normative wish than an analytical statement. Private governments (in the present case, corporations) also formulate constituent policy in two broad ways.

First, corporations have their own internal structures of government. The charter of the corporation sets forth the purposes of the corporation, the responsibilities of the directors, the rights of stockholders, and so forth. Additionally, the usual rules and regulations divide responsibility in any large organization. For corporations that are public policy-making entities in their own right, the charter and other procedural policies are also constituent policy for the society as a whole.

But this internal structure is only the most routine and universal form of corporate constituent policy. Less frequent, but more important, are those instances in which corporations are constituent policy-makers not for themselves but directly for governmental bodies. The most blatant example is the old style company town, which still exists, although in declining numbers, particularly in the South. We need not re-enter the hoary community power debate to note that the local political life of some small communities is *totally* dominated by a single industry. There is, for example, the case of St. Mary's, Georgia, chillingly documented by Peter Schuck and Harrison Wellford.[26] The town is a fiefdom of the Gilman Paper Company, which employs nearly all the town's workers. The town's attorney is also the mill's attorney and was the state representative for the district. The town mayor is a mill employee and is also president of his union local which is, de facto, a company union. The political machine of the town is run directly within the company's plant. In 1970 a local doctor, Carl Drury, narrowly managed to unseat the mill's incumbent candidate for state representative (he lost in St. Mary's but carried the surrounding area of the legislative district). Subsequently, he was framed on a rape charge allegedly orchestrated by the company/town attorney (and former incumbent). Although the case fell apart when brought to the grand jury, Drury later paid a price for his independence when he was badly beaten up. In spite of the several eye witnesses, the assailant was acquitted by a jury dominated by mill employees or their relatives. Additionally, during Drury's campaign, the mill spied on employees to ferret out any who might be supporting Drury. Several were fired, businessmen in the surrounding county who supported Drury or were merely suspected of supporting him suffered economic retaliation.

Of course, a major reason for the extraordinary efforts at total domination is the resulting economic advantage. By running the town the paper company, in effect, can set its own local taxes—with a very advantageous result for itself. But given the economic dependence of the town on the company, such advantages would probably accrue anyway. Schuck and Wellford suggest that domination is craved also for its own sake. They note that "there is a traditional view among southern mill owners, captured by W. J. Cash in his *Mind of the South,* that it's no one else's damn business how they run their town." In short, the paper company runs the show in St. Mary's. Furthermore, the traditional pluralist safeguards are absent. The local press is not independent (the only local paper is controlled by mill interests and gave no coverage to the election), and no countervailing interest groups exist.

The system of campaign financing is the most pervasive form of constituent policy. Unlike the other corporate public policies, this form is directly traceable to the decisions (or lack thereof) of governmental bodies and the needs of politicians in the electoral system as it is presently constituted. Campaigns cost a lot of money. In the absence of provisions for public financing of campaigns or of effective limits on spending, corporations have the ability to deliver the requisite funds (usually by various subterfuges), and they have the incentive to use their economic resources to invest in politicians they deem favorable to their own interests. If public financing of campaigns in the future would be a public policy, corporate financing is currently a public policy with the specific allocations of resources being determined by each corporation.

Conclusion

Our thesis all along has been that it is extremely shortsighted to limit our conception and analysis of public policy to only those policies emanating from governments. We have argued that private governments, particularly giant corporations, are significant public policy-makers. It is equally important, however, not to go overboard in utilizing this broader conception of public policy—there are still limits to what can be considered privately made public policy. Specifically we issue three caveats.

Caveats

First, not all the effects of corporate enterprise upon citizens can be considered to be public policies. Probably most of the impact of corporations on society is due to the social and economic consequences of modern technology, a pervasive capitalist ideology, and large-scale industrial organization. One must distinguish these generalized conditions from specific instances of corporate public policy-making—which requires intentional policies that are specifically identifiable. The line between specific policy and social environment may sometimes be vague, but it should be kept in mind. Even with specifiable policies, the line between those that are purely private and those that are public is not precise. In this respect the situation is analogous to the fuzzy line between public and private organizations. Further research and analysis must precede an attempt to establish more exact criteria of "publicness" for both organizations and policies.

Second, the thesis being advanced is not a conspiracy or a "power elite" theory. We make no claim that hidden powerful interests are pulling the strings of government or that government is nothing more than a reflection of powerful economic interests. What we are asserting, rather, is that a significant amount of *public* policy is made by corporations and other private governments without having to go through formal government authority. Furthermore, there is no claim here that all or even most public policies do so originate—enough to warrant increased public and academic concern.

Finally, it is not contended that all the effects of corporate policy-making are evil. While we need not accept the conservative view that the only valid criteria for assessing business performance are economic, it should still be emphasized that large corporations provide such benefits as goods, services, and employment. Most of this activity, however, does not constitute public policy-making. Corporate participation in the Urban Coalition and other such enterprises indicates that corporate policy-making may be beneficent and may coincide with the interests of other groups in society. Furthermore, the corporate policy-makers have some economic limits on their power and they may exercise self-restraint in using their political power.

Implications

There are two sets of implications of this conception of public policy: one relates to the study of politics, and one relates to democratic values. One major implication for political studies has been stated earlier with reference to the problem of nondecisions. Public policy research can be organized around the analysis of what constitutes a particular policy and the determination of who makes the policy. Indeed such a strategy is essential if we accept the validity of the concept of nongovernmental public policy. A second implication concerns the study and importance of policy impact. Impact studies have traditionally related only to the outputs of governments and have assumed that such outputs were the totality of public policy in a given area. The present broader conception of policy, however, alters this focus in two ways. First, the impact of a policy must include the outputs of all the relevant policy-makers— including the nongovernmental policy-makers. Otherwise we will deal only with partial impacts in such areas as health care, transportation, occupational safety, and other fields with a heavy nongovernmental policy component. Second, impact is not a separable sphere of inquiry but rather is a defining characteristic of what constitutes a *public* policy. Again, although the lines are still blurred, a public policy is any policy whose fundamental impact is a binding allocation of values for a significant segment of society. The final implication relates to the "relevance" of political science. As noted above, David Easton among others argues that extending the concept of public policy beyond the formal government would hopelessly broaden and dilute political science. Yet I would argue that another risk is even more pressing. Limiting the concept of public policy to government policy tends to trivialize political science in that such a narrow concept misses some of the most significant allocations of values for citizens. Furthermore, these nongovernmental allocations are increasingly intertwined with the activities of formal government. To factor out only governmental outputs for research thus tends to make policy studies a heuristic exercise divorced from the real world of policy-making and policy impacts. Such a limited concept is analogous to prebehavioral political science, in which the focus was on the legal and formal institutions of government to the exclusion of much of the world of political behavior. Similarly, the challenge now is to analyze public policy—whatever its source.

The second set of implications concerns political accountability and democratic theory. Nongovernmental policy-makers may be benevolent and restrained in their exercise of power. But, as noted by Morton Baratz, "this is hardly a satisfactory arrangement for a society which places a high value on a decentralized power structure."[27] Baratz approvingly cites Peter Drucker who writes, "the important fact about 'enlightened despotism'—also the one fact 'enlightened despots' always forget—is that while it appears as enlightenment to those in power it is despotism pure and simple to those under it." [28]

This last point is at the heart of the problem. We would not countenance a totally nonelected self-perpetuating oligarchy in government merely because many of the policies of that oligarchy were beneficent. Corporations also make public policy. When they do so, however, there is not even the formal accountability to the public that we have in government. The task for scholars and the public alike is to assess the amount of public policy that is privately made and to formulate ways of limiting such policy-making power—or at least of making it more accountable.

References

1. *Policy Studies Journal* 1 (Autumn 1972): 2.
2. "The Analysis of Public Policy: A Search for Theories and Roles," in Austin Ranney, ed., *Political Science and Public Policy* (Chicago: Markham, 1968): 152.
3. Sanford A. Lakoff, ed., *Private Government* (Glenview, Ill.: Scott, Foresman and Co., 1973).
4. *Public and Private Government* (New Haven, Conn.: Yale University Press, 1944).
5. *Politics, Economics, and Welfare* (New York: Harper and Bros., 1953): 9–16.
6. Robert A. Dahl, *After the Revolution?* (New Haven, Conn.: Yale University Press, 1970): 120.
7. *Private Wants, Public Means* (New York: Basic Books, 1970): 53.
8. See, for example, William W. Kaufman, *The McNamara Strategy* (New York: Harper and Bros., 1964): 168–203.
9. "Local Strength in the American Federal System: The Mobilization of Private-Public Influence," in Marian D. Irish, ed., *Continuing Crisis in American Politics* (Englewood Cliffs, N.J.: Prentice-Hall, 1963).
10. "A Prelude to Corporate Reform," *Business and Society Review* 1 (Spring 1972): 18.
11. *Private Power and American Democracy* (New York: Alfred A. Knopf, 1966).
12. *The End of Liberalism* (New York: W. W. Norton and Co., 1966).
13. "Two Faces of Power," *American Political Science Review* 56 (December 1962) 947–952.
14. Matthew Crenson, *The Un-Politics of Air Pollution* (Baltimore: The Johns Hopkins University Press, 1970).
15. *The Political System* (New York: Alfred A. Knopf, 2nd ed., 1971): 130.
16. David Easton, *A Systems Analysis of Political Life* (New York: John Wiley and Sons, 1965): 352.
17. *Comparative Politics: A Developmental Approach* (Boston: Little, Brown and Co., 1966): 198.
18. *Systems Analysis*, 205–206.
19. *Ibid.*, 349–350.
20. Ralph Nader, *Unsafe at Any Speed* (New York: Grossman Publishers, 1965).
21. *The Folklore of Capitalism* (New Haven: Yale University Press, 1937): 263.
22. *Pricing Power and the Public Interest: A Study Based on Steel* (New York: Harper and Bros., 1962): 20.
23. *Pricing Power*, 43.
24. U.S. Congress, Senate Committee on the Judiciary, *Administered Prices*, Hearings before the Subcommittee on Antitrust Monopoly, 85th Congress, 1st session, 1957: 214.
25. Department of Justice Antitrust Division memorandum on grand jury proceeding, cited by Mark J. Green, *The Closed Enterprise System* (New York: Bantam Books, 1972): 255.
26. "Democracy and the Good Life in a Company Town," *Harper's Magazine* (May 1972): 56–66.
27. "Corporate Giants and the Power Structure," *Western Political Quarterly* 9 (June 1956): 415.
28. *The Concept of Corporation* (New York: John Day Co., 1946): 72.

TO THE STUDENT: A COMMENTARY

"The fact is that older forms of monied power are losing ground." So writes Kevin Phillips. But you have heard it before, haven't you? The same sentence could have been written by Kirkpatrick Sale for "Power Shift." Kevin Phillips also sees a power shift, but not to a Southern Rim, at least not in the article you have just read. Instead it is to a "knowledge community" that constitutes the new elite challenging the older aristocracy, the ancient Establishment.

Who resides in the knowledge community, who operates the knowledge industry? It turns out to be people who dominate the mass media marketplace. It includes writers such as Peter Benchley, author of *Jaws*. There are pop singers like Elton John, Barbra Streisand, Donna Summer, even Dolly Parton. Phillips does not say so, but he could easily add superstar teachers like John Kenneth Galbraith, pollsters such as George Gallup or Louis Harris, television anchors including Walter Cronkite and Dan Rather, or investigative reporter Jack Anderson. (Rather became television's "eight million dollar man" when he signed a lucrative long-term contract to replace Walter Cronkite as CBS anchor; Jack Anderson Enterprises has an annual income of $500,000, substantial but paltry compared to Rather or Elton John!)

"Who cares?" you say. "What does this have to do with politics?" Phillips thinks a lot. "Mediacracy," he writes has displaced aristocracy, at least the older aristocracy: "there *is* an increasingly important media aristocracy in the United States, and the national news media *do* serve as a dissemination system and linchpin of sorts for the views of the so-called Eastern Establishment of think tanks, councils, universities, foundations, and kindred institutions." Here, then, Phillips and Kirpatrick Sale may part company. Remember, Sale argues that the cowboys, not the yankees, are in the ascendancy. Does Phillips suggest, instead, that the so-called knowledge industry, the mediacracy, is a tool reestablishing yankee dominance? It is a point worth debating, one that might prompt you to take a second look at Sale's selection in chapter 5.

Phillips cites other connections between mediacracy and politics. One of those Mark Nadel touches upon briefly in his article as well. It has to do with the financing of election campaigns. Corporate "fat cat" money, argues Phillips, is being squeezed out of campaign finance and "the power of the knowledge-economy organizations is increasing." He gives you the National Education Association as an example. Could that also be an illustration of what David Broder was discussing as special interest, single-issue politics in chapter 6? As you reflect upon that possibility, think also about the apparent difference between Phillips and Nadel regarding the importance of corporate funds to campaign finance. "Apparent" is a useful term here. Nadel seems to be saying that if election campaigns were financed with public funds (money raised through government taxes) corporate clout would decline. Our presidential campaigns are financed by public funds. Could that account for the decline in corporate financing? But if single-issue interest groups and rock stars become, as Phillips says, "the new kingmakers," is that an improvement? We will provide you with some ways to look at that question in chapter 9 that follows, "Same Game, Different Rules, or New Game?"

For the moment, however, consider Nadel's basic point in light of what we have just said about Phillips: the policies that most directly affect our daily lives are not always made by governments, but by private associations. As Nadel notes, political scientists have long recognized that private entities such as business corporations influence what governments do—through campaign contributions, lobbying to influence lawmakers, and even buying influence with money and favors. Moreover, private organizations are miniature political communities in their own right for they have their own internal relationships of power and control, leaders and followers, and procedures for reaching decisions.

But Nadel goes beyond all of that. Like a latter-day Hamlet of scholarly research, he is almost heard to say to his fellow political scientists, "There are more things in heaven and earth, Horatio, than are dreamt of in your philosophy." Horatio in this case is embodied in the political theory of David Easton. In a productive and influential career political scientist David Easton has carefully elaborated a comprehensive theory of political systems. Many political scientists use Easton's "systems approach." That approach has a few critics, but by and large it is the fashion, if not the gospel, of mainstream political science. Here, however, you find Mark Nadel—a mere assistant professor of government when he penned this piece—challenging a key feature of an approach developed by perhaps the foremost theoretician of political science today, namely, the boundary between private and public policy.

For Easton public policy consists of an "authoritative" allocation of values in a society, a binding distribution of rewards and incentives, of punishments and deprivations. But, asks Nadel, what makes a policy authoritative or binding? In Easton's view "public policy is binding because it stems from government." Bindingness lies in who the binder is, government. Nadel doesn't think this is a very helpful way to look at things: "We are left with the circular conclusion that outputs are binding only because they are governmental, and they are governmental because they are binding." Score one for Nadel.

Can we break out of this circle? Yes—if we view bindingness from the perspective of who is bound rather than who binds. The useful thing is not to equate public policy solely with what governments do but to take *any* policy people accept as binding and to examine who made it, be they governmental or nongovernmental. These are the powers that really be! Nadel does precisely this. Along the way he gives you particularly relevant examples of policies that are public and how private governments make them. You can by now probably add several illustrations of your own.

Is all of this belaboring the obvious, straining at gnats? No. To think of policy as Nadel does is nothing less than a redefinition of the scope of politics. Politics now includes all authorities, government and nongovernment, public and private, visible and invisible. In short, any activity that regulates the ways you and others go about living together is grist for the mill—settling arguments, forging agreements, and making society possible. Now, reconsider the earlier question put to you about Phillips' mediacracy: what does it have to do with politics?

Beyond broadening the scope of politics (and, hence, that of watching politics) Nadel's view carries the implications he emphasizes in his conclusions. Especially important are those concerning political accountability in a democracy. If nongovernmental policy makers shape your life, should you not be able to make them accountable for what they do to you? If you object to the actions of a President or congressional official, the voting booth affords some means of complaining, small though it sometimes seems. But what can you do when major oil companies raise their prices, physicians charge higher fees, or colleges demand higher tuitions? This, says Nadel, "is at the heart of the problem." Indeed it is. You will wrestle with it the rest of your life. Learning to watch it now will provide some insights for how best to keep on your feet and off the mat.

Your observations will be improved by reading what others have seen. Among journalistic accounts include:

Kevin Phillips, *Mediacracy*

Ben Bagdikian, *The Information Machines*

Alvin Toffler, *Future Shock*

And by political scientists consider:

Charles O. Jones, *An Introduction to the Study of Public Policy*

Charles E. Lindblom, *The Policy-Making Process*

Carol S. Greenwald, *Group Power*

9 Same Game, Different Rules, or New Game?

INTRODUCTION

With this chapter you come to the close of Part 2 of *Watching American Politics*. You probably discern one or more themes in the presentations. For instance, in Part 1 you found that America is a nation of changing demography, both changing and stable values; that levels of citizens' political involvement is low, their confidence in political leaders varies, and many factors influence how they vote. Perhaps one reason for variable confidence and moderated political activity lies in a popular feeling that "they" rather than "we" govern, "them" and not "us." Power shifts, institutional elites, declines in political party fortunes, the rise of new politicos, and the emergence of new power complexes all seem to force the average citizen to the political sidelines. Such were the themes running through Part 2.

In the wake of such trends many people argue that the American political scene should be reformed. If defects can be removed, obstacles to the citizen's participation will vanish, political institutions will be accountable to your will, and corporate clout, fat cats, special interests, and power elites will meet their match.

This line of thinking was influential in the 1970s. Proposals for reform of elections, campaigns, Congress, the bureaucracy, and other institutions abounded. It was time to clean up politics—quickly and efficiently. Among the reforms that ultimately became law two provide the focal points of this chapter. The first is public financing of presidential campaigns. Rhodes Cook provides a lucid and informative account of reforms and, more importantly, what those reforms have done to us. Cook is a reporter for the *Congressional Quarterly Weekly Report,* known to most people simply as *Congressional Quarterly.* Cook's article, "Public Financing Alters Presidential Politics," is taken from that publication. You are unquestionably familiar with the major news weeklies—*Newsweek, Time,* and *U.S. News and World Report.* All three provide you with useful information to assist your political watching. However, there are two publications—*Congressional Quarterly* and *The National Journal*— that are news weeklies devoted exclusively to politics. A regular reading of either, or both, offers ample opportunity to keep abreast of political events. We trust Cook's article will provoke you to read other features in such publications.

A second area of reform emerging from the 1970s was that of presidential nominating politics. Gerald Pomper in "New Rules and New Games in Presidential Nominations" writes of three key changes in the rules—the increased number of presidential primaries (more than two-thirds of the states held them in 1980), changes in the primary rules, and apportionment of delegates to each party's national convention. Pomper is not simply interested in describing these changes to you; he wants you to understand the impact they have upon the types of people who can and do run for President, who can and do get elected.

Political scientist Gerald Pomper has devoted his career to studying elections in America. In fact, one of his most widely read books has precisely that title, *Elections in America.* In addition he has written a volume about how the political parties select their presidential nominees, *Nominating the President,* and how voters go about choosing between those nominees, *Voters' Choice.* In 1976 it occurred to Pomper and a few of his colleagues that people just might be interested in how political scientists interpret the outcome of elections not two or three years after the election has become ancient history but soon after the outcome. So in early 1977 he published *The Election of 1976,* a volume demonstrating that political scientists—much like the Type III interpretative journalists we described in our prologue—were capable of "instant analysis." The volume was so well received that Pomper undertook a similar project for the 1980 presidential election.

The title of this chapter suggests what to look for as you read the Cook and Pomper selections. Have changes in how we finance presidential campaigns and choose presidential nominees improved presidential politics, i.e., provided a new game? Or is it simply the same game—with same winners and losers—as before reform?

PUBLIC FINANCING ALTERS
PRESIDENTIAL POLITICS

Rhodes Cook

Edited and reprinted from Congressional Quarterly Weekly Report *37 (October 6, 1979): 2227 – 2231.*

No aspect of presidential politics has changed more dramatically in the last decade than campaign finance. And the impact has been far-reaching.

Until 1976 presidential candidates operated under a wide-open system that permitted multimillion-dollar contributions by individuals and unlimited spending. But the Watergate excesses changed all that.

In 1980 candidates will be conducting the second presidential campaign under the Federal Election Campaign Act (FECA).

The law tightly restricts contributions and, to win observance of expenditure limits, offers major party candidates a sizable carrot in the form of matching public funds for primary races and nearly full funding for the general election campaign.

In addition, the Democratic and Republican national committees are provided funds to conduct their parties' national conventions.

Political Ramifications

The major provisions of public funding for presidential campaigns were passed in 1974 with amendments in early 1976. Parts of the law were declared unconstitutional in the January 1976 *Buckley v. Valeo* Supreme Court decision, but the court upheld contribution limits. It also ruled that if a presidential candidate accepted public funds, he must obey the spending ceilings imposed by Congress.

The FECA has won praise from public financing advocates. They claim that it has cleaned up presidential politics by controlling spending and by driving out influence-seeking "fat cats" and special interest groups.

They argue that the law encourages candidates to run tightly organized, efficient campaigns and spurs creativity in fund raising.

Critics counter that the FECA is producing presidential campaigns that are under-financed and overregulated. The contribution and spending ceilings are too low, they claim, forcing candidates to run highly centralized campaigns that curtail grass-roots activity.

Opponents contend that the major beneficiaries of the FECA are lawyers and accountants, whose skills are needed to comply with the detailed provisions of the law.

"If General Washington had to fight the Revolutionary War like we fight our political campaigns," observed political consultant Bob Keefe at an American Enterprise Institute conference in September, "we'd still have a king. . . ."

Spending Curbed

The FECA clearly has helped curb the sharp increase in campaign spending. According to Herbert E. Alexander in his book, *Financing the 1976 Election,* spending for both the pre-convention and general election phases of presidential campaigns jumped by $47 million from 1968 to 1972 (from $91 million to $138 million), but by only $22 million from 1972 to 1976 (to $160 million). General election spending actually went down in 1976 from its level four years earlier.

Before 1976, all campaign money was raised privately, often in large chunks from wealthy contributors or interest groups. That all changed with the FECA. In the 1976 pre-convention period, 36 percent of the funds received by prominent candidates was public money. In the general election, 95 percent of the money collected by the Carter and Ford committees came from public funds. In addition to freezing out "fat cats," the FECA has limited the role of political action committees (PACs) and party organizations. Money from those two sources is not matchable with public funds in the pre-convention phase. With limited exceptions, contributions from those two sources and individuals are barred during the general election.

According to a compilation by Congressional Quarterly of mid-year 1979 campaign reports, 96 percent of the money raised so far by presidential candidates has been individual contributions, virtually all in small chunks of $1,000 or less. PAC contributions have provided barely 1 percent of total receipts, and donations from party committees have accounted for much less than 1 percent.

Together, Jimmy Carter ($63,410) and John Connally ($48,470) have collected about three-quarters of the PAC money, although it has not been a vital source of revenue for either candidate.

In 1976 PACs did not give heavily until it was apparent who would be nominated. In the first half of 1975, for example, Carter received only one PAC donation totaling $500. Sen. Henry M. Jackson, D-Wash., was the top receipient in mid-year 1975 with less than $40,000 in PAC gifts.

In June 1976 after he had wrapped up the nomination, Carter collected more than $200,000 from PACs. But even with the late surge, PAC contributions comprised only 2 percent of Carter's total primary campaign receipts.

Political Party Role

Party sources are playing an even smaller role than PACs in the restructured world of presidential campaign finance. Passage of the FECA has ensured candidates of their financial independence from party sources. Conversely, the law has been nearly as responsible for the declining influence of parties in the nominating process as the proliferation of primaries.

While state and local party organizations can still serve as forums for presidential candidates in meeting party activists, they provide virtually no cash. Of $10.5 million received in contributions by prominent candidates through June 1979, less than $2,500 came from party committees. Carter received the bulk of this paltry sum in small donations from a handful of Democratic county committees in Georgia.

Much more than that has been spent by candidates out of their own pockets on their campaigns. Harold E. Stassen has contributed nearly $16,000 to his effort, while early loans were made by Connally ($50,000) and Philip M. Crane ($15,376) to their campaigns. Still, the $50,000 limit on candidate contributions prevents any candidate accepting public funds from personally financing his campaign as Nelson A. Rockefeller did in 1964 and 1968.

Impact on Campaigns

The FECA's supporters claim that by removing the influence of personal wealth and special interest groups, American presidential campaigns are cleaner than they have ever been.

"Public financing works," remarked Rep. Morris K. Udall, D-Ariz., in 1977. "Carter and Ford had 40 million contributors last year and the largest was the taxpayer who paid one dollar. The system has proven itself in presidential races. . . ."

Critics disagree, complaining that in its effort to prevent another Watergate scandal, the FECA burdens campaigns with bureaucratic rules and red tape.

Officials with Jackson's presidential campaign, for instance, were flabbergasted to find during a crucial stage of the 1976 campaign that they had $70,000 in checks that could not be deposited because the campaign did not have required disclosure information on the contributors.

The law requires candidates to report the names and addresses of contributors of over $100 as well their occupation and place of business. Expenditures over $100 must also be itemized with the amount, date and purpose of the transaction.

The Reagan campaign has had a variety of problems with federal guidelines. In 1976 the Federal Communications Commission questioned the televised showing of movies in which Reagan appeared as an actor. Also, the Federal Election Commission (FEC) has requested more detailed information on campaign expenditures.

In responding to one inquiry in July, Reagan treasurer Bay Buchanan tersely accused the FEC of making "a hypertechnical case out of disclosure, fit only for the aficionados of election law administration."

Other campaigns have also complained about FEC nitpicking, but are spending hundreds of thousands of dollars apiece to comply with the detailed provisions of the law.

Lawyers and accountants are becoming the most valuable members of campaign organizations and their knowledge of the law is considered a basic ingredient in building a successful operation.

The FECA's supporters content that the law has discouraged sloppy bookkeeping and wasteful management and has helped bring about a new era of tightly organized, efficient campaigns.

But critics complain that it has forced campaigns to divert an inordinate amount of their time and money to minor details.

According to Republican Rep. Richard B. Cheney of Wyoming, President Gerald R. Ford's chief of staff from 1975 to 1977, compliance with the law may mean a candidate is "better equipped to serve as director of the Office of Management and Budget than as president."

Longer Campaigns

The FECA has clearly been a major factor in the increasing length of presidential campaigns. With candidates no longer able to finance their campaigns by quickly tapping a small group of wealthy contributors, early starts have become a necessity, especially for long shots who begin with low name identification.

As of early October, all the prominent presidential possibilities except Sen. Edward M. Kennedy, D-Mass., had either announced their candidacy or formed a campaign committee to raise funds.

Time is needed to test direct mail appeals and to organize fund raising in at least 20 states, where $5,000 must be raised in each to qualify for matching federal money.

Yet early success at fund raising is no guarantee of a good showing in the primaries. In mid-1975, for instance, the leaders in raising money were George Wallace ($4.5 million) and Sens. Jackson ($2.3 million) and Lloyd Bentsen, D-Tex. ($1.6 million).

In contrast, President Ford had raised only $10,000, Ronald Reagan had not yet formed his campaign committee, and Jimmy Carter was a little known dark horse who had collected only $350,000 and showed just $8,594 cash-on-hand.

Carter garnered most of his private contributions only after he had begun winning primaries. He received nearly twice as much money in the 10-week period between April 1 and June 8, 1976, as the previous 15-month period.

Although Carter overwhelmed them in the primaries, Wallace, Jackson and Bentsen benefited from early media attention because of their large campaign chests. According to 1976 Democratic aspirant Terry Sanford, qualification for matching federal funds was viewed by the media as a "license to practice," and campaigns were not taken seriously until they qualified.

Campaign finance expert Alexander contends that the law ultimately worked to Carter's advantage by curbing the ability of his better known rivals to collect the large sums of money that they could have raised if there had been no contribution ceiling.

"A vital part of the Carter success story is the FECA," Alexander has written. "Without stringent contribution limits, better-known candidates who had connections with wealthy contributors could have swamped Carter; and without federal subsidies, Carter would have lacked the money to consolidate his early lead."

Ironically, President Carter begins his 1980 campaign in about the opposite position from 1976. He possesses financial connections and a large early lead in fund raising over his potential Democratic rivals.

By the end of June, Carter had already raised more than $1.5 million through a wide range of fund-raising activities that have included direct mail appeals from the president's mother and personal appearances by the first lady, Vice President Walter F. Mondale and a variety of administration officials. The Carter-Mondale campaign committee had nearly $1 million cash-on-hand in mid-1979, more than any other Democratic or Republican candidate committee.

In contrast, the myriad draft-Kennedy committees had raised barely $30,000 through June 30, while the campaign committee of California Gov. Edmund G. Brown Jr. was not formed until late July.

On the Republican side, four candidates—Philip Crane, John Connally, George Bush and Ronald Reagan—already had raised more than $1 million by mid-1979. In spite of having the highest receipts ($2.5 million), Crane's campaign is in a precarious position. His campaign has nearly $800,000 in debts, much of it to conservative direct mail specialist Richard Viguerie who recently bolted to Connally.

Campaign Choice

The spending limits in the FECA force all of the candidates to make some tough decisions. They must choose whether to save their money for a long campaign through all the primaries or to make heavy expenditures in the early ones where a good start is crucial.

With a limited amount of money to spend, most candidates have established highly centralized campaigns run out of a national headquarters. Grass-roots activity is discouraged because any expenditure by an affiliated local group counts against the candidate's spending ceiling.

"The experience of the Ford campaign in 1976," observed ex-Ford aide Cheney at an American Enterprise Institute conference last month, "showed conclusively that it was much easier to discourage grass-roots activity than it was to control it or report it. . . ."

"Given a choice between local spontaneity and enthusiastic participation or control over spending, the cautious campaign manager has little choice but to opt for activities which are controllable," Cheney remarked.

Even with curbs on local involvement, many candidates have criticized the state spending limits as unrealistically low. There are complaints that the ceilings, which are computed primarily on a formula based on voting age population, do not take into account a state's political importance or its delegate selection system.

State limits are not raised for primary states, even though expenses are normally higher for a primary than a caucus. Nor are adjustments made for traditionally important states like New Hampshire. Even though all the prominent candidates are making a major effort in New Hampshire, it has the same spending ceiling as Guam.

The New Hampshire spending limit (presently $264,600) has left most candidates searching for loopholes in order to spend as much as they possibly can. Candidates are staying overnight in neighboring states, placing New Hampshire staff members on their national headquarters' payroll and buying advertising time on Boston television stations. Boston television reaches most New Hampshire households, and nearly the entire advertising cost can be charged against the Massachusetts limit.

Another potential way around the limit is to reject federal campaign funds in early 1980. Theoretically, that would free a candidate to spend an unlimited amount in New Hampshire and then accept public funds at a later date.

The FEC moved to close that loophole in late September by drafting a new regulation that would permit the FEC to deny matching funds to any candidate who prior to seeking federal money "knowingly and willfully" exceeded the spending limit in any state. However, the candidate could become eligible for matching funds by paying a penalty equal to the amount that he exceeded the limit.

Draft Loophole

Some members of Congress are working to plug another loophole that could turn into a significant boon for the numerous draft-Kennedy committees.

In response to an inquiry by a Florida draft-Kennedy committee, the FEC ruled unanimously in August that because Kennedy was not a declared candidate the Florida draft committee was neither bound by the $1,000 limit on individual contributions or the $1.35 million lid on spending within the state. The FEC voted to permit the committee to receive individual contributions up to $5,000 and to spend as much as they pleased.

The FEC did not determine whether the receipts and expenditures of the draft-Kennedy committee would count against the senator's Florida limits if he declared his candidacy. Although the opinion dealt only with the Florida request, it probably applies to draft committees in other states.

But even in its narrowest interpretation, the ruling gives Kennedy forces a fund-raising advantage over Carter in preparing for the Florida presidential preference caucuses Oct. 13 and the state convention in November.

Initial opposition to the FEC ruling has been concentrated among Republican House members. "The noncandidate's unfair advantage is a national irony and a national outrage," Republican Rep. Bill Frenzel of Minnesota told the House Sept. 25.

With the encouragement of GOP congressional leaders, Republican Rep. David F. Emery of Maine is expected to propose legislation after the October recess that would bind draft committees to the same limits that apply to declared candiates.

Emery was rebuffed in the House Rules Committee last month when he sought to have his measure considered on the floor as an amendment to the FEC authorization bill (S 832). All the Republican members present voted for the Emery proposal, and all but two Democratic members voted against it.

Legal Challenges

While the *Buckley v. Valeo* decision upheld the basic provisions of the FECA that govern presidential campaigns, critics still hope parts of the law can be overturned through legal challenges.

The Republican National Committee (RNC) has brought suit against the FEC, challenging the spending limit on publicly financed presidential candidates in the general election. The RNC wants the ceiling removed, arguing that the unrestricted expenditures permitted labor unions for internal communication and voter registration activities give the Democrats an unfair advantage.

The RNC suit does not challenge the constitutionality of public financing or the contribution limits but seeks to allow presidential candidates to spend as much as they could raise in the general election.

Traditionally, the Republicans have outspent the Democrats by a wide margin in presidential contests, but public financing has negated the GOP's advantage.

The suit was filed in a federal district court in New York in 1978. No decision has been reached, but an appeal is expected regardless of the verdict.

Other assaults on the FECA are planned by some of the plaintiffs in the *Buckley v. Valeo* case.

However, unlike *Buckley v. Valeo*, the newest challenge would not be a comprehensive assault on the law's basic provisions but a variety of individual suits attacking specific sections.

Critics have not made a final decision on which provisions of the FECA to challenge, but are likely to focus on the contribution limits and FEC restrictions on independent spending.

NEW RULES AND NEW GAMES IN PRESIDENTIAL NOMINATIONS

GERALD M. POMPER

Edited and reprinted from Journal of Politics *41 (August 1979): 784–805.*

Politics resembles sport in many ways. We each have our favorite players whose performance we watch and rate. Political statistics such as the number of delegates won are examined as avidly as batting percentages. As baseball buffs recall the great games of the past, so political historians recall the great conventions of 1860 or 1952.

One of the basic features of both sports and politics is the formal rules within which the game is played. The rules prescribe the behavior of the players and lead to standards for judging performance. When the rules are changed, the outcome of the contest is also likely to change. Understanding this basic fact, football teams with weak kickers favor restrictions on field goals, and baseball teams with strong pinch hitters favor the use of designated hitters. For similar reasons, advocates of strong national government in 1787 changed the constitutional rules of the United States.

In recent nominating politics, the rule book has been rewritten. From one of the most significant reform periods in American history has come a new game, bringing changes as extensive as those that followed the legalization of the forward pass in football. Although there were other causes, these rules changes are important explanations of the surprising features of the 1976 major party conventions, particularly the victory of Jimmy Carter, and the close race of Ronald Reagan.

New Rules

We will examine the effects of three kinds of rules changes on the 1976 contests: increased use of primaries, changes in primary election rules, and reapportionment of delegates. Most obvious has been the growth of primaries as means of selecting delegates to the national conventions. This latest surge in primaries came after the raucous Democratic convention of 1968 and the subsequent initiation of party reform. By 1976, primaries or preference polls were involved in the selection of 76.9 percent of the Democratic delegates and 71.5 percent of the Republicans. (The figure is a slight exaggeration, for it includes delegates from states holding purely advisory preference polls, such as Vermont and Montana, as well as all delegates from states using mixed systems. The territories are excluded from all calculations.)

A number of related explanations may be offered for the increase in primaries. One factor—both cause and effect—is the decline of the convention as an arena for bargaining. The purpose of the party conclave is no longer to select a nominee, but to legitimize the individual who has proved his mettle and his popularity in the long pre-convention period. Primaries, rather than floor votes, now provide critical information about the relative strength of the contenders and the likely winner of the nomination.

The expansion of the primaries has been abetted by the development of the mass media. Politics has become more open with the development of peering electronic journalism. Television, with its need for a continuing supply of confrontations and excitement, gives great weight to primary results and indeed has made the New Hampshire primary, first in the nation, into a major source of state tourist revenue. After each primary, television and other commentators determine the standing of each candidate, counting their delegates, labeling them as front runners or also-rans, and thereby significantly affecting their chances in future primaries.

In 1976, the federal government provided another cause, money. By providing matching funds for virtually any candidate, more extensive campaigns were facilitated. In the past, restricted finances were an important means of limiting entry into the presidential race. The federal political finance laws which followed Watergate partially removed this restriction. Candidates could at least begin their campaigns relatively easily, as demonstrated by the early proliferation of Democratic candidates.

Increased significance for the primaries is apparently in keeping with the long term trends of American politics toward more public involvement in the parties. Opinion polls consistently show the general public supporting a national presidential primary, and the proliferation of state contests is in keeping with this preference. The arguments against primaries are subtle at best, elitist at worst. It is much simpler to leave the nominating decision to an apparent expression of direct democracy.

A second major change in the rules has been revision of the primaries themselves.

Basically, the change has been one from an emphasis on the representation of state parties, as cohesive and relatively monolithic political units, to the representation of party voters, acting as individuals. This change parallels the shift from the convention as the site of bargaining between state parties to the convention as simply the formal expression of the preferences of the activist electorate.

Primaries come in three basic varieties. In the "winner-take-all," or plurality system, all of the state's delegates are awarded to the candidate who receives the most votes, whether or not a numerical majority. If there is a strong party organization, this system magnifies the influence of those leaders who can deliver a sizable bloc of delegates to their preferred candidate. Even if no strong organization exists, the larger states still become valuable prizes and candidates therefore are likely to give greater weight to the demands of their citizens. In 1976, only California Republicans used this system.

The winner-take-all system in nominations is based on an analogy to the Electoral College, emphasizing the federal character of the political system and giving power to large and cohesive units. Philosophically and politically opposed to this scheme are those which emphasize the representation of the individual voter, seeking to give each person, or at least each substantial minority, some voice in the relevant political decision. In the election of the President, the conclusion follows that electoral votes should either be divided proportionally in each state or that the chief executive should be chosen directly.

Proposals for proportional representation are based on the similar premise that individuals or minority groups within the states should have some measurable effect. The premise led to the Democratic mandate of 1976 that delegates from each state should be chosen in a manner which fairly reflects the division of preferences expressed by those who participate in the presidential nominating process in each state. States would no longer be treated as units, and state parties would not be allowed to bargain as monolithic units.

But the Democrats went one step further, providing not only for proportionality, but for localism. A system of proportional representation can be applied to districts of varying size. Smaller districts reward insular groups with limited general appeal. In 1976, the Democrats went in this direction, by requiring that at least three-fourths of the delegates of any state be chosen below the state-wide level. Overall, proportional representation was the most common system employed.

In the final rules, however, the Democrats avoided complete local proportionality by making two reservations to the general principle. Delegates could be chosen from areas as large as congressional districts, so that the plurality winner in such a district could win all of the delegates. Second, candidates would be entitled to delegates only if they won at least 15 percent of the votes in the relevant district. These two rules provided some means of limiting the fractionalization of preferences by eliminating very small minorities and by providing for a degree of cumulation up to the congressional district level. This "loophole" system was almost as common in 1976 as proportional division.

A third change in recent years has been the reapportionment of delegates among the states, shifting the basic resources of the conventions, delegate votes, among the states and therefore increasing the opportunities of some candidates and detracting from the opportunities of others.

Until the 1912 convention, the basis of convention apportionment was clear and unchallenged. Delegates were distributed among the states in accord with electoral votes, usually a simple multiple of this figure. The result in the 1912 Republican convention was that William Howard Taft gained many delegates from Southern states which had sufficient population to have large numbers of delegates but which had few Republican voters. It was these controlled southern delegations which enabled Taft to beat off the Progressive challenge of Theodore Roosevelt.

The Republican party maintained this traditional system largely intact throughout 1976, while adding "bonus" delegates to each state which voted for the party's candidate for president, or governor, or senator in the last election. For the 1976 convention, the effect of this system was to provide a bonus reward to virtually every state, since the Republicans had won all but Massachusetts in the previous presidential election. The G.O.P. system emphasized only victory, not the number of Republican members or votes for the party in a state. Its result therefore was to strengthen the one party states, rather than the competitive ones, and the less liberal states.

The Democrats after 1968 shifted to a new basis for apportionment. For the electoral college basis and the bonus votes, they substituted a formula which provided essential equal weight to a state's population and to its past Democratic vote. The obvious effect of this system was to give more votes to the larger, more competitive and more liberal states. Because electoral victory as such was not rewarded, there was very little change in apportionment after the disastrous defeat of McGovern in 1972.

The changes in apportionment, like those in the primary election rules, represent a shift in the total political system. Apportionment on the basis of the electoral college was a recognition of the state as political units. Providing bonus votes for successful state parties still treats them as separate groups, but adds a national element, for they are relatively advantaged or disadvantaged as they contribute to overall national success. The Democratic shift disregards the state parties as other than convenient units. Individual citizens or individual Democratic voters are the basis of apportionment. The rules formally recognize only voters and a national party; there are no intermediary institutions, the state parties. The same implication runs through the requirement of proportional representation. It is the closest approach any major American party has made to populist democracy.

New Games

I will seek to discern the effects of the rules changes by examining the differential success of the candidates in different structural situations. We will assume that the effects seen in states using a particular set of rules would apply to all states if they all adopted the same rules. Admittedly, this assumption of uniform effects is an oversimplification and other causes of political change must be acknowledged.

Effects of Primaries

Table 26 indicates the effect of the first major change, the spread of primaries. The first row comprises those states adopting this system after 1968. The broadening of the direct electoral system was clearly of benefit to Carter and to Reagan. The Georgian won nearly two-thirds of the delegates from these thirteen new primary states and the Californian won close to sixty percent of their votes. Without the aid of these supporters, it is conceivable that Carter would have been denied the Democratic nomination. (In this analysis, we are trying to isolate the effects of the primaries from post-primary bandwagons and the conventions. The figures reported for the Democrats thus are the best estimates after the primaries or caucuses themselves, including uncommitted votes. In the actual convention balloting, Carter received far more votes, as his opponents dropped out and the uncommitted came over to his side. In the Republican case, the uncommitted are counted as they actually voted in the convention, since these delegates were essentially in one camp or the other from the beginning, despite their nominal status. Delegates required to vote for a particular candidate, even if personally opposed, are also held to that legal requirement in this analysis. The territories are excluded.) Carter was far weaker in the states with long histories of primary participation or which still chose delegates in caucuses. In these two areas, where state parties presumably had greater influence, he won only about a third of the delegates.

The same point is made in the bottom part of the table, which shows, in vertical columns, the distribution of each candidate's strength. Carter received a disproportionate share of his convention delegates from these new primary states. He fell below a random distribution in both the states with older primaries and those which relied on more traditional methods of caucuses and conventions. If the parties had been stronger, and better able to control the nominating procedures, Carter might have been stopped.

The other Democrats were quite different. Jackson's support came overwhelmingly from the areas which had not changed the rules greatly from the past. He did best in the older primary states, specifically Massachusetts and New York, and the bulk of his votes came from these areas. The most statistically normal candidates were the ideologically diverse pair, Udall and Wallace. They did about as well in each of the three categories of states and their delegates were gathered in proportion to the total distribution of delegates.

Carter's victory can be attributed, in part, to the opportunity provided by the extension of the primaries to new states. To be sure, the opportunity needed to be exploited skillfully. Moreover, we cannot know how Carter would have done under the old rules. It is certainly possible that he would have won as many delegates from the southern delegations of Arkansas, Georgia, Kentucky, North Carolina, and Tennessee. It is more doubtful that he could have overcome the favorite son candidacy of Lloyd Bentsen in Texas without a direct primary. In Michigan, it is also possible that many delegates would have been withheld if the process were controlled by the state party, as in the past.

In the Republican case, Reagan ran best in the new primary states, and might have won the Republican designation if the primary system had been extended to more states in 1976. He also did well in the caucus areas where the zeal of his ideological supporters could be brought to bear. Reagan's weakness was in the older primary states, in which nearly half of the delegates were chosen, but where Reagan won only a third. Ford won his nomination in these areas, but it was not a personal victory. The margin of the former President in these states came almost entirely from New York and Pennsylvania where delegates were elected as formally uncommitted. The strong party organizations in these states eventually brought the bulk of these delegates to Ford, and they are included in his totals. In contrast to Carter, who circumvented the state parties, Ford owed his victory to these organizations. His was the victory of an older politics, in which strong state parties had real influence on the nominations.

TABLE 26 Sources of Candidate Strength in 1976 Primaries

State Category	Democrats							Republicans		
	Carter	Udall	Jackson	Wallace	Brown	Others	(N)	Ford	Reagan	(N)
Distribution of Delegates by Areas [a]										
New Primary States	65.8	11.2	1.8	6.4	2.4	12.4	(623)	41.2	58.8	(532)
Old Primary States	32.7	10.8	11.1	6.5	13.0	25.9	(1665)	67.3	32.7	(1072)
Pure Caucus States	31.8	12.4	6.3	4.2	1.0	44.3	(686)	43.3	56.7	(639)
Distribution of Delegates by Candidate [b]										
New Primary States	35.0	21.0	4.6	22.5	6.3	9.5	(20.9%)	18.0	30.5	(23.7%)
Old Primary States	46.4	53.6	77.4	61.2	90.8	53.1	(56.0%)	59.2	34.2	(47.8%)
Pure Caucus States	18.6	25.4	18.0	16.3	2.9	37.4	(23.1%)	22.8	35.3	(28.5%)
(N)	(1172)	(334)	(239)	(178)	(238)	(813)	(2974)	(1217)	(1026)	(2243)

[a] Entries are percentages which add horizontally by rows.
[b] Entries are percentages which add vertically by columns.

Effects of Proportionality

The second major change was the shift toward proportional representation in the primaries. It is possible to estimate the results which would have followed if any of the three systems in use had been universally applied. Results can differ significantly, depending on the system employed. On the basis of the actual results, and a considerable number of speculative operationalizations, we can reconstruct the 1976 primaries *as if* there were consistent rules in all states. Table 27 summarizes these results.

In the actual primaries, Carter won over forty percent of the delegates. This proportion is strikingly close to that which has been previously calculated as the convention roll call percentage which leads to victorious bandwagons. In nominating history, candidates achieving over forty percent commonly have been able to move on quickly to victory. Carter's bandwagon rolled in the states rather than on the convention floor, but the process was similar. As victory seemed likely, opponents left the race, uncommitted delegates joined the front runner, and a voting majority was secured.

But the result was not inevitable. If delegates had been distributed in accord with strict principles of proportional representation, applied state-wide and with no minimum quota, Carter would still have led, but in this case with only 36 percent of the delegates. As the leader, but still distant from victory, he would have been the obvious target for a coalition of minorities. Moreover, proportional representation would have diminished Carter's impact in precisely those earlier primaries in which his strength was exaggerated by the legal structure and by the mass media. Through February and March, Carter would have gained but 86 delegates in the primaries under this alternative, rather than the 104 he actually won, excluding the special case of Illinois. The numbers are small in either case compared to the total number of delegates, but it is possible that the Carter drive, short of money and attention in its early stages, would have been halted if different rules had been in existence.

More generally, Carter almost always got better than a proportionate share of the delegates. Electoral systems of any kind tend to exaggerate the share of seats won by

TABLE 27   Hypothetical Outcomes of 1976 Primary Contests

Candidate	Actual	P.R.	Winner-Take-All	Districted
	Democrats			
Carter	954 (41.7%)	828 (36.2%)	1278 (55.8%)	1107 (48.4%)
Udall	249 (10.9)	293 (12.8)	0 (0.0)	195 (8.5)
Jackson	196 (8.6)	213 (9.3)	378 (16.5)	196 (8.6)
Wallace	149 (6.5)	254 (11.1)	35 (1.5)	65 (2.8)
Brown	231 (10.1)	212 (9.3)	366 (16.0)	348 (15.2)
Others	509 (22.2)	488 (21.3)	231 (10.1)	377 (16.5)
Totals	2288 (100%)	2288 (100%)	2288 (99.9%)	2288 (100%)
	Republicans			
Ford	634 (39.5%)	675 (42.1%)	756 (47.1%)	685 (42.7%)
Reagan	669 (41.7)	672 (41.9)	591 (36.8)	662 (41.3)
Other	301 (18.8)	257 (16.0)	257 (16.0)	257 (16.0)
Ford, with N.Y., Pa.	940 (58.6)	902 (56.2)	1013 (63.2)	912 (56.8)
Reagan, with N.Y., Pa.	664 (41.4)	702 (43.8)	591 (36.8)	692 (43.1)

the leading faction, and this same tendency was evident in the Democratic front runner's drive. In the seven largest states, for example, Carter got large bonuses in Texas, Michigan, Ohio, and California, received his fair share in Pennsylvania and New York and was disadvantaged only in Illinois, where the preference poll he led was unrelated to the selection of delegates dominated by the Daley organization.

As Carter was advantaged, his rivals lost votes they would have won under proportional representation. Jackson, Udall, and Wallace together would then have had a third of the delegates, rather then the quarter they actually secured. The strategic situation would have been altered as well. With more delegates in hand, these—and other—candidates would have found fundraising easier, would have been better able to resist Carter pressures in state caucuses and other primary states, and would have been more likely to remain in the race and accumulate delegates who eventually were won by Carter.

The opposite system would be that of winner-take-all. From the cumulative results, it would appear that Carter would have been the biggest gainer under this system. He would have won a decisive majority of all primary delegates, and presumably would have secured the nomination even earlier than occurred in fact. Senator Henry Jackson and Governor Jerry Brown still would have have lost the nomination but their delegate totals would have been higher than they actually achieved. The general effect of this system would be quickly to eliminate minor candidates and to focus the race on two or three contenders, just as plurality systems tend to eliminate minor parties and to reduce elections to contests between two major parties. An example of this likely tendency in 1976 is provided by Morris Udall, who never came in first in a primary, but was able to sustain his campaign because he did accumulate delegates even while he repeatedly, often narrowly, missed victory.

If the rules were different, strategies would also change. If the plurality system were widespread, Brown, being fairly confident of a late sweep of the California delegation, might have entered the campaign more vigorously and earlier. Jackson's fortunes would certainly have improved. The Washington Senator actually won both of the two largest primaries in the earliest stage, those of Massachusetts and New York. If these had been winner-take-all elections, he would have come up to the critical Pennsylvania contest with 378 delegates, while Carter would have had but 239 (assuming that he could not win Illinois in an open contest with an organization candidate). Jackson would then have had the media title of front runner and would not have suffered the burden of appearing to be but a stand-in for a reluctant Hubert Humphrey. A Carter defeat in Pennsylvania would severely damage his campaign under these rules and would most likely prevent the future sweeps which inflate his final total under the hypothetical winner-take-all system. George Wallace would have been most severely damaged.

The district system, as might be expected, shares some of the effect of the plurality system, but to a lesser degree. Carter's share of the delegates would be exaggerated beyond proportional representation and sufficiently to assure his victory. It would have deflated the support of Udall and Wallace and of minor challengers. Realizing these effects, Carter forces at the convention in 1976 unsuccessfully sought to maintain the loophole in the future as a means to limit any challenge to Carter for a second term.

Speculations cannot prove a case, and we cannot actually rerun history, either statistically or in reality. We can be assured that if the rules had been different, the strategies of the candidates, and the interpretations of results, would have been different. Contrary to some observers, I conclude that the change in the Democratic rules did have an effect, and that Carter's effort would have been handicapped, although not necessarily repulsed, by a pure system of proportional representation. A pure system of plurality elections might have further sped the Carter bandwagon, but it can also be argued that it would have made Jackson the early front runner.

The rules' effects are different in the Republican party. They are also more difficult to estimate, because there was no state wide ballot in New York and Reagan did not enter the Pennsylvania preference poll, making unavailable an index of relative popularity in that state. Reagan for one believed that he would have won the nomination if a pure system of proportional representation had been in effect.

A winner-take-all system certainly would have benefited Ford. In reality, the only pure plurality system existed in California and worked to Reagan's advantage. If universal, this system would have widened the margin between the two Republicans by more than a hundred delegates, even excluding New York and Pennsylvania. If Ford also were to win these states on a plurality basis—the most likely outcome—he would have virtually won the nomination on the basis of primary victories alone.

The other two systems, universally applied, would not in themselves have aided Ford. In the primary elections as held, Ford won nearly forty percent of the delegates, actually trailing Reagan in committed delegates. On a pure proportional system, he would have won 42.1 percent and, under the pure district system, 42.7 percent, gaining a thin margin in both cases. Reagan too would have gained under either of these systems, but only slightly, adding 51 delegates under pure proportionality and 41 delegates in an unmixed district system. The real difference came again from the two critical states of New York and Pennsylvania. Their large blocs of delegates brought Ford victory. It is likely—but unprovable—that he would have won these delegates in open primary contests. Their decisive impact, however, must be partially attributed to the strength of the party organizations in these states, and their old-fashioned ability to deliver, rather than to the personal popularity of the incumbent president.

Not only the final results, but the strategic environment would have been different under different rules. An important part of the environment in nominating contests is the temporal sequence of primaries. Early victories can be decisive, as they give the legendary quality of "momentum" to the first bandwagons and eliminate potential rivals. Recall the Republican campaign, which had three distinct pre-convention stages: initial Ford victories, a string of stunning Reagan successes in early May, and see-saw outcomes in the final weeks. In past years, these early Ford triumphs would have led to an unstoppable surge of party support. New rules, however, limited the effect of these victories, and Reagan was able to hold on, aided by federal financing, until he recouped in later contests.

Let us reconstruct those early results under hypothetically revised rules. Through the time of the Pennsylvania primary, Ford won 252 delegates in the direct elections, compared to Reagan's 80, a ratio of 3.2:1. As seen in Table 28, a plurality system would have magnified these victories considerably. If New York and Pennsylvania are included as Ford delegations, the Ford margin would have been overwhelming, probably causing Reagan to withdraw from the race. By contrast, a pure proportional system in these early races would have left the candidates at a virtual standoff if the two eastern states are excluded or would have considerably reduced Ford's lead even

TABLE 28 Hypothetical Results of Early Republican Primaries [a]

Electoral System	Ford Delegates	Reagan Delegates	Ford/Reagan Ratio
Actual	252	80	3.2
Pure Plurality	294	54	5.4
Pure Plurality (with N.Y., Pa.)	551	54	10.2
Pure P.R.	199	149	1.3
Pure P.R. (with N.Y., Pa.)	426	179	2.4
Pure District	260	88	3.0
Pure District (with N.Y., Pa.)	487	118	4.1

[a] Primaries held before May 1, 1976 are included.

if they are counted in his column. Ford's weaknesses would have been more obvious under this system, and it might well have provided the small increment needed to bring Reagan the nomination. In the real world, the rules prevented either a quick decision in the Republican party favoring Ford or an early stunning blow by Reagan.

Effects of Apportionment

The apportionment of delegates among the states is the third important rules change. The effect of this change is particularly evident in the Republican party. In general, delegates have been transferred from the older sections of the nation and the historic bases of the party in the Northeast and the Midwest to the newly emerging Sunbelt in the South, Southwest and Far West. These shifts are partially caused by the movement of the national population. They are accented by the Republican bonus rules which award delegates in relatively equal numbers to states won by Republicans, regardless of the size of the state's population or the number of votes cast for Republicans.

The results can be seen if we undertake another hypothetical reconstruction, this time of the convention roll call for the presidential nomination. In Table 29, we present both the actual 1976 roll call and the hypothetical distribution of votes under the apportionment of 1952. Delegations are split between Ford and Reagan in the same proportions as they actually divided in 1976. However, each state's numerical distribution is different because of the lower total number of delegates in 1952 (1185, compared to 2190 in 1976), and because of the different allocation in effect in the year of Eisenhower's first nomination. (Since no fractional votes are permitted in Republican conventions, delegate votes in 1952 are rounded to the nearest whole number. Alaska, Hawaii, and District of Columbia and the territories are excluded from these calculations, lowering the total number of delegates below those actually present at the conventions.)

The 1952 convention is an appropriate benchmark for this comparison. Like the contest of 1976, the earlier conclave was essentially a two-man race in which an avowed ideological conservative fought an acolyte of the traditional party establishment. In both years, the decision was not determined until a rules dispute was settled on the convention floor and, in both years, the nomination was not final until the counting of a single dramatic roll call. The 1952 convention also marks the end of the more traditional era of party nominations before television became fully intrusive,

TABLE 29   The Effects of Republican Reapportionment in Order of Relative Gain in Delegates

State	1976 Apportionment		1952 Apportionment		Comparative Ratio
	Ford	Reagan	Ford	Reagan	
Gaining States					
Mississippi	16	14	3	2	3.25
S. C.	9	27	1	5	3.25
Florida	43	23	12	6	1.98
Georgia		48		17	1.53
Louisiana	5	36	2	13	1.45
Alabama		37		14	1.43
Texas		100		38	1.42
Montana		20		8	1.35
Arkansas	10	17	4	7	1.33
California		167		70	1.29
R. I.	19		8		1.28
Oklahoma		36		16	1.22
Virginia	16	35	7	16	1.20
Tennessee	21	22	10	10	1.16
Arizona	2	27	1	13	1.12
N. C.	25	29	12	14	1.12
Missouri	18	31	10	16	1.02
Relatively Stable States					
Kentucky	19	18	10	10	1.00
Michigan	55	29	30	16	.99
Maryland	43		24		.97
N. J.	63	4	36	2	.95
W. Virginia	20	8	11	5	.95
Ohio	91	6	53	3	.94
Colorado	5	26	3	15	.93
Indiana	9	45	5	27	.91
Illinois	86	14	51	9	.90
Oregon	16	14	10	8	.90
Losing States					
New York	134	20	83	13	.87
Connecticut	35		22		.86
Washington	7	31	4	20	.86
Kansas	30	4	19	3	.84
Idaho	4	17	3	11	.81
Minnesota	32	10	21	7	.81
Nevada	5	13	3	9	.81
N. H.	18	3	12	2	.81
N. M.		21		14	.81
Vermont	18		12		.81
Wisconsin	45		30		.81
Penna.	93	10	63	7	.80
Delaware	15	2	11	1	.77
S. D.	9	11	6	8	.77
Utah		20		14	.77
Wyoming	7	10	5	7	.77
Iowa	19	17	14	12	.75
Nebraska	7	18	5	13	.75
N. D.	11	7	9	5	.70
Maine	15	5	12	4	.68
Massachusetts	28	15	25	13	.61
Totals	1123 (51.2%)	1067 (48.8%)	662 (55.9%)	523 (44.1%)	

before the impact of widespread population movements, and before the onset of party reform efforts.

Comparing the real and hypothetical roll calls shows the vital effect of apportionment. In 1976, Ford won a very narrow victory, gaining only some 51 percent of the delegates from the 48 states which could participate in both elections. If the old apportionment had been in effect, he would have won a considerably more comfortable victory, garnering almost 56 percent of these delegates.

The political character of the shift can be seen further in the ordering of the states. This ranking is based on the last column of the table, which presents a ratio comparing the increases in delegates among the states. All states had more delegates in 1976 than in 1952, since the total size of the convention had increased by a factor of 1.85. To calculate the last column, the proportionate increase in each state is normalized by this overall ratio. Where states gained more than this average figure, they show a ratio above 1.0; where they lost in relative strength, the ratio is below 1.0. (States of equal rank are listed alphabetically.)

There is a striking relationship between gains in apportionment and support for Reagan and, conversely, losses in relative position and support of Ford. Of seventeen states increasing in relative power, all but Florida and Rhode Island voted for Reagan. Of those losing in relative position, two-thirds voted for Ford. Among large states declining in relative convention representation, only Indiana voted for Reagan. Otherwise, the pattern was consistent: the traditional areas of Republican power— such as New York, Pennsylvania, Ohio, and even Kansas and North Dakota, stayed with the nominal head of the party even as these states' grip on the party was loosening. The new fortresses of the G.O.P., such as South Carolina, Texas and California, were predominately in support of the challenger, Reagan. The rules reflected a geographical transfer of power and almost promoted a personal transfer of power as well.

The effect of these rules is not likely to be changed in the near future. Reapportionment for the 1980 Republican convention will operate under the same bonus system as in 1976. While the effect of the Carter victory will be to take some seats from southern delegations, amid an overall reduction in the size of the convention, these shifts will not in themselves affect the ideological character of the party. In fact, if we recalculate the 1976 votes, while Reagan would lose only 129, the big losers among the states will be such Ford bastions as New York, Pennsylvania and Ohio. California will actually gain one delegate, and the changes in the South will affect states which supported Ford such as Florida and Kentucky, almost as much as the Reagan areas such as South Carolina and Georgia. Thus the rules will continue to foster conservatism in the Republican party and perhaps will again aid a Reagan candidacy. (This calculation includes all of the units voting in the 1976 convention, including the territories. The allocation of delegates can be expected to change somewhat as a result of the 1978 elections, with states electing Republican governors, senators and congressmen receiving more seats.)

The results are quite different if we make a similar calculation for the Democrats. In this case, we use the 1960 apportionment, since the convention saw a neat confrontation between a liberal Northern candidate, John Kennedy, and a diverse field, and the convention roll call was almost evenly divided between Kennedy and his combined rivals. If that apportionment had been in effect in 1976, Carter actually would have done better than he did in reality, as his percentage of the total delegates would have been two percent higher.

Carter endured this small disadvantage in the 1976 convention because the new apportionment system of the Democrats gave less weight to the South. Instead of rewarding states for electoral victories as such, it gave premiums to those areas with large populations and large Democratic turnout. The advantaged areas therefore were the traditional key states in presidential elections, the industrial areas of the Northeast and Midwest.

Implications

The rules changes of the past years appear to have some important effects. The spread of primaries to new states aided the presential nomination efforts of Carter and Reagan. The particular rules of 1976 worked to the benefit of Carter, who would have lost delegates under a strict system of proportional representation and might have been at a strategic disadvantage as well under a universal system of winner-take-all elections. In the Republican party, proportional representation might have worked to Reagan's advantage in the early campaign, while a plurality system would have benefited President Ford. The reapportionment of delegates has had contrary effects in the two parties. Among Republicans, power has shifted to the South and Southwest, and will continue to benefit relatively conservative candidates. Among Democrats, the new allocation of delegates has increased the relative power of the large industrial states. While this change worked to the advantage of McGovern in 1972, it was mildly disadvantageous to Carter in 1976.

From these data, we can readily imagine different results in the major decision of the 1976 conventions. *If* no new states had enacted primary laws after 1968, and/or *if* the primaries had been conducted under a purer system of proportional representation, and/or *if* Democratic reapportionment had been even more radical, Jimmy Carter might well be back permanently in Georgia. Among Republicans, a spread of primaries to additional states, fuller use of the proportional principle, and larger allocations of bonus votes (unrelated to state population and Republican votes) would probably have made Ronald Reagan the candidate, and perhaps the president.

A full explanation of the nominations of Carter and Ford must also take account of other factors. American politics has been significantly changed by the decline of partisan attachment and the weakening of party organizations. These trends have come close to transforming the nominating conventions into ritualistic institutions, which only ratify decisions reached in other places. The power of state parties has been supplanted by that of candidate centered organizations and by the mass media. New elites and ideological activists have arisen, creating and manipulating new rules. Furthermore, in politics, the individual qualities and skills of participants will always have an influence. It remains true, however, that all political actors must operate within the established set of rules. As the rules change, candidates and organizations will seek to bend them to their purposes, but some will be better able to adapt than others. Rules are neither neutral nor infinitely flexible. In 1976, they do not provide a sufficient explanation of the outcomes, but they are necessary elements in any analysis.

Beyond the fortunes of individual men and even beyond the policy outcomes which follow, the changes in nomination procedures affect the character of our political parties. We are evolving a party system different from the accepted textbook descriptions of decentralized, cadre organizations. The recent burst of party change ("reform" may be inappropriate) is converting our parties to national organizations. The shift of delegates from one state to another is a constituent act of a dominant political body, a manifestation of sovereignty comparable to the Congress' reapportionment of state representatives. The outlawing of winner-take-all primaries and imposition of requirements for proportional representation is an assertion of power by the parties as against the state legislatures, and a destruction of the previous autonomy of state parties. This movement is more advanced in the Democratic party, but the principle of national party supremacy has been at least stated by the Republicans as well.

To speak of sovereign parties suggests the development of strength in these national institutions. The Democratic party indeed seems to be evolving into an organization of considerable scope and power. It has in place functioning bodies with executive, legislative and judicial powers, a formal party charter, and biennial conferences. Yet this presumptively strong organization is unable to control its most vital decision, the choice of a leader. In 1976, it was a mechanism available to the most aggressive and able mechanic, and was ultimately driven by the aspirant with weak support from the states using more traditional means of delegate selection. Gerald Ford, on the other hand, won his narrow victory by relying on the less modernized means of delegate selection and the less nationalized appeals.

The new nationalization of the parties does not mean, at least not yet, the development of strong national party organizations. There is a different character to the new party system, particularly evident among the Democrats. It has an individualist base and plebiscitarian tone. The extension of the primaries, the emphasis on "making each vote count" through proportional representation, and the allocation of delegates are alike in their focus on the individual voter. The state party as a distinct organization is not accorded a legitimate role. It does not choose the delegates, it cannot operate as a unified delegation on the convention floor and, indeed, it has almost no ability to bargain over the presidential nomination at all. But nominations are no longer seen as the decision of distinct and legitimate factions whose interests must be compromised, or vindicated, or vanquished, but at least acknowledged. Rather they are now reviewed purely as the decisions of a collectivity of individuals, and all barriers which distort their opinion must be removed. Primaries must therefore replace state conventions; proportional representation must replace plurality systems; and delegates must be reapportioned. The same reasoning supports a national presidential primary and direct election of the president. The plebiscite is replacing political organization.

Direct democracy has its problems, however, as the history of the initiative and referendum demonstrate. In limiting the federal character of the party system and diminishing the role of the party organizations, we are also reducing the importance of intermediate organizations and voluntary groups which stand between the individual and the overarching national state. Watergate should have made us aware again of the dangers of concentrated power, as American life should remind us daily of the need for more intimate communities. Tocqueville warned, "There are no countries in which associations are more needed to prevent the despotism of faction or the arbitrary power of a prince than those which are democratically constituted." We would do well to heed that warning.

TO THE STUDENT: A COMMENTARY

Now that you have read Rhodes Cook's assessment of the impact of public financing on presidential politics, it will help you to think about his views if you put them into the perspective of what public funding means. The fact is that most Americans simply do not know how we finance our presidential campaigns. In each of two years, 1979 and 1980, one of the editors of this volume, Dan Nimmo, was involved in a nationwide survey of more than 1,600 Americans per year that tried to find out what citizens knew about public financing. When asked to explain how the presidential election campaigns of 1976 had been funded, and how those of 1980 would be, only 16 percent of persons sampled could correctly respond in 1979, only 14 percent in 1980. Asked what "public financing" means, less than 20 percent could say correctly in either year.

So, what is public financing of presidential campaigns? It means two things. First, the federal government gives matching amounts of money to candidates seeking their party's nomination in presidential primaries and caucuses. The general election campaigns of Republican and Democratic nominees are now financed almost entirely by public funds. To qualify for federal money in seeking nominations candidates must raise $5,000 in each of 20 states from individual donations of not more than $250. Once qualified, a candidate has contributions of $250 or less matched by the federal government on a dollar-for-dollar basis.

But, second, there is a catch. Supporters of public funding regard it minor, critics think it crippling—as Cook points out. The catch is that if candidates want to spend public money to get nominated/elected they must accept limits on how much can be spent and on contributions. In prenomination campaigning there are spending limits at both national and state levels. The national limit is $10 million, adjusted for inflation—hence a little over $13 million in 1980. And, if you are seeking your party's nomination there are state ceilings with the amount of the limit calculated by taking the number of people in the state of voting age population, multiplying by $.16, and adjusting for inflation. But, if you add up all state limits they total about twice the $13 million national restriction. So, in this respect the catch is a Catch-22. Finally, if you win your party's nomination, you are limited in what you can spend to defeat the other party's candidate—a little over $26 million in 1980, $21.8 million in 1976.

Limits on contributions round out the catch. In seeking a party's presidential nomination a candidate may accept only $1000 from individuals, $5,000 from political action committees (PACs). And, should you choose to play the nomination game (if you have reached the age of eligibility, i.e., "ID" required), you can spend only $50,000 of your own money.

Add two items. One: a candidate can refuse public funding, thus avoiding spending limits, but not most contribution limits (but can contribute more than $50,000 to one's own campaign). Two: if you don't want to run as a Democrat or Republican but as an independent or a third party candidate, the going is tough; you get federal funds only if you ultimately receive more than 5 percent of the votes—which scarcely helps you before the election! In 1980 there were examples of both items: John Connally refused public financing in his bid for the Republican nomination; John Anderson ran as an independent.

Supporters of public financing are pleased with its success in presidential campaigns. Cook tells you why. So pleased are they, in fact, that public financing of congressional campaigns seems an attractive proposal. Opponents shudder. As Cook suggests, they complain of the red tape, the length of campaigns forced by public funding, the "license to practice" candidacy implied, and of the declining role of party but increased influence of PACs and special interests—all, they say, derived from public financing.

The pros and cons are worth your thought. Take one as an example—PACs. When David Broder told you parties were in trouble and Kevin Phillips detected the rise of the knowledge industry, both pointed to how PACs foster single-issue, special interest politics. But does public financing promote PACs? Cook argues yes, at least in presidential politics. But consider congressional campaigns, where there is not public financing. The menace of the PACs—if menace it is—is even greater. In 1974 PAC donations to congressional candidates were $12.5 million, in 1976 $22.5 million, in 1978 $35.1 million, and in 1980 as high as $50 million. More than 1,100 PACs were active in the late 1970s—contributing money to congressional campaigns on behalf of groups such as trade associations, corporations, labor unions, professional associations, and others. After election those same groups lobby those same congressional officials for favorable legislation.

So perhaps the thing to do is restrict by law what PACs can give to candidates for Congress, then make that up by public financing. Simple? No. Congressional officials who reap the harvest of PAC donations are not eager to restrict them. For example, a PAC can contribute only $10,000 to a House or Senate candidate—$5,000 in the primary election, $5,000 in the general election. But as of mid-1980 there was no limit on the total amount all PACs could give a candidate. A proposal to change all of that—at least as of this writing in mid-1980—has not fared well in Congress. It would change the $5,000 limits to $3,000 limits, place a $70,000 limit from all PACs to a candidate in a two-year election cycle.

The other proposal, i.e., public financing of congressional elections, has fared no better. In one way or another Congress has considered public financing proposals for congressional elections since 1977, but without passage. There have been several reasons. One is that there is no assurance citizens want public financing. Nationwide surveys differ considerably on this score. Gallup surveys consistently indicate a majority of Americans favor public financing of congressional campaigns, but surveys of Civic Service, Inc. find clear-cut majorities opposed. Perhaps citizens' opinions mirror the confusion—i.e., just what would be the impact of public financing? Would special interests gain or lose? Would the political parties gain or lose? Would *you* gain or lose?

One lesson you *can* take from this discussion of public financing is that the consequences of a reform are never easily gauged. Not before the reform is passed, and not always easily after the fact. Gerald Pomper underscores this point in a different way in his discussion of new rules and new games of presidential nominations.

Pomper's major points and the evidence to support them are clear. Only a brief recap is necessary. The first point is that the number and influence of primaries in the process of nominating presidential candidates has increased. The increase parallels a decline in the convention as an arena of bargaining, the pervasive influence of the mass media, public financing, and greater public involvement in the nominating process.

Second, rules of presidential primaries have changed. Party voters rather than state parties express preferences through primary elections. Whether the arrangement is for a winner-take-all (plurality), proportional, or mixed localized means of selecting delegates, the result has been for state party organizations to decline in influence. Here an addition should be made to Pomper's argument, especially in light of the presidential primaries of 1980. The point is that in some states not only the strength of state parties gets diluted through the primaries, so also does the influence of a party's members. Consider the 1980 candidacy of Republican John Anderson. Before deciding to seek the presidency as an independent, Anderson ran in Republican primaries. But his appeal was less to Republican voters than to independents and to Democrats who might pass up the Democratic party's primary and vote instead for Anderson in the Republican contest.

And, argues Pomper, there are new rules for apportioning delegates to nominating conventions. Those rules, you will note, work in the Republican party to advantage in states with long-term Republican loyalties, but in the Democratic party to benefit large industrial, liberal states. In the Democratic party, again, state organizations take second fiddle to direct representation of the wishes of party members.

A question you have been asked, and asked yourself, before arises—so what? Pomper thinks that such rule changes have added new games as well. In 1976 at least the increased number of presidential primaries worked to the advantage of Jimmy Carter and Ronald Reagan. Reagan lost the 1976 nomination to Gerald Ford, but came close to victory. Both Carter and Reagan ran very strong in the new primary states. Pomper was prophetic. In 1980 it was Carter and Reagan as party victors and, in part, for reasons much like those outlined by Pomper for 1976. Pomper also believes and pointedly states that rule changes regarding the awarding of delegates to primary victors and losers and the apportioning of delegates among the states were critical to the outcome of the 1976 nomination struggles. So, we pose a problem for you—i.e., looking back at the 1980 Democratic and Republican contests for presidential nominations, do you think Pomper's views still hold? Was 1980 foretold earlier, or was 1980 unique in its own right?

There is another item you need to speculate about with respect to Pomper's article—an item equally relevant for Cook's analysis of public financing and certainly related to all of the selections you have read in Part 2. Pomper implies that in the effort to convert our political parties into tools for popular participation in the nomination of presidential candidates we have, in effect, but pounded one more nail into the coffin of party politics. Rather than help create strong national party organizations that might hold public officials accountable to us, we have further weakened state parties. What have we replaced them with? "Nothing" would be too optimistic an answer. No, "the plebiscite is replacing political organizations," writes Pomper. Is this good?

As a watcher of politics that is a question you must debate, perhaps even decide. There are pros and cons. The ideal of interested, informed, and rational citizens going to the polls to select party nominees and public officials—even policies—has goaded reformers throughout this century. But what if, as we noted in chapter 3, citizens aren't like that? Do you want them making such decisions? Do you want yourself to make them?

The question will not be easily, even permanently resolved. Indeed, as proposals pour forth for eliminating the Electoral College, for electing the President by direct popular vote, for limiting the President to one six-year term, for financing more and more elections through public funds, etc., the debate will continue. To assist you in taking part you might wish to consult what others have argued. Accounts with both a practical and journalistic flavor include:

Neil Staebler, *The Campaign Finance Revolution*
Arthur Hadley, *The Invisible Primary*
Jules Witcover, *Marathon*

And there are analyses by political scientists:

Herbert Alexander, *Financing Politics*
David Nichols, *Financing Elections*
Richard Watson, *The Presidential Contest*

PART 3 FOLLOWING THE NEWS

10 Politics in the News

INTRODUCTION

Many of the articles you have read in this volume thus far have alluded to the influential part that mass communication, especially television, plays in American politics. Moreover, unless you are markedly unlike other Americans, chances are television and newspapers are your chief source of political information. Nationwide surveys conducted each year for the past two decades indicate that now almost two-thirds of Americans rely upon TV as a news source and one-half rely upon newspapers (usually in conjunction with TV). Fewer than one in twenty citizens acquire political information from other people. And, asked which medium they believe most one-half of Americans say TV, one-fourth newspapers.

Hence, given the importance of the media of mass communication in the political life of the nation and to the lives of individual citizens, it is important to ask how the mass media present politics to us and what difference that presentation makes. In this chapter we begin that task by looking first at one format of TV news, then at how newspapers and television news contribute to political reasoning. With chapter 11 we examine the overall impact of television upon American politics. Finally, in chapter 12 we explore a growing trend among political journalists and politicians alike, i.e., the use of opinion polls in politics.

"Disco News" by Edwin Diamond is one increasingly fashionable format of TV news programs. In many instances *what* the news is has less impact upon people than *how* it is presented to them. Indeed the form of a news story may determine its content. Consider the nightly network TV news programs. Because of the limits imposed by the brevity of a 30-minute program, the news consists of little more than a series of headlines read by a series of TV anchors. The result—as we noted in our prologue—is to provide viewers with an acquaintance with things, but little knowledge about them.

Diamond, however, is concerned with more than simply the headline aspects of TV news. The disco format refers to the placement of news stories and the pacing of news programs. As you read his selection consider the alternative formats for news programing familiar to you. Are the likely consequences of each the same as those implied by Diamond?

In their companion selection to Diamond's piece, Peter Clarke and Eric Fredin go beyond the format of a single medium such as television. Instead they compare the effects of newspapers and television upon people's levels of political information and citizens abilities to reason about politics. Note that "reasoning" is narrowly defined, that is, simply having reasons for favoring or rejecting political alternatives, not the ways people think through political problems to reach those preferences. In short, Clarke and Fredin come close to saying that having political information and political reasoning are the same thing. Before reading their argument, think back on something you reflected upon while studying the contents of chapter 3. There we considered the qualities citizens must have to make democracy work. Are Clarke and Fredin talking about the same thing; do they reach the same conclusions?

Peter Clarke is a professor of journalism at the University of Michigan. He has written extensively about the relationship of mass communication to political behavior since receiving his Ph.D. in mass communication from the University of Minnesota. Among his many published works is the edited volume, *New Models for Mass Communication Research.* His coauthor, Eric Fredin, was a graduate student in mass communication at the time he worked with Clarke on the article you will read. Since you have already met Edwin Diamond in conjunction with his article analyzing the making of television commercials for Ford and Carter in 1976, nothing need be added about him here. Hence, consider now what he has to say about disco news.

DISCO NEWS

Edwin Diamond

Edited and reprinted from Washington Journalism Review *1 (September/October 1979): 26, 28.*

Fifty-three years ago, the American philosopher George Herbert Mead suggested that there are two models of journalism. One form he called the information model. Information journalism reported facts, such as election results, it emphasized the "truth value" of news. The other journalistic form Mead called the story model. Story journalism emphasized the enjoyability and "consumatory value" of news; story news was presented in such a way as to create satisfying esthetic experiences, and to help people relate events to their own lives. A refreshing as well as an original thinker, Mead rather approved of story journalism; he thought it was natural that popular newspapers sent out their reporters to get a story, rather than just the facts.

There was no way, of course, for Mead to be able to foresee that the story form in the late 1970's would pursue enjoyability toward a model of journalism that is practically all entertainment, and practically zero information. This new form, most instantly recognizable on some television news and public affairs programs, emphasizes style over substance. Programs must have pace. On-air talent must be contemporary

Now-looking people. What is said, the reporting and narration, becomes less and less important than how people look when they are saying it. There are lights, action, bright colors, pulsing music, a fast beat and, overall, a general mindlessness. In a word, it is Disco News.

But we're getting ahead of the story. Though Mead was interested in the newspaper journalism of the 1920's, contemporary consumers of the media have no difficulty relating his models to our current experience. A serious newspaper model of the 1920's, the *New York Times,* is an even better practitioner of information journalism today, and the *Times* has been joined by other serious newspapers, such as the *Washington Post, Washington Star* and the *Los Angeles Times.* Since the 1920's, popular newspapers, in Mead's terms, have been paying more attention to fact reporting (see, for example, the changes at the *New York Daily News,* the largest circulation daily in the country). The story telling mode has been taken over, first by news magazines and, more recently, by television news.

It is hardly news to anyone that the big journalistic success stories of the last decade involve practitioners of the story model—*People* magazine in print and CBS' News *60 Minutes* on television. They package the news into entertaining and smoothly consumed stories; and because success breeds imitation, *People* and *60 Minutes* are being widely copied, the former by clones like *Us* and the new *Media People* by the old-line news magazines, and the latter by story-model television shows such as NBC's new *Prime Time Sunday* and ABC's revamped *20/20* program.

What is news, however, is the extent to which the journalists who engage in story form news are unaware of how pervasively certain esthetic values—for example, considerations of pace, "look," the feel of it all—rather than news values shape their work. Commentators have sniffed around the edges of this development when they worried about a "television generation." Such talk was always done in a hand-wringing way; how awful it would be when people who never learned to read or write properly would grow up and take charge of the world, etc., etc., etc. Well, some of them *are* taking over now. Television is in a transitional period from the story form to a new form that I call Disco News.

Obviously, Disco News is an exaggeration, a journalistic critic's hype as outrageous as the form it rails against. Walter Cronkite will always deliver the news goods straight, in a serious responsible fashion. When he goes, reliable Roger Mudd will continue to uphold the standards. John Chancellor will retain his calm, professorial mien. Frank Reynolds, Max Robinson, Barbara Walters . . . we'll never see them in Disco News blazers.

But can we really be sure? Cronkite, Chancellor et al. and the executives who have nurtured them over the last 20 years represent the first, or 1960's, television generation. Almost all these men and women came from newspapers, wire services or magazines. They were trained in the print information model. The transitional generation of television journalists is made up of 1970's figures like Tom Snyder, Tom Brokaw and the younger men and women who produce programs like *Prime Time Sunday, Today.* . . . Their experience is almost solely in broadcasting; their reporting and writing experience is somewhat limited. The world of the two-minute standupper and the 10-second react may be the only world they know. They may have keen eyes for format but no real ear for content.

I had a chance to observe this tone deafness a while back in what turned out to be a beautiful experimental setting. It didn't start that way. I had invited a highly intelligent and sensible television producer to a seminar at MIT to show some videotape samples of the network news program she worked on. Proudly, she played for the class the videotape cassette of an economic report that led the newscast the previous night—the top of the show.

There was the anchor wishing us good evening; cut to the Washington reporter with the latest inflation bad news; then quickly three consumer reports from around the country; then a U.S. map with graphics showing cost of living rates; back to the anchor and then the Washington reporter, followed by tape and sound "bites"—15-second quotes—from Congressional leaders and Cabinet officers. Finally, a Wall Street reaction . . . and then break for commercial. In all, no more than three minutes had elapsed.

As the various tape, sound and graphics parts in the economics package gave way to each other, the producer snapped her fingers, and whispered "hit it . . ." right in time with each element. She was proud of the network's handiwork, but the students in the classroom shot up their hands. What was that all about? What did it mean? What were you trying to tell us about the economy? Of course, college students relish nothing more than deflating establishment (in their eyes) types; and if the guest is a friend of the professor, so much the better. But when we all watched the videotape once again from the point of view of the audience—people who know little about the effort that goes into the smooth mingling of tape and sound and videofonts and slides, and care even less—we had to admit that it was difficult to grasp, sort out and understand the news somewhere underneath all the production.

I am more empathetic of television than the students. Jim Snyder, a superb television news director of the old school, once told me that producing a daily news program for television was like "wrestling with a big bear." The challenges of bringing the human and technical problems together are prodigious. Another old school journalist, Bill Moyers, uses a different but equally vivid figure of speech. After completing twenty-six weeks of his *Journal* on public television early this summer, he observed that Christopher Columbus and television producers have a lot in common. Columbus didn't know where he was going, didn't know where he was when he got there, and didn't know where he had been when he returned—and television producers find themselves in that same boat week after week.

Jim Snyder, Moyers and members of the older generation of television journalism are perhaps more modest about their abilities than the newer breed, and more sensitive to the prospects of story-form news becoming Disco News. Once you've been to the disco, it's hard for anyone not to get caught up in the beat. A few days ago, someone asked me what I thought of the July 25 Jimmy Carter speech on television. "Well," I began, "I thought he *looked* good. . . ." The question, "but what about what he *said*," what about his proposals, sharply brought me out of the disco mode.

In any argument about the entertainment gloss on television news and public affairs, someone can always say reassuringly, "these show business values won't take over the evening news." Or, as a second line of defense, the argument might be, "even if television goes disco, we'll still have serious print outlets." As for the first argument, I can only wonder. The ineffable Tom Snyder was quoted the other day as saying he thinks that he'd rather become the next host of the NBC *Tonight* show—succeeding Johnny Carson—than the next anchor of the NBC *Nightly News*—succeeding John Chancellor. But who's giving him that choice?

As for the fall-back argument about the sanctity of print, everyone knows that *People* magazine was designed to look like undemanding, consumatory, enjoyable television—big pictures, small captions, beautiful people, no issues. We also know that supposedly serious magazines and newspapers are now trying to look like *People* magazine. What happens to the news when everyone goes disco?

NEWSPAPERS, TELEVISION AND POLITICAL REASONING

PETER CLARKE AND ERIC FREDIN

Edited and reprinted from Public Opinion Quarterly *42 (Summer 1978): 143–160.*

One of the most powerful hopes advanced by theories of representative government is that news media remain free so they may educate the public in making political choices. Ignorance condemns people to sway with the most available rhetoric. The uninformed person chooses randomly or out of habit to support candidates or policies. Often he or she avoids the political arena altogether—perhaps because of hedonism or alienation.

Researchers should take pains, therefore, to plot the educational role of journalism. The nature of this role, and how different media share in it, may yield hints about the future for rationality and order in American political life. Studies have recently confirmed that this educational role exists, despite solemn, sociological pronouncements a few years back about "minimal effects." Agenda setting by media is widely recognized now. Learning about public affairs from media has been documented, holding competing explanations constant.

This article presents two amplifications to recent documentation. The first details the relative contributions of newspapers and television to the public informing process. These contributions may interest prophets of the American political future who note the steady slippage in per capita circulation of newspapers and the persistent rise in minutes spent viewing television news. Although this shift may produce changes in levels of political understanding, it is also possible that informing functions traditionally served by newspapers are being assumed by electronic journalism. The first findings reported below shed light on these alternative possibilities.

A second goal is to discern whether characteristics of media offered to citizens play a part in how informed people are. For reasons that will be made clear, amount of newspaper competition in markets is a key to understanding public information about political affairs. Since competition among newspapers is thought to be declining, any relationship between competition and levels of information would have implications for the future course of American political behavior.

Knowing about Public Affairs

What is the proper definition of being "informed"? The present analysis argues that possessing information about public affairs means *having reasons for favoring or rejecting political alternatives.* Having reasons for perceiving or acting equips a person to explain choices—to self as well as others—lending order and pattern to political action. Reasons provide a framework for acquiring and processing additional information. Helping people develop reasons (to suit their own beliefs) is a goal to which schools and news media aspire.

This survey interviewed people at length about their reasons for supporting or rejecting political contenders in an important race—the election for United States senator in their state. (Other arenas of choice would also have been appropriate.) The senatorial contest can be used to compare the informing functions of two competing media systems, daily newspapers and television.

The analysis does not dwell on the specific reasons people offer. As one would expect, some citizens have no choice at all for U.S. senator or, having chosen, can present no explanation for their preference. Other people express reasons of a discouragingly conventional sort. A tiny minority fulfill the hopes of their civics teachers by enlarging on the candidates' policy positions or advantages that would accrue to certain groups if one were elected instead of the other. Expressing some reasons for senatorial choice, however primitive, is a precondition for having an elaborate point of view. The following analysis might be described as tracing the *minimum conditions* for an informed citizenry.

Contrary to popular opinion, research demonstrates that the public relies on newspapers somewhat more than on television for political news. Both vehicles are especially important in state and local affairs untouched by magazine journalism. This study considers extent of exposure to newspapers and television news as potentially informing vehicles and notes whether people discriminate political messages in these media. As the findings show, message discrimination represents a more direct and powerful contribution to learning than extent of exposure.

The concept of message discrimination (examined elsewhere) is meant to replace the conventional idea of gross media use as evidence that communication events have transpired. Instead, the amount of communication people have experienced is reflected by their reports of having discriminated symbols about specified topics, not by minutes spent exposed to media or frequency of reading or viewing. To measure message discrimination, the interview asked two kinds of questions that provided maximum opportunity to relate the political messages people found in media. One is whether they had read or seen anything having to do with an election campaign, recently concluded. The other is whether they had read or seen messages having to do with national political issues that they noted as important earlier in the interview. As with information holding, the concept of message discrimination provides latitude for people to report behavior they feel relevant to the political scene.

A variety of factors surely affect relationships between what the media convey about politics and growth in public awareness. Statistical controls might be imposed for many variables—race, income, sex of respondent, and more. A narrower path is followed here in order to concentrate attention on people's skills in making effective use of media and on their likely motivations for doing so. One step is to hold constant the level of formal education. This major stratification variable correlates powerfully with use of media and with knowing and participating in public affairs. Furthermore, media differ in the educational attainment of the audiences they reach. In the present analysis, education serves as a shorthand measure of ability.

People differ, also, in their willingness to follow public affairs. Some have been socialized by circumstances as well as institutions to concern themselves with political outcomes.

With education and interest controlled, there is some assurance that the remaining variance arises from the information environment to which people are exposed. This environment can fluctuate according to the demands of political events and the way in which events, like campaigns, are reported.

Research Methods

Data originate from detailed personal interviews with a weighted sample of 1,883 adults, a cross-section of the American public in states with Senate elections in 1974. The sample was selected by multistage, probability methods. Research design, field supervision of data collection, coding, and documentation were conducted according to high standards of the Center for Political Studies in the Institute for Social Research at Michigan.

Interviewing took place following the off-year congressional election; this analysis is confined to 25 states in the continental region where the Center had designated sample points and where senatorial elections were underway. Sample clusters of households represent 67 media markets, ranging from metropolitan giants like New York and San Francisco to rural hamlets in Pitt County, North Carolina and Randolph County, Illinois. In the middle are such varied media locales as Louisville, Tulsa, Salt Lake City, Tulare, Bridgeport, and more.

One may examine these data in two ways: first, at the level of individual behavior, correlating variables across persons; or second, by aggregating data within media markets and correlating across them. The second strategy is followed in order to focus toward the end on a characteristic of media markets that may be associated with how informed people are. This characteristic is the level of media competition—the potential, at least, for a diversity of voices about public affairs, or a multitude of news presentations available to the public.

Measures

The criterion variable is having reasons for liking or disliking the two major party candidates for Senate. The main questions read: "Was there anything in particular about the Democratic (Republican) candidate for Senator that made you want to vote for (against) him (her)?" Respondents were quizzed extensively about likes and dislikes, and as many as 12 responses were coded into an elaborate system of content categories.

Admittedly, the measure favors people who consider themselves participants in the political process. Respondents who resolved not to vote after they studied the contenders and decided neither was worth support might have disclaimed having reasons to "vote for" or "against." They would thus be misclassified in terms of the meaning we attach to this measure—a reflection of having reasons for political choice.

Reading newspapers and viewing television news were measured with conventional items. Message discrimination, as already explained, used one set of questions asking whether the respondent had read anything or seen any programs about the recent campaign, and another battery inquired into reading and viewing about an important national problem the respondent had noted and discussed earlier in the interview. Descriptions of these messages were also content analyzed according to a detailed coding scheme.

Interest in public affairs was measured early in the interview with the following item: "Some people seem to follow what's going on in government and public affairs most of the time, whether there's an election going on or not. Others aren't that interested. Would you say you follow what's going on in government and public affairs most of the time, some of the time, only now and then, or hardly at all?"

Results

Predicting Information Holding

Correlations are first examined between having reasons for choice between senatorial candidates and use of news media. Table 30 shows zero-order coefficients between all predictors and information level. Correlations have been calculated between mean levels for each pair of variables across the 67 news markets in which there were elections for U.S. Senate in 1974.

The limited contribution of television coverage to public information is immediately apparent. Neither TV news viewing nor message discrimination in any television programing correlates significantly with knowing about senatorial contenders. Newspapers contrast by showing large correlations for both number of papers read and amount of message discrimination. Of course, levels of education and political interest in the 67 markets are associated with average information holding.

TABLE 30   Zero-order Correlations between All Predictors and Number of Reasons for Senate Choice

	r
Exposure to TV news throughout day	.10
Number of newspapers read	.45
Discriminating problem and campaign messages on TV	.16
Discriminating problem and campaign messages in papers	.57
Interest in public affairs	.49
Education	.33

$r_{.05} = .24$.
$N = 67$ markets, less one market in the case of TV news exposure for which there were insufficient data.

A more stringent test can be performed for the informing value of television and newspapers, controlling for education and political interest and distinguishing between types of communication variables measured in this study. Only a minority in the audience is devoted to television news or reads newspapers heavily for their political content. To assess political informing functions one should hold media exposure constant, along with education and interest in public affairs.

Multiple regression simultaneously invoking all predictors represents the appropriate analysis. Overall news viewing and newspaper reading are eliminated as correlates of knowing about senatorial candidates. Discriminating messages in newspapers remains a strong predictor; discriminating messages on television shows a *negative* relationship that approaches the .05 level of significance.

The correlations supply persuasive evidence for a unique educational role by newspapers. Messages in newspapers confer information beyond what can be expected from general exposure levels. Television may actually exert an inhibiting effect on knowing about politics.

Is this because people simply do not find messages about public affairs on television? Not according to this survey. Average scores are alike for measures of following the campaign and problems in newspapers and television.

Are people who discriminate messages in newspapers fundamentally different from people who report this experience with television? Possibly. But that kind of explanation must confront the *positive* correlation between these two communication behaviors.

Are there substantial differences in the kinds of messages people can read and those they can view and hear? Undoubtedly. But any differences do not extend to the *topics* those messages cover. We content-analyzed topics reported by newspapers (front pages only) and tape-recorded television news broadcasts before the election. Conclusion of this part of the research awaits coding of more of the news programs taped in the 67 markets. However, topic emphasis by a few stations that have been analyzed correlates highly with the same-city newspaper coverage, suggesting one would find more similarities than differences between media in their treatment of public affairs. One is left for the moment with familiar speculations about why newspapers convey more information—their greater content and detail, audience control over the pace of exposure, and so forth.

Summary

Results are drawn from a nationwide sample including many media outlets. Findings underscore the superiority of newspapers as agents of information to help people identify assets and liabilities of important political contenders.

One cannot determine with these data why television should demonstrate a suppressing effect on information. Viewing and recalling political messages is strongly related to television news exposure, and is even related to message discrimination in newspapers. But when appropriate controls are made in analysis, areas where people use television for political news emerge as less informed than areas of equal education and political interest where people avoid the medium.

Much remains to be learned about causal paths among richness of communication resources, public attention to these resources, skill and motivation to decipher messages, and retention of information. And one must distinguish between long-term developments in political understanding and the foreshortened learning that may take place between candidate nominations and election day, especially when new political figures emerge.

The present analysis has not been able to separate candidate attributes long familiar to the public (an incumbent's record in public office, for example) from attributes only recently communicated (e.g., a challenger's image of honesty or sincerity). Recent learning may correlate more than older learning with patterns of mass media use. Television portrayals may be especially important for learning during the closing days of a campaign—when apathetic citizens first pay attention to the passing political parade. All differences in time span and recency of learning have inevitably been mixed in the cross-sectional data analysis presented here.

Our results do not dismiss television as a political force in America. The data simply call into question television's power to convey candidates' policy positions or personality in such a way that heavy viewers will retain more of this information than light viewers.

Results suggest we can legitimately feel unease over declining newspaper circulation and over any industry developments that limit the amount of newspaper competition within markets. Opportunity to reason about political events requires *having* reasons. If communication assets that are linked to public reasoning weaken, the quality of public judgments about partisan contenders may be in jeopardy.

TO THE STUDENT: A COMMENTARY

Diamond makes an important point at the beginning of his article. Drawing upon the philosopher George Herbert Mead he contrasts information journalism with story journalism. This distinction should not be new to you. It is related to the distinction we made in our prologue between a scientific versus dramatic approach to understanding, to acquiring knowledge about something in addition to acquaintance with it. Information journalism presents facts, analyses of those facts, and interpretations. It is akin to what a social scientist does or the reporting undertaken by a Type III, interpretative, journalist. In story journalism the emphasis is upon narration, entertainment, and drama. This, writes Diamond, is the format of TV news.

Let us pause for a minor disagreement with Diamond. He argues, correctly, that since the 1920s popular newspapers have moved in the direction of more information journalism, less story journalism. Story journalism became the format of, first, news magazines, then, television. There is nothing wrong in that general view if we remember that the difference between information and story journalism is one of emphasis, not of kind. What Diamond calls the "serious newspaper model" still carries within it a considerable body of story journalism. Facts do not exist solely for facts alone, nor for reporting information. Facts also entertain. So, if you pick up a copy of a "serious" newspaper, don't be surprised to find in it a great portion of content devoted to entertaining news, narration, and dramatic presentation.

In its infancy the format of TV news derived from the way newspapers and radio reported information. Early TV news programs minimized visual content. Instead a "talking head" merely read the news, often as though newspaper headlines were being read, and in a format borrowed from radio news programs. And much of that has changed. TV news now has a format of its own, and disco is part of it. But it can be argued that the TV news format no longer is the stepchild of newspapers or radio but, in contrast, now shapes the formats of the other news media. Diamond even suggests this to some degree—*People* magazine has an open, breezy, quick-paced format that apes the TV format. Or, consider that the major news weeklies have redesigned their formats in recent years to appear more like television—open margins, glossy color photos, dramatic pictures, cutesy headlines. A similar format adaptation has hit newspapers, whether they be the popular *National Enquirer* or "serious" journals such as the *New York Times* (examine its Sunday *Magazine* or "Week in Review"), *Washington Post, Washington Star,* or *Los Angeles Times.*

What, then, is the format of TV news? In part it is as Diamond describes—a fast-paced mixture of sight, sound, graphics, and breathless reporting. All of this centers on one or more superstars whose popularity and credibility capture and hold interested audiences. The *ABC World News Tonight* is but the leading example. Anchors in New York, Washington, Chicago, and London switch to one another and hopscotch from story to story in a manner reminiscent of reporters stationed around a two-mile oval stock car race track as they call the race.

But the format of TV news is something more. It is not only disco, it is soap opera. Although nightly reports of them may be brief, stories are—like the melodrama of a soap opera—continuous. That is, they must last awhile and consist of rising and falling drama, preferably with a climax. The story of 1980 clearly exemplifying the soap opera motif was coverage of the presidential election—from the caucuses in Iowa in January through election day in November. There unveiled was conflict between combatants (the candidates), resolutions by outside forces (voters), rising and falling expectations (reported as the results of pre- and post-election polls), an overall plot (a race to the White House), and a cast of heroes, villains, and fools (think, for instance, of the "heroic quest of John Anderson"). There are, of course, other soap operas—the hostage crisis in Iran, the Soviet invasion of Afghanistan, the Jonestown Massacre, the perils of Three Mile Island, and numerous examples you could add to the list.

Assume, in spite of our minor quibble about newspapers still carrying a great deal of story journalism, that Diamond is right. Assume, then, that newspapers emphasize information journalism, television story journalism. You might then speculate that there would be a difference in how people respond to the news, a difference based upon whether they get their news from newspapers or television. Clarke and Fredin say as much.

Clarke and Fredin begin by stating their view of what the minimum conditions for an informed citizenry are in a democracy. You are, they argue, informed if you possess facts about a political question and are able to give reasons for making the choices you do with respect to it. How can such minimum conditions be measured? Clarke and Fredin insist it takes more than just finding out how much you read the newspaper or watch TV news. Whether you can discriminate the information you receive is crucial. That means two things: (1) do you recall seeing or reading anything about particular political events, and (2) do you recall seeing or reading anything about key political issues you think important? Using a cross-section sampling of Americans in 1974 Clarke and Fredin examined varying levels of message discrimination, reasons for voting for U.S. senatorial candidates, and levels of newspaper reading and TV news viewing.

With the experience you have had thus far, we are confident you recognize the analytical techniques Clarke and Fredin use to derive their conclusions—correlations, multiple regression, levels of statistical significance, etc. What, then, do they find? First, newspaper reading correlates positively with having reasons to prefer one senatorial candidate over another; TV exposure correlates negatively with such "reasoning." In fact, "television may actually exert an inhibiting effect on knowing about politics."

In a scientific investigation of the kind Clarke and Fredin engage in it is not enough merely to uncover an interesting finding. There must be some effort to explain that result. Why do newspapers play a unique information role? Clarke and Fredin dismiss several possibilities for you. It is not, for example, a question of people who read newspapers being different in levels of education and political interest from those who watch TV news. Nor is it because there is less news on TV about public affairs. And, the kinds of messages in newspapers and TV news don't make the difference either. In a portion of their article that we have omitted, Clarke and Fredin report the results of an analysis of the relationship between competition between newspapers in market areas and levels of political reasoning. They find that news markets with competition among daily newspapers show greater levels of political information than exist in monopoly areas. This, of course, does not say why newspaper readers and television viewers differ in political reasoning but does imply that as newspaper competition decreases and people are forced to turn more toward television, citizens' understanding of politics may weaken.

On the basis of what we said earlier we invite you to speculate about one other possibility. To the degree that newspapers employ information more than story journalism while TV news does the reverse (remember it is all a matter of emphasis rather than either/or), people thus heed and recall information rather than drama if they are newspaper readers. And, if newspapers disappear Clarke and Fredin may be right, i.e., people forced to turn to television may surrender their "political reasoning." But the forecast could be even more dire—at least if you believe that a democratic citizenry should be informed and rational. As newspapers try to compete with television as information/entertainment media, they too may adopt disco-melodrama formats. On a daily basis outlets for information journalism may disappear. What then of an informed citizenry?

The nature of news formats and the effect of differing formats upon the citizen's understanding of politics has received only limited attention from students of journalism and politics, journalists, and politicians. But there are some important volumes you can turn to for assistance in thinking about the problem. A few worthy accounts by journalists include:

Edwin Diamond, *Good News, Bad News*

David Halberstam, *The Powers That Be*

Fred Friendly, *Due to Circumstances Beyond Our Control*

Paul Gates, *Air Time: The Inside Story of CBS News*

And among those by social scientists consider:

David L. Altheide and Robert P. Snow, *Media Logic*

Thomas E. Patterson and Robert D. McClure, *The Unseeing Eye*

Gaye Tuchman, *Making News*

James David Barber, *Race for the Presidency* (especially chapters 2 and 3)

11 TV Politics

INTRODUCTION

If you are like most Americans today, by the time you reached 18 years of age you had spent more time viewing television than sitting in the classroom. For the most part watching politics has meant watching television. The politics you saw was not limited to the content of what TV executives call "public affairs programming," i.e., news, documentaries, coverage of presidential activities and congressional hearings, interviews, political speeches, and news magazines (such as *60 Minutes*). You also saw paid political advertising in the form of spot commercials, as described in chapter 7. And beyond that, you witnessed political content in entertainment programming. Sometimes it was obvious as in docudramas about the lives of political figures, political satire on *Saturday Night Live* and other shows, and political films like *The Candidate* or *Washington Behind Closed Doors.* Sometimes the political content of entertainment programs was not so apparent, as in daily soap operas or seemingly unending reruns of *Star Trek,* but was still implicit.

What political effects has all this viewing had, some 15,000 hours before age 18 for the average person growing up today? Commentators disagree. Some condemn TV for every ill Americans suffer—from the breakup of the family to the buildup of nuclear arsenals. Others dismiss television as of scarcely any political consequence at all. Arrayed between these poles are a host of other views, pro and con, regarding TV's impact.

The two selections in this chapter offer you the flavor of the debate. Actually there are three articles. The piece that follows by George Will, "Television: Paper Tiger, Not Political Giant," consists of two commentaries he wrote for *Newsweek* magazine. We have put them together to provide you with a rounded version of Will's views. The first section, "Prisoners of TV," provides you with his thoughts on TV's role in our society; the second, "The Not-So-Mighty Tube," is Will's rejoinder to those who believe that television is a force that reworks our daily lives and political institutions.

As you will note, one of those persons George Will seeks to rebut is political scientist

Michael Robinson, the author of the second article you read, "Prime Time Chic." In fact, Will takes issue with a 1977 article Robinson wrote. In that article Robinson sounded a theme that he has emphasized for several years, namely, that in the 1950s TV reflected Americans' social and political values; today TV molds them. It is a theme sounded once more in "Prime Time Chic," an article appearing in 1979, two years later than the piece that provoked Will's ire.

Mike Robinson teaches politics at Catholic University in Washington, D.C. He received his Ph.D. in political science from the University of Michigan. His dissertation, *Public Affairs Television and the Growth of Political Malaise,* was considered the best written by any political scientist in 1973 and received a major award from the American Political Science Association. In it Robinson acted the iconoclast. The dictionary says an iconoclast is one "who attacks and seeks to overthrow traditional or popular ideas or institutions." Mike Robinson does not necessarily seek to overthrow conventional ways of viewing politics, but he does enjoy attacking them. In his dissertation he disputed the reigning view of political scientists that TV had little impact upon politics. Instead, he wrote, political television was a major factor shaping Americans' feelings of frustration and futility in the 1960s, perhaps a key factor underlying the crisis of confidence you read so much about in chapter 2.

George Will was once a political scientist. He taught the subject at three universities, then worked as an assistant to U.S. Senator Gordon Allott of Colorado. But then he took up journalism, writing first for the conservative *National Review.* His writing was so sprightly that the liberal *Washington Post* added him as a columnist in 1973. In 1977 he received a Pulitzer Prize for distinguished commentary. So his credentials as a Type III journalist are solid. That does not, however, mean he gets the better of Robinson. Or does he? You decide.

TELEVISION: PAPER TIGER, NOT POLITICAL GIANT

George F. Will

Edited and reprinted from "Prisoners of TV" and "The Not-So-Mighty Tube" in Newsweek *January 10, 1977: 76, and August 8, 1977: 84, respectively.*

Prisoners of TV

Disparagement of television is second only to watching television as an American pastime. And most disparagement of television is a series of footnotes to Fred Allen, who called television "chewing gum for the eyes." He meant that television is not nourishing.

Most of it is unnourishing. But so is most criticism of it. And recently Eric Sevareid, who has brought a touch of class to print and broadcast journalism, rounded on the critics.

"For TV," he said, "the demand-supply equation is monstrously distorted . . . TV programing consumes 18 to 24 hours a day, 365 days of the year. No other medium of information or entertainment ever tried anything like that. How many good new plays appear in the theaters of this country each year? How many fine new motion pictures? Add it all together and perhaps you could fill twenty evenings out of the 365."

As a station manager says, "Hell, there isn't even enough mediocrity to go around." Certainly, it is sentimental to believe that "Our Miss Brooks" on radio was superior to "Mary Tyler Moore" on television. And it is nutty to suppose that people would read more Virginia Woolf if they watched less "Laverne & Shirley." It may even be true that, as Sevareid insists, television stimulates more conversation than it suppresses: "Nonconversing families were always that way." And the theory that television kills reading is a theory killed by a fact: since television, book sales have grown much faster than the population has grown.

Concern with Content

It is not true that sponsors control the content of television entertainment. True, the gas utility that sponsored the drama "Judgment at Nuremberg" bleeped out the words "gas ovens" from references to Nazi crimes. But television would be better if sponsors concerned themselves with content by boycotting gratuitously violent shows like "Starsky and Hutch." To its great credit J. Walter Thompson, the largest advertising agency, is warning sponsors about their complicity in what the agency calls, "the desensitization of America."

As the networks scramble for audiences, they do contribute to the coarsening of American life by edging ever closer to the soft-core pornography of violence and sex. But without excusing the networks, it must be said that they are pulled along, downward, by movies. Television increases the dosages of shocking material in order to grab the attention of audiences that have become blasé about the sort of mayhem in movies like "Taxi Driver" and "Marathon Man." The most violent *entertainment* on television recently was in movies like "The Godfather" and "The Wild Bunch." Of course worse violence was in news stories from Beirut.

Television news is, it seems, a burr under the nation's saddle. It is watched, voluntarily, by scores of millions, and it is criticized, incessantly, by (it sometimes seems) as many.

Part of the problem is that television news is so brief. Subtract commercials and there are 22 minutes in the news portion. A two-minute story is longer than most. It has been noted that a transcript of the network news would not fill half the front page of *The New York Times.* But such quantitative comparisons miss this point: a page of print cannot have the unique impact of, say, 30 seconds of film showing Joe McCarthy bullying a witness, or retreating Vietnamese soldiers clinging to helicopters.

Viewer as Volunteer

Taking 22 minutes to cover the world *is* a bit like taking a teacup to empty the ocean. And the compression of television journalism magnifies the importance of editorial judgments, and hence magnifies the suspicion of "bias." The viewer is a volunteer, but he also is, in a sense, as Sevareid says, a prisoner: ". . . A newspaper or magazine reader can be his or her own editor in a vital sense. He can glance over it and decide what to read, what to pass by. The TV viewer is a restless prisoner, obliged to sit through what does not interest him to get to what may interest him."

Recently David Brinkley wondered why NBC had routinely run a two-minute story of indecisive, unremarkable fighting in Beirut. It was, he believes, a story of interest to only a tiny fraction of NBC's viewers. Brinkley thinks the problem is that television has adopted newspapers' standards of news, standards that are inappropriate for television because viewers, unlike readers, cannot "skip around." But viewers *can* skip around, to competing programs. And they may skip unless a program provides a steady dosage of what a camera provides best, *entertaining action.*

When wondering why NBC aired the story of meaningless Beirut violence, Brinkley concluded: "We couldn't even use the excuse that the story was easy to get. It wasn't. It was hard, dangerous work for a correspondent and a camera crew and it was sent to the U.S. by satellite, which is expensive." But the difficulty of getting a story, far from being an excuse for not getting it, can be a "reason" for getting it. The Beirut story *was* hard to get. But *only* television could get the sight and sound of battle.

"And in the end," Brinkley asks, "after all the work, danger, time and money, who really wanted to see it? In my opinion, almost nobody." I disagree. Perhaps the Beirut war scenes are *precisely* the sort of things viewers want to see.

Boring the Audience

Brinkley, a superb professional, assumes people watch news in order to see newsworthy things. So, regarding the scenes of meaningless Beirut violence, he asks, "Why bore the audience any more than necessary?" *Bore* the audience? With *war*? Not likely. Brinkley's audience does not consist of Brinkleys. His news show is a brief information program, sandwiched between an afternoon of entertainment and an evening of entertainment. A lot of people turn on news shows in search of . . . entertainment.

Television's raison d'être is the camera. Television is not always "chewing gum for the eyes," but it always is *for the eyes.* People do not stare at their refrigerators. They stare at their television sets, expecting remarkable sights to appear there. And even unnewsworthy fighting is a riveting *sight.* As a news-gathering instrument a camera is at once powerful and limited. It can never produce a picture of an idea. It always can produce vivid pictures of action. Such pictures *can* be invaluable journalism. They can hardly fail to be entertaining.

While Brinkley and Sevareid and other good people in television journalism have been working to make their powerful technology serve the public good, some bad people in television entertainment have their own uses for Beirut. NBC's "Saturday Night," which fancies itself satire, saw comic potential in a ghastly picture of a body being dragged behind a car through Beirut. The "Saturday Night" satirists superimposed a "Just Married" sign on the car. That's entertainment, at least for "Saturday Night's" desensitized young audience, television's children.

The Not-So-Mighty Tube

In simpler days it was said that the hand that rocked the cradle ruled the world. Today, says Prof. Michael J. Robinson of Catholic University (in *The Public Interest*), the rule of television rocks the world: "In the 1950s television was a *reflection* of our social and political opinions, but by the 1960s it was an important *cause* of them." He insists that television journalism did "engender" fundamental changes, "moving us" toward conservatism, and entertainment programing is a "fomenter" of social liberalism, "fostering" and "pushing us toward" change:

"Mary Tyler Moore and 'Mary Tyler Mooreism' seem to have been unusually effective in 'consciousness raising.' Between 1958 and 1969, the percentage of women accepting the idea that a woman could serve effectively as President actually *declined* by 3 per cent. But between 1969 and 1972, the proportion of women who came to accept the idea of a female President *increased* by 19 percent. . . . During those first two seasons in which Mary Richards and Rhoda Morgenstern came to television, the level of public support among women for a female President increased more than among any other two-year—or ten-year—period since the 1930s."

What Makes the Sun Come Up?

The *post hoc, ergo propter hoc* fallacy involves mistaking mere antecedents for causes: the cock crows and then the sun rises, so the crowing caused the sunrise. Did prim Mary cause consciousness to rise? Does the water wheel move the river? Television conforms entertainment to market research, struggling to paddle as fast as the current. Robinson finds it ironic that entertainment programing, the servant of commerce, is supportive of "social liberalism," which he identifies with "hedonism and libertarianism" (and "Maude"). But commerce, which profits from the sovereignty of appetites, has never been a conservative force.

Television is not always benign or even innocuous. When vacuous or violent it is enervating and desensitizing; and it has influenced, often unfortunately, the way Americans campaign for office and for change. But it is more mirror than lever.

Robinson believes the "audio-visual orgy of the 1960s" shifted "power" upward toward the President and downward toward "have-nots" such as the civil-rights movement, and other "groups wretched or angry or clever enough to do what was needed to become photogenic." But Kennedy, constantly on television and consistently stymied by Congress, learned that conspicuousness is not power. Jimmy Carter, who uses television even more assiduously than Kennedy did, is learning that television does not make governing easier. Americans have developed fine filters for what they consider static, commercial and political, so Carter's media blitz about the energy crisis was like water thrown on sand: it left little trace. Thanks in part to broadcasting, political rhetoric has become like advertising, audible wallpaper, always there but rarely noticed.

Setting the Political Agenda

Robinson notes that the 1963 "March on Washington" ("the greatest public-relations gambit ever staged") capped five months of intense civil-rights coverage, during which the percentage of Americans regarding civil rights as "the most important problem facing America" soared from 4 to 52. But it is unhistorical to say that this means the networks had begun "to define our political agenda."

Television did not give civil-rights leaders the idea of a March on Washington or make the idea effective. In 1941 the mere threat (by A. Philip Randolph) of a march frightened FDR into important policy changes. The civil-rights movement did not start with television, but with the moral and social changes wrought by the second world war. The movement's first great victory was the Supreme Court's 1954 desegregation decision, when television was in its infancy. (During the two television decades the least "photogenic" branch of government, the judiciary, has grown in importance relative to the other branches.) The movement had on its side great leaders, centuries of grievances, the Constitution, and justice. It benefited from television, but did not depend upon it. Television hastened change a bit, but probably did not determine the direction or extent of change. What television did on its own (for example, manufacturing Stokely Carmichael as a "black leader") was as evanescent as most shoddy fiction.

When Robinson says "Nixon would have lost in 1968 had it not been for network news coverage of politics between 1964 and his election," he must mean either that LBJ would have been re-elected but for disintegration at home and defeat abroad; or that without television Americans would not have minded disintegration and defeat; or that without television there would not have been disintegration and defeat. The first idea is true but trivial; the last two are false.

The U.S. has never had national newspapers, so the focus of news was local. But network news is "national news." So, Robinson says, television has shifted frustrations toward the national government. But the centralization of power in Washington began well before television and would have "nationalized" news, and frustrations, with no help from television. Robinson believes that television journalism, although accused of liberal bias, has recently stimulated political conservatism. But the limitations of government would have become apparent, and the conservative impulse would have had its day, even if television had developed only as an entertainment industry.

To represent situation-comedy shows as shapers of the nation's consciousness is to portray the public as more passive and plastic than it is. To represent television journalism as a fundamentally transforming force is to make the nation's politics seem less purposeful, more mindless, more a matter of random causes than is the case. The contours of history are not determined by communications technolgoy, however much it pleases people to think that history is what, and only what, can be seen at home. To see the rise of blacks, or the fall of LBJ, as primarily a consequence of television is to hollow out history. It discounts the noble and ignoble ideas and passions, heroes and villains and common people who make history.

"They" Did It

In the silly movie "Network," millions of Americans are prompted by a deranged anchor man to sprint to their windows to shout, "We're mad as hell and we won't take it any more." Modern man, proudly sovereign beneath a blank heaven, is prone to believe that "they" (evil persons, irresistible impulses, impersonal forces) control the world. Astrology, vulgar Marxism and Freudianism, and other doctrines nourish this need. So does the exaggeration of media influence. Journalists and perhaps even serious scholars, such as Robinson, who study television, are prone to believe that it turns the world. But the world is not that easy to turn.

PRIME TIME CHIC

Michael J. Robinson

Edited and reprinted from Public Opinion 2 *(March/May 1979): 42–48.*

For the past two years, the Lawrences have been living very sexy lives. The Lawrences are the family in "Family," one of the few television programs on ABC that has been consistently popular with the critics as well as the public.

Popularity isn't the only thing consistent about "Family." So is sex—not just "cutesy-pooh," play sex that traditionally comes over prime time, but serious, adult sex.

Howard Rosenberg, TV critic of the *Los Angeles Times,* kept a record and found that during their first eighteen months on ABC, four of the five Lawrences had some sort of pre-, post-, or extra-marital tangle.

Brother Willie, twenty-one, had an affair with a married woman.

Sister Nancy, twenty-seven, had three lovers—one of whom was her *former* husband.

Sister Buddy, sixteen, had a homosexual teacher and a steady boyfriend who tried to change Buddy into a woman (and barely missed).

Father Doug admitted to one past "indiscretion," and almost committed a very contemporary second.

Five of this season's first eleven episodes on "Family" had serious sex as the theme. So far, only Mother Kate has managed to stay within the confines of marriage, and nobody is making any promises about her.

If illicit sex was conspicuously present in "Family" during the fall season, guilt was just as conspicuously absent. And almost all of this season's original hits, including "Taxi," "Just Friends," and "Fantasy Island," followed the same pattern—lots of sex, very little remorse.

With few exceptions, prime time has become a plug for sexual openness and freedom. But the plug doesn't stop there. Entertainment television serves as a soft-core, progressive statement about love, marriage, drugs, blacks, women, and gays. Between the news breaks and the commercials, the values on prime-time television are consistently liberal chic.

Programs like "Laverne and Shirley" can dilute but can't neutralize what has developed into a schedule of socially hedonistic, superficially liberal shows.

This season's top twenty contains both kinds of liberal chic—the political and the social. We still watch "M.A.S.H.," a show that satirizes war, the military, U.S. foreign policy, and "All in the Family," the Norman Lear production that made liberal chic legitimate on TV, even in its most blatant political theme.

A good percentage of the newer shows in the top twenty this season are less political, but are every bit as socially liberal as the last generation of programming—shows like "One Day at a Time" that paint life as a socio-sexual odyssey in which mothers and daughters discuss their intimate lives as if they were the weather. Or shows like "Soap" that treat WASP values and behavior as if they were diseases. Shows like "What's Happening" in which blacks act like whites, only better. Or shows like "Three's Company"—last fall's highest rated show—which regards multiple cohabitation as the preferred living arrangement and implies that group sex isn't so much immoral as confusing.

Politically liberal prime time started with the "Smothers Brothers" and ended, more or less, with "Maude." But the social liberalism of "Laugh-In" remains very much alive. The only programs that are willing (dare?) to offer traditional social values are the *nostalgia* shows like "The Waltons," "Happy Days" or "Little House on the Prairie." Contemporary settings almost always mean liberal chic on network television.

While the era of "All in the Family" may be fading, the Lear revolution has been preserved by painting hookers, housewives, and homosexuals as heroes, junkies as misunderstood kids, and blacks, Indians, and Puerto Ricans as the noblest of all Americans. In the new TV world, bad guys are white, suburban, thirtyish, and straight.

But what can we expect to be the implications of all this? After ten years of prime-time chic, we may finally be seeing some results "out there"—not just in the corporate boards rooms and suburban bedrooms, where women, blacks, and gays are asserting themselves in all manner of ways—but in the polls, where more and more Americans are accepting the unconventional, progressive or liberal social behavior that people in prime time either practice or condone. So, although my own values *support* gay rights, feminism, integration, and sexual freedom, I think it's time for admission and recognition by liberals like me, and everybody else, that prime-time chic exists—and that it matters.

A Shift to the Right . . . And the Left?

People don't admit to being liberal anymore. Between 1963 and 1976, the portion of the public labeling itself "liberal" fell from 49 percent to 26 percent. Between 1964 and 1974, the percentage of people who preferred membership in a conservative party jumped from 49 to 57. In November's elections, the Republicans picked up seats in *both* the House and the Senate—the first time they've done that since 1966. Liberals like Udall run as progressive and Jerry Brown is preaching the political economy of Calvin Coolidge.

But the same public which began shifting to the right *politically* in the late sixties has been shifting to the left *socially* since about the same time and at about the same rate. The Gallup poll and Harris poll find that between 1969 and 1977—

* The portion of the public regarding premarital sex as "not at all wrong" increased 16 percent.
* The portion believing that an abortion decision should be left up to a woman and her doctor increased by 13 percent. By 1978 less than 20 percent of the population believed abortions should be illegal in all circumstances.
* The portion regarding marijuana as "a serious problem" decreased by 19 percent.
* The portion admitting to having tried marijuana increased by a factor of six!

The country has even mellowed about gay rights over the last five years. According to last June's Gallup poll, a clear majority—56 percent—now thinks that homosexuals deserve equality in job opportunities. Anita Bryant has not spoken for a silent majority.

Race relations follow the same pattern. The percentage approving of interracial marriage—in theory at least—has almost doubled since 1968. The percentage willing to vote for a qualified black as president has more than doubled in the last twenty years. As of summer 1978, 77 percent of the white population said that they would support a qualified black.

TV Is Divided into Two Parts

One thing that could help explain why the country has been moving in two directions at once is television. At the networks, television comes in two basic styles—news and entertainment. Although news and entertainment often look alike, they make for different kinds of effects.

Despite the brouhaha about elitist, liberal commentators controlling the airwaves, a good case can be made for believing that over the past decade and a half network news has been helping to move national opinion toward political conservatism.

With its unique audience and with a unique penchant for the sensational, the bizarre, and the negative—especially when it comes to scandals and snafus in Washington—network journalism has played a role in undermining public confidence in national governments, New Deal-style or otherwise.

Tying forty million nightly viewers to the day's most "newsworthy" film clips—as networks define newsworthy—would produce public frustration with almost any imaginable administration or set of policies, and has since 1963. My own research shows that people who depend upon TV news for following current events are more hostile toward the national government and more alienated from politics than people who don't. In addition, people who were most hooked on network news back in the late sixties were also more committed to George Wallace, psychologically and at the polls, than anybody else in the electorate.

Of course, Watts, Vietnam, Watergate, and stagflation were real events as well as media events. None of them made big government look like the bargain that the Roosevelt generation had led us to expect. The about-face of the political right can thus be seen as part medium, part message—and not very surprising.

What is surprising has been the continuing drift in the other direction—toward social liberalism.

Fingering entertainment television as the cause of any social phenomenon—good or bad—has developed into a new form of national pastime. But in this instance, a little fingering is probably deserved. One can make at least as strong a case for arguing that prime time has helped to shift the public toward the "social left" as for arguing that news time has moved us the other way. In fact, the case for prime-time liberalism is easier. Arguing that TV news causes conservative opinion requires subtlety, if not a little intellectual sleight of hand. Arguing that prime time causes social liberalism is very direct.

What's on TV?

We can start with the content. Prime time has been pushing liberal social themes since just after the free speech movement began at Berkeley. Some prime-time critics feel that entertainment television still lacks any sort of solid, liberal credentials. Muriel Cantor, Professor of Communications at American University and long-time analyst of television production, says that despite the new image of prime time, "TV is one of the most conservative of media—an instrument of social control . . . themes which appear to be liberal are really cover-ups." And Cantor is hardly alone in painting prime time as a lesson in corporate state values.

But a growing number of critics think that prime time *is* socially liberal—especially compared with its former shadow self.

Much of the griping about prime-time liberalism comes from the fundamentalist,

Christian right wing—groups that send out packets on how to monitor TV programs for indecency or how to get the FCC to stop licensing licentious broadcasters. But social scientists also find that television has plenty of "progressive" social values built into it and that the trend may be getting stronger. The clearest example, as any fundamentalist will tell you, is sex.

Nobody in his right mind could argue that television is hard-core. Sex never happens on serial TV. It has *just* happened or is *about* to happen. But prime time is heavily sex-oriented and getting more so, as producers challenge the censors and, more importantly, as the networks themselves try to compensate viewers for recent cutbacks in violence.

Television loves sex—especially sex between consenting adults who happen *not* to be married to each other. The Summer, 1978 edition of the *Journal of Communication,* perhaps the most distinguished of the scholarly journals that trace popular culture and the media, contains an article that analyzes fifty-eight hours of entertainment TV—one episode from each prime time and Saturday morning dramatic series from the 1976–77 season. In their research, the four authors (Collado, Greenberg, Korzenny, and Atkin) counted and found (actual or implied) "five instances of homosexual or heterosexual rape, seven instances of homosexual acts, twenty-eight instances of prostitution, forty-one instances of sexual intercourse ('unmarried'), and only six instances of sexual intercourse between 'marriage partners.' " Unmarried triumphed over married sex almost seven to one! A second study just completed by Eli Rubinstein at Stony Brook indicates that the level of sexual innuendo in prime time increased by a factor of five between 1975 and 1977.

Neither study makes clear whether all this sex is pictured positively or negatively. But with unmarried sex outdistancing married sex seven-to-one in prime time, network TV can hardly be criticized for reflecting traditional sexual values, although it might be attacked for reflecting contemporary reality.

Of course, prime time rarely takes a dim view of sexuality in any of its hybrid forms. The pilot for ABC's new crime show, "Vega$," turns a teenage hooker into a heroine. In the pilot for "Flying High," CBS's less than adequate answer to "Charlie's Angels," all three female leads, playing stewardesses, try to have sex with the same man—the very unlikely Jim Hutton. As the plot developed, Hutton would have had them all (and they him) except he fell asleep with bachelorette number one and got too sunburned to be touched by bachelorette number two. The end of the show was vintage prime-time chic. The one stewardess (Kathryn Witt) who made the Hutton connection gets applause—not chastisement—from her roommates along with all the flight passengers after they finally figure out what Witt and Hutton have been up to.

Even the straightest of shows practices the same permissive sex. "Love Boat," television's version of Noah's Ark, in which ABC brings on board one of every stereotypic species known to situation comedy, moves back and forth between old-fashioned and new-style permissiveness. "Love Boat's" captain, Gavin MacLeod—the same guy who played hopelessly straight Murray on the old "Mary Tyler Moore Show"—now supports mature, open sexuality among consenting, passenger adults, including himself.

On one show last season MacLeod welcomed aboard a divorced high school crush of thirty years earlier, played by Jessica Walter. MacLeod wooed her until she seduced him. As "Love Boat" reaches its destination, Walter tells the captain that it's been great, but now it's over. In a classic, made-for-modern-TV, sex-role reversal, woman tells man that she's going back to her career and that captains aren't supposed to abandon ship after every affair. It's prime time's vapid version of Bergman telling Bogart what to do—to wise up and get on the plane.

Women of Prime Time

Prime time isn't just sexually progressive—some programs work almost harder at being socially liberal than being libertine. For instance, feminism has been doing much better on prime time than feminist-oriented critics ever admit.

The "Mary Tyler Moore Show" became an ironic target for organized feminist criticism two years ago when the U.S. Civil Rights Commission published its first edition of *Window Dressing on the Set: Women and Minorities in Television.* The Commission report criticized Mary Tyler Moore for calling her boss "Mr. Grant" even though everyone else calls him "Lou," an egregious act that the Commission considered a sign that women on TV "still tend to be subordinate to men in their lives."

But most critics saw Mary Richards—Moore's *nomme de tube*—as a proto-feminist, at the very least. As a single, sexually interested TV producer, Richards was more independent and professional than most mid-thirties American women—and so was Rhoda—and so were all the MTM female leads that spun off from Mary Tyler Moore.

In fact, between 1969 and 1974, 15 percent of the prime-time white females played roles as professional women, according to the very same Rights Commission study that tried to crucify the networks for their continuous sexist programming. That figure of 15 percent not only overstated the percent of professional women "out there," it was greater than the figure for professional black males on TV and wasn't all that far behind the percent for white males.

Judging from the newest edition of *Window Dressing,* published this January, one has to wonder as much about the objectivity of the Commission as the alleged insensitivity of the networks to women. The Commission's own "Update" shows that women are not only doing better on TV but have caught up with men in some important dimensions. Comparing the 1975–1977 performances to 1969–1974, Commission records show that the number of white women depicted in prime time as "professional" had risen to 18 percent, while for white men, the number had fallen to 19 percent. Seven of this season's Top Twenty shows have female leads, and in the new genre of prime time, most of the female leads are smarter and more independent than many of the males. Charlie's "angels"—favorite targets of both Christian and feminist critics—forsake their own dates, à la James Bond, week by week to solve crimes committed by men that the angels always manage to outsmart. Even Laverne and Shirley, who get hung in effigy by critics of all shapes and descriptions, depend on each other, not on their men. Their two male friends, Lenny and Squiggy, play Lucy and Ethel, while Shirley and Laverne really play Ricky and Fred—dumb, but less dumb.

It's hard to make a case for liberated commercials. Ads are the last real frontier for TV's once unrelenting sexist values. Between 1970 and 1976, according to William and Karen O'Donnell, the percentage of women in commercials pictured in the home stayed about the same—80 percent! It's almost as if the industry is willing to gamble with feminism in entertainment but less willing to take a gamble on the really important stuff—the ads.

Blacks Are Oreos

Pseudo progressive values and images extend to race issues, too.

Television treats race relations "liberally," not only by producing more black-oriented programs year by year, but also by removing blacks from criminal roles or unflattering roles of any type.

Joe Dominick, Professor of Journalism at the University of Georgia, identified this tendency for prime time to pour bleach on all the bad guys and have them turn out whiter than white in an article he wrote for *Public Opinion Quarterly* in 1973. Dominick's analysis showed that only 7 percent of the prime-time criminals were black. FBI statistics from that year indicate that blacks accounted for 30 percent of the criminal arrests.

As early as 1970, communications research was discovering that on network television about half of all blacks were portrayed upper middle class and that trend hasn't really abated. The new routine, however, is to put blacks in black settings and have them behave like the better part of the bourgeoisie.

Perhaps the most telling development in black prime time is Norman Lear's recent attempt to do a new series this spring about a black male who serves as a member of the House of Representatives. The plot was built, in part, around the congressman's foolish antics with his staff. The point was apparently to poke fun at a less than competent congressman who *happened* to be black. At first, it seemed like another breakthrough for Lear, but it wasn't to be. As of last month, the word was that under pressure from black members of Congress, who allegedly threatened to sponsor legislation to control some phases of broadcasting, CBS and Lear dropped the show. Prime-time chic and politics mean that, for some time to come, only white males will play frivolous politicians.

Gays Are Victims

Last season's favorite prime-time sop was clearly the misunderstood, harassed homosexual—always white (black gayness is still a bit too much for TV), always professional, and always the innocent victim.

On "Family," last year's theme homosexual was Buddy's teacher, who in the course of the show loses Buddy's respect, since the community bigots have maliciously publicized the fact that she, the teacher, is a lesbian. In the end, the community and Buddy accept the teacher for what she is—a great teacher—and beat down the redneck styled element who try to have her fired.

On "Starsky and Hutch," the obligatory pro-gay program involved a police detective who gets murdered and is then discovered to have been a closet homosexual. He was, however, also a great cop and a close friend of both Starsky and Hutch, who, by show's end, find the killer (not gay) and express their newfound empathy for the plight of homosexuals. Gay is not beautiful on prime time—but since the early seventies it has never been ugly or sinister, let alone evil.

Networks aren't (can't be) as liberal as other media and progressive themes in prime time usually do fade out by the end of the show when traditional values make a minor comeback. On CBS's "One Day at a Time," last summer's number one rated series, Julie, an eighteen-year-old daughter of Ann Romano, moves in with her boyfriend. Mom loses the fight to bring Julie home—but only for the first half of the episode. Julie eventually comes home intact—and before consummating her lease or her relationship. But traditional? Mom and Julie treat the whole thing as a casual lesson learned—no remorse, no recrimination, no "I told you so." To national audiences that may well come across more as, "living with my boyfriend isn't for me, but it's okay for somebody else"—the essence of TV's social liberalism and what the polls show as a continuing acceptance of other people's lifestyles.

The real criticism that applies from both left and right is that prime-time programming is underdeveloped, vapid and plastic—not that it's traditional. Pseudo-liberal, yes; traditional, no. Radical, never.

Sit-Com's the Thing

Things weren't always so liberal on prime time; just think back to Desi and Lucy and Ralph and Alice. The evolution began with the "Smothers Brothers Comedy Hour," continued through "Laugh In," and came of age with "All in the Family." All comedies.

There's no accident to the fact that comedy has led the way toward liberal chic. Comedy has always been important to the networks, not only because comedy excuses so much but because it also sells. CBS used comedy to replace NBC as the number one network back in the fifties. Three seasons back, ABC used comedy, especially situation comedy, to strip CBS of its leadership.

But sit-com may be as important to sociology as it is to the networks. Next to soap opera, sit-com is the most value-packed kind of programming there is. Sit-coms sell values because they don't have much else to sell—no variety, no action, no violence, no suspense. Programs are based on a situation that day-to-day social values have somehow made comic.

A second reason that sit-coms have led the way toward liberal chic is that they have become the very heart of prime time. The Nielsen "Top Ten" list for the last twenty-five years makes the growing importance of situation comedy perfectly clear. In 1956 only two of the top ten shows were situation comedies—"I Love Lucy" and "December Bride." In 1966 there were six sit-coms in the top ten—"Andy Griffith," "The Lucy Show," "Green Acres," "Bewitched," "The Beverly Hillbillies," and "Gomer Pyle USMC." Last season produced a record-tying eight: "Laverne and Shirley," "Happy Days," "Three's Company," "M.A.S.H.," "One Day at a Time," "All in the Family," "Soap," and "Alice." The qualitative differences aren't as great as the quantitative. But compare "One Day at a Time" with "December Bride," or "Three's Company" with "Andy Griffith," or "Soap" with anything.

The only type of programming that even approaches sit-com as a purveyor of social values is soap opera. But soaps are "serious"—they have to meet tougher standards of censorship. On soaps, people who break any of the commandments have to pay—either in guilt, divorce, miscarriage, or impotence. By comparison, sit-com characters get away with murder—or at least promiscuity.

Besides an ability to slip past the censor, sit-coms have other characteristics that make them especially important to anybody trying to explain TV's effects. Popular sit-com characters, who appear every week, who rarely threaten anybody's ego, who lay their own values down gently and humorously on the coffee table and walk away, have a unique potential for affecting their audiences.

If the viewer doesn't like the values being offered he or she can dismiss them as merely satirical or humorous (as liberals do with Archie Bunker). If the viewer agrees with the values, everything is fine.

As for the bulk of viewers in the middle, or the viewers not-too-sensitive about social issues generally, the values of situation comedy may eventually become part of their own. More likely, the program's values will lead those viewers to think that if decent people like Mary Richards (McKinney now) act that way, that's probably a legitimate way to behave. Either way—whether the viewer actually adopts liberal chic values or just accepts their legitimacy—that attitude looks like liberalism in the polls.

Why Liberal Chic?

Nobody denies that television production people are socially liberal. Although Muriel Cantor challenges the premise that programs are really liberal, she is convinced that the writers, actors, and producers are.

Cantor, whose 1969 Ph.D. thesis at UCLA was a sociological analysis of television producers, says that producers and writers are not only Democratic and liberal, they are also Jewish, urban, and from one coast or the other. (Spiro Agnew, where are you?)

Ben Stein, author of a new and controversial book, *The View from Sunset Boulevard* (a work he foreshadowed in his article in *Public Opinion* in August/September 1978), thinks that TV production, based almost totally in Los Angeles, reflects Hollywood more than personal, deep-seated liberal philosophy. While Stein acknowledges that the values of these people are socially progressive, he sees their liberalism only going so far. "Their values are permissive," says Stein, "but their own personal lives are clean cut." "There was more sex in the White House than out here in Norman Lear's company," a charge made even more remarkable by the fact that Stein worked in Richard Nixon's White House. (Stein is the only man in history who will have worked for both Richard Nixon and Norman Lear.)

But the real fight is not over just how liberal the producers and writers are— everyone agrees they are more liberal than their average viewers; the debate is whether they stick their own values into their programs. As expected, critics on the left say no; critics on the right say definitely.

Cantor, who labels herself "pretty radical," thinks that the TV people "clearly are not espousing their own values" when they produce their shows and that the liberals who worked in television during the early seventies couldn't take it any more and have since left. But Stein, a thinking man's conservative, ridicules what he considers a ludicrous theory—that television people don't bring their own social values to their work with them. And there are some leftist critics who agree with him. Jerry Mander, whose new book, *Four Arguments for the Elimination of Television,* takes a position almost as radical as its title, writes that the "Movement people of the 1960s who were not willing to go to terrorism began dropping out, moving to farms in Vermont or Oregon. Or, and I know many who have done this, they got jobs writing television serials. They justified this with the explanation that they were still reaching the people with an occasional revolutionary message, fitted ingeniously into the dialogue."

All serious analysts of television realize that prime time doesn't merely reflect the social values of L.A. producers, or New York executives, or even advertisers. Ratings, affiliates, the FCC, the NAM—all help shape the content. Values are just part of programming.

But some TV analysts see programming as much a case study in social engineering as anything else—a sort of values conspiracy theory. One network executive, a liberal working in audience research in New York, told me that he thinks L.A. production houses, as well as the corporate executives back in New York, figure out how far they can go by using the Midwest—the nation's most traditional region outside the South—as their least common denominator. According to his theory, programs present themes that are acceptable to television production people until the networks or the producers decide that the show won't play in Peoria—a new role for Richard Nixon's favorite barometer.

Is Anybody Out There Listening?

Nobody is certain about the effects of prime time, and some social scientists argue that entertainment television has no impact at all on social values. Some research even makes a case for prime-time television as a *conservatizing* influence. Russell Weigel and Richard Jessor, two behavioral psychologists from the University of Colorado, claim to have found a link between TV watching and conventional attitudes about religion, drugs, politics, and personal freedom. But most of their work was done in 1970, before the industry turned around. George Gerbner, Director of the Annenberg School of Communications in Philadelphia, also finds that watching television and worrying about crime go very much in hand—that "crime-time" television has made Americans more suspicious of each other and more neurotic about the society they share. The end product of all that is, as Gerbner sees it, more support for governmental crackdowns—in short, more conservatism.

But the fact is there isn't much conclusive evidence one way or the other about prime time. Most of the academic studies have been anything but exciting—discovering, for example, that people who consider "All in the Family" to be funny are more likely to watch it. Part of the analytical problem involves finding an acceptable technique for proving that TV per se, actually *causes* something. But beyond that, the problem too has been a lack of real interest. The best talent in the academy has been out studying the impact of prime time on violent behavior, not on attitudes toward sex, drugs, or women's issues. While violence research has been getting funding, values research has been getting the crumbs.

Most of the work done on violence, especially the mammoth *Surgeon General's Report,* argues that TV causes aggression, especially among young people. It seems apparent that if violent programming can cause violence, liberal programming should be able to "cause" liberalism. In fact, because many social scientists think that it is easier to influence attitudes than behavior, the impact of TV on attitudes should be greater than on aggression.

Critics who doubt the impact of entertainment television stress the chicken-and-the-egg problem, arguing that it's impossible to tell what's causing what. Or, alternatively, they argue that television always follows social change and never leads it. While the first argument is hard to dismiss, the second one isn't. Themes on prime time do follow a leader, but the leader in expressed or implied values isn't the public as much as most critics think. Dominant values in much prime-time television, and changes in those dominant values, don't come from the heartland. From civil rights to disco, social movements start in places like New York and L.A., and the media move them out to the boonies. Television gets much of its values and themes from other, classier media (books, and especially magazines), and, to a lesser degree, from an urban-based intelligentsia. Television edits those messages, obviously, before it passes them along as TV chic. But by touching millions, instead of thousands, prime time becomes a highly visible, national, and immediate cause of changing social norms. TV may not be a first cause, but it is a highly apparent one.

Prime time helps to make the social values of the coastline elites the social values of the nation. For decades, prime-time social values have been making us less regional and less heterogeneous. But until the late sixties, that meant national taste in clothes, music, dancing, or accent. With television moving into more serious social themes, the effect is on values, not just tastes. Thus, we find the nation moving into the Global Village that Marshall McLuhan named and predicted—with television in the role of a tribal medicine man who takes his cues from the higher circles but makes the messages palatable, acceptable and enjoyable to the rest of the villagers.

This is not to argue that prime time has single-handedly transformed social values in America. Television reflects and magnifies change as well as produces it. Moreover, there are at least two alternative interpretations that help to explain the growth of social liberalism, both of which are based in demography. One interpretation stems from the accepted fact that the "young" have socially progressive opinions, the other from the more recent view that the "educated" also have such views. Thus, so the theories go, as the country has grown younger and better educated, it has also grown more socially liberal.

But ignoring television as a factor in social liberalism seems foolish. Prime time has so many qualities that make for effective social learning—vast audiences, close involvement between actors and viewers, programs that center around relevant social relationships and social issues. Theoretically, prime time has more going for it as a teaching device than most college classes, which often go without audience, involvement, or relevance. All that the shows lack is a grading system. As long as prime time continues to be progressive—compared to Cincinnati, not to Sausalito—the lessons should continue to stick.

What Next?

Progressive prime time isn't inevitable. In the fifties television was anything but progressive—and it was much more likely to reflect than mold national folkways or attitudes.

It's doubtful that anything could return television to that wretched state, but it is conceivable that prime time could find a different set of social values to build into its programs. One way would be through pressure.

The newest thing in television is the growth of increasingly powerful organizations that try to change something about network programming that the organizations find offensive. (The PTA is at the top of the list when it comes to pressuring networks these days.)

The toughest assaults against prime time have come from the anti-violence people. And they have been successful in reducing the amount and the intensity of violence, but at an ironic cost. Networks tend to substitute sit-com and social relevance for violence. So, the conservative and religious groups that have pushed the networks out of action-adventure have moved programming even more in the direction of liberal chic.

The irony doesn't stop there. Liberal critics who have organized to end sexist commercials and sexist stereotyping sometimes help the groups and causes that they most want to inhibit—the fundamentalist Christian world. Richard Levinson, who wrote "Columbo" and *The Execution of Private Slovic,* says that the "primary bias of prime-time TV in the last several years has been liberal," but that the liberal trend may generate conservative counterpressures that could one day move the industry out of serious drama and back into cutesy, inoffensive programming. So far, however, that day is nowhere in sight.

The "new" season which started in February and the "new, new" season which started in March show that we've reached a near equilibrium. Gratuitous violence is down, sexy sit-com is up, and liberal chic is pretty much everywhere.

TO THE STUDENT: A COMMENTARY

Are you a prisoner of TV? Think about it for it is an important question. You probably think, "Not me; I can take it or leave it, in fact, seldom watch the thing." But that is not what George Will is talking about. Granted you can take it or leave it, when you take it must you sit through what does not interest you to get to what may? If so, you are in that sense a prisoner. And, as Will writes, this worries people who make decisions about TV programming. They don't want to lost you by boring you. "The concept of boredom is the dominant element in a political broadcaster's view of his audience."[1] So wrote an experienced television producer of several years standing. Obviously George Will agrees.

Now what does this imply? Two things. First, TV is a visual medium. To be reported so as not to bore, stories must be visually interesting. Second, interesting means entertaining. Hence, there is a demand for entertaining action. Put the two together and you get what Edwin Diamond called in chapter 10, disco news. Put differently, the line between what is public affairs programming (news) and entertainment programming (show biz) fades, perhaps even vanishes. The overall consequence, says Will, is a desensitized audience, "television's children" (YOU).

That is as far as Will chooses to go. TV, "when vacuous or violent" is "enervating and desensitizing." And it has influenced how politicians campaign for office, something you are well aware of after reading the selections in Part 2. But "it is more mirror than lever."

Here then is where George Will and Michael Robinson differ. Undaunted by Will's attack on his 1977 article, Robinson in "Prime Time Chic" (1979) polishes up his act. He repeats his basic argument that TV's portrayal of political events and social practices can change your beliefs, values, and behavior. The result is a two-part, not two-party, America. TV news leads to public frustration with politics, loss of confidence in government, and a sense of political hopelessness. This adds up to "conservative opinion," writes Robinson. At the same time, however, entertainment programming produces a shift to social liberalism. Confusing? Even Robinson admits that it is: "Arguing that TV news causes conservative opinion requires subtlety, if not a little intellectual sleight of hand. Arguing that prime time causes social liberalism is very direct." Robinson goes in a "very direct" fashion to precisely that point, citing a variety of studies that you may not be familiar with but also noting numerous prime time TV shows that you probably are.

Go back to Will for a moment, to his section "What Makes the Sun Come Up?" What is cause and what is effect? Will thinks Robinson makes a mistake in assuming that simply because TV existed prior to a shift to social liberalism, it thereby produced it. Similarly, simply because TV existed at the time of the civil rights movement it did not define "our political agenda." Robinson now gets his opportunity to rebut in "Prime Time Chic." He notes that critics who doubt the impact of TV's entertainment programming either (1) say that it is impossible to say what causes what, the chicken-or-the-egg problem, or (2) argue that TV follows and does not lead social change—i.e., Will saying TV is "more mirror than lever." Robinson dismisses the second argument easily—indeed, perhaps too glibly. TV, he says, spreads the values of the "coastline elites" (apparently yankees in New York and cowboys in Los Angeles) and transmits them to America's heartland. The result is change—in our values, in our expectations, even our life styles. Is this so? Frankly, we can't say. Nor is Robinson willing to go all the way out on the limb. Note that in one sentence he claims that prime time TV is a "highly visible, national, and immediate cause of changing social norms" but in the next recognizes TV not as a "first cause, but it is a highly apparent one." And what of the chicken-or-egg problem? Robinson finds it "hard to dismiss," and doesn't say more. Give George Will the edge on that one.

Aside from the substantive question of the effects of TV on political and social values, the question Will and Robinson debate, there is another point to be learned from the exchange. As a political watcher there are many times when you will be tempted to ask the "big questions." Consider these: Do we have an imperial or impotent presidency? Is Congress corrupt? Does the Establishment run the country? Should we junk the Electoral College? Is there a crisis of confidence?

These are important questions to be sure. But are the answers so readily apparent that you can stake out a fixed position and hold to it without reservation? Probably not. Such is the problem with assessing the impact of TV upon politics. It flies in the face of common sense either to dismiss television as having "minimal effects" (the conventional wisdom among many political scientists in the 1950s and 1960s) or to say TV is a prime mover. To their credit neither Will nor Robinson so argue. Will thinks TV not so mighty but demurs, "television is not always benign or even innocuous." Robinson thinks TV changes our values but "this is not to argue that prime time has single-handedly transformed social values in America."

But the difficulty extends beyond simply accepting the fact that unqualified assertions are seldom warranted. It extends to how such questions are asked. Certainly TV influences us, but not always. The proper question for watchers of politics is, "Under what conditions does TV programming—public affairs and/or entertainment—change values?" So put, the exercise may seem less exciting than bold assertions about television's "power," but once you enter into the effort, discovering the conditions under which things happen can be every bit as fascinating as watching what happens and searching for single causes.

Efforts to say precisely what TV means to us both socially and politically abound. Many of the books recommended to you at the close of chapter 10 speak to the point. In addition you'll want to consult two books by part-time teacher/writer Robert Cirino and another by free-lance writer Anne Saldich:

Robert Cirino, *Power to Persuade*

Robert Cirino, *We're Being More Than Entertained*

Anne Rawley Saldich, *Electronic Democracy*

Members of the academic community have contributed their views too:

Horace Newcomb, *TV: The Most Popular Art*

Bernard Rubin, *Media, Politics, and Democracy*

James David Barber, *The Pulse of Politics: Electing Presidents in the Media Age*

References

1. Anthony Smith, "A Maturing Telocracy," in Louis Maisel, ed., *Changing Campaign Techniques* (Beverly Hills: Sage Publications 1976): 212.

12 Pollenium?

INTRODUCTION

Rare is the major newspaper that does not on at least one day of the week carry the results of a poll taken to measure how people feel about the President, congressional officials, candidates, or burning issues. Weekly news magazines feature polls as a routine item for news coverage. The national TV networks highlight polls in their daily news programming. Polls it seems are almost as important to political news as the pols. And the pols themselves use polls. One of the first consultants a politician seeking high office employs is the pollster. Moreover, as we saw in chapter 2, policy makers rely upon polls extensively for readings of the public mood, as did President Carter in his discovery of the "crisis of confidence" of 1979. Finally, the polls are a key technique that social scientists use to explain what influences political behavior (even though the term "polls" takes a backseat to a more scholarly reference to "survey research").

Polling is now so pervasive in our society that Alex Edelstein, director of the School of Communications at the University of Washington, once spoke at a scholarly meeting on the topic, "Have We Reached the Pollenium?" His play on words was both amusing and troubling. One standard definition of "millennium," according to the dictionary, is a "hoped for period of joy, serenity, prosperity, and justice." A millennium is obviously something worthy of attainment. But is a pollenium?

Pollsters argue that what they do is essential to making popular government work. How better to assure that citizens' views will prevail than to find out what they are through polls, inform politicians and public officials, then hold those elective and appointive officials accountable? So regarded polls are the pulse of democracy. Pollster George Gallup, certainly one of the most prestigious in the business, even proposes that polls be used to conduct a "public opinion referendum" on a regular basis, thus telling policy makers what you and other Americans want.

But would that be the pollenium it's cracked up to be? To help you think about that question we have reprinted two articles in this chapter that deal with the political uses of public opinion polls. Both refer to how politicians running for office use polls rather than polls used by the news media. However, the problems encountered in using polls that each article implies hold for polls generally—news polls, politicians' polls, scholarly polls, etc.

First, Adam Clymer tells you how polls employed during the 1978 congressional elections were much like a dog chasing its tail—voters tell pollsters their concerns, pollsters report these concerns to candidates, candidates then turn around and tell voters what to worry about. Is such a tight circle of self-fulfilling prophesy a pollenium? You decide.

Second, Eugene DeClerq provides you with a description of 1974 congressional campaigns that successfully used public opinion polls to achieve victory. Moreover, he details the factors that seem to be associated with candidates' decisions to rely upon such polling.

You met Eugene DeClerq earlier in chapter 5 when you read about power elites. DeClerq has been interested in campaign politics for some time and his research into the use of polls by congressional candidates reflects that concern. At the time he prepared the article you will read he was teaching political science at Bryant College. Adam Clymer has covered politics for the *Baltimore Sun, New York Daily News,* and *New York Times.* He has regularly reported on the findings of the *New York Times*/CBS News Poll, so he knows whereof he speaks in discussing the strengths and limitations of opinion polling.

THE VOTERS ARE TELLING
THE POLLSTERS TO TELL
THE CANDIDATES TO TELL
THE VOTERS

ADAM CLYMER

Edited and reprinted from Public Opinion 1 *(September/October 1978): 49–51.*

The polls are telling the consultants to tell the candidates that voters this year are very, very upset about inflation, and very upset about taxes. But they are also telling them the electorate distrusts anybody's solutions and many distrust simple solutions the most.

So how's a consultant to earn a fee? Give classes in canvassing? More likely, he will tell his candidate that even though it's important to sound concerned about inflation and taxes, the candidate cannot expect to win on that issue because his opponent will be against them, too. Thus, the campaign staff must look elsewhere through printouts for the key subject that can turn a vulnerable portion of the electorate around. But no adviser worth a fee this fall is failing to tell his candidate that even if inflation offers no panaceas for election, the polls are showing that it is a matter of profound concern for the voters.

John Gorman of *Cambridge Survey Report* tells of a continual series of national polls asking respondents to list the two most important problems before the nation. Inflation has hung steadily in the mid-thirties for a couple of years, and in January it was cited by 35 percent of those who answered. Then in early summer it shot up to 54 percent. It is not just Gorman (and partner Pat Caddell) or their Democratic clients who are hearing that sort of thing. Wilma Goldstein, associate campaign director at the Republican Congressional Committee, has been seeing polls for more than 100 Republican candidates for the House and finds a steady run of 50 to 60 percent citations of inflation as the single most important problem before the nation. Robert M. Teeter of Market Opinion Research in Detroit tells his Republican clients that inflation is being cited as the most important problem at two or three times the rate it was identified in the 1966 and 1968 elections, when Republicans also sought to make it an issue.

When a good pro combines the numbers and the way things sound as he travels about he comes up with an analysis like that offered by Mark Shields, the peripatetic Democratic adviser: "Inflation is all by itself. It's everywhere. Across all groups. I think double-digit inflation is a seminal event, as frightening for this generation as the Depression was for our parents."

What, then, should a candidate do? "You cannot say 'I have a solution,' it just won't sell," reports Republican consultant Edward Mahe. "But you've always got to have a TV spot talking about it." Shields concurs and emphasizes that a candidate can empathize credibly on the issue and gain an advantage over a less sympathetic candidate, even if neither of them has a solution for inflation.

Moreover, even if few voters take the candidates' solutions seriously, that may not mean they don't have any of their own. Gorman reports that a question that has been asked for years showed a surprising turnaround in results this summer. Respondents were asked if they agreed with the statement, "We've got to learn to live with high inflation. Prices will never be stable again." In 1974, about 25 percent agreed, and after the reality of double-digit inflation, the percentages rose into the forties in 1975. By January 1978, 55 percent said they agreed. But in early summer, the number who agreed had dropped to 35 percent. Why has a fifth of the population suddenly decided that inflation can be stopped?

One possible explanation comes through mixes of other data. Many pollsters report that a growing number of people think government spending is the chief cause of inflation. For a number of years, about a third of the public named government as the chief cause, about a third blamed business and labor, while another third blamed outside events like the weather and the oil embargo. Now, however, Teeter says his state-by-state polls are frequently finding as many as half the respondents think government spending is the chief cause of inflation and labor is now being blamed far more often than business. If people believe inflation is caused by government spending, Proposition 13 in California may have suddenly encouraged them to think there is indeed a solution: they themselves can cut spending, and thus put a brake on inflation, by voting for Proposition 13s across the country.

The idea may have been at hand even before the publicity about the California vote and such phenomena as Howard Jarvis appearing on "Meet the Press," the cover of *Time* magazine, and on Capitol Hill, where conservative Republican senators greeted him open-mouthed, like a group of regional sales managers for a struggling snake-oil firm, convened to meet the man who had redesigned the bottle and the label and would make them all rich. Consider a nationwide poll of 1,500 persons taken by Decision Making Information earlier this year for Citizens of the Republic, Ronald Reagan's political action committee. Here are the question and the results:

"Some people think there should be an absolute limit on the percentage of national income the government can take in taxes, to control the growth of government spending. Others think the government should be allowed to tax and spend as much as it decides it needs. Where would you place yourself?"

Limit	1	2	3	4	5	6	7	No Limit
	40%	16%	18%	15%	4%	2%	5%	

Only 11 percent opposed a limit, 15 percent gave a neutral response, and of the 74 percent that wanted an absolute limit, more than half took a flat-out stand. As Lyn Nofziger, executive director of the Reagan group, points out, this poll was taken *before* the Proposition 13 vote, suggesting that the country today is not just sunning itself in the afterglow of the California action. Tax fever has been around for awhile.

The Tax Lesson

Is there a magic formula here? The electoral pattern may seem uneven. In California, Governor Edmund G. Brown, Jr., was an outspoken opponent of Proposition 13 before the vote, but his fancy footwork afterwards left people forgetting his earlier stand. In Massachusetts, the voters did not forget: Governor Michael S. Dukakis was elected there four years ago with a promise not to raise taxes. By no stretch of the imagination has his administration since then been a free spender, but when he found the state's finances in terrible shape, he *did* raise taxes. This September, the voters meted out their punishment, choosing conservative Edward J. King over Dukakis in the Democratic primary.

Two Senate primaries this fall have also suggested that federal tax-cutting positions have real value, at least if the candidate concentrates on them hard enough and long enough so that they do not seem like gimmicks. For both victors, Republican Jeffrey Bell of New Jersey and Democrat Robert Short of Minnesota, while there were other factors that were more important to their triumph, the call for lower taxes was a significant part of their primary races. Nonetheless, as of September, both Bell and Short appeared to be unlikely winners in the general election. Adding it all up, the lesson appears to be that a strong campaign in favor of tax cuts is no guarantee of ultimate victory, but to be successfully pictured as pro-spending and pro-taxes is probably the country's shortest road to political extinction.

A Year of Many Passions But Few Issues

The distrust that pollsters and consultants all report finding for "solutions" does not mean they are offering their candidates nothing substantive to say on the matter. And the simple fact that a campaign line has been around for many years without great apparent impact does not mean it will never pay off. In Minnesota, where Robert Short spent $800,000 of his own funds in winning the Senate primary, his billboards labeling Donald Fraser as a spender have represented the high-budget version of what quite a few Republican managers are urging their candidates to do—attack the opponent's votes for bills that cost a lot of money.

On the other side, pollster Peter Hart, who finds this "one of your less cataclysmic elections" with little in the way of issues, says that from his polls, he tells Democrats "the key issue is government waste" and they should find a way to oppose it. Caddell believes Democrats can exploit the waste issue by stressing President Carter's civil service legislation. While that issue showed up hardly at all in spring and summer campaigning, Representative Morris K. Udall of Arizona, the bill's floor manager, was telling colleagues as early as June that political audiences were responding to his pitch on the bill as a way to rein in bureaucracy. September's 385 to 10 vote on House passage may show his message got through.

Nonetheless, there is general agreement among pollsters this fall that in this election few issues are affecting very many votes. (Indeed, there haven't been very many votes, as one low turnout after another during the primary season has underlined the public's distrust of politicians.) To some extent, the lack of definable issues with clear opportunities for differentiating candidates results from the dominance of inflation. As Mahe notes, when open-ended questions about important problems get 50 or 60 percent of the people giving one answer, other responses are so widely scattered as to fail to make much impact on polling statistics.

President Carter's stunning success at Camp David came relatively late in the campaign season, not too late to be seized on by Democrats but well after most candidates had made a set decision about how they would run. Teeter's first reaction to the summit was that the skill Democrats had already shown in separating themselves from Carter would make it hard for them to get much benefit from his diplomatic triumph. Still, if there is merit, and there seems to be, in Yale professor Edward Tufte's thesis that a president's popularity and the year-to-year change in real income affect off-year elections, the Democrats are bound to be helped by Camp David, at least a little.

Some candidates this fall have been citing defense as an important issue, or at least as the issue of the future. Republican pollster Bob Teeter finds, however, that while there is a trend toward more traditional attitudes in favor of a very strong national defense, only 5–7 percent of respondents believe it is an important issue. At the GOP Congressional Committee, Mrs. Goldstein scoffs, "For two years, I've been hearing it's a coming issue, but I haven't seen it yet."

The one other issue on a barren agenda appears to be taxes, which may be a part of the inflation issue for many voters. Its dominance varies greatly from state to state, depending on whether taxes have gone up sharply or whether the issue has become acute. Michigan is likely to attract more and more national attention this fall as voters try to decide on two major tax referenda. In Illinois, Democrat Michael Bakalis has used taxes to mount a much stronger challenge than expected to Republican Governor James Thompson, pushing a cumbersome property tax circuit breaker through the legislature which Thompson vetoed and then making further gains when a Thompson petition drive for an advisory referendum on spending turned out to have an embarrassing number of phony signatures—not embarrassing by ordinary Illinois standards, perhaps, but embarrassing for the super-clean ex-prosecutor.

The Kemp-Roth bill, which Republicans are trying to exploit, may be an exception to the warning against simple solutions, although Mrs. Goldstein warns that if it is not carefully explained, voters may turn off on it as just another gimmick. But the attention it's getting is at least as much the result of press interest as polling figures. Reporters and Republican leaders, for that matter, are fascinated by seeing the Republicans on the offensive with a positive economic plan. And, as Republican consultant John P. Sears says, the Democrats have some difficulty counterattacking. "They're not used to calling funny-money schemes irresponsible. That was always our bag."

The "No Frills Survey Module"

The weakness of issues in the campaign has not turned politicians away from pollsters, who are doing more business than ever, promoting their wares with handy little packages like DMI's black, yellow, and orange booklet describing the $9,540 "No Frills Survey Module," which consists of three polls—"Benchmark, Follow-up and Quick-Look."

Political consultants employ such polling material in all sorts of ways that go beyond basic strategy planning. Nofziger observes, as usual joking less than he says he is, "I use these things to show reporters that people agree with us." That's just another version of leaking the raw percentages of a positive poll in order to discourage the other side. David Keene, another Republican consultant, says "I don't need a survey to tell someone not to run like a right-wing nut, for example, but having the numbers may help me convince him, especially if he has a lot of conservative friends back home who keep saying, 'Why aren't you talking more about the Panama Canal?'"

Polls can thus prove a lot of negatives, showing that a particular issue does not matter, at least to voters who are still undecided. But polls offer opportunities, too. They can tell a candidate like John Pucciano, a Republican running for the House in New Haven, that federal aid for housing is very important to people in his district, or that his opponent, Robert N. Giaimo, is more highly regarded by both Democrats and Republicans than by independents. They can also tell a party where to target its resources. This year, for example, the Republican National Committee took a number of polls to locate districts where middle-ranking and senior Democratic incumbents might be weaker than generally thought. Their findings have a lot to do with where Republicans are making major efforts, and if the GOP does score significant gains next month, they may be a major reason.

Political polls this year provide no sure-fire schemes for election victory—and probably little that has even as much impact as David Garth's discovery that by getting Ed Koch to hammer on capital punishment, he could toughen up the candidate's image and get him elected mayor. They do offer a number of warning signs to smart campaign managers and they do suggest opportunities. Still, there's only so much anyone should expect from the polls. They cannot tell a candidate how to make himself credible, nor can they tell him how to whip inflation—not even many economists are sure of that anymore.

THE USE OF POLLING IN CONGRESSIONAL CAMPAIGNS

Eugene DeClerq

Edited and reprinted from Public Opinion Quarterly 42 *(Summer 1978): 247–258.*

The use of private political polls by candidates has become an object of increasing public interest. Most of the attention has focused on the use of polling in national and state elections. Polling's role in campaigns for the U.S. House of Representatives has received far less attention, despite the finding a decade ago that a majority of congressmen in competitive races used polls and that a substantial proportion (85 percent) of those using them found the polls helpful in their campaigns. In the period since that study, a number of factors (e.g., increased professionalization of campaign management, higher levels of campaign funding, increased levels of awareness concerning the benefits of polling) have combined to make it even more likely that polling plays an important role in the campaign process. The purpose of this article is to systematically examine what role polling played in campaigns for the U.S. House of Representatives in 1974.

Our findings are based on interviews with congressmen or their staff members identified as most knowledgeable about the 1974 campaign. Every office in which the candidate was opposed in 1974 was contacted, and even some unopposed members were contacted to see if polling might have been done as a precaution for future elections (it was not). In all, 421 offices were contacted, and virtually complete interviews were done in 100 instances. Since we have, in essence, the entire population of winning poll-users, only descriptive statistics will be used. The respondents were: the congressman (5), his administrative aide (61), legislative aide (13), other staff aides (15), or press secretary (6). Respondents were generally quite knowledgeable about both the campaign in general and the use of polling (almost one-third of them had been managers of the 1974 campaign). The interviews focused on several general questions:

- In what types of campaigns was polling used?
- When and how often was the polling done?
- How was the polling carried out?
- What kinds of information were gathered in the polls?
- How was the information used in the campaign?

Where Was Polling Used?

Table 31 presents the critical groups in our analysis. Keep in mind that our data are only on poll-users who *won* the election and we do not generalize beyond that group. The essential comparison is obviously between those who used polls and the winners who did not. For comparative purposes, we present the same breakdowns for those congressmen who were either not contacted or who refused to answer the screening question. Since most of these members were unopposed for reelection and were, typically, southern Democrats, much of the data in column three appears anomalous. For example, these members are older, more conservative, have less competitive races, and represent poorer districts with higher proportions of blacks than either of the other groups. Of far more interest and importance is the comparison between those who used polling and those who did not, and this will be the basis of our discussion.

The single factor that best characterizes races that involve polling is their competitiveness, as Table 31 illustrates. The average vote for a candidate using polling was 58 percent compared to 69 percent for those who did not. Likewise, 76 percent of those using polling won with less than 60 percent of the vote, compared to only 31 percent for non-poll-users. The relationship between the use of polling and the competitiveness of the race is not surprising. It is in competitive races that factors such as campaign organization, the use of media, and polling data may make the difference

TABLE 31   Characteristics of Districts Where Polling Was Used and Those Who Used It

	Poll Users' Districts (100)	Non-poll-users (311)	Not Contacted or Refused to Answer (24)
Political characteristics of district			
% votes for winner 1974 (mean)	58%	69%	85%
% of winners with less than 60% of the vote 1974	76%	31%	8%
% votes for Rep. House candidate 1968–74 (mean)	50%	47%	19%
Campaign expenditure of winner 1974 (mean)	$99,967	$70,097 [a]	—
Demographic characteristics of district [b]			
Median age of voting age population	42.5	50.3	42.0
Median family income	$10,243	$9,818	$8,862
Median school years completed by population over 25	12.0	12.3	11.8
% homes owner occupied	66%	64%	62%
% population black	6%	12%	15%
Candidate characteristics			
% freshman (94th Congress)	49%	15%	0
% Republicans (94th Congress)	43%	31%	14%
Party loyalty—1975	74%	68%	61%
Conservative coalition support 1975	47%	53%	60%
Participation—1975	94%	90%	92%
Average age—1975	45	51	55

[a] Three hundred and seventy-five races with two major party candidates.
[b] Figures as of 1970 census.

between victory and defeat. It is also competitive races that draw the heaviest campaign contributions and have the highest expenditures. Costs for a professional survey of a district are usually between $6,000 (telephone interviews) and $10,000 (personal interviews) and can be covered only in races where expenditures are substantial. These costs are based on the typical sample size of 400 used in congressional districts and costs of $15 per interview for telephone surveys and $25 for personal interviews. As Table 31 indicates, candidates who used polling spent about 40 percent more than the average winner in 1974.

One might argue that competitiveness in the 1975 race is not as important to the form of the campaign as competition in previous House races in the district. In highly competitive districts, parties are usually well organized, races generate greater interest in the electorate, and attractive candidates are easier to recruit. All these factors could contribute to the use of polling and, in fact, an examination of votes for each party from 1968 to 1972 in our sample of districts indicates that on the whole, competitiveness was common in House races in these districts. The average vote in these districts for the 1974 winners' party from 1968 to 1972 was only 54 percent. Because of the present party imbalance in Congress, to say that the districts in our sample are generally more competitive implies greater support for Republican candidates than the national average. That is indeed the case, with Republican House candidates averaging 3 percent more votes from 1968 to 1974 than the average for non-poll-users. Also, President Nixon won these districts in 1972 with 64 percent of the vote, compared to 60 percent in the districts without polling. For the most part, the district demographic data presented in Table 31 indicates that districts where polling is used have slightly larger affluent, young, white populations. These characteristics largely conform to the "Republicanness" of the districts noted above.

Some studies of political campaigning have suggested that Republican candidates, in order to help make up for their smaller share of partisans in the electorate, are more likely to adopt new campaign techniques and put a greater emphasis on running an effective campaign than Democratic candidates. If that is true, then the use of polling should be more prevalent among winning Republican candidates, and that appears to be the case—43 percent of our sample are Republican, compared to 31 percent of the nonusers. Of course, as we noted earlier, our districts supported Republican candidates more strongly than the nation as a whole and hence, since our sample includes only winners, we cannot be certain the relationship exists for all candidates. Almost one half of our sample is made up of freshmen, while they constitute only 15 percent of the nonusers. Nonincumbents in close races are likely to rely on polling data to provide them with information on a constituency that may be somewhat new to them. Once in office, the Republican members of our sample correspond almost precisely to the entire Republican membership in the House in terms of party loyalty, conservative coalition support, and voting participation. On the other hand, Democrats who used polling, have slightly higher party loyalty scores and support the conservative coalition less than their party colleagues, largely because few of the Democrats who used polling were from the South.

Our sample was, on the average, 45 years old, with about 5 years of prior experience in elected office before entering the House, which means that many probably first ran for office in the mid and late sixties, when the virtues of polling were becoming more apparent to candidates. In contrast, the majority of the House received its early electoral experience when polling was less well understood and certainly less widely used.

In summary, we can say that for successful House candidates in 1974 polling was most likely done by nonincumbents in close races in districts generally more supportive of Republican candidates than most. The campaigns feature high expenditures and candidates who are generally younger than the House as a whole and who in turn must appeal to a constituency that is younger than the national average.

When and How Often Was Polling Done?

The average number of polls taken by members of our sample was 2.5—respondents took either one (32 percent), two (29 percent), three (15 percent), four (11 percent), or five or more polls (13 percent). Figure 4 illustrates the timing of the polls. It may surprise some to see so much polling done so far in advance of the general election. Early polling is partly a function of getting ready for a primary. Those with primary contests normally began polling by May while those unopposed in primaries usually did not begin polling until July. However, the fact that in almost 70 percent of the cases where polling was used the first poll was completed by the end of July indicates the potential importance of polling data to the establishment of basic campaign strategy. This conclusion is reinforced by the fact that 55 percent of our respondents indicated that a precampaign poll was taken.

FIGURE 4
Timing of Polls

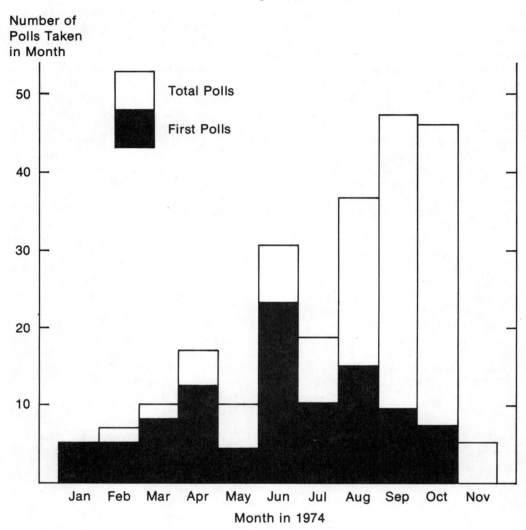

How Was the Polling Carried Out?

Almost one half (46 percent) of those in our sample used professional pollsters to write and carry out the polls. Another 27 percent relied on a combination of a professional pollster and some of their own staff to design, administer, and interpret the surveys, while 13 percent used campaign workers exclusively. Of the services provided by the professional pollster, the most utilized were questionnaire design (91 percent of those using a professional) and sample selection (87 percent), followed by interviewer training (84 percent), coordination (81 percent), and hiring (71 percent). In about half the cases where a professional was used, the services above were provided only for the first poll with subsequent polls carried out by campaign workers, sometimes in consultation with the pollsters. While a few campaigns used mail questionnaires or made polling part of their canvassing effort, the techniques most commonly relied on were personal interviews (45 percent) and telephone interviews (75 percent). In cases where both were used, the normal pattern would be to begin with a poll based on personal interviews and then turn to telephone surveys for further tracking of electorate opinion. The heavy use of telephone interviews reflects not only their ease of administration and the speed with which they can be carried out, but also their substantially lower costs.

What Types of Information Were Gathered?

Table 32 presents the types of information collected in the surveys. Candidate standing is clearly the type of data most consistently collected. The charting of "horse race" findings such as these is an important element in adjusting campaign planning to fit the progress (or lack of progress) of the campaign, although pollsters frequently emphasize the importance of other kinds of information. Initial ambiguity as to who an opponent will be may be the reason this type of data is more likely to be collected in polls subsequent to the first one. Also, for an unknown candidate, a simple assessment of standing is often meaningless, not to mention discouraging.

The distinctions in the use of the first poll compared to subsequent ones is interesting. Of substantial importance in the first poll is the determination of the issues that are critical to the electorate. This type of information is often used to establish the basic themes of a campaign. Issue concerns are monitored continually in most campaigns, but the value of these data diminishes once a basic campaign plan is agreed upon. In a majority of races in our sample, information on the candidate's personal image and the opposition's strengths and weaknesses is gathered in the first poll as well as in subsequent ones. Some campaign managers have argued that polling plays a crucial role in assessing the value of different media to the campaign. Although this may be true in statewide and national races which conform more easily to media markets, few gather such information in races for the House.

TABLE 32 Information Gathered in the Polls

Type of Information	First Poll (N = 100) Number	Subsequent Polls (N = 68) Number	% of Those Doing More Than One Poll
Issues important to the electorate	81	41	60%
Candidate standing vs. opponent	74	57	84
Public view of candidate's personality	55	34	50
Opposition's strength and weaknesses	53	41	60
Assessing the value of various media	22	10	15

How Was Polling Data Used in the Campaign?

To assess how polling was used in the campaigns we asked a series of questions concerning the importance of polling to a variety of areas of campaign strategy and planning. The results are presented in Table 33. Survey data are most important in the selection of issues and the determination of candidate standing. It is in these areas that traditional sources of such information (e.g., talking to campaign workers, reading letters to the editor) may be highly biased, and therefore survey data satisfy a critical need. Polling is also useful in determining the degree of support for the opposition, the role of the candidate's personal image, and the assessment of group attitudes. In some races, a candidate's standing in private polls is a critical factor in establishing the credibility of a campaign to potential financial supporters. On the whole, however, very few respondents felt that polling played an important role in the generation of campaign contributions. Party success in the 1972 campaign appears to be a factor for those indicating that survey results were important in fund raising. The party of candidates who felt that polling was important or very important to fund raising had averaged 6 percent fewer votes in the previous election than those indicating polling was not important or very unimportant (for Democrats the difference was more than 10 percent). Therefore, while survey results are generally not important in fund raising, in cases of poor party showings in the last election, they play a minor role in generating contributions.

TABLE 33   The Use of Polling Information in the Campaign

| | % Responding That Polling Was Important or Very Important | | | | | | | | |
| | Democrats (57) | | | Republicans (43) | | | Overall (100) | | |
Area of Campaign	Impor-tant	Impor-tant	Total	I	VI	T	I	VI	T
Selection of issues	36%	43%	79%	37%	51%	88%	36%	47%	83%
Determining candidate standing	39	39	77	24	64	88	32	50	82
Developing overall campaign strategy	46	29	75	38	50	88	43	37	80
Deciding which elements on the candidate's image to stress	47	22	69	59	23	82	52	22	74
Assessing the opposition's strengths and weaknesses	41	32	73	40	33	73	41	32	73
Drawing an accurate picture of attitudes of different groups in the electorate	45	27	71	42	18	61	44	23	67
Generating campaign contributions	16	7	23	24	3	26	19	5	24

What Factors Determine How Polling Is Used?

We examined a number of factors that might have influenced how polling was used in the campaign. Most (incumbency, competitiveness of the race, district characteristics, the background and ideology of the candidates) had little or no impact on the use of polling, as measured by such factors as how many polls were completed, what kinds of information were gathered, and the role of survey data in campaign planning. The lack of influence of such factors may be surprising to some. We feel it can be best explained by the fact that, as noted earlier, polling tends to be used in certain types of races and by particular kinds of candidates, and given the frequent use of professionals and the communication that occurs between candidates, the actual use of survey data does not vary greatly across the variables cited above.

The way polling was used did vary somewhat according to three factors: party of the candidate, the level of expenditures, and the use of professional pollsters. Previous studies have discovered differences in the way Democrats and Republicans organize and carry out their campaigns. Table 33 illustrates some clear distinctions. Polling was considered very important to the development of overall strategy in 29 percent of the Democratic campaigns, compared to 50 percent of the Republican campaigns. Also, polling was more important in Republican campaigns in determining candidate standing, the selection of issues, and the use of the candidate's personal image. In only one instance did the Democrats rely more heavily on polling, and that was in the use of polling to assess group attitudes. This finding supports those who view the success of Democratic candidates as being more dependent on the pulling together of a coalition of groups than is the case in Republican candidacies. Party affiliation was also related to the use of professional pollsters: 61 percent of the Republican candidates relied solely on professionals for their polling, while 36 percent of the Democratic candidates did so. Democrats were more likely to rely on a combination of a professional and their own campaign workers. On the whole, polling played a somewhat bigger role in planning Republican campaigns than in Democratic ones.

Both the use of a professional and the level of campaign expenditures were related to the number of polls taken. In campaigns where professionals completely controlled the polling, fewer polls were taken (see Table 34). The costs of having a professional do all a candidate's polling are substantially higher than when a combination of pro-

TABLE 34   The Use of Professional Pollsters and the Frequency of Polling

Number of Polls Taken	*Who Wrote and Conducted the Polls?*		
	Campaign Workers Only *(12)*	*Professional Pollster Only* *(44)*	*Professional Pollster and Campaign Workers* *(27)*
1	25%	39%	22%
2	50	32	15
3	0	23	11
4	0	5	26
5+	25	2	26
Total	100%	101%	100%
Average Number of Polls	3.0	2.0	3.6

fessional pollsters and campaign staff are used. Therefore, those using the latter approach can do more polling. Our data do not permit us to assess the direction of causality in this case, however, and it may be that a desire to do more polling results in the use of campaign workers to conduct extra polls. The question of cost is also reflected in the fact that those who completed one or two polls had an average campaign expenditure of $93,417 while those doing three or more polls averaged $114,008 in expenditures.

The use of a professional pollster also influenced the way in which polling was used in the campaign, as illustrated in Table 35. Candidates who use only a professional generally rely more heavily on polling in the areas of issue selection, candidate image, assessment of the opposition candidate, and overall strategy. Those whose polls are carried out completely by campaign workers show more interest in candidate standing and group attitudes. The importance of polling in determining candidate standing is often viewed as typical of amateur campaigns. Professional pollsters emphasize the wealth of insights that they provide, with candidate standing, at least at the outset of the campaign, being of minimal importance. In fact, the differences in the pattern of using polls illustrated by the first two columns of the table are a good indication of the advantages of using a professional pollster. On the whole, Republican candidates are much more likely to use a professional pollster and in turn rely on polling more heavily in developing basic campaign strategy.

Another factor that may influence the use of polling information in the campaign is the perceived accuracy of the data. If the campaign decision makers have doubts concerning the quality of the polling data, they will hardly be likely to rely on it very heavily in the campaign. In the overwhelming majority of cases, the surveys were perceived as accurate. We asked respondents to rate the accuracy of the information gathered in the polls, particularly in the prediction of the vote totals, and most stated that they were almost perfect (20 percent), very accurate (42 percent) or somewhat accurate (23 percent). Somewhat surprisingly, however, perceived accuracy of the polls was only weakly related to how the polls were used. Finally, we should note that the number of polls taken, the amount of information gathered, and the use of survey results in the campaign were related to each other in the expected directions. The larger the number of polls taken, the greater the amount of information gathered in the polls, and the more important was polling to the campaign.

TABLE 35   The Use of Professional Pollsters and the Importance of Polling Information in the Campaign (% stating polling was important or very important)

	Who Wrote and Conducted the Polls?		
Area of Campaign	*Campaign Workers Only (13)*	*Professional Pollster Only (44)*	*Professional Pollster and Campaign Workers (27)*
Selection of issues	63%	91%	82%
Determining candidate standing	84	78	77
Developing overall strategy	66	89	77
Candidate image	67	78	78
Assessing opposition	50	70	92
Group attitudes	75	69	66
Campaign contributions	17	14	32

Summary and Conclusions

This article has attempted to clarify how polling fits into the overall campaign process. Several findings are of interest to students of political campaigning. First, the most important factor determining whether or not a winning candidate used survey data appears to be the competitiveness of the district, both historically and in this 1974 race. A substantial majority of those using survey data were involved in races that, at least at the outset, appeared to be close. A second factor related to the use of polling was, not surprisingly, the availability of funds to pay for them. Polling is most likely to be used in competitive races with well-funded campaigns.

Of more interest is the way in which polling was used. Those who used polling generally began polling early, particularly if they had a primary contest, and usually polled more than once. The information they gathered depended to some extent on the stage of the race. Issues were emphasized in early polls, and candidate standing was of importance in the latter stages of the campaign. The data collected in the polls were useful in several areas of the campaign, particularly in selecting key issues to emphasize in the campaign, monitoring candidate standing, and developing overall strategy. How polling was used was related to party affiliation, the use of a professional pollster, and the level of campaign expenditures.

This study's findings suggest the need for further research, which we hope will develop along several lines. First, an examination of the campaigns of *losing* candidates as well as winners would enable us to asssess to what extent campaign strategy in general, and polling in particular, varies between winning and losing candidates. There is also a need for comparative research on campaigns across different levels, to determine how well the findings noted above applied to campaigns for city, county, state, or national elective office. As a result of research of this nature we will begin to get a fuller understanding of the influence of polling on campaign politics.

TO THE STUDENT: A COMMENTARY

In 1976 a young lawyer in a southern state decided to run for Congress. With no opposition he easily became his party's nominee. His task was to defeat a highly popular incumbent who had held the congressional seat for several terms. In the past the incumbent had faced only token challenges. Two years earlier, for example, a taxi cab driver had run against the congressman, did not campaign, and received only 33 percent of the vote. That fact encouraged the young lawyer. If a taxi cab driver who mounted no campaign could get one-third of the vote then a more experienced candidate like the lawyer who campaigned vigorously just might pull off an upset. But the lawyer wanted more reassurance. So he hired a pollster, a nationally known and reputable polling firm. Since the pollster was conducting a statewide survey for a presidential candidate at the time, he simply added a question to the statewide poll. That question would be asked of all persons polled in the lawyer's congressional district. The lawyer was ecstatic with the results: 40 percent of those polled favored him over the incumbent. Dedication, hard work, drive would produce results. On the basis of optimistic poll results the lawyer spent $50,000, worked very hard, campaigned all over the district, and hoped. Meanwhile his opponent geared up his normal group of loyal volunteers, put up yard signs, sent out a few brochures, and pondered his next term. Election day arrived. The challenge fell short. Countless hours of campaigning, $50,000 and all of his media blitz accomplished little. The lawyer captured 36 percent of the vote, only three more than the lackadaisical taxi driver!

There is a lesson in this little saga, one that goes beyond what Clymer and DeClerq have told you. Clymer makes it clear that there are valuable insights a candidate can obtain from polls. These are primarily insights into what troubles voters. But polls do not uncover solutions for those problems. Hence, it may well be a mistake for pollsters and candidates to assume that what voters say they want should automatically become what politicians say they should want. Clymer notes other uses of polls. One is to make news. By making news candidates might discourage their opponents. Also by making news candidates can manage expectations. Many a candidate has leaked a poll to the press showing him "behind" and an "underdog" in a race. This not only lulls the opposition and galvanizes one's supporters, it also permits the candidate to claim, no matter how poor the showing, that he or she did "better than expected," hence claiming victory even in defeat. DeClerq suggests to you other uses of polls—to measure a candidate's image and strengths and weaknesses of the opposition, give financial supporters confidence when they "place their bets," and assess the value of various campaign media.

Our campaign-weary and financially drained lawyer friend used his poll for every one of these purposes. If you have read Clymer and DeClerq closely you realize that was his first mistake. For example, Clymer writes of the "no frills survey module." Recall that the module is a do-it-yourself polling kit developed by Decision Making Information, a major polling firm that worked on behalf of Ronald Reagan (among others) in 1978 and 1980. A key aspect of that package is that it consists of three surveys—benchmark, follow-up, and quick-look. Recall also that DeClerq found that two-thirds of successful congressional candidates he surveyed employed more than one poll. Candidates polled early and frequently. But not our lawyer friend, Mr. 36 Percent. On the basis of a single-shot poll well after a May primary he committed $50,000 to campaign for a November election.

DeClerq alludes to another item that our defeated lawyer should have considered before placing too much faith in his poll. That item is accuracy. Almost two-thirds of DeClerq's respondents regarded their polls as very accurate or better. Mr. 36 Percent might have said so too (although since DeClerq studied winners, not losers, our lawyer friend would not even make the cut!). But any poll result must be interpreted in the light of potential inaccuracies. Some adjustment, for instance, must be made for "sampling error." This refers to the range of probable error produced by projecting poll figures from a sample to a larger population. Put differently, when our young lawyer found that 40 percent of those sampled in his poll favored his candidacy, how could he know 40 percent would indeed vote for him?

The fact is he couldn't! And for a number of reasons. One is obvious to you. Simply because someone favors your candidacy on September 15 doesn't mean that person will vote for you in November. People change their minds. Moreover, saying you favor Candidate A in response to a pollster does not guarantee you will not vote for Candidate B in the polling booth. The context of being interviewed is not that of voting.

But there are other reasons. One has to do with the nature of polling. If samples of people are randomly drawn from a larger population the very act of sampling introduces some error. How much error depends upon a number of factors—how the sample is selected, the characteristics of the population, etc. For any given number of people in a sample the range of sampling error can be estimated. A sample of 10,000 people (a prohibitive size because of the costs) has a range of error of 1 percent. A sample of 1,500 persons has an error range of 2 to 3 percent. One of 200 has a range of 7 to 9 percent.

Suppose, then, you sampled 200 people in a congressional district and 40 percent said they favored your candidacy. Being informed about sampling techniques you would know that this meant an error range of at least plus or minus 7 percent. That is, based upon your sample of 200, you would know that in the total congressional district 33 to 47 percent favored your candidacy. Our chagrined lawyer faced precisely these figures—but did not know that! His pollster sampled 200 people in his district and reported a 40 percent support. In actuality that could have been as low as 33 percent (the taxi driver's earlier vote) or as high as 47 percent. Our candidate thought 40 meant 40, was encouraged, and rode off on his charger to do battle. His incumbent opponent in the meantime had a series of polls, each of 600 persons (with an error of plus or minus 4 percent) that showed he could expect 60 percent of the vote. His head rested easily upon his pillow.

Whether you watch politics because you might yourself become a candidate or because you simply want to be informed, there is one other key factor you should take into account in reading the polls. Be on the lookout for sloppy, biased, or loaded question wordings. Sometimes misleading question wordings are deliberate, but more likely the cause lies in the fact that any word, no matter how neutral on the surface, provokes some degree of pro or con sentiment. Here is an example related to a problem we talked about in chapter 9, public financing of congressional campaigns. In 1977 a Gallup Poll asked over 1,500 people the following: "It has been suggested the federal government provide a fixed amount of money for the election campaigns of candidates for Congress and that all private contributions from other sources be prohibited. Do you think this is a good idea or a poor idea?" The results were that 57 percent thought it a good idea, 32 percent a poor idea, and 11 percent had no opinion. Surely as a congressional official you would think people supported public financing. But don't jump too quickly. That same year another polling firm, Civic Service Inc., conducted a nationwide sampling of 2,500 people. The question read: "It has been proposed in Congress that the federal government provide public financing for congressional campaigns to the U.S. House of Representatives and Senate. Would you approve or disapprove of the proposal to use public funds, federal money, to pay the costs of congressional campaigns?" Thirty-three percent approved, 63 percent opposed, and the remainder were of no opinion. Both Gallup and Civic Service polls were in the same year (even in the same month of March). On other items included in both polls findings coincided. Yet on the question of public financing one poll found a majority of persons in favor, the other a larger majority of persons opposed. Why the difference? Look at how the two questions were worded. As you can see each has its share of loaded words. In all likelihood each set tapped different sentiments. So it may be that neither measured opinions about public financing. Rather, both may have gauged conditioned responses to key code words.

Such are a few of the problems any watcher of politics has in interpreting the results of public opinion polls. Politicians have them. Journalists have them. Political scientists have them. And you have them. Since polls are so much of our political lives now it behooves us to learn more about them and to judge the relative merit of the current pollenium. Some useful books that will assist in that endeavor (in addition to those listed at the close of chapter 2) are:

George Gallup, *The Sophisticated Poll Watcher's Guide*
Charles Roll and Albert Cantril, *Polls: Their Use and Misuse in Politics*

Those two books are written by pollsters. A social scientist's view can be found in:

Leo Bogart, *Silent Politics: Polls and the Awareness of Public Opinion*

EPILOGUE

WATCHING AND KNOWING, BUT KNOWING WHAT?

INTRODUCTION

In the preceding chapters of this book we have urged that if you want to understand politics you must watch it. One way to do that is through your personal experience; that is, get involved in political activity and find out what is going on. But for those of you who do not have the time, energy, money, or other resources to take part in politics all or most of the time, there is another way to be a political watcher. That, of course, is by reading what seasoned observers of the political scene have to say. Their descriptions, accounts, analyses, interpretations, and speculations can give you a good grasp of the political life even if it is secondhand.

We have recommended two types of political observers to you. First, there are political journalists who keep close to political goings-on and report their observations. As we have noted such observers are not limited simply to people who work regularly in the news media, but may even include politicians, political consultants, pollsters, and others who write to you about politics, take part in radio and television programs, or simply free-lance their views. Second, there are the social scientists—especially political scientists and communication scientists—who research and write about politics. Having sampled their wares along with those of political journalists, you undoubtedly recognize that they too have something to say to you.

We hope, therefore, that this book will not be the end of watching American politics for you. We hope that you will turn to the observations of professional political watchers whenever you get the opportunity. However, in making that recommendation we would be remiss in closing this book without raising an important question about political watching. Simply put the question is, "How do we know what we see is real?" How, in short, do you know the political realities reported to you by journalists and scientists are what really happens, what politics is really all about? If you don't experience politics firsthand, how can you be certain other political observers are telling it like it is?

The question of the fidelity of political reports and analyses is what we ask you to address in this chapter. We are not talking so much about whether or not political observers try to deceive you. Instead we are raising the question, or possibility, that there may be something in the nature of political watching—be it political journalism or political science—that obscures your political vision. There just may be something that makes it very difficult to add knowledge about politics to acquaintance with it. If there is, how can you deal with it?

The first selection in this epilogue is by the same person you met in the first selection of the prologue, Bill Rivers. Rivers has written a book that argues, in part, that political correspondents constitute "The Other Government." By digging out what goes on and reporting it, political correspondents perform a vital governing function as important in many respects in a democracy as what presidents, congressional officials, judges, or other politicians do. In the selection that follows from that book Rivers warns you of the pitfalls that lie in the path of political correspondents when they try to report politics like it is. Read what he says carefully, then ask yourself if Walter Cronkite for all those years as anchorman of the CBS News was accurate in closing his broadcasts with "and that's the way it is."

But political scientists have problems telling it like it is, too. Those problems disturb political scientist Lee McDonald, author of the second selection we call "The Other Knowledge?" McDonald argues that the very language of politics obscures whatever political realities there may be. The language of politics, he argues, is replete with myth. But, he goes on to argue, so is the language of those scientists who study politics. The language of political science is also mythical in much of its content. The result is that what passes for political knowledge about politics may in fact be political mythology.

Lest you think that the problems facing political journalists discourage Bill Rivers, or those hounding political scientists depress Lee McDonald, be forewarned that they do not. The very awareness that such problems exist offers hope. And, we believe that if you too achieve that awareness, your appetite for political watching will be stimulated every bit as much as your skills for doing so have been sharpened by reading the thoughtful articles by political journalists and scientists in the preceding pages.

THE OTHER GOVERNMENT?

William L. Rivers

An Original Essay.

The vast diversity of Americans rely on The Other Government, but few know the pitfalls that confront the correspondents as they struggle with facts and what masquerade as facts. Consider what occurs:

1. Something happens in government.
2. Government officials decide how to announce or present this occurrence. This may differ from (1).

3. Through a press secretary, the news media are presented with the government's announcement of the occurrence. This may differ from (1) and (2).
4. A reporter produces a story about the occurrence. This may differ from (1), (2), and (3).
5. The media organization processes the reporter's story for presentation to the public, either directly or through its client newspapers and broadcast stations. This may differ from (1), (2), (3), and (4).
6. The public retina receives an image of the occurrence. This may differ from (1), (2), (3), (4) and (5).

From initiation to presentation, a news story must hurdle four crucial obstacles. Hurdle #1 is set up by government officials. The official responsible for the news-making occurrence will winnow an announcement from the work of many subordinates—a process which may displease them. Nonetheless, the official contracts the announcement, which is necessary, in a way that will please *him*. Next, ordinarily he relies on a press secretary (or one known as a public-information specialist), who may think well of the new-minnowed bulletin, or not. He submits the announcement to a journalist. At that point, the press secretary has an unusual role, for he is there to answer questions. If he is questioned perceptively, he has an unusual opportunity to suggest that the journalist check with the higher official—or to answer the questions himself in the way *he* prefers, or even to guide the journalist to an unhappy subordinate. In many cases the journalist is in a hurry—or is lazy—and will print or broadcast what he is given. Often these days, however, he is an adversary journalist, one who questions closely and looks beyond the announcement. When he finds what is or seems to be lying or corruption—or the beginnings of it—he faces a high obstacle: his editor. It is usual for the editor to pass the bland story as it is written. That encourages the journalist not to look for, say, unethical or illegal behavior. But more and more often, the journalist has a vision of fame and prizes, which increases his ardor. The editor, however, has final authority. Whatever decisions are made, the occurrence presented to the public is an image—often highly distorted—certainly not the reality.

What can the public do about the distorted images that pass before us as though they were real? Clearly, we are *always* helpless. We speak as though we know. Yet how *do* we know that Barbara Walters, one prominent member of The Other Government, is paid $1 million a year while the other television anchormen are paid much less? Was this a triumph of women's liberation when she changed from NBC to ABC?

If you were one of the 20 million viewers of John Chancellor's NBC evening broadcast, you heard him say: "NBC valued Barbara's services highly, but the negotiations for a renewal of her contract involved a million dollars and other privileges, and this afternoon NBC pulled out of the negotiations, leaving her a clear path to ABC." What Chancellor failed to say was that the path ended earlier; she had weighed both offers, decided in favor of ABC, and signed the contract. Only *then* did NBC give up, which is quite different from pulling out of negotiations. Moreover, NBC spokesmen called newspapers and wire services to say that NBC had withdrawn its offer to Walters. It was a lie.

Even if you read the Associated Press story, which was published by nearly all the American newspapers, you would surely believe that she is paid twice as much as the three others who work on the same kind of program. The Associated Press story, which was read by scores of millions, said only that Barbara Walters will be paid $1 million dollars a year as a co-anchor worker on ABC and said nothing about her additional work. If you were also one of the three million subscribers to *Newsweek*, you probably read the story in the issue of May 3, 1976, headed "The $5 Million Woman."

The second paragraph of the story reads: "To persuade NBC's daytime queen to defect, ABC handed her a five-year, $1 million-a-year contract—thereby enshrining Walters as the highest-paid newscaster in the history of the medium (Walter Cronkite, John Chancellor, and Reasoner each earn about $400,000 a year)." Later, it said, "In addition to doubling Walters' $500,000-a-year income, her new contract calls for her to anchor four prime-time specials each year (to be put together by her own production company), to occasionally host ABC's Sunday "Issues and Answers" series and to appear on a number of the network's other news and documentary programs." Are these specials in *addition* to her $1 million a year?

Your strongest impression might be either confusion, or the belief that Walters is being paid $1 million for working as a co-anchor. Only if you had read *Broadcasting* magazine, which has a circulation of less than 75,000, would it become clear that only $500,000 is paid to her to anchor the news. One paragraph asserts: "Actually, only half of the annual million dollars will be salary for the evening news role. The rest will come from fees for four prime-time specials she will anchor for each year, produced by her own production company with ABC financing. She also will anchor eight of the ABC News *Issues and Answers* public-affairs series each year and will contribute to other ABC News documentary programs."

When the *San Francisco Chronicle* had its photographic reporter ask readers, "Is Barbara Walters worth a million?" *everyone* thought she was paid only to share the anchor position. As one responded, "No, a million for an anchor person is ridiculous."

And the bulk of public opinion is nestled in that response. What proportion of the public has an informed opinion on Walters? Much less than 1 percent—excluding those who asked the question.

Do you know the President? Have you seen him? On television? Of course—but there he is on display. The reality of the man is not the man you see through the good offices of the media.

We live in a synthetic environment. What most of us know is based primarily on second-hand information. We don't *know* the President, or our Senators, or perhaps even our Congressmen; probably not even our mayors. We are seldom at the center of each world crisis, nor in the policy-making councils of government. What we do know about events around us, local or international, is almost always based on information provided us by the news media.

Most of us seldom acknowledge that fact. We act as though our view of the world were based on direct, first-hand experience; as if our information was naturally accurate and trustworthy. We rarely, if ever, consider the methods by which information is *processed,* and therefore often altered. The very structure of the mass media—with its machines, technicians, gatekeepers, constraints of time and space—affects the substance of what is transmitted. But we respond to that end product as if it were a pristine re-creation of reality, mainly because we know so little about the process in between.

Nor do we really know what the media are doing or even what they are trying to do.

The extent of our ignorance is highlighted by a story told by the manager of a television station. A viewer kept calling him to complain about some of the programs being broadcast. After many polite explanations, the frustrated station manager finally solved the problem. "Look," he told the viewer, "if you call here once more I'm going to unplug your set from this end." Of course, no such thing is possible—but the viewer never called again.

The news media are often termed the "mirror on the world." But the process is a double-mirror, and selectively narrow. Indeed, even that mixed metaphor may be too simple an analogy. The news media may be better understood as a prism, which picks up rays of information from all directions and refracts them, bends them, before sending them out again. The image is sent to many diverse audiences for information—and thus back to the original source, where a politician or other news-maker responds to the media image of himself. Each facet of the media—television, radio, newspapers, magazines—has its own particular angle. Refracting according to structural limitations of time, space, film, and deadlines each medium sends out its uniquely altered message. What you hear on the five-minute radio news will not, of course, be the same as what you see on television. Neither report is precisely the same version one gets in the newspaper, and *all* will differ from the account offered by magazines.

We should recognize that the information we receive about government is not the same thing as government itself. While we are not often deliberately deceived, we must be wary of our tendency to respond to the image rather than the reality. To put it simply: When we vote, are we electing people according to what we really know, or are our ballots cast according to what we see in brief bursts of film on the 6 o'clock news? When we decide to support—or not support—our government's foreign policy, is the decision made on the basis of solid information, or on an article in a weekly news-magazine?

Whether we read newspapers and magazines, listen to radio news or watch television news, most of us protect ourselves and our opinions from the overwhelming confusion that is in the news media. We have developed three filtering processes, in various degrees, to reject information that does not square with our views of the world. We protect our opinions by *selective exposure*—keeping up with the news that reinforces our opinions, rejecting much that is opposed to it. For example, a larger percentage of Democrats than Republicans watched the telecasts of the Senate hearings on the Watergate case.

Second, we also tend to register what we want to register—*selective perception*—a process that psychologists have demonstrated so often that many are now no more interested in probing its existence than a mathematician is interested in proving that two-plus-two equals four. Many people go to extravagant lengths to perceive "facts" that will support their prejudices. It has been shown, for example, that some people who are strongly anti-Semitic can look at an editorial cartoon that plainly ridicules religious bias and see it in reverse—as a glorification of Anglo-Saxon lineage.

By the same uneasy token, whoever you are, it is much more likely that you are politically independent. In responding to poll surveys, more and more often Americans are "undecided" almost until the election itself is at hand. Moreover, as the *New York Times* put it in a headline on Page 1: POLLING ENCOUNTERS PUBLIC RESISTANCE: DECISION-MAKING PROCESS IS THREATENED. Mervin Field, president of the Field Research Corporation in California, was quoted in the story: "Twenty years ago, we could figure on getting 85 percent with reasonable effort. Now we're hard-pressed to get 60 percent."

Moreover, when the public opinion pollsters surveyed nationally, they found that many of those who were surveyed did not care *who* became President. Early in 1976, the *Wall Street Journal* reported that:

"There is a belief that the [political] process is so unresponsive and dishonest that it cannot be used by voters for their purposes" says Patrick Caddell, a pollster for many Democrats. His

Cambridge Survey Research surveys show that fully "four out of 10 respondents say it doesn't make any difference who wins" elections.

A grim array of polling evidence indicates that alienation and cynicism toward politics and government have become pervasive after a confidence-shattering decade stretching from Vietnam through Watergate and a deep recession. Items:

—By a margin of almost two to one, a Caddell poll finds that people believe "most politicians don't really care about me."

—58% believe that "people with power are out to take advantage of me," according to the Louis Harris Survey.

—49% believe that "quite a few of the people running the government are a little crooked," according to Market Opinion Research Inc., the polling firm for President Ford's campaign.

—68% feel that "over the last 10 years, this country's leaders have consistently lied to the American people," a Caddell poll finds.

—57% believe that "both the Democratic and Republican parties are in favor of big business rather than the average worker," according to a survey by Peter Hart, a pollster for many Democrats.

America's reluctance to decide for a political candidate indicates the next turn in political journalism. We may be passing from the stage of interpretive reporting, for which a struggle was waged for decades, to a new kind of news writing. This beginning of a story about a black general, written by William Greider of the *Washington Post,* may indicate the changes ahead:

The general is a man of heavy presence, tall and broad-shouldered, with a deep and serious voice, a natural "command voice" that subtly extracts deference from those around him.

So it was a rare moment, listening to this man after hours, over drinks, in the standard red-brick general's house assigned to the base's vice commander. His voice turned soft and rheumy as he stretched out in the lounge chair and sketched word pictures from his past.

"When I was going to school with my mother, we always did shows," he said. "We'd have an Easter operetta, a Fourth of July patriotic blast and I'd have the largest speaking parts."

Lt. Gen. Daniel James, Jr., 55, talked about a small boy nicknamed "Chappie" standing on a stage, dressed in a pink tuxedo with white lapels while his cousin Mabel sang to him a song written by his older sister.

The general's voice shifted to a falsetto imitation of his cousin Mabel and he began to sing:

"Handsome is as handsome does, so the wise man say. Feathers fine may make fine birds, but folks are not that way.

"It's what is in your heart that counts, deny it if you can. I'm not impressed with how you dress, cause clothes don't make the man."

The general laughed at his own singing. Why, he wondered, do those words stick in his memory after all these years? He was growing up poor in Pensacola, Fla., only he didn't know it. His mother never told him. . . .

In this profile, Greider creates both General James and the South in which he lived as a black officer. This kind of reporting is lonely among the many kinds of news and feature stories that appear in newspapers, but, perhaps, not for long.

To compete with television, the correspondents for newspapers and magazines must study Greider's story. *What is it?* It can be described simply: visual writing. How can it compete with television? Television is by definition visual. In almost all cases, the watchers of TV news programs are opting to take their information with the least exertion possible, inviting the pictures to wash over them. If correspondents will learn to write visually, the work of their readers will be easy because of the sheer joy of reading.

For example, consider Ed Asner, who plays Lou Grant, the city editor of the *Los Angeles Tribune* in the televised production. If correspondents have seen him, which is probable, it is still unlikely that they can describe him in more than a sentence: "He's short, stocky, and balding." To describe Lou Grant in much more than a sentence, most correspondents would have to make a strong and unaccustomed effort. They must make that extra effort. Long before television was invented, a great novelist, Joseph Conrad, wrote: "My task is to make you hear, to make you feel—it is, before all, to make you *see.*"

Newspaper and magazine correspondents should also consider the way *Time* magazine described Larry O'Brien when he was the chairman of the 1972 Democratic Convention:

> O'Brien picked up the huge gavel. Too heavy, he thought. Why not get an electric buzzer next time? He whacked it down, and the great spectacle of Miami Beach was on. He made an early decision. The noisy mass below him had to be managed. Somehow led through four days of business, but more important were the millions of Americans who were watching through those blinking red eyes directly in front of him. Talk to them, he told himself, wondering what the man in San Clemente would be seeing in a few hours.
>
> The convention was already behind time when O'Brien started his speech. That was deliberate. Don't harass or push. Stay loose, he kept telling himself. The noise on the floor hardly subsided as he talked—the old Irish rasp, the square sentences full of platitudes, annoyingly interspersed with film clips. Yet here and there people began to listen. It was not the familiar polemic against Richard Nixon. It was not the extravagant praise of the Democratic past. He talked about "the crisis of truth," of the Democrats being "on trial." He did not avoid blame for problems, and he tried to warn his youthful audience that the world is not remade by "a stroke of the pen."

This kind of interior monologue will demand much stronger efforts from the correspondents. Even though this kind of reporting should be true to the standards of the most reliable standard reportage, it seeks a larger truth than is possible through merely compiling facts.

How much of Washington reportage is compilation of facts plus a bit of learned commentary? Nearly all of it—as though the correspondents were afraid or lazy. The Other Government has many powerful writers who can make events come alive with reality, or at least something closer to "lived" reality. Writers who came to Washington from local-reporting assignments notice almost immediately the loss of the sense of "real life" in their reports. Jim Naughton, former White House correspondent for the *New York Times* finds this loss "the only significant difference" between his Washington reports and his writing in Cleveland. "We deal so often with issues rather than people," he says. "We don't humanize the content of the news in Washington in ways that you can do elsewhere in this country: related to the lives of the readers. We probably could do a lot better than we do. That is one of the reasons I wanted to get on at the White House. I get so tired of writing about plastic figures, from a distance. I really wanted to write, for a change, about live human beings."

I believe that many of the correspondents are ready for such reporting. Reducing the distance between the image and the reality will require that visual writing come to political journalism. Writing such stories would make the correspondents aware that government itself can be made to live for the public—just as Greider made General James live on the page, just as *Time* made Larry O'Brien live.

I have chosen to close with a discussion of the new journalism because the issues that subject raises underscore the guiding themes of this book: the immense power, generic limitations, and concomitant responsibilities of the news media. In the course of several hundred pages, I have attempted to show again and again that the only— literally the only—knowledge which most citizens have of their federal government comes from information provided by the media. But, as I have tried repeatedly to show, the information we receive through our lone source is, by its very nature, deceptive. "You had to be there" is a phrase often used by story-tellers when their narrative capacity fails; it is also a phrase much heard among journalists.

Television, as I hope I have demonstrated, is even more deceptive than the print media as a transmitter of news. Television pictures give a sense of immediacy, a feeling of "being there," but what they present in their tiny flashes of real-life drama is never much more than a caricature of the grainy reality. When wielded by a news-gatherer and news-interpreter dedicated to impartial service of the public's right-to-know, the techniques of fiction could bring us closer to the daily life of government. I am convinced that correspondents, because they comprise The Other Government, must act on their increasingly great sense of public accountability. And I believe that their responsibility extends not only to accuracy and diligence in reporting, but also to the development of whatever techniques can help overcome the enormous obstacles facing correspondents in the age of Heisenberg.

The press has for two centuries been the public's ear in the District of Columbia. But in a time of vastly increasing federal authority, the public has every right to ask its Other Government to represent its first, third, fourth, fifth, and even sixth senses in Washington. Like the muckraking journalism of an earlier era, the new journalism of our own time may one day be seen as a necessary response to changes in the reality of government. As the official government searches its official soul in the wake of the Sixties and Seventies, correspondents should be well aware that a new time is upon us and that it may require of them a new journalism.

THE OTHER KNOWLEDGE?

Lee C. McDonald

Edited and reprinted from "Myths, Politics and Political Science," Western Political Quarterly *22 (March 1969): 141–150.*

1. *Is the language of politics inefficacious without mythical elements?*
2. *Is the language of political science inefficacious with mythical elements?*
3. *What is the relationship between the answer to question one and the answer to question two?*

I

If any language should prove invulnerable to mythological infiltration it would seem to be that language which is direct, literal, and used more to *do* something than to *mean* something. Such language was called by J. L. Austin "performative" language, that is, language which performs an action rather than states anything, as does our more common "constative" utterances. An example of a performative is the "verdictive" judgment: "We the jury do hereby find the defendant guilty." Another would be the "exercitive" action: "I vote 'no!'" Still another might be the "commissive" utterance: "I pledge you my support." Are mythical elements alien to such speech-acts?

To answer this question we must ask another and try to answer it, however sketchily: what is myth?

In frequent usage today "myth" is treated as a synonym for "illusion," usually to be contrasted with "reality." Such usages are understandable, but they sadly shrink a once virile term.

The Greek "*mythos*" was "a tale uttered by the mouth," generally associated with religious ceremony. It had a narrative and dramatic quality and pointed toward the divine, that is, the unknown. It attempted to capture in terms conceivable to humans some of the indeterminate qualities of this divine unknown. The language of these stories was consequently figurative, metaphorical, and ambiguous. Myths are poetry, but a special kind of poetry—the poetry men live by. As the bearer of other meanings, larger meanings, meanings beyond, myths have the concreteness of images found in private poetry, but also a certain universality. Hence, we have often been told that myth "does not tell truths, but does tell the truth"; a myth is something that "never was, but always is."

Live myths have potency even, or especially, when we are unaware of them as myths. The opaqueness of dead myths—Zeus, Perseus, Hercules—make them museum pieces. But the transparency of live myths make them very much like pieces of music; they have a character of their own, but are always subject to reinterpretation.

The transparency of myth is of a piece with the transparency of metaphor, by which, through juxtaposition, the ordinary is seen as extraordinary. The possibilities of metaphor are infinite and omnipresent. Because of what metaphor can do, we can never be sure that the ordinary will remain only ordinary. Indeed, the simplest descriptive terms may turn out to have something of this quality. They may be bearers of built-in conceptions we have taken for granted, but which condition the very perceptions the terms are intended to describe. It is unlikely, as Ernst Cassirer constantly reminds us, that we can ever get outside of, or get behind, our most basic language in order to perceive things purely and unconditionally. For example, the Greek *men*, or moon, means "the measuring one," suggesting that periodic recurrence is what is important about the moon. The Latin *luna* means "the shining one," suggesting that visual excitation is what is important about the moon. Myth, says Cassirer (he should have said metaphor at this point) is not just the shadow language throws on thought; it generates its own light.

To conclude our definitional excursion, we may lean on Philip Wheelwright, who says that metaphorical language, and by extension mythical language, is unique to the degree that it is tensive, diaphoric, and epiphoric. That is, to the degree that it is capable of holding tensions within it, can accomplish transferences from one thing to another, and is presentational rather than representational. It follows that those elements of reality that are born in conflict, that are coalescent rather than dichotomous, that are presentational (that move into view and then out), can be expressed only very poorly in literal language and probably cannot be expressed at all in that most literal of languages, mathematics. (Lest we are tempted to try to get along without language at all, it is well to be reminded, as Michael Polyani does for us, that when humans are denied all use of verbal communication, their performance in getting out of mazes turns out to be less intelligent than that of rats.)

So, back to our direct, supposedly literal political performatives. Can we be sure that the verdict of "guilty" does not carry with it some lingering overtones of betrayal of the gods and betrayal of the tribe? May not the jury that finds guilt feel without conscious articulation the etymological link between *juris* and "jury"? Is our negative voter perhaps in some small degree still the religious votary making his sacred vow? Is our politician's pledge of support, however platitudinous, still tinged with the thought of giving physical security as his Germanic linguistic forebears would have done? The most routine bureaucratic definition of "citizen" does not destroy altogether the memory of the citizen as member of a city and the memory of a city as more than buildings. The most unimaginative use of the word "party" cannot quite obscure the conception of party as part *of* something.

But the citation of political words with long etymologies would prove my point too easily. Myth runs deeper into political experience than its penetration into words. It runs also into sentences and even paragraphs. Even a prosaic President leading a pragmatic people finds it impossible to stick with literal language. Lyndon B. Johnson began his third State of the Union message,

> I come before you to report on the State of the Union for the third time.
> I come to thank you, and to add my tribute once more to the Nation's gratitude. For this Congress has already reserved for itself an honored chapter in the history of America.

We could easily translate these three sentences into more literal language:

> This is the third time I have been here to talk to you about some of the problems some of the people in the federal government have been working on. I thank you members of Congress—or some of you—and quite a few other people probably do, too, because you passed some legislation and did some other things that I liked and that some other people liked, too. Maybe some people living in future times will like them also.

The more literal of the two statements (which still has about four metaphors in it) is more easily subject to verification; but the object of this type of political speech is not to transmit empirically verifiable propositions, but to renew the authority of the speaker and to invigorate the sense of community among the auditors. Each is a means to the other. By this standard the latter statement requires thirty-three more words to achieve a lesser effect than the former statement. It is awkward, undignified, and bears no one any honor. By contrast, "come before" suggests the formality and dignity of a state occasion, and also a degree of obeisance. The phrase registers a sense of eventfulness, as in "I come bearing gifts." One seems to see a tired but elated warrior dismounting from his steed amid cheers from the multitude, having ridden at breakneck speed from the neighboring kingdom.

The dignity of Roman office still hovers over the word "tribute," from the Latin *tribus,* or tribe, and later the tax paid by the tribes. The whole American nation is personified and given a single emotion in "the Nation's gratitude." And that the Eighty-ninth Congress should have a whole chapter in the history of America suggests, among other things, that the history of America is a book with chapters, with an author, who must surely be God.

Because of its eventfulness, its malleability, and its transparency, myth is uniquely able to bridge old and new, to absorb new meanings, to give structure to the inchoate. For this reason, authority as a structuring agency always employs myth. Historical myths, as opposed to nature myths, have had a special appeal to political authorities. Primordiality becomes authenticity. Indeed, as the Greek *mythos* was a tale told by the mouth, the Roman *auctoritas* was one who declared or told and by telling brought something new into existence. Historical places as well as historical persons can absorb meanings in myth-like fashion, can become "happenings" that bring a people consciousness of itself. Political authorities are links in a process that brings new collective consciousness out of old collective consciousness: Valley Forge: Washington; Gettysburg: Lincoln; Dallas: Kennedy; Berkeley: Reagan.

But collective consciousness goes back beyond the life-span of any people, back into the dark unrecorded past where thought itself was born. The infinite variety of mythological applications is only matched by the remarkable uniformity of underlying mythical themes. Every culture seems to have some variation of the sky father who impregnates the earth mother, the divine-human hero who overcomes the night-dwelling devil; paradise and the place of the dead; holocaust and inundation; the primal seizure of fire from the heavens. That God is father is not unrelated to the assertion that Washington was the father of his country. That in Christ we become a new being is not unrelated to the new Soviet—or, better, new Chinese—man, born again in the travail of revolution. Three astronauts dying in a vehicle named *Apollo* are better remembered than three civil rights workers dying in a ditch, as a Classics Professor reminds us in a recent issue of the *New Republic.* The fallen Achilles named Kennedy is memorialized in poetry full of mythical allusions, and in an automotive age, a riderless horse marches in the funeral parade in hopes that historical memory can save us from an awful meaninglessness.

Hence does the authority of a founder like Solon pass down from ruler to ruler, both as a creature of the earth and as a creature of the mind—from Plato's philosopher-king to Machiavelli's prince to Hobbes' sovereign to Rousseau's Legislator to every modern hero-ruler.

Politics is not necessarily the primary medium of mythological conceptions. In our day the economic sphere may be a more likely medium. On television we can find Adam and Eve strolling in the Salem cigaret paradise, juxtaposed with the hell of science-fiction robots and uncontrollable stomach acid. The royal tiger is in your tank, the indestructible hero is James Bond, and the earth-mother is a fold-out. But without myths there is no authority and without authority there is no politics. Without some mythical elements the language of politics is inefficacious. We must answer question number one in the affirmative.

II

My claim regarding the language of political science is probably more contentious than my claim regarding the language of politics. Here, too, I assert, myth and authority dwell hand in hand; but in a more concealed fashion.

What is science? It is impossible but fortunately needless to develop here a rounded position on what science is. Among other things, scientific activity suggests: (a) the existence of criteria of evidence and methods of validating empirical observations authorized by a community of scholars; (b) systematic explanation; (c) future orientation.

As to claim (a), little need be said at present except to note that although political authority and scientific authority have different objects, *as authority* the two are comparable. The relevance of this comment may become clearer in a moment. What I mean to assert by claim (b) is that the demand for explanation and even understanding or *verstehen* is a legitimate scientific demand. It is a call for more than data, however rewarding the data-gathering process may be. Sometimes impressive work in political science is less explanatory than it might be because it rests content with mere data. Any number of articles illustrate this tendency. One example is "Some Effects of Interest Group Strength in State Politics," by Lewis Froman.[1] The article offers some interesting statistics, imaginatively arrived at, to show that states with strong pressure groups, compared with states with weak pressure groups, had more elected officials, more elected judges, with shorter terms, under constitutions easier to amend. The data are interesting; but still they are only data. Why these correlations occurred, what they show about the ways of interest groups or state governments, or what their implication is for present experience or future change are left unexamined.

Someone must, of course, gather data, and the scholar need not, indeed, cannot, work on all fronts at once. After all, one can say, all our attempts to formulate hypotheses, patterns, paradigms, and models are but attempts to "make sense" of data. Moreover, although mere data are never "self-explanatory," the transformation of random impressions into data can have the effect of flattening out, making level, making observable from above, so to speak, the phenomena under study. This is the original meaning of "explain." My plea for explanation is, therefore, strictly speaking a plea for elucidation—which originally meant to shed light upon. Data-making can be a useful process of reduction and denominating; but data shed no light. If Cassirer is correct, myth does.

But whether we call it explanation, elucidation, insight, or understanding— whether flattening, lighting, looking, or standing under—the quest for knowledge requires not only data, but what Stephen Pepper calls "danda."[2] Data is evidence refined through multiplicative corroboration, by repetitive tests, or by observations of a similar kind made by a series of observers. Danda is evidence refined through structural corroboration, by measuring conformity to a preexisting construct. The distinction, it is important to note, is not that between observation and nonobservation. Observers seeking data on the strength of a chair will have a series of different observers perform the same strength test on it. Observers seeking danda on the strength of the same chair will seek to find a concurrence between different aspects of the chair—quality of wood, character of the design, reputation of the maker, etc.

Data-gathering is clearly a more "social" enterprise than danda-gathering since collaborators are absolutely essential. Is it possible that data-gathering studies receive more professional attention than nonmultiplicative studies, partly because data-gatherers must be gregarious and danda-gatherers need not be so much so? Data can be discredited more easily than danda, which is at once its strength and its weakness—strength because data is without ambiguity, weakness because it is easily displaced and hence transient. Ghosts at one point in time were taken as data. When discredited as data, they could still live on as danda, entities explainable by reference to something else.

Since the whole world—or for that matter, any "world": the planet called world, the world of the Enlightenment, the world of the U.S. Senate, the world of Sammy Davis, Jr.—since none of these can be experienced as data, all world hypotheses require danda for validation; but world hypotheses also come into existence prior to any system by which they may be validated. They rest on what Pepper calls "root metaphors." Even views of reality that are hostile to metaphor, themselves rest on root metaphors. (One is reminded of John Locke in *Essay Concerning Human Understanding*. In one very short passage [Bk. III, ch. 10, sec. 34] which argues that metaphor misleads judgment, Locke is forced to employ about ten metaphors.) Systematic inquiry into the world of politics has always been built on different kinds of root metaphors. Aristotle was biological. Hobbes was physicalistic. Bentham was mechanistic. Karl Deutsch is neurological. David Easton is electronic. Easton's *Systems Analysis of Political Life* has as its admitted cognitive parent the computer (even though "life" is a biological term).

There is nothing wrong either with seeking political data that can be digested by a computer, or with conceiving political systems *as if* they were computer systems—so long as one is clear about what one is doing, and is reasonably modest about it. Easton is usually clear, but he sometimes forgets the "as if," and treats the figurative as the literal. His macroscopic analyses of system inputs, outputs, and feedback loops are well known. Let us plug in at random to a discussion of "the systemic feedback loop":

> Through the interlocking chain of feedback loops, all of the participating members of any one loop may be coupled, if only loosely, with many other members in the system. To point this up, I have deliberately selected the participants in the various feedback diads so that an unbroken line could be drawn through the six different actors who make up the six pairs of the six different loops. If we look at each loop as a link in a continuous chain—which they indeed form pictorially *and literally*—we can appreciate that the interaction around any one feedback loop has the potential, if it is strong enough, to pass its influence down the chain to other units in the system.[3]

But what does it mean to say that the chain is both pictorial and literal? It is surely not literal in reference to what Mayor Daley actually does, or to what the Rev. James Bevel or Saul Alinsky do to Mayor Daley. Is it then literal in reference to what a figurative political computer would do?

Easton declares that this system is not yet ready for microscopic data (which means, presumably, data about specific human beings):

> At this preliminary state in a theory of political systems, when we are still trying to get our general bearings, a detailed analysis of this kind cannot and need not be undertaken. . . . for purposes of macroanalysis we do not need to push any more deeply. . . . It is as though we were initially reconciling ourselves to use a telescope rather than a microscope because we

are not yet sufficiently confident of the units and processes that we want to lay open to detailed analysis.[4]

This is a very strange analogy. We do not yet know what to put under our microscopes; but we will know if we spend more time looking at stars through our telescopes. Easton's telescope is a strange metaphor. But it may suggest a truth, nevertheless, a possibility even for bad metaphors. It suggests that in cognition wholeness precedes particularity, danda precedes data. There must be some coherent entity by which to comprehend a set of particulars. Raw empiricism is not enough. As Polanyi notes, one does not come to understand the purpose of a watch by taking it apart.

The future orientation of Easton's remarks are also worthy of note, but comment on that comes later. For now, my point is that Easton—whom I do not deny is acting like a scientist—is building his whole system not on data or literal experience, but on analogy, metaphor, and possibly myth. The terminology of the computer pervades even his discussion of history, a history in which the computer was unknown. Under the heading "Rules for the retrieval of stored experiences," he refers to "a social memory bank" as a "potential resource for the authorities."

> Members could not possibly recall the whole of history transmitted to each generation, even if it were desirable or necessary. Retrieval is always selective. What a person recalls will hinge on those rules governing the ways in which he scans his memory, the criteria of appropriateness used to make selections from the information retrieved, and the rules regulating the way he goes about synthesizing and reorganizing the knowledge recalled for immediate use. ... The rules themselves constitute part of the available resources necessary for handling feedback response.[5]

President Johnson's metaphorical language was translated into literal language only by increasing the number of words. In this case one might attempt the same thing and actually shorten the number of words. We might read this passage to say: "Habit affects memory and people remember from history what is useful for them to remember." In the case of both Johnson and Easton, the metaphorical base renews the authority of the speaker in his own communal context. In one case it is historical grandeur appealing to the citizen and legislator; in the other case it is computer-talk appealing to the scientist of the computer age.

My conclusion at this juncture is that satisfying explanation or elucidation requires more than data and once we are beyond data we find ourselves leaning on the metaphors and myths that stand between us and the unknown. We must use the known to get at the unknown and this is what myth primordially does. Sisyphus may have started out as a datum; but he became a myth by giving shape and meaning to all the elusive Sisyphian experiences man has had.

The third aspect of science worthy of note here is its future orientation. Thomas Kuhn in his splendid little book, *The Structure of Scientific Revolutions,*[6] shows by historical study how important the sense of forward motion is to the scientific community. Scientific paradigms provide the structure within which researchers can work and feel they are "making progress." When unusually creative men come up with new paradigms that give promise of greater forward movement, old paradigms can lose their grip on the imagination with remarkable rapidity.

When Renaissance painters were concerned with perfecting the techniques of linear perspective, of transforming three-dimensional vision onto a two-dimensional surface, they thought of themselves as scientists. When perspective ceased to be an interesting problem to them, they stopped being scientists and began calling themselves artists. Copernicus destroyed but did not replace the earlier view of terrestrial motion, and the same could be said for Newton on gravity, Lavoisier on the property of metals, and Einstein on space and time. This is what Kuhn calls the incommensurability of scientific paradigms.

It is interesting that both David Truman in his 1965 presidential address to the American Political Science Association, and Gabriel Almond in his 1966 presidential address to the same body, mentioned Kuhn's book. They did so because he supports the claim that the concept of system is central to the scientific endeavor. Truman uses Kuhn with great caution, but Almond, in citing Kuhn, glides over the principle of incommensurability and the phenomenon of futurism. Being suddenly and overtly mythical, Almond says that an older generation—Herring, Schattschneider, Odegard, Key—saw a new land on the horizon, and a newer generation—Truman, Easton, Dahl, Deutsch— "have been moving across the Jordan to possess it." [7] But what Kuhn seems to me to be saying is that science is not as cumulative as we have thought it to be. Knowledge produced by a scientific system cannot be "possessed" the way land can be possessed.

One cannot help but be struck by the sense of movement into the future that animates so much political science writing, a sense that communicates itself in often quite metaphorical language. The September 1966 issue of *The American Political Science Review* may be taken as a representative example. Eight of the eleven articles could be called future-oriented (of these eight, incidentally, seven are quantitative. Of the three present-oriented articles, two are nonquantitative). What I mean by future-orientation is indicated by conclusions like these:

... the social scientific examination into the complexities of judicial decision-making has barely commenced. It is no shame that we are only now at the state of hypothesis formulation and technique development. The first toddles are always the shakiest.[8]

Inter-nation simulation and man-computer simulation in general may be considered way stations on the path to all-computer simulations.[9]

... the intention of the present investigation [is] to make an initial excursion into this uncharted area.[10]

This study can be interpreted as an introductory exploration of the processes by which more general political beliefs and behavior are affected by the local community.[11]

Future analyses of recruitment need not be confined to the simple categories used for illustrative purposes here.[12]

And so on.

Am I suggesting that the conquest of the future is the underlying myth of all science and therefore of political science? Not quite. For one thing, myths themselves are past-oriented, not future-oriented. They are composed of images from the past that illumine the present by revitalizing the past. By contrast, ideology is uniquely future-oriented. It "explains" the future by logical projection. Ideology is abstract whereas myth is concrete. Because it may be used for purposes of control, measurement, and prediction in human affairs, ideology is like a science. But it is a pseudo-science, for it cannot deliver on its promises and projections. Myth, on the other hand, makes no promises. It just is. There is a singular "logic" to ideologies like Marxism, racism, or John Birchism, that "explains" more than it is entitled to. There is no such singular logic to myth. It illuminates precisely because of its tensive, diaphoric, and epiphoric qualities; but these very qualities also mean that the same myth can mean sharply different things to different people. Perhaps we can say that while Promethean and Faustian myths are relevant to science, the conquest and control of the future is not the myth but the ideology of science.

Is the language of political science inefficacious so long as mythical elements remain? If science means only the collection of quantitative data the answer is yes. If science means also explanation and elucidation by the structural corroborations of danda, the answer is no. The coherences we seek in trying to relate and explain the various linguistic phenomena of politics cannot be expressed in an utterly precise and univocal manner so long as mythical or metaphorical elements remain; but these elements do not necessarily negate and they may enhance the explanatory function.

III

What is the relationship between the answer to question one and the answer to question two?

The "X" on a ballot is the result of a sublingual act, and it is exceptionally objectifiable. It comes into being at a clearly identifiable moment in time and it stays in place. Voting statistics are admirable as data, and it is not surprising therefore that political science most fulfills the requirements of quantitative science in the area of voting studies. But the content of most political behavior is linguistic: bargaining, conciliating, threatening, exhorting, persuading, reporting. All this goes on somewhere between the two poles of violence, which is speechless, and contemplation, which is speechless. Michael Polanyi notes that for an observer to say "the stone is rolling" involves two logical levels, one for the observer and his statement, a second for the stone. When an observer says "the cat sees a rat" a third level is introduced, requiring of the observer some awareness of the experience of seeing that he shares with the cat.[13] Polanyi's argument is that significant knowledge is always personal knowledge. The personality of the knower is bound up with the object of his knowing and must be. If the scientific observer is not looking at a looking cat, but speaking to a speaking citizen, and the citizen says, "Ronald Reagan says he believes in individualism" we are confronted with about five logical levels with which the political scientist must deal.

Politicking and the analysis of politicking are, of course, sharply different enterprises. If unexamined myth is omnipresent on the stump it need not be in the professional journals. Politics is drama. Need the drama critic be dramatic? No necessity requires him to be; but he will shed little light unless he is. Where would scientific political analysis be without concepts like election, vote, rule, law, power, authority, represent, community, govern, charisma, republic, democratic, liberty, equality, fraternity—words whose contextual meanings are so steeped in the historic experiences of concrete communities that a lack of awareness of those invested meanings leads to impoverished understanding? The aim of methodological precision drives us away from the figurative toward the literal in the hopes of finding a neutral language. But if political language is always contextual and contextual language is never neutral, the price we pay for neutral language may be loss of touch with politics itself.

I am not, of course, advocating surrender to imprecision. We can use controlled metaphor to explain rampant metaphor. We can use conscious myth to explain unconscious myth. But if we try too hard to avoid dependence upon metaphors, we may succeed, becoming literal but lifeless. If we try too hard to live without myth, we may only wind up enslaved to ideology, thereby closing down what is, in fact, an open future.

References

1. *American Political Science Review* 60 (December 1966): 952–962.
2. *World Hypotheses* (Berkeley: University of California Press, 1961).
3. David Easton, *Systems Analysis of Political Life* (New York: John Wiley and Sons, 1965): 376. Italics added.
4. *Ibid.*, 376–377.
5. *Op cit.*, 458.
6. Thomas Kuhn, *The Structure of Scientific Revolutions* (Chicago: University of Chicago Press, 1962).
7. "Political Theory and Political Science," *American Political Science Review* 60 (December 1966): 875.
8. Theodore Becker, "A Survey of Hawaiian Judges," *American Political Review* 60 (September 1966): 680.
9. William Coplin, "Inter-National Simulation and Contemporary Theories of International Relations," *American Political Science Review* 60 (September 1966): 578.
10. Jack Dennis, "Support for the Party System in the Mass Public," *American Political Science Review* 60 (September 1966): 613.
11. Robert Putnam, "Political Attitudes and the Local Community," *American Political Science Review* 60 (September 1966): 652.
12. Leo Snowiss, "Congressional Recruitment and Representation," *American Political Science Review* 60 (September 1966): 639.
13. *The Study of Man* (Chicago: University of Chicago Press, 1963): 74–77.

TO THE STUDENT: A COMMENTARY

In 1976 a professor of psychiatry, Paul Watzlawick at Stanford University, published a provocative little book entitled *How Real Is Real?* (New York: Vintage Books). He opened his work with a statement that some readers might find puzzling, others disturbing, still others obvious. "This book," he wrote, "is about the way in which communication creates what we call reality." He went on to acknowledge that such a statement might seem "peculiar" for "surely reality is what it is, and communication is merely a way of expressing or explaining it." He disagreed. "Not at all," he argued, "our everyday traditional ideas of reality are delusions." The most dangerous of such delusions, he stressed, "is that there is only one reality." Then came his key point:

> What there are, in fact, are many different versions of reality, some of which are contradictory, but all of which are the results of communication and not reflections of eternal, objective truths.

What, you ask, does this have to do with watching American politics? A great deal. What you watch and what you see of politics is but one of "many different versions" of political reality. Through the pages of this book, in fact, you have been introduced to diverse versions of political reality, i.e., to multiple political realities. Consider just a few examples from the preceding chapters:

- Was Ted Kennedy correct in challenging a sitting President for his party's nomination in 1980? Ben Wattenberg's version of political reality says Kennedy was correct (chapter 1) but other versions disagree.
- President Jimmy Carter's reality in 1979 spoke of a crisis of confidence (chapter 2); others' realities did not.
- There are numerous realities allegedly explaining Americans' voting and nonvoting habits (chapters 3 and 4).
- Is it a political reality that America is governed by an Establishment (chapter 5); if so what are the realities of power elites?
- Realities of partisan politics say the party's over, or do they (chapter 6)?
- In reality mediacracy has replaced democracy; the real consequences of political reform counter that shift, or do they (chapters 7, 8, 9)?
- Really, TV makes things happen (Mike Robinson's reality expressed in chapter 11); no, says George Will, TV only reflects social values.

We could go on but by now you get the point. So, if there are multiple political realities derived from political watching, what does this say about trying to observe politics secondhand through the accounts provided by political journalists and political scientists? Bill Rivers and Lee McDonald have spoken to you on this point.

Rivers recognizes that "we live in a synthetic environment." Secondhand information substitutes for direct, firsthand experience. His account of how people perceived and reported Barbara Walters' move from NBC to ABC illustrates for you his important point, i.e., that what the news presents to the public "is an image—often highly distorted—certainly not the reality." Again, referring to the President, Rivers informs you that the reality of the man you see on TV is but one reality, the one "on display," and not necessarily even close to realities presented in other displays—when in the Oval Office, meeting with heads of state, dealing with congressional officials, relaxing with his family, etc.

The upshot of this complicates your life as a political watcher, but not to the point that you need despair. The complication flows from something Rivers realizes: "We should recognize that the information we receive about government is not the same thing as government itself." Hence, "we must be wary of our tendency to respond to the image rather than the reality." In short, if you are to be a sensitive political watcher you must constantly be aware that the secondhand realities of politics you encounter through the news media are not direct but *mediated political realities*. Thus, to Watzlawick's suggestion that political realities (all realities) are multiple there is the implication in Rivers' article that those multiple realities are mediated.

All right, you say, that is all well and good. It is not too surprising, is it, that political journalists trying to gather, report, and interpret an endless array of political happenings may distort them? That The Other Government's members—like yourself—are victims of selective exposure, perception, and retention is clear enough. That news accounts, to return to Watzlawick's statement, are "many different versions of reality, some of which are contradictory," simply means we should adopt a skeptical stance toward them. But need this be so with scientific accounts, surely they are "reflections of eternal, objective truths" in spite of Watzlawick's assertions.

Lee McDonald thinks not. His account is more complex, you may think even more esoteric, than Rivers', but the gist is similar. A brief review of what he is saying will help you catch the drift.

First, McDonald says that much of politics is mythical. You have encountered this notion before, i.e., in chapter 7 when Jim Combs wrote to you about how political advertising is myth making. What is myth? To begin with it is, as McDonald says, a dramatic narrative, an account that attempts to make the unknown known in ways people will understand and believe. Through metaphor and other devices myths give the impression of yielding knowledge about things rather than mere acquaintance with them. They are versions of reality and, like Rivers' "images," they may be distorted. Their truth, or lack thereof, is difficult to test. What counts is not their truth or falsity but that people *believe* and *act* upon them.

Metaphors pervade politics, thereby making politics mythical. As you learned long ago a metaphor is a figure of speech, one that takes a quality of one object and implies by comparison or analogy that another object possesses that quality. The chapters you have read in this book are full of political metaphors. "Crisis" of confidence is one. A crisis is a crucial point, a turning point in an event or scheme of things. In announcing a crisis of confidence in 1979, President Jimmy Carter implied a turning point in our nation's history, a point brought on by a "crisis of the spirit" and yet another "crisis," the energy crisis. Or recall other obvious examples: "parties in trouble" and "the party's over;" "mediacracy;" "watershed election;" and on through a laundry (clean or dirty wash?) list of illustrations.

As McDonald argues, it is not too hard to demonstrate that politics possesses mythical elements. But his second major point, i.e., that political science is mythical as well, is more difficult. Nonetheless McDonald does it. He provides you an example that you have encountered before. Recall in chapter 8 that Mark Nadel in writing about the hidden dimension of public policy was severe in his criticism of political scientist David Easton's views. McDonald also turns to Easton. Reread that section, for what McDonald says of Easton—that Easton "is building his whole system not on data or literal experience, but on analogy, metaphor, and possibly myth"—could also be asserted about other scholarly watchers of politics. Indeed McDonald provides several examples extracted from the pages of scholarly journals. With little difficulty you could easily go back through preceding chapters and make your own comparable list of quotes of political metaphors.

But is this bad? McDonald is not decrying the presence of metaphor and myth in political scientists' accounts of politics. Unless science is nothing more than the gathering of facts for facts' sake, metaphorical elements must exist. They help provide elaborations and elucidations. Accounts too literal in content are, he says, lifeless.

By the same token Rivers in the opening two paragraphs of "The Other Government" shares with you his understanding that political correspondents can not and do not report facts as facts. Multiple realities intervene. Those realities intrude upon any political observer—you, us, journalists, scientists—in the form of images, myths, metaphors, etc.

Now if Rivers and McDonald realize that multiple versions of reality not only do but must exist, what is the message they want to leave? It is the same for both. Rivers wants political correspondents to be *aware* of the problem of multiple, mediated realities so that they can better cope with the demands of political reporting. McDonald wants political scientists to be *aware* of the myth-making aspects of their craft, not to "surrender to imprecision" but to avoid enslavement to ideology, to avoid closing down "an open future."

Both Rivers and McDonald look ahead, Rivers to a "new journalism" for a "new time," McDonald to an open future. And we urge you to look ahead as well. Political journalists and political scientists will always have something to say to you as a political watcher. If you too are aware that their accounts are but a sampling of diverse versions of reality, *possible* not absolute truths, your watching of politics will grow more informed, more critical. Then, even though most of what you see as politics is second-hand, you need not be a slave to any journalist's or scientist's version of the political scene, but are liberated to create your own version. There is an old adage that politics is the art of the possible. We trust for you that watching politics will be the art of creating, discovering, and entertaining possibilities.